Toward a Political
Economy of Culture

Recent Titles in the Series

Critical Communication Theory: Power, Media, Gender, and Technology,
    Sue Curry Jansen
Digital Disability: The Social Construction of Disability in New Media,
    Gerard Goggin and Christopher Newell
Principles of Publicity and Press Freedom,
    Slavko Splichal
Internet Governance in Transition: Who Is the Master of This Domain?
    Daniel J. Pare
Recovering a Public Vision for Public Television,
    Glenda R. Balas
Reality TV: The Work of Being Watched,
    Mark Andrejevic
Contesting Media Power: Alternative Media in a Networked World,
    edited by Nick Couldry and James Curran
Herbert Schiller,
    Richard Maxwell
Harold Innis,
    Paul Heyer
Toward a Political Economy of Culture: Capitalism and Communication in the Twenty-First Century,
    edited by Andrew Calabrese and Colin Sparks

Forthcoming in the Series

Public Service Broadcasting in Italy,
    Cinzia Padovani
Changing Concepts of Time,
    Harold A. Innis
Many Voices, One World,
    Seán MacBride
Film Industries and Cultures in Transition,
    Dina Iordanova
Globalizing Political Communication,
    Gerald Sussman
The Blame Game: Why Television Is Not Our Fault,
    Eileen R. Meehan
Mass Communication and Social Thought,
    edited by John Durham Peters and Peter Simonson
Entertaining the Citizen: When Politics and Popular Culture Converge,
    Liesbet van Zoonen
Elusive Autonomy: Brazilian Communications Policy,
    Sergio Euclides de Souza

Toward a Political Economy of Culture

Capitalism and Communication in the Twenty-First Century

Edited by
Andrew Calabrese and Colin Sparks

ROWMAN & LITTLEFIELD PUBLISHERS, INC.
Lanham • *Boulder* • *New York* • *Toronto* • *Oxford*

ROWMAN & LITTLEFIELD PUBLISHERS, INC.

Published in the United States of America
by Rowman & Littlefield Publishers, Inc.
A wholly owned subsidiary of The Rowman & Littlefield Publishing Group, Inc.
4501 Forbes Boulevard, Suite 200, Lanham, Maryland 20706
www.rowmanlittlefield.com

P.O. Box 317, Oxford OX2 9RU, United Kingdom

British Library Cataloguing in Publication Information Available

Library of Congress Cataloging-in-Publication Data

Toward a political economy of culture : capitalism and communication in the
twenty-first century / edited by Andrew Calabrese and Colin Sparks.
    p. cm. (Critical media studies)
Includes bibliographical references and index.
  ISBN 0-7425-2683-6 (alk. paper) — ISBN 0-7425-2684-4 (pbk. : alk. paper)
  1.   Communication—Social aspects. 2. Mass media—Social aspects. 3.
Culture. 4. Capitalism. 5. Information society. I. Calabrese, Andrew,
1956– II. Sparks, Colin, 1947– III. Series.
  HM1206 .T65 2004
  302.2—dc21

                                                                    2003009118

Printed in the United States of America

♾™The paper used in this publication meets the minimum requirements of
American National Standard for Information Sciences—Permanence of Paper for
Printed Library Materials, ANSI/NISO Z39.48-1992.

This book is dedicated to Nicholas Garnham, in honor and respect for his excellent mind, intellectual honesty, and moral commitment to the theory and practice of public communication.

Contents

Acknowledgments   xi

**Part I Taking Stock of the Political Economy of Communication
and Culture**

1   Toward a Political Economy of Culture   1
    Andrew Calabrese

2   The Rise of the Westminster School   13
    James Curran

3   Making a Molehill out of a Mountain: The Sad State of Political
    Economy in U.S. Media Studies   41
    Robert McChesney

Part II Capitalism, Communication, and the Public Sphere

4   "The Marketplace of Ideas": A History of the Concept   65
    John Durham Peters

5   Capitalism and Communication: A New Era of Society
    or the Accentuation of Long-Term Tendencies?   83
    Bernard Miège

6   *Kugai:* The Lost Public Sphere in Japanese History   95
    Tatsuro Hanada

7   Truth Commissions, Nation Building, and International
    Human Rights: The South African Experience and the Politics
    of Human Rights Post-9/11   111
    Robert Horwitz

Part III The Political Economy of Film and Broadcasting

8   Show Me the Money: Challenging Hollywood Economics   131
    Janet Wasko

9   The Fight for Proportionality in Broadcasting   151
    Richard Collins

10 Broadcasting and the Market: The Case of Public Television 178
    Giuseppe Richeri

11 Living with Monsters: Can Broadcasting Regulation
    Make a Difference?   194
    Sylvia Harvey

Part IV New Media, the Information Society, and Other
         Obscure Objects

12 Capitalism's Chernobyl? From Ground Zero to Cyberspace
    and Back Again   211
    Vincent Mosco

13 New Media and the Forces of Capitalism   228
    Robin Mansell and Michèle Javary

14 Dismantling the Digital Divide: Rethinking the Dynamics
    of Participation and Exclusion   244
    Graham Murdock and Peter Golding

15 Building the Information Society in EU Candidate Countries:
    A Long Way to Go   261
    *Jean-Claude Burgelman, Elissaveta Gourova, and
    Marc Bogdanowicz*

16 Romanticism in Business Culture: The Internet, the 1990s,
    and the Origins of Irrational Exuberance   286
    Thomas Streeter

17 The Impact of the Internet on the Existing Media   307
    Colin Sparks

Part V Extending the Boundaries of Political Economy

18   Audiences on Demand   327
     Oscar H. Gandy Jr.

19   Feminist Theory and the Political Economy of Communication   342
     Ellen Riordan

Index   357

About the Contributors   371

Acknowledgments

The idea for this project originated from efforts to plan a conference in June 2002 to honor the work of Professor Nicholas Garnham on the occasion of his retirement from the faculty of the University of Westminster. Garnham's valuable contributions to establishing a field of the political economy of culture are known and appreciated around the world. Although this book is dedicated to Garnham, it is not a Festschrift, as it was never our intention to suggest that the study of capitalism and communication be grounded in the work of a single strand of influence, and Garnham would be the first to counsel against such an error. Indeed, some of the chapters printed here are distinctly critical of positions that have been closely identified with Garnham in the past. Rather, this book points to the fertile interdisciplinary field that Garnham's work has tilled, and it demonstrates the continued vitality and importance of work in this tradition.

The editors owe debts of gratitude to many people who made the conference and the subsequent volume possible. In particular, at the University of Westminster, we are indebted to the vice-chancellor, Dr. Geoffrey Copland, who provided the generous finance that made it so much easier to gather together a wide range of scholars from around the world. His continuing support has been an important factor in the development of the Centre, and in that of its successor, the Communication and Media Research Institute. There are many other people at Westminster to whom we have different sorts of debts, but among them we must single out Ms. Alison Sorrell, the research officer responsible for the Centre, whose hard work and attention to detail meant that the conference ran extremely smoothly.

The journey from a collection of disparate conference papers to a coherent published volume was made easy due to the understanding and professionalism of the staff of the publishers, Rowman & Littlefield. Among them, we must mention the acquisitions editor, Brenda Hadenfeldt, and the production editor, April Leo, both of whom put up with more than their normal quota of academic sloth and prevarication.

We both owe immense personal debts of many kinds to our families. We are truly thankful that we have been privileged to receive nothing but support and understanding, even when we did not deserve it. We have nothing but love and admiration for Sue and Katharine Sparks and Bridget Bacon and Emma and Rosa Calabrese.

Boulder, Colorado, and London, England
September 2003

1

Toward a Political Economy of Culture

Andrew Calabrese

This book is about the political economy of communication and culture at the start of a new millennium. It can be read as a status report on an important research tradition that explains the role played by the means of communication in the modern world. As in many other areas of inquiry in the human sciences, the boundaries of political economy shift over time, due to both historical transformations in the object of study—the institutions and technologies we know as "the media"—and the intellectual developments that are characteristic of any lively research tradition. The chapters in this volume are a testimony to the vitality of that tradition.

What is "political economy," and what is the nature of its relationship to communication and culture? These questions have captured the attention of many scholars, several of whom are contributors to this volume. Perhaps the most detailed and accessible introduction to the subject is Vincent Mosco's *The Political Economy of Communication* (1996). In answering the question "What is political economy?" Mosco provides an extended and enlightening introduction to the heritage of modern political economy by examining the contributions of many key thinkers, including Adam Smith, David Ricardo, Thomas Malthus, Karl Marx, Jeremy Bentham, J. S. Mill, Alfred Marshall, John Maynard Keynes, and numerous others. Mosco's account is not a neutral catalog; instead, it focuses primarily on what we might generally refer to as a "critical political economy," emphasizing Marxian or materialist thought in particular. Of more importance at this historical moment is the attention Mosco pays to the *political* in political economy, noting how the discipline and language of contemporary economics have evolved to profess value neutrality. Unlike political economy, contemporary economics tends not to explicitly engage moral considerations and political questions that have historically been central to political economists.

Moving from "political economy" to the "political economy of communication," Mosco provides a comprehensive review of work in the field that spans several generations and continents, from the pioneering work of Dallas Smythe and Herbert Schiller to that of Nicholas Garnham, Graham Murdock, Dan Schiller, Peter Golding, Janet Wasko, Armand Mattelart, Bernard Miège, Jill Hills, Manjunath Pendakur, Robin Mansell, Robert McChesney, and numerous others. In one way or another, all of these authors have been preoccupied with how the dynamics of capital accumulation and class power manifest themselves in the capitalist mode of production, particularly the institutional structure, organization, and production processes of the media industries.

Another writer who has reflected at length and in depth on the political economy of communication is Nicholas Garnham. Over the course of more than three decades, Garnham has been influential in British media politics and academic circles through a body of theory and research that goes far beyond Britain in defining the field. Garnham defines political economy across a number of his books and essays, emphasizing first and foremost that "it is always concerned with analyzing a structure of social relations and of social power. But it is particularly concerned to analyze the peculiarities of that system of social power called capitalism" (Garnham 1990a, 7). He notes a starting assumption of political economy: "the historically observable unequal distribution of the surplus product, from an essentially collaborative enterprise, as between capital and labor requires explanation, is historically contingent and is the result of the specific structure of the mode of production" (8). Elsewhere, he characterizes this inequality, as it applies to communication, in the following way:

> A delimited social group, pursuing economic or political ends, determines which meanings circulate and which do not, which stories are told about what, which arguments are given prominence and what cultural resources are made available and to whom. The analysis of this process is vital to an understanding of the power relationships involved in culture and their relationship to wider structures of domination. (Garnham 1995, 65)

It is worth noting that Garnham and others tend to interchange the phrases "political economy of communication" and "political economy of communication and *culture*" (e.g., Garnham 1990a, 8). The explicit attention that this book's title brings to the latter term is meant both to take into account where the field has in fact already been and where it must focus more intensively in the future. The degree to which the media constitute, define, or otherwise influence what we take to be the realm of the "cultural" in the modern world is certainly a matter for dispute. What is indisputable is that no conception of culture in the modern world is complete if it fails to account for the space occupied by "the media"—the institutional and technological means of communication and information. Although the media do not offer sufficient grounds for outlining the domain of a political economy of culture, they are a necessary and central aspect of that field. To the extent that this book aims to stay true to its agenda—*toward a political economy of culture*—it does so by demonstrating where some of that necessity lies: in examining the material foundations of what we have come to call the "public sphere," in understanding our news and entertainment industries as capitalist enterprises, in media policy and regulation, and on the frontiers of "new media" development. Before moving to the following chapters that address these subjects, we should consider some of the unique features that shape the context of a critical political economy of communication and culture in the first years of the new millennium.

In the last decade of the twentieth century, we witnessed many profound changes that have in various ways shaped the political economy of communication and culture, including the "velvet revolutions" that brought an end to communist governments in Central and Eastern Europe and thus an end to the Cold War; the ascent of neoliberal economic theory and, related to this, the declining influence of Keynesian economic theory and the sharp erosion of the post–World War II social policy settlements of many affluent capitalist democracies; massive industrial reorganization in most capitalist countries, especially in mass media, information technology, and telecommunications; the formation of new regional trading blocs (e.g., the European Union, NAFTA, Mercosul); and the intensive expansion and consolidation of Western (particularly U.S.) control over global trade and investment policy and regulation. At the end of the twentieth century and the beginning of the twenty-first, we witnessed a "global contagion" of failing currencies in many countries in Asia, Eastern Europe, and South America, marking the beginning of a world economic recession; the September 11 suicide attacks on American targets in New York City and Washington, D.C., followed by the U.S.-led military invasion of the Taliban regime and al Qaeda bases in Afghanistan; and a "preemptive war" waged by the United States and Great Britain against Iraq. This is far from an exhaustive list of key events over the past decade or so, but it gives a sense of the major geopolitical events at the dawn of the new millennium.

It is impossible to calculate the number of new risks that have arisen in the wake of these developments, but some specific doubts, with particular reference to the United States, are worth highlighting. During most of the "go-go" years of the 1990s, the triumph of Western-dominated global capitalism and the principles of liberal democracy that undergird it seemed to many to be irreversible. Economic crises occurred in Russia, Brazil, Thailand, Indonesia, Argentina, and elsewhere in what appeared to be a domino effect, or what the *New York Times* termed "global contagion" (Kristof et al. 1999). For many journalists, academics, and politicians, these events called into question the economic foundation of the triumphalist mantra that had been resounding in the business and political press in the United States and elsewhere. When the American new economy's "dot-com bubble" burst, Wall Street traders couldn't dump their Internet shares fast enough, as they discovered that telecommunications and information services could not meet the unrealistic earnings expectations that had been placed on them. This downturn happened just as the Clinton presidency was winding down. When George W. Bush became president, he found himself in a much less secure economic situation than his predecessor. Clinton rode the wave of unprecedented stock market growth just long enough to see it wash ashore as his presidency ended. Seeing that whoever followed Clinton would inherit a troubled economy, Bush emphasized in his election campaign that the key to economic recovery and long-term prosperity lay in stimulating investor confidence, which he proposed to accomplish mainly through a program of radical tax cuts. A short time after taking office, Bush fulfilled his promise and got the Congress to approve a modified version of his plan. In June 2001 he signed into law a $1.35 trillion, ten-year tax cut. Meanwhile, the stock market continued to slide as unemployment continued to rise in the United States while consumer confidence declined. Only a few months later, the dramatic and tragic events of September 11, 2001, drew the eyes of the world toward the United States. Shortly after, Bush declared that his presidency would be dedicated to leading a "war on terrorism," and his first front would be a conventional attack against the Taliban regime and al Qaeda forces based in Afghanistan.

Although arguably these two events—the worldwide recession and the terrorist attack on the United States—have no direct connection, they are related in the sense that they both signal in different ways a change of status for the last remaining superpower in the eyes of the world, and they raise new questions about the future of global leadership. The Bush presidency began with an economic plan that was generally premised on the continuity of a world safe for American capitalism. That premise was threatened by a direct assault on symbols of American financial and military power—the spaces and occupants of the World Trade Center and the Pentagon. For the Bush administration, 9/11 became the basis on which some of its most controversial policy ambitions found popular support, including radically intensified domestic surveillance of American citizens and foreign nationals living in the United States (Chang 2002; American Civil Liberties Union 2003) and, with the support of the British government, the unilateral invasion of Iraq in March 2003. It is too soon to say what the long-term consequences of these actions will be, although predictions range widely.

What was happening in the communication and information industries during the past two decades? In the 1990s, the U.S. government was busily revamping and consolidating the regulatory reforms that had reached a crescendo with the breakup of AT&T in the early 1980s.[1] This momentous event was a watershed in U.S. policy making that also became a model for telecommunications deregulation, privatization, and liberalization in many countries. Industries and policy makers began to tout the benefits of "open networks" as they labored to reconfigure the emerging new media environment, aiming toward the convergence of previously separated industries. During this time, telephone companies, newspaper chains, cable television systems, satellite services, data communication companies, television and radio broadcasters, research and development firms, hardware suppliers, pundits, media researchers, and policy makers shared in imagining an information age that could reinvigorate the spirit of capitalism. Despite continued growth in the size and penetrating influence of the U.S. government, regulators in several industries, especially in media and telecommunications, belligerently ratified the article of faith that the "public interest" is best served by the market. Government is at best a necessary evil, a damaging force, the presence of which must be minimized. In terms of media policy, government's role should be limited to advancing the movement of the means of communication as central to the mode of production, particularly by intervening in the realm of ownership policies. A pressing concern is to eliminate barriers to cross-media ownership and promote the global expansion of corporate property rights within the reconfiguring industries. By the end of the 1980s, the collective will was widely in place to reinvent the new and emerging means of communication to meet the specifications of flexible accumulation by deeply embedding their uses into the worlds of work, politics, finance, culture, and our most intimate spheres of everyday life. In many ways, media and telecommunications developments and policies of the 1980s and 1990s have shaped and also reflect the prevailing market, or neoliberal, conception of what the information society should look like.

By the early 1990s, two globally significant patterns of media development were under way: the Internet "revolution," that is, rapid diffusion in the use of digital networks for work and leisure, and the transnational "harmonization" of telecommunications regulatory policy. The Uruguay Round of the General Agreement on Tariffs and Trade (GATT), concluded by the end of 1993, established much of the framework for what became the World Trade Organization (WTO). In 1993 the director general of the WTO, Renato Ruggiero, said in a speech, "We are writing the constitution for a single global economy."[2] The WTO has become a powerful force in the transnational enforcement of intellectual property rights (IPR) and the arbitration of IPR disputes. Today the WTO, together with other multilateral organizations, exercises broad powers to secure the shareholder interests of the world's largest corporations, wherever they operate. Sweeping national and international regulatory reform in the communications and information industries underlies much of what glob-alization theorists point to as change at the structural level, and the national player that by most accounts has had the greatest influence in these develop-ments is the United States. Through direct pressure on many foreign governments and by example the U.S. government has exercised a forceful foreign policy in shaping the new global media environment, which can hardly be called a level playing field.[3]

Concurrent with powerful efforts to globalize and harmonize trade and in-vestment policies affecting the media, the early 1990s saw the prospect of a commercially viable form of digital communication (the Internet) emerge. The World Wide Web and user-friendly graphic displays on web browsers made the corporate world sit up and take notice of a business opportunity in what previously had been viewed as an arcane realm that only computer nerds and egg-headed academics could navigate. Within a short period of time, the celebrated "information superhighway," as U.S. Vice President Al Gore famously (or infamously) called it, came to be viewed as a new Athen-ian agora. Soon word began to spread that not everyone would be able to afford the technology, and among those who could many would lack the education to use it effectively. Thus was born what is now treated as a world-wide social policy issue: the digital divide. Convergences of previously sep-arate media and telecommunications industries led to new thinking about what sorts of communication needs would have to be met among the have-nots in a global information society. The old industry models for public ser-vice broadcasting and universal telephone service would require rethinking.

In the United States, as new Internet companies began to sprout, policy makers and the corporate lobbies that supported them began to recognize the remaining myriad legal and regulatory obstacles that interfered with the realization of shared dreams of a technologically and industrially converged digital media environment. Thus fresh efforts were made to fulfill a widely held dream of comprehensively rewriting the patchwork of U.S. communi-cations law, particularly in the wake of the breakup of AT&T. The dream be-came reality when President Bill Clinton signed the Telecommunications Act of 1996 into law. It has done much to accelerate the already dizzying pace of industry concentration, vertical integration, and conglomeration among pre-viously separate telecommunications and mass media behemoths. Concerns that further unrestricted industry concentration would mean greater shrink-age in the number of voices in news, public affairs, and entertainment and that market censorship would impede public awareness and stifle public de-bate had little chance to be aired. The companies that were in the best posi-tions to relay concerns about foul play in policy making to the public, and to offer forums to consider the consequences, were also frontrunners in the race to achieve the blissful state of "synergy" that the new policies promised. The prospect of coupling massive technological innovation to a bonanza of mergers and acquisitions and the promise of untold profits far outweighed what nay-sayers were claiming about threats to the health of the public sphere. Today, the U.S. Federal Communications Commission (FCC), the primary domestic regulatory body for enforcing telecommunications and mass media policy at the national level, endorses industry rhetoric that media concentration is a path to not only greater economies of scale but also greater editorial diversity. In classic doublespeak, the prevailing view emanating from the FCC is that media concentration is good for America and, of course, for the world (Calabrese, in press).

What risks are associated with the declining number of independent voices? Historically, antitrust law has been based on the reasoning that the public is disserved by a lack of competition for price and quality of service. Moreover, the realm of public communication has had a unique status in regard to industry regulation. "Pure" economic competition arguments have always been balanced in liberal legal theory against concerns about such general interests as freedom of expression and the public's "right to know." Media concentration has been subject to prophylactic regulation based on the belief that a lack of editorial diversity threatens to undermine the breadth, depth, and overall quality of public knowledge and discussion about issues of vital importance, including matters of war and peace, public health and safety, and social and economic well-being.[4] Such risks reflect the sort of inequality in which a "delimited social group, pursuing economic or political ends, determines which meanings circulate and which do not" (Garnham 1990a, 8). Indeed, the possibility of an autonomous political culture or the autonomy of culture in general is called into question.

Garnham has emphasized the link between the political economy of the means of communication on the one hand, and the political culture it enables on the other. Like others who have advanced the ideals of a rational public sphere, however, he neglected, in his initial treatment of the public–private dichotomy, the high barriers that exist for many who seek to establish the legitimacy of their interests and their moral claims. Like Habermas's initial treatment of the public sphere, Garnham in "The Media and the Public Sphere" (1990b) said little about how or why vernacular rhetoric can or should be heard within the hallowed and idealized public sphere of rational deliberation among privileged elites. For this reason, among others, a rationalist and patriarchal concept of the public sphere has been found lacking by numerous critics (e.g., Calhoun 1992; White 1995; Young 2000). Not surprisingly, the terms of this debate are played out across the human sciences. In a subsequent but much different essay by the same title, Garnham (1992) advanced his position as he contributed to the sharper criticism of Habermas by responding to the increasingly acknowledged need to think about the public sphere in more ecumenical terms. More recently, in appealing to a "nonfoundational" concept of reason, Garnham (2000, 8) pits the "overweening rational subject" against "doubt," the latter being identified with what he characterizes as the true spirit of the Enlightenment project. He identifies his concept of reason as Kantian, based on ideals of "open debate among free citizens," as opposed to a Cartesian concept (180). Garnham argues that Habermas seeks to wed Kant's view of public reason with "a "search for foundationalism in the basic structure of communicative action which is both unnecessary and probably unsustainable" (181). Whether Habermas lacks an intersubjective concept of reason is arguable, especially if we consider his sustained treatment of the subject in his later work. Regarding his views on the media, in various publications, Habermas has conceded much to criticism of his early work, and in his underdeveloped references to the subject he has generally departed from the concept of an undifferentiated mass society by acknowledging that politics and popular culture are more intimately connected than perhaps he had previously recognized (e.g., Habermas 1992, 438–39).

Of more immediate importance is an aporia in Garnham's own nonfoundational epistemology, which seems to run against the grain of the argument he makes elsewhere in claiming that cultural studies rejects the notion of false consciousness and treats it as the "temporary effect of discourse" (Garnham 1995, 69). Whether it is true that this is a view generally held within the multiperspective field of cultural studies, Garnham further argues that "without some notion of grounded truth the ideas of emancipation, resistance, and progressiveness become meaningless" (69). How do we reconcile this compelling claim with Garnham's appeal to the contingent, which is ever present in a nonfoundational, intersubjective conception of reason? We cannot have it both ways. And although intersubjective reason was never at odds with Enlightenment ideals, with Kant being the most notable exponent of the principle (and Habermas arguably being his closest contemporary exponent), Garnham does not instruct us on how his own nonfoundational epistemology should be distinguished from the nonfoundational frameworks he rejects for being postmodern. At one extreme, we have been duly cautioned against embracing the negative ideal of the overweening rational subject, but at the other boundary, like so many other cautions against postmodern relativism, Garnham's is fuzzy. On the one hand, he tells us we should distinguish a critique of false consciousness that is founded on the negative rationalist ideal from one based on intersubjective reason. On the other hand, how do we defend an intersubjective position that critiques "false consciousness" from the charge that such a position is simply the product of an overweening rational subject? A sympathetic reading might be that his appeal to "grounded truth" is more dialectical, more grounded in a historical materialist theory of power, than his comments here suggest. In any case, is it the question of false consciousness that divides political economy and cultural studies? Equally important, is there a unified view of ideology within critical political economy? And if so, what might that be?

Whatever one concludes, Garnham's provocative views on the media and the public sphere deserve close attention, particularly because they represent an intelligent and sustained appeal to the Enlightenment project, an uncomfortable position to take while prevailing winds have been blowing in a different direction for many years. This has been done mainly through a career-long project to contribute to a historical materialist political economy of communication and culture. But much remains to be done in advancing this tradition, particularly if it is to engage with the idea of the "cultural" in ways that go beyond aging debates with cultural studies. Has common ground been discovered between these two fields? An increasingly common interest is policy analysis, criticism, and intervention, long a preoccupation of political economists and more recently an area in which cultural theorists have demonstrated interest (e.g., Bennett 1998; Miller 1998). A key area of shared concern centers on the *meaning of citizenship*, not only in terms of rights and responsibilities associated with government but also with respect to the rightfully contested terrain of "civil society."

Another area of common interest, which overlaps with the shared concerns about citizenship, entails questions about media audiences, including questions of continued importance about how audiences are commodified (e.g., Meehan 1990, 1993; Wasko and Hagen 1999). Oscar Gandy's innovative work on audiences, including his essay in this book, demonstrates the significance of understanding the range of implications of audience surveillance and market segmentation, as a means of not only commodification but also inclusion and exclusion. Perhaps this growing interest in the audience will establish the common empirical ground that is lacking and needed in efforts to develop more fruitful dialogue, and even collaboration, between practitioners of political economy and cultural studies. Equally important for political economists is that a focus on the audience makes it possible to respond more effectively to the types of issues raised by Garnham about how a political economy of culture can claim to know which meanings do or do not circulate, which stories are told, and which arguments are most prominent as a result of inequality in the social relations of production. In short, audience research enables us to answer empirical questions about what we think we know regarding *the production and circulation of meaning*, which is not of negligible importance, given claims on which the work of political economists rest. To address such issues, political economists must respond to research that attempts to answer these empirical questions, as well as make a more active contribution. Such a move necessitates not only that we view the means of communication as the means of production, but also that we understand the mode of production in terms that extend beyond a narrow industrial focus. In the *Grundrisse*, Marx's introduction to the critique of political economy, he implicitly counsels against an undialectical tendency to treat production and consumption as binary opposites:

> Production, then is also immediately consumption, consumption is also immediately production. Each is immediately its opposite. But at the same time

a mediating movement takes place between the two. Production mediates consumption; it creates the latter's material; without it consumption would lack an object. But consumption also mediates production, in that it alone creates for the products the subject for whom they are products. The product only obtains its "last finish" in consumption. . . . Consumption produces production in a double way, (1) because a product becomes a real product only by being consumed; (2) because consumption creates the need for *new* production, that is it creates the ideal, internally impelling cause for production, which is its presupposition. (Marx 1973, 91)

Applied to media audiences, these words underscore the need to avoid seeing the audience as being on the "other side" of production. Real and meaningful differences do not just disappear when we recognize shared interests between political economy and cultural studies, nor should this be the goal. Highlighting common empirical ground is not a call for false consensus on important substantive questions about determination, the autonomy of culture, and human agency, or about the relationships among class, race, gender, and other bases of inequality. But the broad field of critical media and cultural studies is too small, and the domain it professes to explain is too vast, to afford the luxury of divisive misunderstanding and indifference where interested and respectful engagement would prove far more fruitful. As Graham Murdock wisely counsels, "The aim must be to work toward the construction of a more complete account of the central dynamics of contemporary culture and to mobilize these insights to defend the symbolic resources required to extend the rights and duties of citizenship in the service of revitalizing democracy" (1995, 94). These are worthy aspirations for a coherent critical theory of communication and culture.

Critical research about the political economy of communication and culture has made important contributions to a wide range of theory and practice related to media industries and policies, technology studies, and political and cultural theories about the institutional pressures and constraints on public discourse and the public sphere. The chapters in this volume offer a snapshot of that legacy as it continues to thrive. The contributors include several of the leading political economists of communication working today. The authors have varied backgrounds of education and research experience, and they represent a wide range of career stages. They turn their attention to a rich mix of topics and issues that link to the heritage of political economy work, policy studies, and research and theory about the public sphere. Familiar but still exceedingly important topics in critical political economy studies are well represented here: market structures and media concentration, regulation and policy, technological impacts on particular media sectors, information poverty, and media access. New and important contributions for political economy research are charted, and relatively unexplored but fruitful lines of inquiry are presented, including work on racism in audience research, the value and need for feminist approaches to political economy studies, and the relationship between the discourse of media finance and the behavior of markets.

The idea for this project originated amid efforts to plan a conference in honor of the work of Professor Nicholas Garnham. Garnham's work is unique in the set of concerns he has brought to bear in political economy studies. He has steadfastly contributed to important interdisciplinary dialogues about the relationships among political communication, cultural practices, industry structures, technological innovation, state power, and the logic of capital accumulation. Chapter 2, by James Curran, pays homage to the Westminster School of political economy work, behind which Garnham's work is a primary force. Curran thoughtfully outlines the important influence of that legacy in contemporary work on the political economy of culture. The other chapters focus on various issues and topics of importance in the contemporary political economy of communication and culture. Most, but not all, of the contributors offer explicitly critical perspectives on how capitalism has shaped and been shaped by the public and private media institutions of the twenty-first century.

NOTES

1. The best chronicle of this history is Horwitz 1989.
2. Renato Ruggiero, director general of the World Trade Organization, in a speech presented to the UCTAD Trade and Development Board on October 8, 1996. Quoted on the Public Citizen Global Trade Watch website: www.citizen.org.
3. For an overview of the sources of U.S. influence in media-related trade negotiations through the Uruguay Round, see Calabrese and Redal 1995. See Ó Siochrú, Girard, and Mahan 2002 for an excellent overview of "global media governance," with historically informed introductions to all major governance bodies.
4. A competitive media environment, not just a highly concentrated one, is also prey to the harms of market censorship, as industry pressures to safely define and conform to prevailing audience tastes can lead to homogeneity.

REFERENCES

American Civil Liberties Union. 2003. *Bigger Monster, Weaker Chains: The Growth of an American Surveillance Society*. New York: American Civil Liberties Union. Available at www.aclu.org.
Bennett, Tony. 1998. *Culture: A Reformer's Science*. London: Sage.
Calabrese, Andrew. Forthcoming. "Stealth Regulation." *New Media and Society*.
Calabrese, Andrew, and Wendy Redal. 1995. "Is There a U.S. Foreign Policy in Telecommunications? Transatlantic Trade Policy as a Case Study." *Telematics and Informatics* 12: 35–56.
Calhoun, Craig, ed. 1992. *Habermas and the Public Sphere*. Cambridge: MIT Press.
Chang, Nancy. 2002. *Silencing Political Dissent*. New York: Seven Stories.

Garnham, Nicholas. 1990a. "Media Theory and the Political Future of Mass Communication." In *Capitalism and Communication: Global Culture and the Economics of Information*. London: Sage.

———. 1990b. "The Media and the Public Sphere." In *Capitalism and Communication: Global Culture and the Economics of Information*. London: Sage. Originally published in 1986.

———. 1992. "The Media and the Public Sphere." In *Habermas and the Public Sphere*, edited by Craig Calhoun, 359–75. Cambridge: MIT Press.

Habermas, Jürgen. 1992. "Further Reflections on the Public Sphere." In *Habermas and the Public Sphere*, edited by Craig Calhoun, 421–61. Cambridge: MIT Press.

———. 1995. "Political Economy and Cultural Studies: Reconciliation or Divorce?" *Critical Studies in Mass Communication*, March, 62–71.

2000. Introduction to *Emancipation, the Media, and Modernity: Arguments about the Media and Social Theory*. Oxford: Oxford University Press.

Horwitz, Robert Britt. 1989. *The Irony of Regulatory Reform*. New York: Oxford University Press.

Kristof, Nicholas D., Edward Wyatt, David Sanger, and Sheryl WuDunn. 1999. "Global Contagion: A Narrative." *New York Times,* February 15, 16, 17, 18. Available at www.nytimes.com.

Marx, Karl. 1973 [1939]. *Grundrisse*. Translated by Martin Nicolaus. New York: Vintage.

Meehan, Eileen R. 1990. "Why We Don't Count: The Commodity Audience." In *Logics of Television*, edited by Patricia Mellencamp, 117–37. Bloomington: Indiana University Press/BFI Books.

———. 1993. "Commodity Audience, Actual Audience: The Blindspot Debate." In *Illuminating the Blindspots: Essays Honoring Dallas W. Smythe*, edited by Janet Wasko, Vincent Mosco, Manjunath Pendakur, 378–97. Norwood, N.J.: Ablex.

Miller, Toby. 1998. *Technologies of Truth: Cultural Citizenship and the Popular Media*. Minneapolis: University of Minnesota Press.

Mosco, Vincent. 1996. *The Political Economy of Communication: Rethinking and Renewal*. London: Sage.

Murdock, Graham. 1995. "Across the Great Divide: Cultural Analysis and the Condition of Democracy." *Critical Studies in Mass Communication*, March, 89–95.

Ó Siochrú, Seán, Bruce Girard, and Amy Mahan. 2002. *Global Media Governance: A Beginner's Guide*. Lanham, Md.: Rowman & Littlefield.

Wasko, Janet, and Ingunn Hagen, eds. 1999. *Consuming Audiences? Production and Reception in Media Research*. Cresskill, N.J.: Hampton.

White, Stephen K., ed. 1995. *The Cambridge Companion to Habermas*. Cambridge: Cambridge University Press.

Young, Iris Marion. 2000. "Inclusive Political Communication." In *Inclusion and Democracy*. Oxford: Oxford University Press.

2

The Rise of the Westminster School

James Curran

The role of the Birmingham School in the development of cultural studies in Britain is well known. It is the subject of competitive reminiscence (Clarke 1991; Hall 1992, 1996; Brunsdon 1996), the target of recurrent criticism (e.g., Thornton and Gelder 1997), and a focal point of a good textbook history of British cultural studies (Turner 2002).

By contrast, the history of media studies in Britain has yet to be written, and the part played by different traditions in its development remains obscure. This chapter will look at a pioneering group of academics—the Westminster School—because it played a prominent role in shaping the definition of British media studies. The areas that the School identified as important and the distinctive approach it adopted crucially influenced the development of media research in Britain.

The Westminster School originated in the early 1970s in the Media Department of the Polytechnic of Central London (PCL, renamed the University of Westminster in 1992). Its founders introduced the first media studies degree in Britain in 1975. In 1979 they launched *Media, Culture, and Society*, now the largest subscription media academic journal in Europe. Though centered at the University of Westminster, the Westminster School has since outgrown its corporate origins and is no longer confined to people linked to the university.

Early Formative Influences

In the early 1960s, an unprecedented number of people educated at elite universities went to work in the media. This was a time when films were hailed as a great art form. London's Royal Court was undermining the genteel hegemony of Rattigan and Coward, and regional novelists like Baistow and Sillitoe were making an acclaimed breakthrough. Above all, the British Broadcasting Corporation (BBC), in particular BBC2 (launched in 1964), was producing groundbreaking drama. The media seemed to be an arena of artistic experiment, progressive ideas, glamour, and influence.

Their siren call attracted two avant-garde film enthusiasts with an elite educational background: Nicholas Garnham (Winchester and Cambridge) and Vincent Porter (Rugby and Oxford). Garnham became the coproducer of the BBC2 fortnightly program *The Movies*, while Porter became a documentary filmmaker, based mainly at Shell Films. They wrote critically about the media, became involved in television and film union (Association of Cinematographic and Television Technicians, ACTT) politics, and started teaching, initially as part-time lecturers in film. Garnham became head of media studies at PCL and designed Britain's first media studies degree course, while Porter established a pioneering postgraduate diploma (later a master's) in film also at PCL.

The new media studies degree course (building on an earlier diploma) was intended to establish a seminary for critical media workers, with a strong sense of vocation. It was justified as a way of fostering "media literacy"—1970s educational jargon meaning the cultivation of informed and discriminating responses to the media. This was an echo of the Leavisite drive to engage critically with popular culture, expressed in its manifesto, *Discrimination and Popular Culture* (Thompson 1964). However, the principal inspiration behind the new degree was not Leavisite disdain for commercialized culture, but rather a critical love affair with the media. In Garnham's case, this began with cool jazz and "auteur" theory in a half "gap year" in Paris. It blossomed into a celebration of commercial culture as art in the films of Samuel Fuller, in an elegantly written book that refers nostalgically to Garnham's "love born in the dark womb of Sunday afternoon moviehouses in rain-drenched provincial towns and the seedier areas of London" (Garnham 1971, 7). It was expressed in a more characteristically acerbic tone in a coauthored book of interviews with broadcasters (Bakewell and Garnham 1970), in which Garnham lamented "the decline of serious programming" in British television during the later 1960s (Garnham 1970, 203). Yet he remained hopeful about the future possibilities of broadcasting. The drive behind educational innovation was fueled by optimism of both will and intellect. The Westminster pioneers believed that the academy could play a part in ensuring that the media fulfilled their progressive potential.

The creation of a new degree course generated its own research demands, since gaps in the relevant literature had to be filled. It also established a strong institutional base despite being located at the margins of educational privilege, in a polytechnic. Media studies fitted the polytechnic mission: it was different, vocational, and "relevant." The Polytechnic of Central London did everything in its power to make the launch of undergraduate media studies a success, introducing teaching sabbaticals to assist preparation of the new degree and recruiting new staff to teach it. Its successor body, the University of Westminster, continued this careful husbandry. In 1992, Westminster's media academics were the only group in any discipline in the former polytechnic sector to gain the top, "international excellence," research ranking in the official audit of universities. The Westminster department's reputation continued to grow and became a magnet for research students around the world. From an outsider's viewpoint, its staff sometimes seemed unaware of the extent to which they were being supported because they were so protected from the harsh winds that blew elsewhere. Yet the resource backing they received was crucial in both incubating and *maintaining* the Westminster tradition. By contrast, two other pioneer centers at Birmingham and Leicester Universities were housed in more traditional institutions that viewed the study of the media and popular culture with suspicion. These centers were given much less support, and were eventually closed down.

One tradition influencing the early work of the Westminster School was a media policy debate extending back in Britain to the 1920s. The development of film policy had been paved by a succession of public reports (e.g., HMSO 1936, 1949a, 1968, 1976), and a notable think tank report (*Political and Economic Planning [PEP]* 1952), framed for the most part in terms of economic analysis and objectives. Successive inquiries into broadcasting had culminated in an influential indictment of the market and a call for the reform of commercial television, which drew on both economics and literary studies (HMSO 1962a). A well-researched think tank report (*PEP* 1938) advocated professionalism and self-regulation as the solutions to media concentration and falling standards—a view adopted by the first Royal Commission on the Press (HMSO 1949b). Its successor drew heavily on radical Keynesian economics for its analysis, though not its conclusions (HMSO 1962b). Thus there already existed a way of discussing the media that was heavily indebted to economics (then in its expansive, confident, Keynesian phase) before media studies was born in Britain. It was given house room in the emergent Westminster tradition.

The other two influences that shaped the Westminster School were Marxism and literary studies. Most of the Westminster pioneers had studied English literature at university, and many of them were affected by the radicalization that took place in universities during the late 1960s and early 1970s. Westminster's roots in the study of literature was one of the things that made it different from the Leicester/Loughborough tradition, which originated, and remained grounded, in sociology.[1] What is more difficult to explain is why the Westminster tradition should have parted company from the two traditions represented by the journal *Screen* and by the Birmingham

Centre for Contemporary Cultural Studies, since these were also strongly influenced by Marxism and literary studies. Yet the *Screen* and Birmingham
traditions took the idealist high road and followed a winding mountain path
through textual analysis, structuralism, psychoanalytic theory, ideology,
postmodernism, and audience discourse. By contrast, the Westminster
School took the materialist low road and grubbed around the political economy of the media, its institutions, regulation, technology, and history.

Part of the explanation for this divergence has to do with the media involvement of Westminster staff, in contrast to most Birmingham researchers.
Nicholas Garnham had worked in television for ten years as a film editor and
director, and he was consequently acutely aware of the importance of resource allocation and institutional processes in the making of programs. Similarly, Vincent Porter's jaundiced experience as a documentary filmmaker
prompted him to conclude in a coauthored book that "it is virtually impossible to exhibit an independent short film profitably in Britain" (Knight and
Porter 1967, 139). Some of their colleagues, with no prior media background,
became involved in political journalism. James Curran edited the Labour Party
magazine, *New Socialist*, and became a weekly columnist for *The Times*; Colin
Sparks edited the Socialist Workers Party magazine, *Socialist Review*, while
Irene Brennan, a colleague in PCL's School of Communication, was on the editorial board of the Communist Party magazine, *Marxism Today*. Moreover,
the PCL/Westminster department differed from the theory-centered Birmingham center in that half its staff (all ex-media professionals) taught how-to-do-
it media production courses, a major component of its undergraduate degree.
Recognition of the central importance of institutional processes, resource allocation, and markets was part of the culture of the Westminster tradition, an
extension of its multiple links to the media industries.

STATE REFORMISM

One of the distinctive features of the Westminster tradition was that it developed a reformist view of the democratic state as an empowering agency that
could enhance potentially the contribution that the media made to society.
This reformist view was sometimes contested or qualified, and increasingly
set in a wider context, by writers in the Westminster tradition. It was not a
straightforwardly positive view of the benign role of "big government." But
the fact that numerous Westminster writers adopted a statist approach made
them different from the majority in the radical tradition of media research
during the 1970s. It also tended to set them apart from the prevailing view of
society during the neoliberal hegemony of the 1980s and 1990s (which left
its imprint on the development of cultural studies).

The troubled nature of the Westminster School's statism, indeed the rather
reluctant way in which it moved against the grain of radical consensus, is

perhaps best illustrated by Nicholas Garnham's early wanderings in the desert. In 1973, he argued that the BBC and Independent Television (ITV) "manipulate the public" in the interests of the "power elite" (Garnham 1973, 12). This was attributed largely to flows of official influence in which the "state exercises a daily influence on the output and general behaviour of the broadcasters" and in which the "price of independence has been eternal obedience" (Garnham 1973, 15). This pattern of control, supposedly exemplified by the BBC's subservience to the government in the 1922 general strike, was, according to Garnham, underpinned by the recruitment of broadcasters from a narrow class and educational base, hierarchical management within broadcasting organizations, and an ideology of objectivity that masked adherence to mainstream opinion. The solution lay in root-and-branch transformation of British broadcasting in which "we must build our new structures from the margins in to the centre" (Garnham 1973, 42). This could be achieved through the creation of devolved television structures accountable to grassroots and worker control (which Garnham specified in the fastidious detail of a Fabian Society pamphlet).

This approach was typical of much radical analysis during this period. For example, Philip Schlesinger—for a time a squatter at the Regent Street headquarters of the Polytechnic of Central London—argued that broadcasters' strategy for presenting themselves as neutral and coping with the pressure of time was to use formal debates conducted through the institutions of the state as the basis for framing discussion of current affairs. "For being impartial in terms broadly pre-defined by the state," wrote Philip Schlesinger, "it [the BBC] is rewarded with the gift of independence" (Schlesinger 1978, 168). This led to "depreciation" of the radical politics of student protests, factory occupations, and public demonstrations.

By the later 1970s, Garnham was having second thoughts. In 1978, he made an enigmatic reference to the deficiencies of both liberal and Marxist views of the state (Garnham 1978, 49), and expressed reservations about syndicalist and decentralizing solutions (Garnham 1978, 7–8). A year later, he expressed unease about "unproblematic acceptance" of the view that the media are "ideological tools of ruling-class domination" as a consequence of being privately owned or controlled through the state (Garnham 1990a, 27). This was later widened to a critique of "hegemonic" accounts of state power and the professional ideology of objectivity. All too often, he warned, this led to "idealist formulations of free communications" proposed in a grassroots form (Garnham 1990a, 106). Without saying so, Garnham was attacking his former self.

His first means of escape from classical Marxism (or, at least, one version of it) was to attack its base/superstructure model—the assumption that the economic base determines the superstructure of thought. In the same essay, he also challenged the counterclaim that ideas are free-floating and autonomous. What was needed, he argued, was a middle way that examines "the specificities of the shifting relationships between economic, ideological and political levels" (Garnham 1990a, 27). The implication of this was that the nature of the state, and the relationship of the media to it, varied in different historical contexts that needed to be investigated rather than preordained by simplifying theory.

His second route out of fundamentalist Marxism was Habermas. Garnham reinterpreted Habermas's *Structural Transformation of the Public Sphere* in a way that was enormously influential. Habermas (1989) argued that growing numbers of the bourgeoisie in eighteenth century Britain, France, and Germany had engaged in critical discussion of public affairs through the pages of the press, and through face-to-face interactions in drawing rooms and coffeehouses. These discussions had been directed, at least in principle, toward the public good, and had given rise to reason-based public opinion that influenced government policy. However, this public sphere of reasoning debate had been undermined subsequently by the extension of corporate and state power, and by the development of manipulative and commodified forms of communication. With imaginative flair, Garnham extracted from this then relatively obscure book (which he first encountered in French translation) a normative model of the media's role in the contemporary democratic system. In effect, he advocated the reincarnation of the eighteenth century restricted public sphere as an enlarged public space between the state and the economy in which different views could be freely expressed in a rational, universalistic and inclusive form directed toward the public good. This then led, in the next crucial step of Garnham's argument, to the conclusion that the public service model of broadcasting was the "embodiment of the principles of the public sphere" (Garnham 1990a, 109). This "requires us to revalue the public service model" and defend public service broadcasting (Garnham 1990a, 114).

Garnham thus derived from Habermas a normative model of how broadcasting ought to be. Since only the state could bring this model into being, it followed that the role of state should be reassessed. This prompted Garnham to attack other leftists for their antistatist attitudes (e.g., Garnham 1990a, 106). His reorientation was achieved, at least in terms of published work, not through a conjunctural appraisal of the state in contemporary society—based on an examination of the shifting relation between the economic, political, and ideological—which Garnham had earlier advocated in principle. This would have entailed wading in deep waters since Garnham was writing during the height of the Thatcherite ascendancy. Instead, he extrapolated from Habermas's interpretation of the past an essentially liberal argument[2] and transplanted it to the present. This entailed sidelining the more radical (and simplistic) part of Habermas's *The Structural Transformation of the Public Sphere*, and by implication repudiating its account of the enlarged state and electronic media as subverters of the public sphere.

Garnham's reinterpretation of Habermas had a clear parallel with Hall's reinterpretation of Gramsci, during broadly the same period. Both Gramsci and Habermas were "known" Marxists and provided intellectually respectable sources from which to import liberal ideas. A highly selective as-similation of Gramsci's thought provided for radical cultural studies a way of integrating ethnicity and gender into new conceptual maps, and of opening an escape hatch out of its version of radical functionalism understood in terms of ideological class domination. In a similar way, Habermas was uti-lized to break free from a political economy version of radical functionalism (typified by Miliband 1973), based partly on the idea that broadcasting is controlled by the capitalist state.

The first fruit of this escape was a wide-ranging discussion of the nature of the contemporary public sphere, with contributions from around the world.[3] In essence, this was a debate about the media and the democratic system that moved backwards and forwards between the descriptive ("how it is") and the normative ("how it ought to be"). It was a debate to which Westminster pio-neers made a significant contribution. Among other things, Garnham (1986, 1992) made the key point that the original conception of the public sphere as an aggregation of interacting individuals was inadequate, and needed to take account of organized groupings and their relationship to the media—something that Habermas (1996) subsequently attempted to do in an ambi-tious reworking of his original thesis. Garnham (2000) went on to offer a wide-ranging defense of the idea of public reason that underlies most under-standings of the public sphere in opposition to some versions of postmod-ernist and feminist criticism. Another Westminster School veteran, John Keane (1996), argued that the public sphere should be reconceived as micro-, meso- and macropublic spheres, by which he meant, broadly, local, subcultural, re-gional, national, international, and global public spheres. This prompted James Curran to pose the question, how should media systems respond to the erosion of national government power in favor of global financial markets, transnational business, and international regulatory agencies? He answered in part that public service broadcasting should renegotiate its his-torical legacy as the product of the nation, giving more attention to the new multilayered system of global power and the forces that were seeking to hold it to account (Curran 2002a). He went on to examine the role of global Inter-net journalism in building an international civil society (Curran 2003) and called for suprastate sponsorship of an independent, global public service in-ternet (Curran and Seaton 2003).

Public sphere theory also informed evaluations of media content by West-minster analysts. John Corner (1995) explored its implication in terms of news, documentaries, and advertising, while Peter Dahlgren (1992) drew at-tention to the role of media entertainment in forging a sense of symbolic community and mutual obligation. Dahlgren's analysis implied that media entertainment provides important channels of public debate and contributes to collective self-rule through norm-based social regulation. In a celebrated essay, Paddy Scannell (1989) argued that public service broadcasting en-hances the "reasonable, as distinct from the rational, character of daily life in public and private contexts." Reasonableness, he continues, means that "people accept mutual obligations to each other, acknowledge that they are answerable and accountable to each other—in short, deal with each other as equals" (Scannell 1989, 342). By augmenting "claims to communicative entitlements"—the right to know, understand, speak, hold to account, listen, and be heard—and by fostering a sense of community membership, public service broadcasting underpins a culture of democratic sociality.

Most versions of public sphere theory argue that the media should offer a free and open forum of debate, promote public knowledge, and foster forms of discourse that are directed toward the general good. This provided a basis for examining (and also valorizing) the work of public service broadcasting. For example, James Curran drew attention to the way in which young journalists—mostly women—were attempting to redefine the conventions of journalism in a regular BBC current affairs program *Newsnight*. The injunction to "get away from white men in suits" and "broaden our political coverage away from Westminster" contained in one internal memo (cited in Curran 2002b, 182–83) typified an attempt to find new ways of extending public participation in debate, breaking free from elite news sources and developing alternative strategies of reporting. A similarly upbeat view was offered of British television news between 1975 and 1999. It was claimed that—despite increasing market pressures—British mass television offered adequate amounts of foreign and political coverage within a more differentiated news service because it was publicly funded and regulated (Barnett, Seymour, and Gaber 2000).

The same general orientation informed studies of broadcasting organization. A key theme of Barnett and Curry's (1994) portrait of the BBC during the Thatcher years was that its institutional fundamentals—its goals, public funding, tradition of risk taking and sense of purpose, and collective memory—enabled the corporation to maintain high standards despite political pressure and attack, budget cuts, restructuring, and flawed leadership. Other writers in the Westminster tradition offer less sanguine assessments of the BBC during this period (O'Malley 1994; Leys 2001; Curran and Seaton 2003), though from a position sympathetic to the ideals of public sphere journalism.

However, a positive view of the democratic state as a sponsor of journalism serving the public sphere was subject to growing qualification at a time when neoliberal administrations around the world were promoting free market policies. The main theme of Jill Hill's comparative study of telecommunications deregulation in Britain, the United States, and Japan was that it was "reregulation" in the interest of big business (Hills 1986). Similarly, Vincent Porter (1991) argues that the extension of national and international copyright protection was designed to assist not "authors" but broadcasting and record companies. Peter Goodwin (1998) portrayed Conservative broadcasting policy between 1979 and 1997 as being driven by a desire to advance the market at the expense of public service, combined with the promotion of authoritarian controls. A subtheme of his book is that this pursuit of a seemingly resolute agenda was often ad hoc, ambivalent, constrained, and sometimes ineffectual. A broadly similar theme is found in Vincent Porter and Suzanne Hasselbach (1991), who argue that the right-wing coalition government's drive to promote market "reforms" of broadcasting in Germany during the 1980s was powerfully constrained, not least by the Federal Constitutional Court's judgments upholding the right of public access to diverse information enshrined in West Germany's Basic Law.

Thus a theoretical view of a repressive bourgeois state and a normative view of the enlightened state as the sponsor of public sphere openness and freedom gave way to a more contextualized understanding of the role of the state in relation to the media. An especially informative example of this situated approach is Colin Sparks's political economy of the media[4] in Eastern Europe before and after 1989 (Sparks 1998). His central argument is that the fall of communism gave rise to a political rather than a social revolution. It resulted in a recomposition of the ruling elite to include former members of the communist state bureaucracy, former dissidents, and local businesspeople, often with links to Western capital, rather than to a more profound transformation of society. Yet it gave rise to a significant shift from highly concentrated power centered on the leadership of the national Communist party, to competition between groups of rulers. This competition was played out in the context of authoritarian political cultures that limited media diversity. Public broadcasting tended to be controlled by the party in power; commercial broadcasting was distorted when franchises were awarded to political allies, who became further involved in politics in order to seek regulatory favors. The press, often controlled by former members of the *nomenklatura,* tended to be initially critical of government. In this general account—allowing for significant variations between countries—newly created democratic states were not custodians of hands-off public interest regulation that served the welfare of society. However, the greater fragmentation of power that followed the ending of Communist party rule and the introduction of electoral democracy promoted the development of a more pluralistic—though still flawed—media system.

In short, the Westminster tradition developed a strong interest in the "political" aspect of the political economy tradition, marking a break from the narrow materialism represented by pioneers like Dallas Smythe. While increasingly stressing the need to contextualize and differentiate, it retained a generally reformist view of the democratic state as potentially a sponsor of enlightened media reform.

MARKET CENSORSHIP

A positive view of the state went hand in hand with a critical view of the market. The Westminster School developed a sustained critique of the market's distorting influence on the democratic performance of the media.

Thus James Curran argued that the rise of market entry costs, the growth of advertising finance, and increasing oligopoly rendered the press unrepresentative (Curran 1977). Working with two undergraduates, he examined the market dynamics causing the growing depoliticization of the national popular press (Curran, Douglas, and Whannel 1980). Publishers' market research over a forty-year period showed that coverage of public affairs had a minority appeal concentrated especially among older and male readers, whereas human interest stories and certain entertainment features were read extensively by all social groups. The intensification of market pressures led to the erosion of public affairs coverage in favor of content with a common denominator appeal. Curran also investigated advertising influence on the press in a number of essays. Generous editorial space was allocated, he argued, to certain content categories with limited reader appeal as a way of organizing readers into suitable job lots for advertisers (Curran 1978). Arguing that blackmailing pressure by advertisers was overstated (Curran 1980), he concluded that advertising influence operated in a largely impersonal and unsought way. Advertising is a subsidy system that reflects and reproduces social inequality by distorting the structure of the press, and sometimes the type of reader courted by publishers (Curran 1981; cf. Sparks 1999). His overall contention was that the market has fostered right-wing big business ownership of the press, as well as a split between a heavily subsidized elite press and an underprivileged, depoliticized mass press that has tended to promote a conservative form of "common sense" (Curran and Seaton 1981). However, this portrayal of "market censorship" acknowledged a residual democratic element:

> In its entertainment sections, tabloid newspapers do not simply impose a view of the world on its readers, but start from their experiences and interests and work them into a form that is pleasurable and entertaining. Since the majority of tabloid readers [before the spread of the tabloid format] are working class, and experience life in a way that is partly different from representations of reality within the dominant culture, this generates tensions and contradictions within the pages of the popular press. (Curran and Sparks 1991, 232; cf. Curran 2002c)

A similar critique of market distortion was developed in relation to other media. Barnett and Seymour (1999) acknowledged that increasing market pressure was undermining the quality of television current affairs (especially on ITV) and drama. They revealed that between 1987–1988 and 1997–1998, foreign coverage dropped from 15 percent to a mere 7 percent of ITV's current affairs program content. This was part of a more general shift in which analysis of economic and political affairs gave ground to "softer" crime and consumer features. More generally, Barnett and Seymour argued, the fiction output of terrestrial television relied increasingly on tried and tested formulas, renewable series, and upbeat story lines. This was reflected in the growing eclipse of the television play, traditionally the place where new ideas and talent had been tried out and demanding scripts accepted. Individual plays declined as a proportion of public service television drama from 23 percent to 10 percent between 1978 and 1998.

An early exploration of market censorship was also mounted in relation to film. Knight and Porter (1967) argued that vertical integration in the film industry led to the systematic exclusion of minority short films in Britain. Similarly, Nicholas Garnham (1990a) showed that control over distribution was the main reason why a small number of Hollywood majors had been able to dominate the world film market for more than a quarter century.

MARKET DEBATES

Nicholas Garnham's attitude toward the market is more complex and multi-layered than his public reputation as an austere, radical political economist suggests. His first major study attacked the elitist cultural assumptions of public service broadcasting, arguing that television entertainment should be guided by public demand and "has little to do with public service" (Garnham 1970, 294–95). He followed that study with a reverent act of homage to commercial art (Garnham 1971) and a scathing attack on British broadcasting. Significantly, Garnham's firepower was directed mainly at the state and a collaborating intelligentsia rather than the market (Garnham 1973). He subsequently came to endorse the view that the market is a productive force that has created the necessary conditions—surplus time and money—for the growth of civil society and democratic freedom. His later work stressed the extended rhythms of change, the embedded nature of certain problems, the limits and uncertain outcome of public action (Garnham 2000a) in a way that is both analytically and temperamentally removed from the mind-set that drafted detailed blueprints for worker control of television in the early 1970s.

Garnham's consistently dirigiste approach to broadcasting was sustained by his unchanging conviction that the democratic system is ill served by an unregulated market. The provision of information about public affairs, the transfer of specialist knowledge, and the fostering of rational dialogue are, he has long argued, essential to the healthy functioning of democracy, and they are best secured through some version of public service broadcasting. By contrast, his attitude toward "culture"—and cultural markets—has been less fixed.

Relatively early on, he rejected the idea that the market system was destroying, in an unproblematic way, "high culture" or subverting "enlightened culture," whether conceived in terms of the values of preindustrial, dissenting England (Leavis) or the urban working class (Hoggart). In the 1980s and early 1990s, he was strongly influenced by Pierre Bourdieu, whose work he helped promote in Britain (Garnham and Williams 1980). Bourdieu (1984) challenged essentialist theories of cultural judgment, arguing that taste and competences are greatly influenced by class and education, and are linked to strategies for joining a desired group and excluding others (Bourdieu 1984). Bourdieu (1993) later portrayed aesthetic judgment as being partly the historical outcome of factional struggles for status and financial rewards in cultural fields of production. These relativizing arguments contributed for a time to Garnham's growing estrangement from traditional aesthetic values, and led to a more positive view of the market as a system for connecting supply and demand. "The market has much to recommend it," he wrote, "provided that consumers enter the market with equal endowments and that concentration of ownership power is reduced, controlled or removed" (Garnham 1990a, 164).

This reorientation led to an influential interlude as an adviser to the left-wing Greater London Council in the early 1980s. The arts policy of the traditional left, in the late 1970s, could be summarized as "bring 'culture' to the people." This translated into more public money for the Arts Council, and more support for regional and educational provision. Arts policy was reinterpreted by the left-wing Greater London Council in the early 1980s as more arts funding for ethnic minorities, women, and progressive groups. Garnham launched an influential attack on both these approaches, arguing that nonmarket provision "has tended either simply to subsidize the existing tastes and habits of the better-off or to create a new form of public culture which has no popular audience" and is directed toward "cultural bureaucrats who pay the bill" (Garnham 1990, 164). It is much better, he argued, to intervene in the cultural industries with a view to creating jobs. Alternative cultural enterprises should also be assisted to adapt better to the market through policies designed to improve their distribution, market expertise, and economies of scale.[5]

Garnham has since elaborated a more traditionalist aesthetic. Challenging the view that cultural judgments are merely the expression of socially defined, transient, subjective taste, he argues that cultural judgments are in fact more enduring than relativistic accounts often acknowledge. Judgments of value based on moral reasoning, truth/insight, and aesthetic pleasure are rightly forged through a "public sphere of critical debate" (Garnham 2000a, 162; cf. Garnham 2001).

But if the general thrust of Westminster School analysis is critical of the role of markets in communications, there is also one notable promarket dissenter. A one-time Leavisite and subsequently a Marxist, Richard Collins shifted in the 1980s to a new position. The deregulatory television policies of the Thatcher government should be broadly welcomed, he argued, because they represented an attempt by a radical middle class to weaken an old elite's control of broadcasting and empower the viewer (Collins 1990). The rise of Silvio Berlusconi, he argued, has also "increased the external pluralism of the Italian media" (Collins 1990, 100).

This was followed by Richard Collins's influential and eloquent championing of what became a "New Labour" perspective. The privatization and liberalization of telecommunications, Collins and Murroni argued, was a success, causing prices to go down and the quality and range of services to improve. But the picture elsewhere, they decided, was more mixed. The new right exaggerated the speed of technological change in the communications industries and was overly optimistic about the extent of genuine competition. "What is needed," they concluded, "is competition policy where competition can thrive in the public interest and regulation where it cannot" (Collins and Murroni 1996, 12), linked to a program of libertarian legal reform. Although making a reverent genuflection to "the benefits of innovation, efficiency and a thriving industrial sector . . . conferred by private ownership and competition" (Collins and Murroni 1996, 182), they actually endorse a quite extensive degree of public regulation. For example, they argue in favor of retaining the BBC as a producer of merit goods, even if its structure should "more closely approximate to the federal business model of Unilever and ICI" (Collins and Murroni 1996, 147). Yet, if the book is directed against the arguments of other members of the Westminster School, it is still manifestly a Westminster School product. It is tuned to the same wavelength in assuming that economic organization and political regulation of the media shapes their contribution to society.

Discussion of the role of the market also developed a comparative dimension. A number of essays in Curran and Park (2001) suggested that the market exerts an emancipatory influence on the media in the context of authoritarian societies. However, Naomi Sakr challenges this argument in her notable study of satellite broadcasting in the Middle East. She shows that owners of satellite TV enterprises often have close ties with Arab states; concentration of satellite TV ownership has restricted pluralism; the flow of advertising is both limited and distorted; and official controls are exerted in a variety of ways, not least through national governments, regional regulation, and a pan-Arab code of ethics underpinned by penal sanctions. What she reveals is a highly politicized and state-penetrated market that sustains limited media autonomy (as does, to a lesser degree, Colin Sparks in his analysis of Eastern Europe). The one key exception she identifies to this regime of control is Al-Jazeera, a state-linked organization in Qatar (not unlike the BBC), whose relative freedom springs from the Qatar government's desire for prestige (Sakr 2001).

If one issue of central concern to the Westminster tradition is the role of markets in the functioning of the media, another is the influence more generally of the industrial production of communications. Drawing on insights from mainstream economics, Nicholas Garnham argued that the economic organization of the media (irrespective of its form of ownership) influences their structure and output. Economies of scale are substantial in the media industries because they have high "first copy" costs and low marginal costs of reproduction. This creates a strong incentive to maximize audiences; to lower unit costs through large-scale production; and to mount an increased drive to sell overseas. In this situation imported programs are often cheaper than indigenous productions (Garnham 1990a; Garnham 2000a; Collins, Garnham and Locksley 1988). In general, big operators tend to prevail over small ones because they are in a better position to respond to the unpredictability of media markets. They can hedge their bets by offering a wider range of products (Garnham 1990a). Their competitive advantage is sometimes reinforced through their control of the distribution system, usually the key locus of power in market systems. But if size tends to prevail, it can also generate higher levels of media product investment and quality—a key reason why Garnham shifted away from his earlier "small is beautiful" grassroots position. It is also why he has consistently criticized the drive to expand the number of television channels, arguing that more outlets will cause limited resources, constrained by the finite time and money of consumers, to be spread more thinly between channels, with a resulting loss of quality (e.g., Garnham 2000a). Some of these general arguments about the economic organization of the media proved to be highly influential, gaining prominence in books outside the orbit of the Westminster tradition (e.g., Hesmondhalgh 2002).

Thus the Westminster tradition challenges the prevailing tradition of British media studies in which content and audiences are the center of study and institutional mediations are ignored. In contrast to this "immaculate conception" perspective of media texts, the Westminster tradition argues that political and economic forms of media organization and regulation strongly influence the output and role of the media. The logical extension of this position was to review what form this regulation should take.

MEDIA POLICY

In the early 1970s, the assumption was that the next television channel would be ITV2. It was ITV's "turn," following the creation of BBC2 in 1964. However, a vociferous lobby of academics and broadcasters challenged this consensus. They argued that the output of the "cozy duopoly" of BBC and ITV was too similar; its staff was too often drawn from a small pool of Oxbridge graduates; its drama was increasingly middlebrow and unadventurous; and its journalism was governed by a restrictive, unspoken centrism.

Prominent among these critics was Nicholas Garnham, not least because he channeled dissatisfaction into demands for wholesale reform. In 1970, he called for BBC radio and television to be separated, and in 1973 for the corporation to be broken up (Garnham 1970, 1973). His coup in 1974 was to persuade a Labour Party media policy study group, chaired by Tony Benn and including senior trade unionists and politicians, to advocate the complete dismantlement of the broadcasting system into "dispersed program units" (Labour Party 1974, 14). The resulting report, *The People and the Media*, gained extensive support within the Labour party partly because it attracted negative media publicity. The appointment of the Annan Committee (HMSO 1977a) in 1974 was a response to this and other expressions of dissatisfaction with the television system.

In the event, the committee recommended the establishment of a new type of television channel. This was a product of a sustained campaign for change mounted by radical academics and broadcasters in which Garnham played a leading role (even if he opposed the creation of Channel 4). This campaign was fueled by research, typified by Collins and Porter's celebration of Cologne television station's backing for the "worker film" movement (Collins and Porter 1981). Channel 4 came into being in 1982 with a brief to innovate for and cater to minorities. It proved to be a successful way of re-newing the public service tradition.

Some members of the Westminster tradition—Nicholas Garnham, James Curran, Steven Barnett, and Jean Seaton—acted as media policy advisers to the Labour Party, serving on an extended shift basis from the 1970s to the 1990s, while Vincent Porter became increasingly central in the progressive Viewers and Listeners Association. They contributed to Labour's sustained opposition to broadcasting deregulation during the Conservative eighteen-year ascendancy, and thus played a part in blunting the New Right's assault on public service broadcasting. Although increasingly sidelined by the con-solidation of New Labour, they continued to advocate broadcasting reforms, such as new ways of appointing BBC governors and members of regulatory authorities that would prevent government "packing" (Barnett and Curry 1994; Collins and Murroni 1996; Curran and Seaton 1997). The halfhearted reform that followed in 2002 failed to adequately distance broadcasters from the long reach of government. Jean Seaton, the new official historian of the BBC, contributed to its creative soul-searching in the early 2000s, not least through a seminal paper that became set reading for BBC governors (Seaton 2000). More generally, the role of Westminster academics in influencing Labour's long-term broadcasting policy is well documented by Des Freed-man (2003).

But if some success met efforts to sustain and renew public service broad-casting, there was virtually no return on efforts to reform the press. James Cur-ran advocated Nordic social market policies (Labour Party 1974), a version of which appeared in Labour's 1983 and 1987 general election manifestos, and was revised in Curran (1986). He switched briefly to a professionalizing ap-proach, initiating the application for funding of *British Journalism Review* (founded in 1990), and made a pitch through New Labour's think tank for strengthening staff rights as a way of divorcing press ownership from control (Curran 1995; cf. Collins and Murroni 1996). Meanwhile Jean Seaton (1990) advocated positive content requirements for the press, modeled on regulation of commercial broadcasting. All initiatives fell on deaf ears. A growing vol-ume of criticism of the press led to the appointment of a Royal Commission on the Press (HMSO 1977b), which failed to offer majority support for any substantial reform and was ignored anyway. That closed the door, as it turned out, for press reform for a generation. The inadequacy of what had been achieved—an ineffectual system of self-regulation—was documented in unsparing detail by John Tulloch (1998) and O'Malley and Soley (2000). Reflecting on the causes of failure, Curran (2000a) pointed to a long-established tradition of united press opposition to any regulation, politicians' fear of alienating publishers, and the absence of a flourishing professional culture in the press of a kind that exists in broadcasting. O'Malley and Soley (2000) countered that even if reformers had encountered resistance, at least they had established the symbolic accountability of the press (cf. O'Malley 1998).

In a more general sense, the Westminster tradition contributed to the structural reorganization of media management. One theme advanced by Curran and Seaton (1981), and elaborated in subsequent editions, was that media policy in Britain was contradictory, and it needed to be rendered coherent through the creation of a single ministry concerned with communications, arts, and entertainment. Somewhat to their perplexity, their argument was taken up by the new right, arguing for the creation of a new ministry that would impose market-based consistency across the full spectrum of communications policy. The Department of National Heritage was established in 1992 and renamed the Department of Culture, Media, and Sport in 1997. In actual practice, responsibility for framing media policy remained divided between the Cabinet Office, Department of Trade and Industry, and the "new" ministry; media policy continued to be incoherent and inconsistent. Rather more effective was Collins and Murroni's (1996) early advocacy of a single Office of Communications to absorb the "alphabet soup" of disparate regulatory agencies in the area of communications. The new Office of Communications was created in 2003.

In addition, Westminster academics outlined optimal models of media systems that were widely translated into foreign languages, but were completely removed from the reality of British media politics. John Keane (1991) proposed a model of a media system that is controlled by neither state nor market (though his small print proposals actually entail an extensive degree of state intervention). James Curran (1991) outlined a radical pluralist model in which different media sectors are organized in different ways to serve different purposes, re-presented as a synthesis of best European practice (Curran 2002a).

MEDIA PERFORMANCE

The monitoring of media performance was a natural outcome of a concern with media policy and of public sphere theory emphasizing the role of the media as a source of public information in liberal democracy. Steven Barnett played a leading role in this, not least in work analyzing television content trends that was cited earlier. However, this is only part of his much larger output. Among other things, Barnett and Gaber (2001) argue that a combination of new pressures—increasing media competition and proliferation, demands for greater productivity in multimedia organizations, the growing casualization of the media workforce, and the increasing blizzard of public relations-generated information—is leading to a demonstrable decline of journalistic standards. Building on this study, Barnett (2002) maintains that a decline of social deference during the 1960s led to more critical journalism, which gave rise to a defensive growth of official and party public relations, which led in turn to a defiant assertion of professional autonomy by journalists. The resulting escalation of conflict between journalists and politicians is, Barnett claims, promoting political disengagement by the public. Earlier, Barnett (2001) revealed in a neat piece of research the way in which the phrasing of questions in opinion polls and the interpretation of their results were manipulated by two papers—*Independent on Sunday* and the *Daily Mail*—to legitimate their claims to speak for the people, in diametrically opposed ways, on the decriminalization of drugs. Drawing on other examples, he argues that the British press frequently resorts to populist manipulation in a way that distorts democracy.[6]

Jean Seaton (1999) criticized television as well as the press in a wide-ranging commentary on the reporting of ethnic conflict in former Yugoslavia, Rwanda, and elsewhere during the post–Cold War period. Journalists' easy recourse to "ethnic enmity" as an explanation of conflict often obscures, she argued, the social and economic realities that underlie and prolong these conflicts. It also implicitly represents them as intractable and inevitable, the product of qualities inherent in the character of the communities involved, in ways that sometimes echo the rhetoric of the nationalistic groups furthering persecution. These and other reporting deficiencies stem partly from the media's commercial concern to engage attention through shocking (but not repellent) visual images and familiar story lines.

The charge that Aeron Davis (2002) advances in a wider study of public relations is rather different. He argues that a corporate public relations battle over the contested takeover of the Forte Group in the mid 1990s distorted the way in which it was reported. It resulted in the press portraying the takeover struggle in terms of what would benefit shareholders and investors while ignoring its implications for consumers, employees, or the wider economy. This illustrates, he argues, the current degeneration of business journalism and the way in which "media dialogue" often takes the form of a horizontal communication between elites that sidelines the public.

In a similarly critical vein, James Curran (2000b) shows that the literary editors of the national press privilege the same kinds of books as their top-hatted antecedents did in Victorian Britain. Their static choice ignores changes that have taken place in the structure of knowledge (e.g., the rise of science and the "social sciences") as well as shifts in public taste.

While other relevant studies from the Westminster tradition could be cited, this *audit* strand of the Westminster tradition is underdeveloped. Indeed, the output of critical studies monitoring empirically the performance of journalism in Britain is in general far smaller than it is in some other countries—most obviously the United States but also in some smaller nations like Sweden.

COMMUNICATIONS TECHNOLOGY

The Westminster tradition's engagement with media policy led to what was at that time an unfashionable interest in communications technology. In 1985, Nicholas Garnham argued against the full restoration of a publicly owned state telecommunications monopoly, advocated by some in the Labour movement, while also making the point that there could never be full competition in this sector (Garnham 1985). Perhaps in response to bemused friends unable to understand why he should be interested in telephone wires, Garnham subsequently set out the case—in 1990—for why telecommunications was centrally important. It provided the essential infrastructure for an advanced economy, the pipeline for new media of communication and a major source of employment. Criticizing the past management and development of telecommunications, he urged the breakup of British Telecom into regional enterprises and the establishment of strong public interest regulation (Garnham 1990b).

Garnham (1998) went on to challenge the most fashionable and admired of the "information society" theories, namely, that advanced by Manuel Castells (1996, 1997). In a wide-ranging critique, Garnham (1998) argued that Castells's thesis is based on a reductionist account of changes in the economy that is inconsistent, logically flawed, and inadequately supported by evidence. In particular, it invests with the weight of epochal revolutionary change what is no more than a significant step in a cumulative shift in methods of production and the part played by information workers. Indeed, the evidence is extremely thin for the weakening of economies of scale and of scope as formative influences in the organization of production, for the diminution of multinational corporate concentration, and even for media "de-massification." Returning to the attack, Garnham (2000b) questioned whether a rapid growth of knowledge work was causing structural unemployment among the working class due to a supposed skills gap. In fact, he suggests, the growth of categories like care work and sales is probably outstripping those in the knowledge industries. The former require attributes like interpersonal social skills that are rarely alluded to in fashionable theories of knowledge as human capital formation (Garnham 2000b). More generally, Garnham claims, the production, distribution, and marketing of goods continue to be the dominant sector of the global economy, while the productivity gains from communication technologies have been greatly overstated. "The Information Society," declared Garnham (in a characteristic turn of phrase), "is a concept with no objective correlative in the real world" (Garnham 2002, 267).

These important arguments scarcely featured in his book-length study, *Emancipation, the Media, and Modernity* (2000a). The scattered publications in which they appear are trailers of work in progress, suggesting that Garnham's retirement is purely nominal. His attack on the notion that information and communication technologies are producing a fundamentally new "network" society is part of a consistent position of opposition to technolog-ical determinist theory found in writing by Garnham and others in the West-minster School. Back in the 1980s, Garnham poured scorn on the view that the creation of the cheap, easy-to-use video recorder was going to inaugurate a brave new world of community television. The availability of accessible technology did not mean that the "people" would be able to take over televi-sion, he pointed out, since control of television resided not just in technology but the allocation of spectrum, the assembling of skills and talent, and also the mobilization of considerable financial resources (Garnham 1990a). Similarly, Curran and Seaton (1991) argued that new printing technology, introduced in the British national press in the mid-1980s with the promise that it would pro duce a flowering of minority journalism, changed very little in the long run. It did not undermine the enormous economic advantages of large press groups that enabled them to continue to dominate the market. This continuity was fa-cilitated by their anticompetition strategy of multiplying newspaper sections (causing entry costs to rise once more). Richard Barbrook pointed to a differ-ent set of constraints limiting the impact of new technology in his study of French media development. The introduction of Minitel during the 1980s did not fulfill dreams of a new Athenian agora because "despite the free distribu-tion of terminals . . . the main users of videotext services were young people and professionals, especially men" (1996, 335).

All these objections argue that the unequal distribution of economic and cultural resources in society influence new technology-based communica tions and constrain their emancipatory effect on society. As Garnham com-mented, "The trick is played by concentrating upon the technical potentialities [of new communications technology] rather than upon the social relations that will determine the form in which those potentialities are realised" (Garnham 1990a, 121). This theme informs much of Westminster School writing on the Internet. For example, Sparks points out that access to the web is structured by language, as well as global and class-based inequalities of income. Web content is shaped by the dominance of business with the result that "it is the discourse of business that dominates cyberspace" (Sparks 2001, 92). The web's likely impact on the press, he argues elsewhere, is to exacerbate "exist-ing tendencies to separate politics and ordinary life, and to concentrate pub-lic debate and information in just a few hands" (Sparks 2000, 289). James Cur-ran adopts a more equivocal position, arguing that the battle between premarket and commercial definitions of the web has not yet been resolved and can still be channeled toward a positive outcome through progressive public policy (Curran and Seaton 2003).

This tradition of Westminster School skepticism prompted Barbrook and Cameron to pose the question, Why has so much "radical" commentary on the net made such inflated claims about its emancipatory impact? Their an-swer is that the "Californian ideology" about the net is the wish fulfillment of members of a defeated radical generation who now belong to a privileged "virtual class" and have turned to antistatism "to reconcile radical and reactionary ideas about technological progress" (Barbrook and Cameron 1996, 10). Yet, argue Barbrook and Cameron, state intervention, along with capitalist entrepreneurship and a grassroots "do-it-yourself" (self-organized) culture, is needed to realize some of the hopes centered on the Internet.

MEDIA HISTORY

The other area that the Westminster tradition identified as a priority was media history. This arose from Nicholas Garnham's insistence that the first degree in media studies, introduced in 1975, should have a course on the "media and the making of modern British society." James Curran was told to draft this course but reported back, after reading piles of books devoted to narrow institutional media histories, that it was impossible to frame a new course in this broad, expansive way. Garnham's response was to say, with an audible sigh, "do the best you can."

Books were written partly to serve the needs of this course. Curran and Seaton coauthored the first general academic history of the British media (1981). Their central, underlying theme was that the press and broadcasting had different relationships to society because they were organized in different ways. The capitalist development of the press stifled the flowering of newspaper pluralism in the early nineteenth century, contributed to the defeat of a militant working-class movement, and fostered—with exceptions—a conservative political culture. By contrast, the development of public service broadcasting contributed to the empowerment of the public and greatly enriched the cultural and social development of British society.

Another lecturer on the PCL media history course, Paddy Scannell, wrote with David Cardiff a magisterial history of the BBC in interwar Britain (Scannell and Cardiff 1991). They show how the corporation, though still caught up in the coils of power, developed independent newsgathering resources of its own, pioneered "talks" programs that conveyed a democratizing message, and, at best, gave voice to weak and marginalized groups in society. They also show how the BBC, partly goaded by rivalry from commercial radio, displayed "growing concern . . . for the needs of the 'ordinary listener'" (Scannell and Cardiff 1991, 244), not least through the development of popular music and comedy shows that helped, in their view, to forge "a genuinely common culture." This study has an epilogue—two illuminating essays that continue its central themes in relation to World War II. The BBC, they argue, braved official fury by staging contentious debate about peacetime reconstruction during the war and catered more successfully to the entertainment needs of different publics. This reflected, they argue, a broader change in the social relations of power in wartime Britain in which the governing elite was compelled to accommodate more fully to the concerns and needs of the people (Cardiff and Scannell 1981, 1986).

A third lecturer on the PCL media history course, Vincent Porter, also made a major contribution to British media history. He wrote a history of British film that highlighted the influence of market and political censorship (Porter 1985), and he was the senior editor of an early history of the British cinema (Curran and Porter 1983). This was followed by a flow of publications about film history that foreground two recurring themes. One is the way in which corporate power shaped the historical development of British film, sometimes leavened by the influence of creative individuals and audience demand (Porter 1997, 2000, 2001a; Harper and Porter 1999). The second, linked theme is that British film accommodated to, but also policed, social and political change. Thus he and his coauthor, Sue Harper, contrast the films of reassurance with which 1950s began with films later in the decade that were critical of social, managerial, and gender hierarchies (Harper and Porter 2003). However, their critical tenor was qualified and contained. Thus some 1950s films espoused gender equality, but in the context of support for traditional morality. Other films challenged the stuffy hierarchies of traditional Britain, but in a form that expressed meritocratic rather than radical egalitarian values (Porter 2001b).

One overriding concern of Westminster media history was to identify connections between media political economy and wider changes in society. This input contributed to a gradual revival of British media history (greatly assisted by the feminist transformation of social history). In 2002, it was relatively easy to document alternative ways of viewing the role of the media in the development of modern British society (Curran 2002d)—something that was almost impossible a quarter of a century earlier.

Another legacy of the Westminster tradition was a significant contribution to the history of communications technology. This began with a year-long visit at PCL by an American academic, Carolyn Marvin, whose pioneering work shed new light on the telephone and electric light (Marvin 1988). She revealed the cumulative nature of technological innovation—the gradual evolution of the electric light from fairground and public spectacle to domestic appliance, the transformation of the telephone from an elite subscription service to a popular mode of communication, and early attempts to develop a proto-radio service in Hungary and elsewhere through the use of telephone lines. She also documented the gradual democratization of this early communications technology, as well as the exaggerated fears and also hopes that this aroused.

These two themes of continuity and exaggerated response also feature in Brian Winston's history of communications technology (Winston 1998). He argues that the fax was first introduced in 1847; the idea of television patented in 1884; digitalization demonstrated in 1938; and the web first anticipated in 1945. Lack of historical knowledge of the cumulative nature of communication transformations has given rise, he suggests, to recurrent displays of gullibility. "Historical consciousness," he writes, "reveals the 'Information Revolution' to be largely an illusion, a rhetorical gambit and an expression of technological ignorance" (Winston 1998, 2). However, Winston's main concern was to demolish the view, central to technological determinism, that the evolution of communications technology follows an inner scientific logic, which in turn leads to a transformed world. On the contrary, Winston argues, the evolution from idea to prototype, "invention," and diffusion has been powerfully conditioned by the technology, economy, corporate structure, and cultural patterns of society during the last two centuries. This explains why some technological developments have lain dormant, others have been suppressed, and still others have mushroomed almost simultaneously in different places. The implication of this debunking history is that communications technology is made by society, instead of society being determined by it.

This contextualizing theme is developed in a different way in Jill Hills's groundbreaking history of the international regulation of communications between the mid-nineteenth century and World War II. The central drama of her account centers on how the United States set about subverting Britain's early global control of communications technology—submarine telecommunication cables—maintained through an international regulatory agency, the International Telegraph Union (ITU). The United States imposed unilateral, domestic regulation and ownership restrictions, and developed a mercantilist strategy for supporting its communications industries. In other words, it did precisely what it deplores others doing, now that it is the dominant communications power. More generally, Hills's account is deeply revealing about the interplay of corporate and national power in shaping the international economic environment in which media industries operate (Hills 2002).

If one aim of the Westminster tradition has been to liberate media history from its traditional straitjacket of narrow institutional history, this has found its apotheosis in Jean Seaton's panoramic account of the communication of conflict. Moving effortlessly from the Roman games and medieval art to the Twin Towers bombing and the second Chechen war, she examines the social meanings of representations of "carnage." These range from the moralizing example of a good death in a gladiatorial ring, the uplift inspired by Christian images of suffering, to media reporting of war that fuels barbaric retribution or alternatively an emotional recoiling from cruelty (Seaton 2004).

RETROSPECT

This account provides a record of the work of a group of pioneer media academics in Britain. It is a history of an ensemble of people who influenced each other and who, while not always agreeing—indeed often disagreeing—sought to explore certain areas in a new field of research. These key areas were media political economy, media policy, media and democratic theory, communications technology, and British media history. This research agenda, and the positions associated with the Westminster tradition, significantly influenced the evolution of media studies in Britain.

This is a necessarily selective and condensed account. It leaves out—unforgivably—important work and important contributors to the Westminster tradition. It has said too little about the weaknesses of this tradition, in particular its underdevelopment of feminist analysis[7] and its early seduction by radical functionalism. Yet it provides an indication of the work of one significant grouping that contributed to the broader, radical tradition of media research.

While this account offers a group portrait, it also foregrounds one person—Nicholas Garnham. Garnham has often criticized the professional disengagement of contemporary intellectuals, and the autonomization of media studies as a subject. His own professional life is a tribute to the virtues of critical engagement in public life and a monument to the value of intellectual curiosity. Garnham has contributed for over thirty years—in good times and in bad—to political debate about the development of media policy. He has also traveled confidently across intellectual frontiers, and imported insights from different disciplines and traditions into media studies. The work of Habermas, Bourdieu, and radical economics were championed by him in a way that significantly influenced the development of British media research. His polymathic learning was displayed, in its most expansive mode, in his most recent book (Garnham 2000a). This relates the analysis of the media to the history of modernity; the social organization of society; the role of intellectuals as servants, critics, and sources of power; the interrelationship of ideas, identity, and action; theories of culture and aesthetics; and issues around communications technology and the information society—among other things. It is a book that returns media studies to its origins as a Renaissance subject. It also embodies an Enlightenment tradition of rationality and public purpose in opposition to the postmodernist currents of cultural studies.

Although Nicholas Garnham's leadership has been primarily intellectual, he has also been good at institutional politics without ever seeming to set much store by it. In the early 1970s, he was a dominating presence on the People and Media Labour policy group, full of able politicians and trade unionists. His political skills and personal charisma helped to inaugurate a new degree, and launch a new field of undergraduate study in Britain. They were also deployed in starting and managing a successful journal, *Media, Culture, and Society*. Above all, Garnham was the central figure in the birth and development of the Westminster tradition of research. Had he remained a *Cahier du Cinéma* caterpillar, instead of evolving into a political economy butterfly, the world of media research would have been very much poorer.

NOTES

This chapter draws on conversations and interviews with some of the pioneers of the Westminster School.

1. The Leicester/Loughborough tradition clearly overlaps with that of Westminster. Thus the former includes a succession of distinguished overviews of media political economy, beginning with the trailblazing Murdock and Golding (1974) and continuing (to date) with Murdock and Golding (2001), as well as many other fine studies (including the exemplary Golding and Middleton 1982).

2. For insight into the way in which Habermas's ideas drew on eighteenth-century liberal thought, see Barker (1998).

3. The key springboard of this discussion was Calhoun (1992).

4. Sparks's emphasis has shifted over the years. In 1985, he saw Nordic-style subsidies as a threat to emancipatory journalism (Sparks 1985, 144). Almost twenty-five years later, he wrote in a relatively approving way about state regulation of commercial broadcasting in Britain (Sparks 1998, 181–82).

5. The Greater London Council (GLC) cultural industries policy was adopted by other local authorities as a model for creating jobs and, in a post-GLC development, as a way of reviving rundown urban areas.

6. However, not all his studies are critical. An earlier piece of research salutes the way in which television sports journalists discovered new sports (Barnett 1990).

7. Helen Baehr, the only woman in Pel's Media department in the 1970s, made a pioneering contribution to feminist media research outside the Westminster tradition.

REFERENCES

Bakewell, J., and N. Garnham. 1970. *The New Priesthood*. London: Allen Lane.

Barbrook, R. 1996. *Media Freedom*. London: Pluto.

Barbrook, R., and A. Cameron. 1996. "The Californian Ideology." *Science as Culture* 6, no. 1: 44–72.

Barker, H. 1998. *Newspapers, Politics, and Public Opinion in Late Eighteenth-Century England*. Oxford: Oxford University Press.

Barnett, S. 1990. *Games and Sets*. London: British Film Institute.

———. 2001. "Distorting Democracy; Public Opinion, Polls, and the Press." In S. Splichal, ed., *Public Opinion and Democracy*. New Jersey: Hampton.

———. 2002. "Culture, Consumerism, and Contempt: Broadcasting and Politics after the Communications Act." Inaugural lecture, University of Westminster. Available at www.wmin.ac.uk/events/Barnett.htm.

Barnett, S., and A. Curry. 1994. *The Battle for the BBC*. London: Aurum.

Barnett, S., and I. Gaber. 2001. *Westminster Tales*. London: Continuum.

Barnett, S., and E. Seymour. 1999. *A Shrinking Iceberg Moving South*. London: Campaign for Quality Television.

Barnett, S., E. Seymour, and I. Gaber. 2000. *From Callaghan to Kosovo*. London: University of Westminster.

Bourdieu, P. 1984. *Distinction*. Cambridge: Harvard University Press.

———. 1993. *Field of Cultural Production*. Cambridge: Polity.

Brundson, C. 1996. "A Thief in the Night: Stories of Feminism in the 1970s at CCCS." In D. Morley and K.-H. Chen, eds., *Stuart Hall*. London: Routledge.

Calhoun, C., ed. 1992. *Habermas and the Public Sphere*. Cambridge, Mass. MIT Press.

Cardiff, D., and P. Scannell. 1981. "Radio in World War II." In *The Historical Development of Popular Culture*. London Taylor & Francis.

———. 1986. "'Good Luck War Workers!' Class, Politics, and Entertainment in Wartime Broadcasting." In T. Bennett, C. Mercer, and J. Woollacott, eds., *Popular Culture and Social Relations*.London: Taylor & Francis.

Castells, M. 1996. *The Rise of the Network Society*. Oxford: Blackwell.

———. 1997. *The Power of Identity*. Oxford: Blackwell.

Clarke, J. 1991. *New Times and Old Enemies*. London: HarperCollins Academic.

Collins, R. 1990. *Television: Policy and Culture*. London: Unwin Hyman.

Collins, R., N. Garnham, and G. Locksley. 1988. *The Economics of Television*. London: Sage.

Collins, R., and C. Murroni. 1996. *New Media, New Policies*. Cambridge: Polity.

Collins, R., and V. Porter. 1981. *WDR and the Arbeiterfilm*. London: British Film Institute.

Corner, J. 1995. *Television Form and Public Address*. London: Arnold.

Curran, J. 1977. "Capitalism and Control of the Press, 1800–1975." In J. Curran, M. Gurevitch, and J. Woollacott, eds., *Mass Communication and Society*. London: Arnold.

———. 1978. "Advertising and the Press." In J. Curran, ed., *The British Press: A Manifesto*. London: Macmillan.

———. 1980. "Advertising as a Patronage System." In H. Christian, ed., *The Sociology of Journalism and the Press*. Sociological Review Monograph, no. 29. Keele, U.K.: Keele University Press.

———. 1981. "The Impact of Advertising on the British Mass Media." *Media, Culture, and Society* 3, no. 1. Reprinted in R. Collins et al., eds., *Media, Culture, and Society· A Critical Reader*. London: Sage.

———. 1986. "The Different Approaches to Media Reform." In J. Curran, J. Ecclestone, G. Oakley, and A. Richardson, eds., *Bending Reality*. London: Pluto.

———. 1991. "Mass Media and Democracy: A Reappraisal." In J. Curran and M. Gurevitch, eds., *Mass Media and Society*. London: Arnold.

———. 1995. *Policy for the Press*. London: Institute for Public Policy Research.

———. 2000a. "Press Reformism 1918–98: A Study of Failure." In H. Tumber, ed., *Media Power, Professionals, and Policies*. London: Routledge.

———. 2000b. "Literary Editors, Social Networks, and Cultural Tradition." In J. Curran, ed., *Media Organisations in Society*. London: Arnold.

———. 2002a. *Media and Power*. London: Routledge.

———. 2002b. "Television Journalism: Theory and Practice, the Case of *Newsnight*." In P. Holland, *Television Handbook*. 2d ed. London: Routledge.

———. 2002c. "The Sociology of the Press." In A. Briggs and P. Cobley, eds., *The Media*. 2d ed. Harlow: Longman.

———. 2002d. "Media and the Making of British Society, c. 1700–2000." *Media History* 8, no. 2.

———. 2003. "Global Journalism: Case Study of the Internet." In N. Couldry and J. Curran, eds., *Contesting Media Power*. Lanham, Md.: Rowman & Littlefield.

Curran, J., A. Douglas, and G. Whannel. 1980. "The Political Economy of the Human-Interest Story." In A. Smith, ed., *Newspapers and Democracy*. Cambridge: MIT Press.

Curran, J., and M.-Y. Park, eds. 2001. *De-Westernizing Media Studies*. London: Routledge.

Curran, J., and V. Porter, eds. 1983. *British Cinema History*. London: Weidenfeld & Nicholson.

Curran, J., and J. Seaton. 1981. M.-Y. Park, eds. *Power without Responsibility*. London: Fontana.

——. 1991. *Power without Responsibility*. 4th ed. London: Routledge.

——. 1997. *Power without Responsibility*. 5th ed. London: Routledge.

——. 2003. *Power without Responsibility*. 6th ed. London: Routledge.

Curran, J., and C. Sparks. 1991. "Press and Popular Culture." *Media, Culture, and Society* 13, no. 2.

Dahlgren, P. 1992. Introduction to P. Dahlgren and C. Sparks, eds., *Journalism and Popular Culture*. London: Sage.

Davis, A. 2002. *Public Relations Democracy*. Manchester, U.K.: Manchester University Press.

Freedman, D. 2003. *Television Policies of the Labour Party, 1951–2001*. London: Cass.

Garnham, N. 1970. Conclusion to J. Bakewell and N. Garnham, eds., *The New Priesthood*. London: Allen Lane.

——. 1971. *Samuel Fuller*. London: Secker & Warburg.

——. 1973. *Structures of Television*. London: British Film Institute.

——. 1978. *Structures of Television*. 2d ed. London: British Film Institute.

——. 1979. "Contribution to a Political Economy of Mass Communication." *Media, Culture, and Society* 1. Reprinted in N. Garnham, *Capitalism and Communication* (London: Sage, 1990).

——. 1985. "Telecommunications Policy in the United Kingdom." *Media, Culture, and Society* 7, no. 1.

——. 1986. "The Media and the Public Sphere." In P. Golding, G. Murdock, and P. Schlesinger, eds., *Communicating Politics*. University of Leicester Press. Reprinted in N. Garnham, *Capitalism and Communication* (London: Sage, 1990).

——. 1990a. *Capitalism and Communication*. London: Sage

——. 1990b. *Telecommunications in the UK: A Policy for the 1990s*. Fabian Society Discussion Paper 1.

——. 1992. "The Media and the Public Sphere." In C. Calhoun, ed., *Habermas and the Public Sphere*. Cambridge: MIT Press.

——. 1998. "Information Society Theory as Ideology: A Critique." *Society and Leisure* 21, no. 1.

——. 2000. *Emancipation, the Media, and Modernity*. Oxford: Oxford University Press.

——. 2001. "Reaching for My Revolver: Problems with the Concept of Culture." *European Review* 9, no. 4.

——. 2002. "'Information Society' as Theory or Ideology: A Critical Perspective on Technology, Education and Employment in the Information Age." In W. Dutton and B. Loader, eds., *Digital Academe*. London: Routledge.

Garnham, N., and R. Williams. 1980. "Pierre Bourdieu and the Sociology of Culture: An Introduction." *Media, Culture, and Society* 2, no. 3.

Golding, P., and S. Middleton. 1982. *Images of Welfare*. Oxford: Martin Robertson.

Goodwin, P. 1998. *Television unter the Tories*. London: Birtish Film Institute.

Habermas, J. 1989 [1962]. *The Structural Transformation of the Public Sphere*. Cambridge: Polity.

——. 1996. *Between Facts and Norms*. Cambridge: Polity.

Hall, S. 1992. "Cultural Studies and Its Theoretical Legacies." In L. Grossberg, C. Nelson, and P. Treichler, eds., *Cultural Studies*. New York: Routledge.

———. 1996. "The Formation of a Diasporic Intellectual: An Interview with Stuart Hall." In D. Morley and K.-H. Chen, eds., *Stuart Hall*. London: Routledge.

Harper, S., and V. Porter. 1999. "Cinema Audience Tastes in 1950s Britain." *Journal of Popular British Cinema* 2.

———. 2003. *British Cinema of 1950s: The Decline of Deference*. Oxford: Oxford University Press.

Hesmondhalgh, D. 2002. *The Cultural Industries*. London: Sage.

Hills, J. 1986. *Deregulating Telecoms*. London: Continuum.

———. 2002. *The Struggle for Control of Global Communication*. Urbana: University of Illinois.

HMSO. 1936. *Report of the Committee Appointed by the Board of Trade*. Moyne Report. London: HMSO.

———. 1949a. *Report of the Working Party on Film Production*. Gater Report. London: HMSO.

———. 1949b. *Royal Commission on the Press 1947-9 Report*. London: HMSO.

———. 1962a. *Report of the Committee on Broadcasting*. Pilkington Report. London: HMSO.

———. 1962b. *Royal Commission on the Press 1961-2 Report*. London: HMSO.

———. 1968. *Board of Trade Review of Films Legislation*. London: HMSO.

———. 1976. *The Prime Minister's Working Party on the Future of the Film Industry*. London: HMSO.

———. 1977a. *Report of the Committee on the Future of Broadcasting*. Annan Report. London: HMSO.

———. 1977b. *Royal Commission on the Press 1974-7 Final Report*. London: HMSO.

Keane, J. 1991. *The Media and Democracy*. Cambridge: Polity.

———. 1996. "Structural Transformations of the Public Sphere." In M. Andersen, ed., *Media and Democracy*. Oslo: University of Oslo Press.

Knight, D., and V. Porter. 1967. *A Long Look at Short Films*. Oxford: Pergamon.

Labour Party. 1974. *The People and the Media*. London: Labour Party.

Leys, C. 2001. *Market-Driven Journalism*. London: Verso.

Marvin, C. 1988. *When Old Technologies Were New*. New York: Oxford University Press.

Miliband, R. 1973. *The State in Capitalist Society*. London: Quartet.

Murdock, G., and P. Golding. 1974. "For a Political Economy of the Mass Media." In R. Miliband and J. Saville, eds., *The Socialist Register 1973*. London: Merlin.

———. 2001. "Digital Possibilities, Market Realities: The Contradictions of Communications Convergence." In L. Panitch and C. Leys, eds., *A World of Contradictions: Socialist Register 2002*. London: Merlin.

O'Malley, T. 1994. *Closedown? The BBC and Government Policy 1979–1992*. London: Pluto.

———. 1998. "Demanding Accountability: The Press, the Royal Commissions, and the Pressure for Reform, 1945–77." In H. Stephenson and M. Bromley, eds., *Sex, Lies, and Democracy*. London: Longman.

O'Malley, T., and C. Soley. 2000. *Regulating the Press*. London: Pluto.

Political and Economic Planning (PEP). 1938. *Report on the British Press*. London: PEP.

———. 1952. *The British Film Industry*. London: PEP.

Porter, V. 1985. *On Cinema*. London: Pluto.

——. 1991. *Beyond the Berne Convention*. London: John Libbey.

——. 1997. "Methodism versus the Marketplace: The Rank Organisation and British Cinema." In R. Murphy, ed., *The British Cinema Book*. London: British Film Institute.

——. 2000. "The Robert Clark Account: Films Released in Britain by Associated British Pictures, British Lion, MGM, and Warner Bros., 1946–57." *Historical Journal of Film, Radio, and Television* 20, no. 4.

——. 2001a. "All Change at Elstree: Warner Bros., ABPC, and British Film Policy, 1945–1961." *Historical Journal of Film, Radio and Television* 21, no. 1.

——. 2001b. "The Hegemonic Turn: Film Comedies in 1950s Britain." *Journal of Popular British Cinema* 4.

Porter, V., and S. Hasselbach. 1991. *Pluralism, Politics, and the Marketplace*. London: Routledge.

Sakr, N. 2001. *Satellite Realms*. London: I. B. Tauris.

Scannell, P. 1989. "Public Service Broadcasting and Modern Life." *Media, Culture, and Society* 11. Reprinted in P. Scannell, P. Schlesinger, and C. Sparks, eds., *Culture and Power*. London: Sage, 1992.

Scannell, P., and D. Cardiff. 1991. *Serving the Nation*. Oxford, U.K.: Blackwell.

Schlesinger, P. 1978. *Putting "Reality" Together*. London: Constable.

Seaton, J. 1990. "Down with Aunt Tabitha: A Modest Media Proposal." In B. Pimlott, ed., *The Alternative*. London: W. H. Allen.

——. 1999. "The New 'Ethnic' Wars and the Media." In T. Allen and J. Seaton, eds., *The Media of Conflict*. London: Zed.

——. 2000. "The BBC's Changing Role." In *E-Britannia*. Luton: University of Luton Press.

——. 2004. *Carnage and the Media*. London: Penguin.

Sparks, C. 1985. "The Working-Class Press: Radical and Revolutionary Alternatives." *Media, Culture, and Society* 7, no. 2.

——. 1998. *Communism, Capitalism, and the New Media*. London: Sage.

——. 1999. "The Press." In J. Stokes and A. Reading, eds., *The Media in Britain*. Basingstoke: Macmillan.

——. 2000. "From Dead Trees to Live Wires: The Internet's Challenge to the Traditional Newspaper." In J. Curran and M. Gurevitch, eds., *Mass Media and Society*. London: Arnold.

——. 2001. "The Internet and the Global Public Sphere." In W. Bennett and R. Entman, eds., *Mediated Politics*. New York: Cambridge University Press.

Thompson, D., ed. 1964. *Discrimination and Popular Culture*. Harmondsworth, U.K.: Penguin.

Thornton, S., and K. Gelder. 1997. *The Subcultures Reader*. London: Routledge.

Tulloch, J. 1998. "Managing the Press in a Medium-Sized European Power." In H. Stephenson and M. Bromley, eds., *Sex, Lies, and Democracy*. London: Longman.

Turner, G. 2002. *British Cultural Studies*. 3d ed. London: Routledge.

Winston, B. 1998. *Media Technology and Society*. London: Routledge.

3

Making a Molehill out of a Mountain
The Sad State of Political Economy in U.S. Media Studies

Robert McChesney

Media and information are at the center of social life in the twenty-first century in the United States and worldwide. This should be the moment in the sun for media studies (a.k.a. communication) at U.S. universities, as it has been for computer science. Indeed, in the not too distant past, that was roundly anticipated to be on the horizon. "I have no doubt that many communication scholars can hardly believe their luck. After years on the margins of intellectual concern and academic power," Nicholas Garnham wrote in the *Journal of Communication* in 1983, "we suddenly find ourselves center stage, with the spotlight of social relevance full upon us" (Garnham 1983, 314). The academic field of communication (or media studies) enjoyed a rapid rise to prominence in the generations following World War II. By the 1970s and into the 1980s important epistemological, theoretical, and political debates were being raised, and the discipline was influenced by the vitality of intellectual life in those times. Since the middle 1980s, and clearly by the 1990s, however, the dynamism has been extinguished, mirroring the overall trend toward quiescence and depoliticization on university campuses. The field of communication has settled into a second-tier role in U.S. academic life, providing mostly inconsequential research of little interest to anyone outside narrow subsets of the field, not to mention anyone outside the field or outside the academy. Were it not for the large undergraduate demand for training and degrees leading to employment in the media/information sector, the very future of the field as a distinct and necessary research enterprise would be open to question.

Are these words concerning the state of U.S. media studies too harsh? Perhaps, and one can always point to impressive communication scholars moving in the opposite direction. But note that my criticism is not original; in fact, it is part of an increasing concern across the field. "With the exception of a few works produced by a handful of notable scholars," a despondent long-time chair of a U.S. communications department wrote upon his retirement in 2000, "most of what passes for 'scholarly research' in media is pretty trivial" (Berkman 2000). Raymie McKerrow, the recent president of the National Communication Association (NCA), one of the three main organizations for media and communication scholars, wrote a scathing critique of the field's irrelevance in the NCA newsletter in 2000. Citing approvingly a seminal article from 1972 by Wander and Jenkins, McKerrow noted that "criticism, at its best, is informed talk about matters of importance" (1972). McKerrow called for "criticism as intervention," for the field to "become more familiar with and influential in public policy deliberations," and for the aggressive spawning of "public intellectuals" (2000). The 2001 annual conference of the International Communication Association (ICA), another of the main scholarly groups in the field, was titled, perhaps to convince itself, "Communication Research Matters." The conference was structured to promote the important work that media and communication scholars can do to assist the public with the fundamental issues of our age.

I argue in this chapter that the trivialization and irrelevance of U.S. media studies is directly related to the marginalization of critical perspectives, and, in particular, political economy. As a result, the field has almost nothing of value to say concerning the crucial policy debates surrounding media and communication policy. It is irrelevant. I also argue that the solution to the problem is to place political economy in a central position in media studies. I do not argue that the political economy of communication should be the dominant component of all communication programs, merely that it have a presence in all of them. I argue that all communication scholars, regardless of their areas of expertise, would benefit from a working knowledge of basic political economic concepts and theory. The relationship between political economy and other branches of communication research is complementary, not antagonistic. At the same time, the political economy of communication is uniquely positioned to provide quality analysis of the most pressing communication issues of our era. It is not the only necessary aspect of the field of communication, but it is one of the cornerstones.

I begin the chapter with a few general words about political economy and critical scholarship in media studies and elsewhere. I then turn to a more specific discussion of the historic role of political economy in U.S. media studies, in an effort to explain its paltry status at present. I concentrate on the United States because it is the terrain I know best. I sense, nonetheless, that some of the points apply to other nations and regions as well. In general, however, the situation for political economy and critical research does not seem as dire in media studies outside the United States. Lord help us if that is not the case.

POLITICAL ECONOMY AND CRITICAL SCHOLARSHIP

What do I mean by the political economy of communication? The scholarly study of the political economy of communication entails two main dimensions. First, it addresses the nature of the relationship between media and communication systems on the one hand and the broader social structure of society on the other. It examines how media and communication systems and content reinforce, challenge, or influence existing class and social relations. It does this with a particular interest in how economic factors influence politics and social relations. In this work it draws heavily from political theory, sociology, and history. Second, the political economy of communication looks specifically at how ownership, support mechanisms (e.g., advertising), and government policies establish media systems and communication technologies and (directly and indirectly) influence media behavior and content. This line of inquiry emphasizes structural factors and the labor process in the production, distribution, and consumption of communication. The political economy of communication cannot provide a comprehensive explanation of all communication activity, but it can explain certain issues extremely well, and it provides a necessary context for most other research questions in communication.[1]

The combination of these two dimensions distinguishes the political economy of communication from other variants of communication or cultural analysis. Cultural studies, for example, often is concerned with the relationship of media to audiences and both of them to existing class and social relations. But it has mostly lost interest in examining the structural factors that influence the production of media content. Media "economics" often provides microanalysis of how media firms and markets operate, but, like mainstream economics, it assumes the existing social and class relations are a given, and a benevolent one at that. Likewise, communication policy studies examine the influence of government policies on media performance, but the work generally presupposes the necessary existence of the market and the broader social situation as the best of all possible worlds. The dominant form of communication research in the United States is drawn from quantitative behavioral social science. This work tends to be the polar opposite of the political economy of communication: it presupposes capitalist society as a given and then discounts structural factors in explaining media behavior, although—I hasten to add—there is nothing intrinsic to quantitative methodology that necessitates these characteristics. Quantitative communication research often generates valuable findings for media studies.

My argument on behalf of political economy of communication is not methodological. I am not especially interested in rehashing old arguments about the merits of qualitative versus quantitative research methods or the strengths of archival history over textual analysis or ethnography. These are important and necessary debates, if done in a collegial manner, but they are beside the point I am trying to make. For my argument, methodologies are like tools. They have their strengths and their limitations. One uses the best tool to accomplish the job at hand. The problem in media studies is not that we have bad tools or that we use them improperly, though we may; it is that we have a poor overall design. We need to immerse the field in the broad and important issues concerning media, capitalism, and democracy that political economy is determined to pursue. For most of these issues a variety of methodologies can be employed. In my view, a healthy field of media studies will be one with tremendous intellectual cross-fertilization and interdisciplinary work among scholars who specialize in different methodologies. Disciplinary or methodological apartheid in communication undermines the best argument for the field's existence as a distinct entity.

This is not merely an "academic" concern. What happens in media studies departments, what happens in universities, affects everyone, eventually. Ideas are important. (That is why the political right has devoted so much energy toward encouraging conservative scholarship over the past two decades.) If media studies provides a substandard education to undergraduate and graduate students alike, we will see the consequences in poorer media, as well as poorer media and communication policies. If communication research tends to avoid fundamental issues, then all the resources devoted to it will be of little use to the citizenry when it looks to experts for assistance in addressing core policy decisions surrounding media, culture, and communication.

By the reasoning so far, my argument might just seem to be a boilerplate argument for political economy that could be applied to sociology, education, history, political science, or any other field in the social sciences. Although it is true that these other fields probably could benefit from more political economy, I want to make a stronger case than that. In my view, political economy and communication have a special relationship. Each deals directly with commercial and material issues and its historic rise is closely tied to the rise of capitalism. Each is ultimately concerned with issues of social justice, human freedom, and political governance. Both political economy and communication are indispensable to democratic theory. In combination, political economy and media studies can make a potent brew. Our communication system is the result of crucial policies, and these policies only come into full view under the light of political economic analysis. While one can be a political economist and have only a passing interest in communication issues, the need to have at least a passing interest has grown considerably in this, the so-called information age. And for scholars of communication, it strikes me as highly questionable not to have a working knowledge of political economy, of how capitalism works, of how democracy functions in a materialist and institutional sense, and of how the media system "triangulates," to employ a term much in fashion these days, with both of them.

In this triangulation, the subject of capitalism looms like the proverbial eight-hundred-pound gorilla. There are important philosophical and intellectual arguments to be made for political economic approaches to the study of media and communication, as well as all the social sciences.[2] Dan Schiller, for example, has provided a compelling historical argument about the importance of studying the labor process and keeping material issues at the center of communication inquiry (1996). But the case can be made even more simply. The central and overriding aspect of our times is the dominance of the market, capitalist social relations, and the primacy of profit. To understand every significant institution in the United States, and across the world, requires a basic grasp of the nature and logic of capitalism and how the system operates in the real world.[3] It is as important to intellectual inquiry in the United States as a critical understanding of communism and the operations of the Communist party were for honest analysts in the old Soviet Union.

The contemporary ideology that the market can do no wrong is deemed neoliberalism, and no assessment of media systems or policies can be complete without a strong understanding and critique of neoliberal claims. They underscore every important trend in media and communication in the United States and the world today. The notion of the competitive media market "giving the people what they want" is a cornerstone for rationalizing the output of the system. The idea that the market is the best and most rational manner to regulate affairs is the philosophical justification for the wave of deregulation, privatization, and commercialization that has swept U.S. and global media and communication systems. The claim that government regulation always holds a far deeper potential for damage to human freedom than market regulation, except in extraordinary and almost unimaginable circumstances, is the ante for admission to media policy-making forums. To grasp core issues surrounding contemporary democracy, globalization, or the Internet without an understanding of capitalism and neoliberalism would be like writing a history of the French Revolution without studying the Enlightenment and European history from 1600 to 1789. Accordingly, no media studies scholar can afford to ignore the "free market" or accept the claims of neoliberal advocates at face value. In this regard, it is the political economic approach to media studies that is best suited to that job.

In some respects my argument is a restatement of the familiar call for more "critical" work in media studies and communication. The notion of "critical" research, drawn from Paul Lazarsfeld's famous formulation of critical versus "administrative" research, remains important and merits elaboration. One way to think of this is to recall the widespread use of the term "bourgeois" by 1960s student radicals to denigrate academics with whom they disagreed. I was offended by the anti-intellectualism of this practice at the time (e.g., the categorical dismissal of someone as a "bourgeois" economist as if they were an academic stool pigeon), but there was a deeper meaning that possibly some of the protesters and I (most certainly) missed at the time. A "bourgeois" scholar is one who presupposes the natural and necessary existence of capitalist social relations and whose work is conducted within that context. Bourgeois scholars can be brilliant and they can produce valuable work, but their work is at times compromised by untested and undebated assumptions about the basic propriety of the status quo. The fundamental structure of society is off-limits to analysis. The range of debate among the elite and the needs of those who dominate society set the boundaries on legitimate inquiry. As Lazarsfeld noted, and as is almost a canon of philosophy of science, this adaptation to the needs and values of those in power in society compromises the scholar's intellectual integrity. Nevertheless, much of U.S. media studies or communication research could be characterized as "administrative," "bourgeois," or the more common term "mainstream."

Critical scholarship, on the other hand, is premised on rejecting the notion that what exists does so because it is natural and good. It begins with a set of values and working assumptions and proceeds to make what Karl Marx famously termed "the *ruthless criticism of all that exists*, ruthless also in the sense that criticism does not fear its results and even less so a struggle with the existing powers" (1979, 30).[4] The range of inquiry for a critical scholar is not bounded by the needs of those who rule society and benefit by the status quo, but by the range of what is determined to be socially possible. Almost by definition, then, critical scholarship will be in a tenuous position in a university or society at large.

Is the call for more "critical" research, and especially for an increased role for the political economy of communication, merely a ruse to smuggle more left-wingers and socialists into academic positions? This is a plausible concern, for two reasons. First, political economy appears to be another name for making historical materialist analysis, and historical materialism is closely associated with Marxism. But there is nothing about historical materialism that necessarily leads to left-wing conclusions. Indeed, much social science today is influenced by historical materialism (consider, for example, any CIA report on the political conditions in a particular nation), but only a fraction of it is socialist or Marxist. Second, it seems that antagonism to capitalism is a prerequisite for being a U.S. critical scholar. To the extent a so-called critical scholar shills for left-wing politicians, causes, or institutions, however, this is a valid criticism, and such a person is no more a critical scholar than is an unthinking advocate of the interests of business. Stuart Hall made the case for honest critical scholarship in British media studies persuasively, and the argument is every bit as true for the United States: "People who are seriously in the business of challenging the state of affairs in Britain cannot, opportunistically, collude with any and every exaggeration provided it casts the *status quo* in a bad light. We have to provide those who are, by and large, at the receiving end of 'media power' with a convincing account—an adequate understanding—of how that power *really* works. Only then will we know why and how the situation needs to be changed. More significantly, only then can we win broad, popular-based support which, in our situation, is our only leverage for change" (Hall 1986, 6).

In my view, critical scholarship is predicated not on socialist principles, but on liberal and democratic principles. It is committed to political enfranchisement, freedom of speech and intellectual inquiry, and social justice. It grows directly out of the Enlightenment experience. If it is done right, it requires scholars to question, interrogate, and possibly alter their own assumptions on a regular basis. Framed this way, critical scholarship is not especially radical; it is Philosophy of Science 101. If the conclusions are locked in by the presuppositions—which are off-limits to criticism—it makes for lousy scholarship regardless of the scholar's values or politics.[5]

A critical approach, then, will by definition question the dominant interests in society. In the case of the United States, and the world today, that means coming to grips with the market and neoliberalism. Critical research does not presuppose that capitalism is evil and unacceptable; there is simply skepticism to the existing order and its theoretical justifications. One can do critical work or political economy and come down on the side of capitalism and the status quo; such a person need only be willing to subject these topics to a withering review. The great Joseph Schumpeter is the classic example of just such a critical political economist (1942). Sadly, few who presume the greatness or the entrenched nature of the status quo have much desire to follow in Schumpeter's footsteps. It seems like a waste of their time. When such a critical approach is applied to nations like China or the old Soviet Union, it will produce criticism of the status quo every bit as pronounced as anything generated in the United States.

This may seem very abstract, so consider a current and important example of this administrative-critical split in the field of communication. The federal government presently is generating crucial policies—sometimes incorrectly dubbed "deregulation"—for the development of the Internet and the media system. The mainstream approach is to study the issues, look at who in power is debating various positions, and then describe the situation with little comment or, if a position is taken, to adopt the side of one of the main contending parties. Adopting a position that is outside the mainstream of debate, even if it may be right, is virtually unthinkable. For example, since the forces that oppose television advertising to children are very weak politically in the United States, mainstream communication scholarship ignores that as an option. It tends to gravitate toward the position that wants only slight modifications to the existing situation, since that is deemed politically realistic. Television advertising to children may well be evil, but it is an unavoidable evil.

The critical position, on the other hand, is to try to understand why the range of legitimate debate is so constricted compared to the range of what is possible and what would be best for all of society, not just the contending business interests. The critical approach is to challenge the legitimacy of existing debate if it fails to serve the interests of the broader public. In the case of television advertising to children, the critical position is to understand why advertising to children is such a massive aspect of our media system. The critical approach then evaluates the research on the effects of television advertising to children, determines the truth as best it can be done, and lets the chips fall where they may. The solutions to the problem are not restricted to what is politically feasible at this moment (i.e., what large corporations can make gobs of money doing) but what is socially possible, and what might get at the cause of the problem. Nations like Sweden and Norway, which prohibit television advertising to children under twelve years of age and have well-funded noncommercial television services for children, become important case studies for democratic policy makers, instead of being dismissed as irrelevant.[6]

But political economy of communication is not synonymous with critical studies in communication. True, it is by definition critical, as it is expressly committed to holding those in power up to the light of day and judging them from a perspective that does not assume their benevolence. But virtually any methodology or tradition can be deployed in a critical manner. In the United States, the most prominent branch of critical work in media studies has been in cultural studies. Regrettably, too much of cultural studies has moved away from a critical stance and has become, to some degree, a variant of mainstream research. This process has taken place in direct relation to cultural studies shedding and eschewing its once considerable interest in matters of political economy.

I do not wish to cast the mainstream-critical categories in stone. There are not two distinct camps in media studies with an iron wall or a barbed wire fence between them. They are two heterogeneous approaches, so to speak, with a very large and fuzzy gray area between them. Jonathan Sterne argues, for example, that even critical icon C. Wright Mills had strong and important links to so-called administrative research (2001). For some, perhaps much, of communication research, whether it is formally framed as critical is not necessarily relevant. My argument is not that everyone in media studies needs to jump and land both feet in the critical camp. To the contrary, my argument is merely that everyone in media studies needs to respect and encourage the role of critical research, especially political economy of communication. In the long run, even for scholars who have made their peace with the existing social structure, it is in the interest of all scholars that critical issues get raised, that mainstream presuppositions get challenged. Otherwise, a field tends to grow weary and stagnate.

That is the crisis we are in today. Critical work, including political economy, is very much on the margins of the field in the United States. If there are two encampments, as I mention above, the mainstream one is the size of Texas, and the critical one is Rhode Island. There are structural reasons for this—that are largely self-evident—and I will return to them below. But structural factors aside, the situation need not be as dire as it is. There are steps we can take to nudge the status of political economy and critical scholarship to a more lucrative stature in media studies within the range of what is currently possible. In a relatively small field like media studies, the actions of a handful of leading figures can go a long way toward setting the tone that influences what issues get examined and debated, what graduate students study, and how the field develops. The leadership in U.S. media studies, with a few notable exceptions, has tended to be unsympathetic to critical approaches. It is not uncommon for some leading media scholars to dismiss critical work categorically as "ideological" and therefore unscientific, while work that assumes the soundness of the status quo is almost never held to that standard. Likewise, when critical scholars work closely with dissident political groups, as they logically should, it is dismissed as partisan activity beneath the role of a scholar; when mainstream academics advise those in power, it is the culmination of their career and a matter of considerable distinction.[7]

In particular, critical analysis of capitalism and neoliberalism, and their implications for media, politics, and culture, is discouraged in mainstream media studies. They are simply taken as a given, as natural and unchangeable, and/or as unimportant. The notion that U.S. democracy is fundamentally flawed, that this is closely related to our inegalitarian profit-driven economy as well as our commercial media system, and that our democracy can be, and should be, radically improved is beyond the pale.

All told, this tends to create a chilling effect, where graduate students and young scholars learn to censor themselves and stay away from controversial issues and arguments. Or scholars learn not to take the argument to its logical conclusion if it lands them outside the range of legitimate debate. It also creates an environment where the evidentiary requirements placed on someone challenging the status quo become significantly, even exponentially higher than the requirements placed on someone reaffirming the soundness of our social order. Anyone who wants to be regarded as legitimate needs to situate his or her work in contrast to the critical position, which is often represented in vulgar and unsympathetic terms.[8] And when in doubt, always claim that the evidence does not establish that the media have any effect on anything, followed by the admonition that everything is too complex anyway to say anything definitive, at least that might be critical of the existing order. Not surprisingly, a familiar migration in U.S. communication is for scholars to make the trek from critical to mainstream. In many cases it may well be a heartfelt transition, but the path is greased by the culture of the field.

In this environment, is it any wonder that U.S. media and communication programs are not generating a body of work that is known and utilized across disciplines or among a broader public?

In fairness to those hostile or at least unsympathetic to political economy and critical approaches to media studies, there are grounds for concern about critical communication research generally, and the political economy of communication specifically. Although I argue for their inclusion in the U.S. media studies program unequivocally, the actual output of U.S. scholars in these areas has been unsatisfactory. Just adopting a critical posture or doing political economy does not mean the resulting work will be of value. Moreover, merely bringing political economy more prominence in media studies will not solve all the field's problems in any calculation. There are several other reforms that would strengthen the field, independent of political economy or critical approaches.[9]

The crisis of media studies would be of far less concern were other disciplines filling the void and providing searing insights into media and communication and their role in the emerging social order. But, alas, such is not the case. Some outstanding work is produced by scholars working in other fields, but they often work against the grain of their discipline. In some respected disciplines, where the political economy of media should be a central concern, it is virtually ignored. Most striking in this regard is political philosophy. One can read the truly brilliant work of political philosophers and theorists like John Rawls, Ronald Dworkin, Cass Sunstein, and Amy Guttmann, among others, and find scarcely a word on the matter.[10] Book after book weighs in with detailed and thoughtful expositions on the necessary social conditions to promote democratic deliberation and viable self-government, often elaborating in detail on the role of educational systems, the evils of censorship, and the best way to construct political parties and electoral systems. But the nature of the media system and how it is structured, and how that might affect the conditions for the informational needs of a democracy, are nowhere to be found. It is a genuine blind spot in their field. This work not only cannot reduce the weight on media studies' shoulders, it needs a thorough dousing in communication research to generate better answers to the important questions it is addressing.

Conversely, there are a range of important works being generated in fields other than media studies that put considerable emphasis on the role of media in our polity and our culture. Some of these books, like the works of Robert Putnam and Derek Bok, are by highly respected scholars and go directly to the basic caliber of our democracy (Putnam 2000; Bok 2001). Others sometimes make dramatic claims about media, in a manner that often makes mainstream communication scholars' skin crawl.[11] These books vary in quality, but all have the virtue of attempting to make strong claims about media and society. Nonetheless these books all suffer, including Putnam's and Bok's, from the weakness of their media analysis. Were there a strong and vibrant literature in media studies—especially the political economy of communication—for these authors to draw on, their books would be the better for it.

Media scholars are justifiably sensitive about the relative lack of importance accorded communication research—mainstream and critical—at major
U.S. research universities. At the University of Wisconsin–Madison, where I
taught for a decade, communication was seemingly regarded by the pooh-
bahs in history, political science, and sociology as having roughly the same
intellectual merit as, say, driver's education. The immediate reaction of some
communication scholars—mainstream and critical—has been to erect the
same type of intellectual barriers-to-entry as mainstream social scientists in
order to justify and exalt the field's existence. To the extent that critical communication scholars engage in this exercise—for example, adopting trendy
but mostly incomprehensible jargon—is the extent to which critical communication scholars insure their irrelevance, even asininity. This is not to stay
that difficult terminology is not sometimes necessary; only that the instances
in which it is necessary are far fewer than the instances such terminology is
presently employed. In short, media studies cannot succeed in academia by
imitating the established fields. We have to boldly strike out in a popular, interdisciplinary and critical manner that runs directly counter to the dominant
trends in the academy.

In view of the perils of the academy, it would be comforting to think that
intellectuals committed to democratic communication could bail out of the
university system and do their work independently, perhaps holding down
"day jobs" or incorporating their intellectual interests into nonacademic employment. But this is not really an option, nor should it be. People outside
the academy are going to have their judgment affected by the positions they
are in, and, while that has positive aspects, it also compromises their vision.
Societies need public intellectuals and they need to provide them with some
autonomy and insulation in the academy. As Harold Innis has argued, it is
the hallmark of a liberal and a democratic society to have an autonomous
university sector, where scholars can provide critical analysis for the benefit
of all of society.[12] More recently, John Michael has made a strong argument
for the necessity of intellectuals in a democratic society (2000). Academics,
accordingly, are granted tremendous privileges and occupational freedom
compared to most people, and with that comes considerable responsibility.
True liberals, in the best sense of the term, fight to defend this vision of the
university even if they disagree with the nature of the scholarship. It is essential for a viable democratic culture. What that means is that the ideal of
critical scholarship, as I have defined it, instead of being on the margins
of the academy, should be at its center. We can defend the tenure system
only on the grounds that it protects the integrity and autonomy of intellectuals, so they can tell the truth without fear of professional consequences. I am
not naive. I know this is an ideal, not a reality. But it is a struggle we can
never abandon.

Let me be clear on this point because it is complicated. I do not mean to
posit university intellectuals as being "objective" because that clearly is not

the case. They have their biases, and those are unavoidable and not necessarily evil. The greatest inherent problem with academics is the prevalence of elitism, which is an occupational hazard. There is no simple solution to this problem, though it can be lessened if not eliminated. But I would say that once one factors in their values—and their self-interest in the university system—university intellectuals can be more objective than those seeing the world from a more narrowly defined vantage point. The great threat to the notion of a liberal or democratic institution today comes from neoliberalism—the notion that scholarship should properly assist the needs of the dominant economic interests and be supported through commercial auspices. It is a noxious and antidemocratic notion of higher education. (Here, too, the similarity of neoliberalism to Soviet-style communism is striking.) As Christopher Lasch wrote in his final, glorious book, the main academic freedom battle on university campuses today is to arrest and roll back the increasing corporate-commercial penetration of higher education. It is inimical to the university tradition. If universities increasingly become subservient to corporate interests, they are less likely to serve those groups or values, or address those issues, disfavored by the commercial patrons. Nor is this entirely recent; it is a core tension in a capitalist society that neoliberalism merely brings to the fore. In the 1940s Innis went so far as to say, "The descent of the university into the market place reflects the lie in the soul of modern society" (quoted in Tudiver 1999, 155).

U.S. MEDIA STUDIES AND CRITICAL APPROACHES: YESTERDAY AND TODAY

Communication study tends to occupy the low rent district of the academy. This marginalization of communication is due to several factors. The least acceptable of them is the tendency to maintain the view that communication is a largely dependent variable with little social significance in its own right. This tendency has been especially pronounced in the United States, where, not coincidentally, the corporate commercial model has been most thoroughly ingrained economically, politically, and ideologically. The corporate media PR drum has been pounding out the message that media are a powerless and democratic reflector of public tastes for seven or eight decades.[13] Ironically, the devotion of much of the field's research to the notion that media have "limited effects" plays directly into the notion that communication is not an especially important area of study. In fact, the case for media studies has been made eloquently elsewhere so I will not repeat it here (Silverstone 1999; Sardar and Van Loon 2000). I share Nicholas Garnham's view that media are fundamental institutions of modern times, having an importance similar to, if not exceeding, religion and educational institutions (Garnham 2000). The mere fact that so much of our lives—by some measures around ten hours per day on average for Americans—is devoted to media in one form or another points to the importance of understanding the place of media in our society.[14] In this the so-called information age, as media and communication issues are woven into the heart of every key social issue of our times, the notion that media are a forgettable dependent variable is decreasingly prevalent. But the legacy of that belief continues in the status of media studies in U.S. universities.

The best reasons for the minor league status of media studies owe to institutional factors within universities. Consider, for example, the field's belated arrival. It developed a generation or two later than the other leading social sciences, largely due to the rapid emergence of communication as a significant social factor at the turn of the century. But being "late to the table" hardly accounts for its current small portions, as the field of computer science attests.

A related explanation for the field's status is to look at communication's extremely heterogeneous antecedents. Modern communication has developed from English departments, speech programs, journalism schools, theater and drama departments, radio-TV departments, and film schools; it has been influenced by economics, political science, psychology, and sociology. On many campuses, like the one I taught in for a decade in Madison, there are two or three departments devoted to communication and there is little rational explanation for which department does what. To the untrained eye this can seem goofy. The contemporary practice of communication research extends from cognitive, experimental, and survey research to rhetorical studies, cultural studies, political economy, law, and archival history. Many, perhaps most, communication scholars have as much in common with people in other fields as they do with people in their own. This breeds the concern that the field can never generate the quality of research that a more defined discipline can, that communication lacks the necessary focus to establish itself as a distinct field. Hence it receives less resources and is taken less seriously.

The methodological apartheid that exists in communication only makes this situation worse. Media studies departments often have quantitative scholars, psychologists, sociologists, historians, legal and policy experts, political economists, and so on. They tend to keep to themselves so the whole is less than the sum of the parts. To outsiders, the media studies faculty in history or law or psychology may not look like scholars with a broad range of knowledge in media studies and a particular area of emphasis; to the contrary, they appear like people lucky to have a university job but too dumb to be employed in the history, law, or psychology departments. Hence communication is classified as a minor league field. (Methodological Stalinists see the problem but argue that the solution is for everyone to recognize one approach—invariably their own—as the proper one for all to use. The real solution is for an interdisciplinary approach, a willingness to tackle big questions, an open mind to critical research questions, and a commitment to addressing the important public issues surrounding media. All of that points strongly to the need for political economy of communication.)

In combination this means that media studies has been caught in a vicious cycle, where its second-tier status prevents it from being given the necessary resources to become first tier. Universities are scarcely meritocracies. It is not a case of the best research and most important topics attracting the most institutional support. Of arguably greater importance is the perceived prestige of the field, and in this area communication suffers greatly in comparison to the other main social sciences. Prestige is only loosely related to quality, and it has a self-fulfilling logic that is difficult to crack. Moreover, it cements an academic system that privileges unoriginal and noncontroversial work. From what I have seen of some of the more prestigious social science departments on leading campuses, the emperor has no clothes. Much of the actual work is mediocre and uninteresting if not banal. Communication researchers are justified in refusing to deem these fields and their scholars superior, but when the prestige standard is applied, communication always falls way short.

For any number of reasons, the pursuit of prestige is an occupational hazard for people in academia, even for those, like myself, who know just how counterproductive it is. The institutional pecking order is as well established in academia as the caste system is in India. Communication is a failure in the prestige game on U.S. campuses for the simple reason that aside from Penn and Stanford, it barely exists on Ivy League and other elite private university campuses. At the crucial big three—Harvard, Yale, and Princeton—it only recently acquired a research presence at Harvard's Kennedy School of Government. Hence the ten leading programs in communication research consist mainly of schools that would rank in the second tier for the other social sciences. So when a dean has to decide between cutting communication or, say, history or sociology, there is tremendous impetus to go for the former. When a dean cuts communication, she or he will get pressure from the likes of Wisconsin, Minnesota, Oregon, and North Carolina to back down. When the dean cuts those other fields, the pressure comes from Chicago, MIT, Harvard, Berkeley, Princeton, and Yale. Barring other factors, it is a bureaucratic no-brainer.

Moreover, the prestige of communication is undermined by its close association—past and present—with the media and communication industries. As communication research is often conducted in departments with course work devoted to professional training, its role in a liberal arts college is legitimately called into question. Communication appears as just a hepped up form of vocational education, while the traditional social sciences sit atop Mount Olympus pondering the fate of the world. I recall, while teaching at Wisconsin, once speaking to the dean of Letters and Sciences, the college in which our department resided. I implored the dean to give us more teaching assistantships, so we could support more graduate students and be more competitive in attracting the best talent to our campus. He responded that TA-ships were not necessary because our graduate students should be able to land part-time jobs working on the local newspaper. It became clear he thought we mostly had professional students, when we had one of the largest Ph.D. programs in communication in the world. And this was *our* dean!

There are very serious grounds for concern about the implications of the linkage of the media industries to media studies departments for communication research. To the extent that it is directly or indirectly dependent on the support of the media industry, it puts distinct limits on the range and nature of what can be and is being done. This theme is underdeveloped in the mainstream treatments of the field, as the mainstream is the beneficiary of this process, producing work that tends to be unthreatening, if not useful, to communication firms.

In the current era of cutbacks and retrenchment, there is even greater pressure from university administrators on communication departments to slap on their kneepads and kiss up to media and communication interests to get them to bankroll an even greater portion of the field's expenses. In these neoliberal times, this acquiescence to private power is simply accepted as an unavoidable fact, even by people who would openly disparage the situation were they not part of it. There is little doubt, however, that this is the most significant threat to communication ever becoming a major league discipline. At a practical level, too, business schools are far better suited to conduct commercially sympathetic research, especially as communication is now a central business activity. Who needs departments predicated on public service, democratic citizenship, and professional principles like journalism or the free flow of information when the whole idea is to maximize profit?

In this context the paltry status of critical approaches, especially the political economy of communication, makes sense. First, insecure disciplines like communication are going to be less willing to take chances on risky and controversial fields; all the pressure is to go in the opposite direction and ape what goes on in the more established departments and disciplines. Second, to the extent much of the field's budgets are based on professional undergraduate programs, critical classes can seem like teaching pacifism at West Point or atheism at Oral Roberts. Third, the link to the corporate media sector puts pressure, usually implicit but at times explicit, to have communication programs that do not question the nature of the media system from which these firms prosper. Moreover, critical and especially political economic research will not be attracting research money from these sources.

Some might respond at this point, "So what? What's the big deal? This is America and that's the way it has always been." In fact, that is not the case at all. There was nothing intrinsic to U.S. media studies that preordained its present configuration. What is striking when one looks at its history, broadly construed, is how significant critical approaches and political economic concerns were from the outset. The real story to be told is how they were so successfully marginalized, why the United States produced such a Milquetoast version of media studies. Recall that media studies came to the academy after most of the other social sciences had been formally established. Schools of journalism were launched in the early years of the twentieth century, but decades passed before they spawned research components that went beyond their origins as professional educators. Some prominent academics, like Robert Park and John Dewey, dabbled in media issues during the Progressive Era, but for the most part the field lay fallow into the 1930s. If we restrict our view to the formal history of media studies and communication at universities, the origins can look relatively drab, or at least a straight shot— more or less—to where we are today.

If we look outside the academy, however, the origins of media studies look considerably different. The United States was undergoing a striking social reconfiguration in the decades following 1890, and nowhere was the turbulence greater than in the realm of media. By the turn of the century, U.S. journalism was increasingly the domain of large commercial interests operating in semicompetitive or monopolistic markets. Social critics ranging from Edward Bellamy to Henry Adams were highly critical of the corrupt, antidemocratic nature of U.S. journalism, owing to its private ownership and its reliance on advertising. Between 1900 and 1920 numerous muckrakers and social commentators wrote damning criticism of the antidemocratic nature of mainstream journalism. In many respects, this was the golden age of media criticism, though it barely showed up on the academic Richter scale. In 1920, Upton Sinclair's *The Brass Check: A Study of American Journalism* was published. This breathtaking 440-page account of the corruption of journalism by moneyed interests sold some 150,000 copies by the mid-1920s (Sinclair 1920, 2003). All but forgotten in the intervening years, it is a book that should be the starting point for all assessments of journalism, if not media, in the United States. The topic of media control became a part of progressive political organizing. The great progressive Robert La Follette devoted a chapter of his book on political philosophy to the crisis of the press. "Money power," he wrote, "controls the newspaper press . . . wherever news items bear in any way upon the control of government by business, the news is colored" (1920).

The first few decades of the twentieth century saw the rise of advertising, public relations, the film industry, and radio broadcasting. The latter two were instrumental in stimulating the rise of formal communication research in the 1930s, but during these years there was also a nonacademic media studies emerging in response to them that was quite critical by nature. In the case of advertising, for example, a large and militant consumer movement emerged by the 1920s and 1930s that was highly critical of advertising and the consumer culture it spawned. It resulted in the formation of groups like Consumers Union. Likewise, with the emergence of commercial radio broadcasting in the early 1930s, a feisty and heterogeneous broadcast reform movement emerged that was piercing in its criticism of the limitations of commercial radio for a democratic society (McChesney 1993). Both of these movements were expressly dedicated to enacting political reform in Washington, D.C., and both generated a sophisticated critique of advertising and media that anticipated the best academic criticism made five or six decades later.

When communication made its grand splash in the academy in the 1930s, it did so by looking at the very big issues. There was the matter of democracy, and what it meant in the age of corporate capitalism and mass media. The master works of Dewey and Walter Lippmann in the 1920s granted the topic sufficient gravitas. There was the matter of propaganda, as it was employed not only by the Soviets and the fascist states, but also in the Western democracies as a routine matter. The question was in whose interests and how would this propaganda be deployed. And there was the matter of media effects. How did our social immersion in a world of media affect us? All of these issues were linked, and they held the potential for a significantly critical approach to media studies. Moreover, the launching pad for communication research was not only at a few large Big Ten universities, but also at the premier Ivy League universities like Princeton, Harvard, Yale, and Columbia. Dan Schiller has written brilliantly on this period, concentrating on the activities of Paul Lazarsfeld and Robert Merton. Schiller notes that all the elements for a powerful radical critique of propaganda were in place in media studies, aided and abetted by a relatively sympathetic political climate, and elites concerned by, and confused by, the world they were entering. But the critical approach was nonetheless unwelcome by commercial media sponsors, university administrations, and the key foundations, especially Rockefeller, which bankrolled much of communication research during these years (Schiller 1996, 49–53).

By the late 1940s, the critical impulse was effectively marginalized, if not purged, from U.S. media studies. Ironically, Lazarsfeld, who had framed communication research to be open to critical inquiry in the 1930s, became the icon of mainstream research. The political climate was changing dramatically. The broad historical and intellectually informed sweep that informed the research of the 1930s and early 1940s was gradually replaced by an ahistorical quantitative approach that accepted the commercial basis of U.S. media and the capitalistic nature of U.S. society as proper and inviolable. Research became more closely tied to the needs of the dominant industry interests (Chaffee 2000, 317–27). When the Hutchins Commission made its seminal study of the press and media in the immediate postwar years, it combined piercing criticism of commercial media with lame pleas for industry self-regulation as the solution (1947). Had the popular movements that opposed commercial broadcasting and advertising in the 1930s been more successful, the notion that commercial media was innately "American" might not have been swallowed hook, line, and sinker in the academy. Instead, the room for critical analysis and study was shrinking, and quickly.

The Cold War encouraged this anticritical process along; indeed, it made it almost mandatory. Christopher Simpson and Timothy Glander, among others, have documented the close relationship of the "founding fathers" of mass communication research to the emerging U.S. national security state in the 1940s and 1950s (Simpson 1994; Glander 2000). In this environment notions that commercial interests might use their control of media to provide propaganda fell from grace; propaganda became something only done by "totalitarian" states and governments. This was a stunning change in both rhetoric and analysis. In the early 1930s, for example, the U.S. advertising industry hailed Adolf Hitler and Josef Goebbels as brilliant fellow propagandists. "Whatever Hitler has done," the trade publication *Printers' Ink* wrote in 1933, "he has depended almost entirely upon slogans made effective by reiteration, made general by American advertising methods." Nor was that all. "Hitler and his advertising man Goebbels issued slogans which the masses could grasp with their limited intelligence. . . . Adolf has some good lines, of present-day application to American advertisers" (McChesney 1997, 16–18). Such candid commentary on the use of propaganda by powerful interests in democratic nations was soon relegated to the lunatic fringe, where, in many respects, it remains. By midcentury the ideas that ownership and control over media were decisive and that media had large and important effects were limited to the Soviet Union and other communist nations. In the United States, structure was irrelevant and/or benign, the system served the interests of the people, and media had limited effects. Had the U.S. political climate in the 1940s veered left—not as absurd a notion as some might think—rather than right, critical media studies might have survived as a viable entity in U.S. universities, and even flourished.[15]

By the 1950s much of the foundation enthusiasm for the importance of communication research had dried up, and the field lost its toehold in the major Ivy League universities. Thereafter, the balance of power shifted to the large public research universities of the Midwest. Critical work was not entirely dead; Kenneth Burke and a bit later George Gerbner, James Carey, and Hanno Hardt, among others, would keep the flame alive. Dallas Smythe and Herbert I. Schiller almost single-handedly put the field of political economy on the map in the United States in the 1950s and 1960s, but as influential as their work was and is, the times did not foster a legion of collaborators for them. Smythe returned to his native Canada in the 1960s to find more fertile soil for critical scholarship. Much critical work on media returned to its traditional status: it was done by people outside the discipline, like educator Paul Goodman and C. Wright Mills, a sociologist at Columbia, and outside the academy. In many ways Mills's work provided a superior framework for the critical evaluation of media; *The Power Elite* remains one of the most brilliant works ever on U.S. politics. It properly locates media within a broader social context without diminishing the importance of communication (1956). Mills's *The Sociological Imagination* (1959) made what may be the most trenchant critique of the limitations of the mainstream quantitative work that was ascending in the academy. Mills's untimely death at age forty-five in 1962 was a dark moment in the history of critical media studies.

The most striking weakness in mainstream media studies (which is a direct reflection of the lack of critical work in the field, especially of a political economic nature) is the unquestioned use of noncritical presuppositions that point the work inexorably in a particular direction while never holding those presuppositions accountable. These presuppositions include a belief in the basic propriety of the U.S. political economy and the justness of the corporate media system. The problem shows up in the conclusions of even the best quantitative studies, when the authors provide weak analysis and lame recommendations that do not and cannot ever escape the status quo assumptions built into the research. For even the most serious problems, the solution often is reduced to further calls for more education, begging those in power to change their ways, or recommending reforms that ignore the root cause of the problem (Moy and Pfau 2000, 186–89; Graber 2001, 180–83). To make matters worse, mainstream media studies evince a bogus neutrality; compromises to power are built into their very terminology. It is now accepted, for example, that public relations and advertising are forms of "persuasive" communication. That nonsensical designation—what communication isn't persuasive?—is said to be neutral and unbiased. Balderdash. In the 1930s PR and advertising were understood to be exactly what they are: propaganda in the interests of business. The industries themselves acknowledged as much. But saying the truth today marks the speaker as subjective, opinionated, biased, and incapable of fair, impartial research. The mainstream has accommodated itself to the ideological needs of the powers that be and defined that accommodation as neutrality.

CONCLUSION

Beginning in the 1970s a second generation and "homegrown" cohort of political economists of communication began to emerge in the United States, inspired by Smythe and Schiller and the emerging political economists in Britain, most notably Peter Golding, Graham Murdock, and Garnham. The main figures included Vincent Mosco, Janet Wasko, Dan Schiller, Eileen Meehan, Stuart Ewen, Oscar Gandy Jr., Gerald Sussman, Manjunath Pendakur, to be followed by another generation in the late 1980s and 1990s. As Mosco has written, this group of scholars produced "a substantial research record, well out of proportion to the institutional support it has received" (1996). In 1983, when the *Journal of Communication* published its massive "Ferment in the Field" special issue where the field's leading figures assessed the state of the discipline, eight or nine of the thirty-five commissioned articles were by people in the political economy tradition, and three or four of the other essays were by critical scholars closely linked to it.

The overall influence of the political economy of communication peaked in the early 1980s, and it has struggled to recover its influence ever since. The high-water mark for the field was not an accident; it accompanied the rise of dissident social movements and anti-imperialist sentiments worldwide in the 1960s and 1970s. It was typified in communication by the movement for a new world information and communication order (NWICO), in which political economists like Herbert Schiller played a large role on a global stage. With the rise of neoliberalism in the 1980s—which, among other things, impaled the movement supporting the NWICO—and the return to generalized depoliticization, the momentum on behalf of political economy of communication began to lessen. In some respects the field has returned to the dark days of the 1950s, when conventional wisdom saw little need or reason for the political economy of communication; if the market is presumed to be synonymous with democracy, what is there to study? Even for some less sanguine about the marriage of capitalism to democracy, the rule of capital seems enshrined for many generations. In this case, why bother studying the political economy of communication if nothing can be changed? The proper course would be to put one's energies where there is the possibility of having some effect.

For an indication of the decline of the political economy of communication over the past two decades, consider the following: When the *Journal of Communication* published its follow-up special edition on the state of the field in the middle 1990s, only three of the twenty essays were by political economists, and only a couple more by critical scholars sympathetic to political economy (Levy and Gurevitch 1994).[16] There are few classes and fewer jobs in the political economy of communication. As it is, there are only a handful of explicit jobs in U.S. universities for people who do political economy of communication. (When I left Wisconsin, despite teaching some of the most popular courses in the department for more than a decade and supervising several Ph.D.s, there was no thought toward hiring someone who did political economy to replace me. That tradition was terminated.) Most political economy scholars in media studies get hired for some other reason (e.g., to teach news writing or new media) and do their research without tremendous encouragement. Nor are their divisions in ICA, NCA, or AEJMC (the professional organizations) devoted to political economy, with journals to publish research. This has a reinforcing effect. Graduate students exposed to political economy are not blind. They see that it is not a viable career option, at least in the United States, and some shift to research that has more prospects for publication and employment down the road.

All is not lost, fortunately. The two previous waves of political economic work in communication—the 1930s and 1940s and the 1960s and 1970s—were directly in response to broader progressive political movements outside the academy. Their decline, likewise, can be attributed to the reactionary political moments that followed. A similar wave of activism is emerging worldwide and media issues are increasingly at the center of popular concerns. The interest in political economy of media, and the issues it addresses, is growing, perhaps even rapidly. Book sales for political economic titles have increased over the past few years, and public talks on political economic issues draw large audiences. The issues that political economy is best suited to addressing—the relationship of media, capitalism, and democracy—have moved to the fore with a vengeance in the era of globalization and the Internet. The core traditions and theorists on which political economy is built are as important and vital as ever. It is institutional support that is lagging, for the reasons described in this chapter. As a result the amount and quality of the work being generated in the political economic tradition is just a smidgen of what is necessary. There is an enormous gap. Some signs are on the horizon, however, that these issues are gaining more attention in the academy, though we are early in the process. If the field of media studies in the United States is going to amount to much more than a hill of beans, it is going to require a cornerstone of political economy on which to stand.

NOTES

1. For the best overview of the subfield, see Mosco 1996.
2. For two books that address this subject, see Staniland 1985; Tabb 1999.
3. For a lovely and balanced recent exposition on the nature of capitalism, see Lindblom 2001.
4. This quote appears in a letter from Marx to Arnold Ruge, September 1843.
5. Much of my own thinking about critical scholarship came from a graduate seminar at the University of Washington in 1986, where we spent most of a term closely examining Kaplan's classic text. See Kaplan 1998.
6. To support a point made above, it is worth noting that opposition to television advertising to children is not necessarily a "left-wing" issue in the United States. Right-wing figures such as Phyllis Schlafly and George Will oppose advertising in schools on principle—eschewing neoliberal orthodoxy—and some conservatives are willing to broach the idea of flat-out bans on TV advertising to children as well.
7. All great social scholarship is guided by a set of political values, and much of it is driven by explicit and immediate partisan political concerns. That does not mean the work is "unscientific." In economics, for example, nearly every great breakthrough in theory has been made by people like Smith, Ricardo, Malthus, Marx, and Keynes, who were weighing in on the great issues of their day. See Dowd 2000. The goal is not to be neutral per se, but to be honest about the assumptions and values that guide our research.

8. See, for example, Demers 1999, 2001; Aufderheide 1997, 157.

9. We should, for starters, demand far more from graduate students. Students who are admitted to a Ph.D. program are almost guaranteed a degree. Consequently, many grad students set their sights low and do just enough to get by, and too few will do whatever it takes to produce great work. While I don't want to see a cutthroat environment, we have to encourage young scholars to become their own toughest critics and to be committed to excellence. We have to cultivate students who are passionate about their research, not just attempting to get a day job to pay the bills.

10. See, for example, Guttmann and Thompson 1996; Young 2000; Dworkin 1996, 2000; Sunstein 1997; Rawls 1999; Lupia and McCubbins 1998. One of the very few works in political philosophy that considers what the best manner to structure the media system would be for a democracy is Howard's *Self-Management and the Crisis of Socialism* (2000).

11. See, for some recent examples, Sommerville 1999; Johnston 2000; Cherny 2000; Berman 2000; Shane 2001; and Scheuer 1999.

12. Discussed splendidly in Carey 1978.

13. For a discussion of this PR campaign in the history of radio broadcasting, see McChesney 1993.

14. For a compilation of figures concerning U.S. media usage, see "Media Use in America," *Mediascope*. March 15, 2000. www.mediascope.org/pubs/ibriefs/mua.htm.

15. Considerable historical research has recast the 1940s as a pivotal decade in recent U.S. history, where progressive political forces were far stronger than much of the conventional thinking had presumed. See, for example, Lipsitz 1994.

16. These essays originally appeared in "Special Issue: The Future of the Field II," *Journal of Communication* 43 (1993): 4. They were later published as a book, Levy and Gurevitch 1994.

REFERENCES

Aufderheide, P. 1997. "Telecommunication and the Public Interest." In *Conglomerates and the Media*, edited by Erik Barnouw et al. New York: New Press.

Berkman, D. 2000. "Living a Professional Lie." *Shepherd Express Metro,* April 6. www.shepherd-express.com/shepherd/21/15/cover_story.html.

Berman, M. 2000. *The Twilight of American Culture*. New York: Norton.

Bok, D. 2001. *The Trouble with Government*. Cambridge: Harvard University Press.

Carey, J. 1978. "A Plea for the University Tradition." *Journalism Quarterly* 55: 846–55.

Chaffee, S. 2000. "George Gallup and Ralph Nafziger: Pioneers of Audience Research." *Mass Communication and Society* 3: 317–27.

Cherny, A. 2000. *The Next Deal: The Future of Public Life in the Information Age.* New York: Basic.

Demers, D. 1999. *Global Media: Menace or Messiah?* Cresskill, N.J.: Hampton.

———. 2001. "Bernard Shaw Makes a Better Journalist Than Media Critic." *Global Media News*, Summer, 6–7.

Dowd, D. 2000. *Capitalism and Its Economics: A Critical History*. London: Pluto.

Dworkin, R. 1996. *Freedom's Law*. Cambridge: Harvard University Press.

———. 2000. *Sovereign Virtue*. Cambridge: Harvard University Press.

Garnham, N. 1983. "Toward a Theory of Cultural Materialism." *Journal of Communication* 33: 314.

———. 2000. *Emancipation, the Media, and Modernity.* Oxford: Oxford University Press.

Glander, T. 2000. *Origins of Mass Communications Research during the American Cold War.* Mahwah, N.J.: Lawrence Erlbaum.

Graber, D. 2001. *Processing Politics.* Chicago: University of Chicago Press.

Guttmann, A., and D. Thompson. 1996. *Democracy and Disagreement.* Cambridge: Belknap.

Hall, S. 1986. "Media Power and Class Power." In J. Curran, J. Ecclestone, G. Oakley, and A. Richardson, eds., *Bending Reality: The State of the Media.* London: Pluto.

Howard, M. 2000. *Self-Management and the Crisis of Socialism.* Lanham, Md.: Rowman & Littlefield.

Hutchins, R. 1947. *A Free and Responsible Press.* Chicago: University of Chicago Press.

Johnston, C. 2000. *Screened Out: How the Media Control Us and What We Can Do about It.* Armonk, N.Y.: M. E. Sharpe.

Kaplan, A. 1998. *The Conduct of Inquiry.* With an introduction by C. Wolf Jr. New Brunswick, N.J.: Transaction.

La Follette, R. 1920. *The Political Philosophy of Robert M. La Follette.* Madison: Robert M. La Follette Co.

Levy, M., and M. Gurevitch, eds. 1994. *Defining Media Studies.* New York: Oxford University Press.

Lindblom, C. 2001. *The Market System.* New Haven: Yale University Press.

Lipsitz, G. 1994. *Rainbow at Midnight.* Urbana: University of Illinois Press.

Lupia, A., and M. McCubbins. 1998. *The Democratic Dilemma: Can Citizens Learn What They Need to Know?* Cambridge: Cambridge University Press.

Marx, K. 1979. *The Letters of Karl Marx.* Edited and translated by S. Padover. Englewood Cliffs, N.J.: Prentice-Hall.

McChesney, R. 1993. *Telecommunications, Mass Media, and Democracy: The Battle for the Control of U.S. Broadcasting, 1928–1935.* New York: Oxford University Press.

———. 1997. "Springtime for Goebbels." *Z Magazine* 10: 16–18.

McKerrow, R. E. 2000. "Scholarship, Influence, and the Intellectual Community." *Spectra* 36: 4.

"Media Use in America." 2000. *Mediascope,* March 15. www.mediascope.org/pubs/ibriefs/mua.htm.

Michael, J. 2000. *Anxious Intellects: Academic Professionals, Public Intellectuals, and Enlightenment Values.* Durham, N.C.: Duke University Press.

Mills, C. 1956. *The Power Elite.* New York: Oxford University Press.

———. 1959. *The Sociological Imagination.* New York: Oxford University Press.

Mosco, V. 1996. *The Political Economy of Communication.* London: Sage.

Moy, P., and M. Pfau. 2000. *With Malice toward All?* Westport, Conn.: Praeger.

Putnam, R. 2000. *Bowling Alone: The Collapse and Revival of American Community.* New York: Simon & Schuster.

Rawls, J. 1999. *The Law of Peoples.* Cambridge: Harvard University Press.

Sardar, Z., and B. Van Loon. 2000. *Introducing Media Studies.* New York: Totem.

Scheuer, J. 1999. *The Sound Bite Society: Television and the American Mind.* New York: Four Walls, Eight Windows.

Schiller, D. 1996. *Theorizing Communication: A History.* New York: Oxford University Press.

Schumpeter, J. 1942. *Capitalism, Socialism, and Democracy.* New York: Harper & Row.

Shane, E. 2001. *Disconnected America: The Consequences of Mass Media in a Narcissistic World.* Armonk, N.Y.: M. E. Sharpe.

Silverstone, R. 1999. *Why Study the Media?* London: Sage.

Simpson, C. 1994. *The Science of Coercion.* New York: Oxford University Press.

Sinclair, U. 1920. *The Brass Check: A Study of American Journalism.* Pasadena: Author.

———. 2003. *The Brass Check: A Study of American Journalism.* With an introduction by R. McChesney and B. Scott. Urbana: University of Illinois Press. A new edition was issued by the University of Illinois Press in 2003, with an introduction by Robert W. McChesney and Ben Scott.

Sommerville, C. 1999. *How the News Makes Us Dumb: The Death of Wisdom in an Information Society.* Downers Grove, Ill.: InterVarsity Press.

Staniland, M. 1985. *What Is Political Economy?* New Haven: Yale University Press.

Sterne, J. 2001. "Ground Zero of the Sociological Imagination: C. Wright Mills at the Bureau of Applied Social Research." Paper presented at the International Communication Association, Washington, D.C.

Sunstein, C. 1997. *Free Markets and Social Justice.* New York: Oxford University Press.

Tabb, W. 1999. *Reconstructing Political Economy.* London: Routledge.

Tudiver, N. 1999. *Universities for Sale.* Toronto: James Lorimar.

Wander, P., and S. Jenkins. 1972. "Rhetoric, Society, and the Critical Response." *Quarterly Journal of Speech* 58: 4.

Young, I. 2000. *Inclusion and Democracy.* New York: Oxford University Press.

4

The "Marketplace of Ideas"
A History of the Concept

John Durham Peters

The liberal tradition's apparent equation of free trade and free speech deserves special interpretive care. Some exult in the ideological camouflage it provides and appreciate old arguments for lending their business interests a democratic patina and venerable intellectual lineage. Others, wanting to differentiate democracy and capitalism and take responsibility for the health and diversity of public life instead of abandoning it to the hurly-burly of the marketplace, recoil at liberalism's marriage of the free market and the free press as an antiquated apologetic and call for its interment in a resurrection-proof vault. These too starkly drawn alternatives offer readers of this volume an easy choice. Yet critical scholars' rejection of the liberal tradition can be too hasty. We shouldn't trust neoliberals or civil libertarians (no matter how sincere) as sole interpreters of the tradition. Further, the thinkers often considered founders (funders?) of the twin doctrine of free market and free press such as John Milton or John Stuart Mill to not unambiguously endorse the market as a normative model for communication. These classic "liberals" do not always like the market; indeed, they may not always be liberals. The "marketplace of ideas" is a powerful but distorting lens for reading the tradition.

In this chapter I hope to clarify the conceptual link between communication and economics by examining the notion of the "marketplace of ideas." This term, especially in the United States, has become a fixture in legal and public debates about freedom of expression and the social responsibility of the media. It is used widely and often unreflectively by mainstream and critical thinkers alike. Robert McChesney, an eminent critic of neoliberal market logic, uses the "marketplace of ideas" uncritically as a measure of ideological diversity (1992). Robert Horwitz (1989, 14–16) more ambivalently ponders the conflict of commerce and dialogue implicit in the term, wanting to shuck its free market connotations and keep its civil libertarian ones (cf. Garnham 2000, 54). Nothing is wrong per se with using words in their everyday acceptations. We have little choice: it would take many lifetimes, as J. L. Austin (1970) said, to be responsible to the whole of one's language. Words are conceptual mausoleums, haunts at which the spirits of the dead continue their debates and threaten to possess the bodies of the unwary. Intellectual history can provide a selective exorcism for conceptual and political clarification. Taking the "marketplace" as the central metaphor for public communication, as we will see, has divergent effects. It packs hefty semantic freight, suggesting that communication and economics are not only analogous but flourish when unregulated, that diversity is essential, and that exchange occurs in a "place" where people congregate and circulate, enter and exit at will. The term often wears the halo of what one might call the libertarian theodicy—the faith that ideas, if they are left to shift for themselves, will be diverse and truth will conquer error in the long run. It implies a rather disembodied vision of public communication, as if the politics of culture were governed by entities so Platonic as "ideas." It is a culturally protected zone where laissez-faire ideology persists in its purest form (Coase 1974). This key word offers us the public sphere "lite." It stacks the conceptual deck against rival terms accounting for communication in public such as ideology, hegemony, *Öffentlichkeit* (public sphere), patriarchy, revelation, solidarity, or objective truth. Though full of contradictions, the "marketplace of ideas" is a normative and critical concept, with resources worthy of an inventory.

RETROACTIVE PREHISTORY: MILTON, MILL, HOLMES

The history of the catchphrase is quite recent, dating only to the 1930s. Its historicist effects, in contrast, reach to the seventeenth century, gathering Milton and Mill, Adam Smith and Thomas Jefferson in its net. Like rabbits in Australia, the new concept quickly took over the landscape, insinuating itself even into the past. Every concept invents its ancestors. The "marketplace of ideas" has been regularly placed in the mouths of several suspects, usually Milton, Smith, Mill, and the American jurist Oliver Wendell Holmes Jr. Yet the term was not used, as far as I have been able to discover, by any of these men, and was not even in wide circulation until the 1950s. Although it captures the long liberal animus against censorship, the term does little justice to the wisdom, warnings, and diversity in the tradition. In historical inquiry, the ways that old texts surprise us are as important as the ways they confirm standing prejudices. The taboo on post hoc imputation on history is a salutary if impossible discipline. Fruitful interpretation requires not only that strange texts be made familiar but that familiar texts be made strange. The classic texts can be neutralized by their canonization; careful reading is often antidote enough.

Take John Milton (1608–1674), who is regularly handcuffed by friendly anachronism. His tract against licensed printing, *Areopagitica* (1644), is a difficult masterpiece—though Milton dismissed his political prose of the 1640s as "writings for the left-hand"—and is usually remembered in one of two ways: as the proclamation that truth, in a "free and open encounter" with error, will triumph, and as a savage attack on Catholicism, as if to expose Milton's hypocrisy. In writings about free expression, fragments often weigh more than whole texts, and the chief retailers of Milton as a market theorist are lawyers and journalists. Legal scholar Thomas Tedford (1997, 371), for instance, states: "Milton demonstrated his belief in what some have called a 'marketplace theory' of free speech—a viewpoint suggesting that ideas 'grapple' in the field (or marketplace) open to merchants of all shades of opinion, and that after due consideration thoughtful consumers 'buy' the product that to them represents truth." Tedford wisely attributes this reading to an unnamed "some," since nothing in *Areopagitica* sustains such a reading. One example would be Jeffery A. Smith (1988, chap. 2), who imputes the notion to a wide range of figures—Milton, Shaftesbury, John Trenchard and Thomas Gordon, Tom Paine, Jefferson, and Thomas Erskine. "The marketplace of ideas concept—the proposition that truth naturally overcomes falsehood when they are allowed to compete—was used continually during the eighteenth century as a justification for freedom of expression" (Smith 1988, 31). Though notions of tolerance, truth triumphant, and press freedom circulated widely in the eighteenth century, there was no such notion as the marketplace of ideas.

Journalism historian Herbert Altschull (1990) offers a richer textual analysis of *Areopagitica* than Tedford or Smith, but his emphasis on "the self-righting principle" misses the mark: Milton simply has no notion of a counterbalancing system, economic or otherwise. Self-righting can be read into a variety of eighteenth-century notions—the deist's solar system, the political theorist's checks and balances, or the political economist's order emerging from the disjunct activities of many buyers and sellers. But Milton is a century too early. The closest Milton gets is his call to build a house of truth from the diverse labors of individuals: "nay rather the perfection consists in this, that out of many moderate varieties and brotherly dissimilitudes that are not vastly disproportional arises the goodly and graceful symmetry that commends the whole pile and structure. Let us therefore be more considerate builders, more wise in spiritual architecture, when great reformation is expected" (Milton 1957, 744). The notion that independent acts cumulatively can form a single "pile and structure" may resemble Smith's economics, but Milton calls for conscious collaboration instead of Smith's order emergent from unorchestrated private enterprise. Richard Schwarzlose (1989, 4–7) rightly notes Milton's theological vision and the absence of clear market language, but then he proceeds to treat Milton's notion of gathering truth as if it were a market anyway. Refreshingly, Nerone and colleagues (1995, 46) grasp Milton's spirit with acuity: "Clearly, Milton did not conceive of public discourse as a marketplace. Rather, he seems to have conceived it as a church; it is easy to imagine him chasing the money changers out of it."

To what extent does Milton use market talk in *Areopagitica?* Two passages employ economic metaphors. In a negative comparison of truth to goods, he states: "Truth and understanding are not such wares as to be monopolized and traded in by tickets, and statutes, and standards. We must not think to make a staple commodity of all the knowledge in the land; to mark and license it like our broadcloth and our woolpacks" (Milton 1957, 736–37). Though he seems to be rejecting economic models for mental life, he is ever the opportunist where a metaphor is concerned: "More than if some enemy at sea should stop up all our havens and ports and creeks, it hinders and retards the importation of our richest merchandise, truth" (741). These two passages—one denying that truth can be traded like wool, one affirming truth as England's richest merchandise—are the closest Milton gets to the "marketplace of ideas." The question turns on what we mean by a market. If we mean that Milton imagines reading and writing taking place in an unrestricted, open-ended, and voluntary space, fair enough. But if we mean that laissez-faire economics is the best way to operate broadcasting and news media, regulation should be scrapped, and the realm of ideas operates like that of commodities, then Milton can end up buying lunch for the media industries. Milton is no neoclassical economist. Forgive my pedantry: in interpreting Milton, at stake is the specification of what is honorable and dangerous about markets as normative frameworks of communication. Call him radical, call him puritan, call him poet, but don't call Milton (neo)liberal.

Milton's central place in the liberal pantheon is, in many respects, a misunderstanding, but it is a fortunate one. *Areopagitica* deserves its place in the intellectual tradition not because it offers a crystal clear defense of openness in communication, but because it advocates a brokered coexistence of good and evil. Milton's understanding of publication is motivated by theological and aesthetic commitments: that passage through a fallen world offers mor(t)al tempering and art allows imaginative trial by contraries (Fish 2001, chap. 5). Aspects of *Areopagitica* do legitimately resonate to a libertarian ear—the pluralism, the call for many minds to build a house of truth, the contempt for compulsion (at least as exercised by others!), and the equation of censorship with murder: "who kills a Man kills a reasonable creature, God's Image; but he who destroys a good book, kills reason itself, kills the Image of God, as it were in the eye. Many a man lives a burden to the Earth;

but a good book is the precious life blood of a master spirit, embalmed and treasured up on purpose to a life beyond life" (Milton 1957, 720)—an extraordinary passage from a man who would be totally blind within eight years. Censorship is not "the slaying of an elemental life, but strikes at that ethereal and fifth essence, the breath of reason itself, slays an immortality rather than a life" (720). Books as bottled souls, spiritual extracts, "the orphan remainders of worthiest men after death" (736): this is a way of thinking more creepy—and interesting—than free-expression commentators usually manage. Milton, unlike most of his "marketplace of ideas" interpreters, does not suffer from an underdeveloped sense of wickedness; as author of *Paradise Lost* and hence of one of the most compelling characters in world literature, Satan, he is one of the great experts on the subject. He hates (what he considers) evil and would gladly put, for instance, Catholics and their books into the furnace, but the heights and depths of his theological and aesthetic vision of liberty (which I hope to cover elsewhere) are hardly fathomed by those who convert this puritan radical and magnificent, dangerous poet into a theorist of the marketplace.

What about John Stuart Mill (1806–1873)? As befits an arch-Socratic figure who believes it our duty to pray for the vigor of our enemies' arguments, Mill has many faces. *On Liberty* (1859) has become part of the canon of First Amendment theory in the United States, thanks in part to its enthusiastic reception by key Supreme Court justices such as Holmes, Brandeis, and Brennan, and its institutionalization in the canon of journalism education. *On Liberty* suggests, in passing, that the philosophy of liberty of thought and discussion parallels that of economic free trade (Mill 1975, 88), and Mill is of course a classic figure in British political economy. But Mill is subtler than most proponents of the "marketplace of ideas." Though he lacks a vision of the structural constraints on consciousness comparable to his London contemporary, Karl Marx, Mill by no means envisions either truth's automatic victory or a hindrance-free zone of open competition. The diffusion of light across public space has no guarantees. Mill has a healthy respect for the obstacles that face communication in public.

First, Mill does not believe that truth, left to shift for itself, will shine. The automatic victory of truth is nothing more than a "pleasant falsehood" (Mill 1975, 29): "It is a piece of idle sentimentality that truth, merely as truth, has any inherent power denied to error of prevailing against the dungeon and the stake" (30). If Milton imagines truth as an undefeated wrestler, Mill's sporting metaphor might be a batting average: truth gets hits some of the time, but strikes out other times. The great risk Mill found in his age was enervation: "the danger which threatens human nature is not the excess, but the deficiency, of personal impulses and preferences" (57–58). Like William James later, Mill wanted a moral equivalent to war, something capable of producing the vigor without the blood and trauma. Public debate, in Mill's account, often had a martial spirit. "Both teachers and learners go to sleep at their post, as soon as there is no enemy in the field" (41). Enlightened discussion was a kind of cold war with both self and other, a constant pre-emptive girding of the loins. The historical tie of belligerent passions and in-tellectual life is ubiquitous in Mill. Yet as a foe of violence and the abuse of power, and a champion of reason, Mill is both a critic and an architect of what a century later would be called mass society. Mill combines a stoic's love for self-command with a romantic's love of eccentricity; modern society threatens both. "Formerly, different ranks, different neighbourhoods, differ-ent trades and professions, lived in what might be called different worlds; at present to a great degree in the same. Comparatively speaking, they now read the same things, listen to the same things, see the same things, go to the same places, have their hopes and fears directed to the same objects, have the same rights and liberties, and the same means of asserting them" (68). Mill has no nostalgia for bygone days of bloodlust; but his project, shared with his father, James Mill, and spiritual grandfather Jeremy Bentham, is the softening of manners, the elimination of torture, the withdrawal of execu-tions from public gawkery, the secret ballot (which Mill came to regret), and sundry other reforms, all of which make public life saner and duller. As a "liberal critic of liberalism" he almost laments his achievements (Habermas 1989, chap. 15). Instead of the glorious site for threshing truth and error so beloved of the eighteenth-century philosophes, the public has become a "miscellaneous collection of a few wise and many foolish individuals" (Mill 1975, 21). This is rather a diminuendo.

Second, Mill is clearly aware of manipulation and puffery. In "Civiliza-tion" (1836), Mill makes resonant points about what we have since learned to call "public relations." In a face-to-face community where everyone knows everyone, he argues, people and products gain the reputation they deserve. (Like many nineteenth-century social thinkers, Mill's modernity is a *Gemeinschaft* to *Gesellschaft* story.) Continued patronage depends on goods or services of high quality. In civilization, in contrast, where "the in-dividual becomes so lost in the crowd," much (too much) depends on image making. By giving goods and services "a gloss, a saleable look," the entrepreneur in a crowded city can make a profit without a single return customer. Signs start to drift apart from their referents. The quackery and puffery of both commerce and intellectual life "are the inevitable fruits of immense competition; of a state of society where any voice, not pitched in an exaggerated key, is lost in the hubbub. Success, in so crowded a field, depends not upon what a person is, but what he seems: mere marketable qualities become the object instead of substantial ones, and a man's labour and capital are expended less in doing anything, than in persuading other people that he has done it. . . . For the first time, arts for attracting public at-tention form a necessary part of the qualifications even of the deserving: and skill in these arts goes farther than any other quality in ensuring suc-cess" (132–33). The critique of people on the make, celebrities who know how to succeed by seeming instead of being, of advertising inverting appearance and reality, is older than we think.

While it is fair to say that Mill is fiercely individualistic, that *On Liberty* imagines a public realm of speakers and writers with more or less equal access to the means of communication, it is not fair to say that he has no sense for hindrances to free circulation of thought, whether social (the tyranny of opinion and norms of propriety), psychological (laziness and torpor), economic (advertising), or political (parliament, newspapers). Mill may underestimate concentrated economic power in the shaping of opinion, but his understandings of debate as warfare, the hazards of argument, the public sphere without guarantees, make him richer than his conscription into the marketplace of ideas. Rescuing Mill from this metaphor can offer our thinking about communication fresh options. An encounter with the past should involve otherness, not just repetition of the same.

With Oliver Wendell Holmes Jr. (1841–1935), we are getting closer to the origins of the phrase. In a famous dissent to a First Amendment decision in the wake of World War I, Holmes wrote: "But when men have realized that time has upset many fighting faiths, they may come to believe even more than they believe the very foundations of their own conduct that the ultimate good desired is better reached by free trade in ideas—that the best test of truth is the power of the thought to get itself accepted in the competition of the market, and that truth is the only ground upon which their wishes safely can be carried out. That at any rate is the theory of our Constitution. It is an experiment, as all life is an experiment" (*Abrams v US*, 250 US 616, 630 [1919]). Here Holmes elucidates the "theory of our Constitution" in a way that is actually quite novel: the Founders would not readily recognize it without first boning up on their Mill, Spencer, and pragmatism. (We know that Holmes read Mill carefully.) In these words, so prized by civil libertarians, Holmes extols the struggle of ideas and the relativizing benefits of historical consciousness: recognizing the transience of old causes lessens one's dogmatism. Yet Holmes had no substantive conception of truth. Truth, he liked to provoke his friends by saying, is the "majority vote of the nation that could lick all the others." Like Pontius Pilate, he enjoyed asking "what is truth?" without staying for an answer. Holmes, a decorated Civil War veteran who was wounded in three separate battles, cultivated a harsh vitality in his laissez-faire economics, strenuous professionalism, cheerful nihilism, even authoritarianism (something he shared with his British friend and colleague, James Fitzjames Stephen). He is a very odd hero for civil libertarians, though some of his decisions in favor of free competition helped him gain the title of "Great Dissenter." Holmes had remarkably little faith in public speech, and other decisions (e.g., *Schenck*) place clear restrictions on expression. He thought the "competition of the market" was dangerous and brutal and could eat people alive; that's one reason he liked it.

To my knowledge Holmes nowhere speaks of the "marketplace of ideas" though many insist that he does, misremembering the language of his *Abrams* decision. To be sure, Holmes invites this metaphor; my point is not to be picky but to attend to the diverse ways that our thoughts are shaped by the minutiae of language practice. In the most recent scholarship, ranging across a variety of political and philosophical perspectives, Holmes is directly tagged. I would agree with Menand's (2001b, 431) analysis but not his attribution: "Holmes's conceit of a 'marketplace of ideas' suffers from the de-· fect of all market theories: exogenous elements are always in play to keep marketplaces from being truly competitive." Magee (2002, 234) also attributes the notion to Holmes directly, and Bunker's critique of free expression theory (2001, 2–8) trots out an anachronistic lineage of marketplace theorists in Milton, Mill, and Holmes. Holmes's vision of public life is a good deal less edifying and optimistic than faith in the marketplace has come to imply. He might get a good chuckle out of the civil libertarian pieties he unwittingly spawned, and might enjoy how even critical theorists have come to find it indispensable to use economic metaphors to talk about liberty of communication.

Thinkers as rich as Milton, Mill, and Holmes deserve more thorough treatment than what I can give them here. There are reasons to read them as friends of the "marketplace of ideas," just as one could be forgiven for calling Cicero and Dante "Italians" (a label invented in the nineteenth century). Imaginative retrojection is inevitable in historical inquiry. But it is not fair to saddle Milton and friends with all the resonances of the catchphrase, a metaphoric kudzu vine whose resources have shaped English-language reflection on public space for the past five decades for good and ill.

HISTORY OF THE TERM "MARKETPLACE OF IDEAS"

The term does not emerge from Holmes, nor from, as far as I can discover, any leading theorists of free expression before 1950 such as Louis Brandeis, Zechariah Chaffee, Learned Hand, or Alexander Meiklejohn. I cannot find it in John Dewey or Walter Lippmann. Electronic text databases provide an unprecedented opportunity to study the conceptual development of key words. The *New York Times* (*NYT*) is now searchable in its entirety, and as the newspaper of record in the United States, it offers an excellent window, though naturally not exhaustive or representative, to the discourse of American elites. Though the *Times* is rather fond of the locution, judging from its frequent use in editorials, most instances occur in quotations. Below I sketch the term's rise and decline (see table 4.1), providing parenthetical references for each passage to the date and page in the *Times*.

Table 4.1.   Number of Articles in *New York Times* Mentioning Marketplace of Ideas

	Market Place of Ideas	Marketplace of Ideas	Total
1930s	2	0	2
1940s	0	1	1
1950s	14	8	22
1960s	17	12	29
1970s	10	40	50
1980s	1	125	126
1990s	3	81	84

Source: Proquest, Historical database, *New York Times.*
Note: "Market-place" added no hits to the search.

The first two uses of the term anticipate its future. In a 1935 letter to the editor, David M. Newbold complained that leaders in the upcoming convention of the Republican Party were threatening to use bloc voting to manipulate the party's presidential nomination instead of giving free rein to the delegates. Newbold wanted the party to nominate one of its senior statesmen, Herbert Hoover or William Borah, via an open process. "If for some reason neither of these two great national leaders is available, then their likes will issue not from a dark room at 2 o'clock in the morning, but as the result of men and issues competing in the market place of ideas where public opinion is formed" (*NYT,* 28 December 1935, 14). Already the term calls for democracy, openness, and competition, and denounces secrecy and elitism in government. The only other mention in the 1930s comes from a speech by Grover A. Whalen, president of the 1939 New York World's Fair: "The fair, planned to entertain and delight every one with its beauty, its comfort, its magnificence, and its variegated amusements . . . will be a market place for ideas, the birthplace of a wonderful new era" (*NYT,* 9 October 1936, 27). Another characteristic theme is evident: a celebration of diversity, and of trade—the World's Fair was, after all, a glorified trade show—as the best way to achieve it. Curiously, the heading to the paragraph containing this quotation is "marketplace of ideas," as if a copy editor thought the term deserved an "of" instead of a "for." Probably the term already enjoyed some currency, perhaps as a popularization of Holmes's *Abrams* dissent.

Usages in the 1940s and 1950s usually belong to civil libertarians of various stripes who resist the McCarthyite muzzling of dissidence and political discussion. The sole instance in the 1940s comes in the American Communist Party platform for the 1948 election. "We Communists seek only the opportunity to compete fairly in the marketplace of ideas, asking only that our program and proposals be considered on their merit" (*NYT,* 7 August 1948, 2). In an essay on civil liberties, the seventy-year-old Norman Thomas, leader of the American Socialist Party, argued—quoting Milton and Mill—that dissent has long been a source of social creativity and progress. The struggle for progress, however, has its casualties and reversals: "Truth in the market place of ideas does not always bear away victory" (*NYT,* 28 November 1954, SM12). Thomas understood his Mill! In a essay on "The Black Silence of Fear," Supreme Court Justice William O. Douglas wrote in defense of diverse ideological competition—and against the specter of communist thought control in the Soviet Union and Asia. "If we are true to our traditions, if we are tolerant of a whole market place of ideas, we will always be strong" (*NYT,* 13 January 1952, SM38). Here the marketplace of ideas is treated as something peculiarly American—and anticommunist. These three selections nicely depict the range of American political opinion to the left of center in the immediate postwar era—communist, socialist, and establishment liberal; all oppose the ideological preemptiveness of McCarthyism and favor open competition, fearless debate, and toleration of diverse doctrines.

Despite its use by the communists, the "marketplace of ideas" quickly took on a Cold War flavor, as noted. A brief notice about the American radio station in Berlin, RIAS, observed: "By its present jamming effort the East German Government is implicitly confessing its political bankruptcy, its inability to compete in the free marketplace of ideas" (*NYT,* 13 November 1953, 26). A reviewer of a book by Justice Douglas queried, "And how much of the most virulent work of the Communists and their fellow-travelers is ever done out in the open market place of ideas, anyway?" (*NYT,* 28 May 1953, 21). The *Times* op-ed page repeatedly plays this tune: "Marxism is a philosophy that cannot win in any free market place of ideas, or even in a market place where there is at least some opposition from other schools of thought" (*NYT,* 26 December 1962, 6). By 1989, the *Times* congratulated Gorbachev's policy of glasnost for giving up "its ideological monopoly to a robust marketplace of ideas" (*NYT,* 11 September 1989, A10). The distinctive feature of the free world, in this rhetoric, is its marketplace of ideas. Two, of course, can play at this game. When NATO bombed Serb state television headquarters in Belgrade in 1999, "Yugoslav officials said NATO was simply trying to destroy the free marketplace of ideas and insure that just one side's 'propaganda' could be propagated" (*NYT,* 24 April 1999, A6).

Concepts that glow with unmitigated righteousness can create mischief. The "marketplace of ideas" often shined a noble light on the press and obscured its profit-making interests with a flattering self-description. A choice mix of anticommunism and self-congratulatory boosterism is present in a 1953 speech comparing American and Soviet newspapers given by Julius Ochs Adler, general manager of the *New York Times*. Their journalism is "a kind of mass narcotic, since the reading of Communist newspapers behind the Iron Curtain tends to lull minds to sleep, to discourage questions, to prevent differences of opinion." American newspapers, in contrast, together with magazines, radio, and television, offer a "real market place of ideas in which different points of view and different opinions compete against each other for public acceptance." The American press is "essentially the product of our free, democratic society" (*NYT,* 15 August 1953, 3). Here the high office of the newspaper, with the *New York Times* the chief high priest, is affirmed in such a way that free expression is conflated with democracy and free markets. That the public sphere needs more than diverse news media, a free press needs more than a free market, and democracy is not the same as capitalism, are thoughts the "marketplace of ideas" concept can make difficult to think. Critics of the marketplace risked being branded as un-American communist scaredy-cats while its friends are lauded for their ability to take the heat of open competition. The "marketplace of ideas"—like all ideas that secure a monopoly of virtue for their proponents—can be morally and politically extortionist.

Advertising copywriters pounced on the term. In a priceless 1961 ad, WNEW-TV announced: "In ancient Greece, where the marketplace of ideas was, literally, a marketplace, people with important things to say would 'enchant souls through words' (Socrates). Today, or rather, tonight the marketplace moves indoors—to the television set in your home—and we are confident that you will be enchanted by the words you will hear and the ideas expressed on these programs" (*NYT,* 12 February 1961, X15). Much could be said about the equation of marketplace of ideas, Athenian agora, and television set, as well as the interiorization of public debate (Habermas 1989, chap. 18). The news media, from the seventeenth-century press to early television, have long spun noble tales about themselves. These tales secure them a lofty lineage and privileged place in democracy and treat the marketplace's civic and commercial dimensions—its voicing of opinions and generation of profits—as seamlessly intertwined (Curran 1996). An ad for *Harper's* magazine called it the "freest, most invigorating marketplace of ideas in America" (*NYT,* 4 December 1977, 298). An ad for the Sears Financial Network, starring a testimonial from Alan Greenspan, stated: "In the marketplace of ideas, just as in the marketplace of goods and services, vigorous competition best serves the American consumer" (*NYT,* 10 June 1985, A17). Even in political rhetoric, the metaphor's commercial aspects were widely exploited. Lamented presidential candidate Richard M. Nixon in 1967: "Ideas should be our greatest export—and yet in the marketplace of ideas, people of other nations are simply not buying American" (*NYT,* 13 September 1967, 26). His opponent in the 1968 election, Hubert H. Humphrey, did not equate ideas and goods (as befits a Democrat): "to insist that something be done my way or I strike or lock the other fellow out, is part of the idea of the marketplace; but it is abhorrent in the marketplace of ideas" (*NYT,* 5 May 1968, 32). From Nixon to Humphrey, from trade balances to civic decency—the term oscillates.

As a site of dialogue across difference, higher education often attracts the term. President Horton of Wellesley College called her campus "this free marketplace of ideas" (*NYT,* 20 May 1953, 15). A letter praised teach-ins: "The college campus is, traditionally, a place for entertaining a free marketplace of ideas, including the dissenting. In view of the usual work pressures on professors, they are to be congratulated rather than criticized for their attention to these issues concerning Vietnam" (*NYT,* 30 May 1965, E11). In 1969 students at City University founded SEEK—Seek for Education, Elevation, and Knowledge—as a "Market Place of Ideas in West Side Hotel" for poor and underprivileged students (*NYT,* 21 May 1969, 49). Colleges and universities, said a 1969 letter to the editor, "must make every effort to insure that dissent retain its full value on what used to be considered the open market place of ideas and opinions" (*NYT,* 5 October 1969, E13). The "used to be" here is a comment on President Nixon's pledge to ignore anti-Vietnam protests. An ad for classes at the New School invited: "Come shop at the marketplace of ideas" (*NYT,* 9 January 1990, B5). The life of the mind as shopping! Hannah Arendt, who taught at the New School, would be rolling in her grave. Critic and historian of ideas Louis Menand (2001) recently used the term as a label for the health of the American university.

Religion is another site; Jewish groups especially take to the term. A plan to promote cooperation among Jewish organizations said that its purpose "is not to seek to suppress or gloss over differences, but to encourage discussion and clarification of differences, with a clear mutual recognition of the right of each view to exist and to compete with the others in the free market place of ideas" (*NYT,* 18 October 1959, 125). Here the term serves as a diplomatic balm, assuring participants of ideological openness. A meeting of rabbis called for an encounter with secular ideas: "Orthodox Judaism welcomes a confrontation with doubt, for out of it can come a deeper understanding. . . . Our religion has had to compete in the marketplace of ideas for centuries and millennia. It has confronted all the philosophies of the ages and has always emerged triumphant" (*NYT,* 21 June 1969, 30). Such optimism comes in sharp contrast with nervousness about anti-Semitism. The American Jewish Committee and the Anti-Defamation League of B'nai B'rith worried in 1971 that the rock opera *Jesus Christ, Superstar* recycled old images of Jews as bloodthirsty crucifiers. But they did not call for censorship: "the authors of the play and the producers have a right to present their thesis in the market place of ideas. . . . We have the same right to present our understanding" (*NYT,* 13 October 1971, 40). The Anti-Defamation League also objected to a passion play on similar grounds but denied calling for censorship: "In the free marketplace of ideas, we all can express a dissent" (*NYT,* 20 July 1982, C9). A Baptist leader responded in 1999 to Jewish and Hindu criticisms of his methods of proselytizing: "The only people who have to fear a free marketplace of ideas are people who are afraid their idea may not have enough currency" (*NYT,* 4 December 1999, A10). Here again market talk shows an antidialogic edge, the arrogance of recoding lack of respect for the other as courage.

The "marketplace of ideas" became the central metaphor for the social responsibility of the mass media in both official and public discourse. The American Civil Liberties Union stated: "Today's market place of ideas is found for the most part in books, magazines, newspapers, radio and television" (*NYT,* 17 November 1965, 27). Justice William O. Douglas was perhaps the first figure to institutionalize the term for legal and public debate about free expression and media. He used "market place of ideas" first in a Supreme Court decision in 1953 (*US v Rumely,* 345 US 41, at 56) in defending the rights of a radical bookseller to refuse to disclose his customers (note the Mc-Carthyist setting). After *Lamont v Postmaster General* (381 US 301 [1965], 308), it became a fixture in Supreme Court decisions (see table 4.2). The history of this term is, in large part, the history of free expression jurisprudence generally since the 1960s. It appears in many of the most significant cases: *Red Lion* (1969), *Miami Herald v Tornillo* (1973), *FCC v Pacifica* (1978), *Hustler v Falwell* (1988), *Texas v Johnson* (1989), and *R.A.V. v City of St. Paul* (1992). *Red Lion* (395 US 367 [1969], 390) sustained the Fairness Doctrine, the duty of broadcasters to provide airtime to "controversial issues of public importance": "It is the purpose of the First Amendment to preserve an uninhibited marketplace of ideas in which truth will ultimately prevail, rather than to countenance monopolization of that market, whether it be by the Government itself or a private licensee." Other cases used the term to defend government neutrality in ideological matters, toleration of offensive or outrageous expression, and "the joust of principles" (*Texas v Johnson,* 491 US 397 [1989], 418). The important circuit court decision about the regulation of pornography, *American Booksellers Association v Hudnut* (1985), which was unanimously upheld by the Supreme Court, gave an official seal of approval to the intellectual lineage of the "marketplace of ideas": "Much of Indianapolis's argument rests on the belief that when speech is 'unanswerable,' and the metaphor that there is a 'marketplace of ideas' does not apply, the First Amendment does not apply either. The metaphor is honored; Milton's *Aeropagitica* and John Stewart [sic] Mill's *On Liberty* defend freedom of speech on the ground that the truth will prevail, and many of the most important cases under the First Amendment recite this position" (771 F. 2d 323, 330).

Outside the courts, this language has become central to discussion of media regulation (Napoli 1999). The report of the mass media group of the National Commission on the Causes and Prevention of Violence stated: "The

Table 4.2. Number of U.S. Supreme Court Decisions Mentioning "Marketplace of Ideas"

	Market Place of Ideas	*Marketplace of Ideas*	*Total*
1950s	1	0	1
1960s	1	4	5
1970s	2	13	15
1980s	2	20	22
1990s	0	14	14

Source: www.findlaw.com.
Note: www.westlaw.com gives slightly discrepant figures. Mentions may include citations of previous opinions. "Market-place" added no hits to the search.

news media can play a significant role in lessening the potential for violence by functioning as a faithful conduit for intergroup communication, providing a true market place of ideas, providing full access to the day's intelligence, and reducing the incentive to confrontation that sometimes erupts in violence" (*NYT,* 13 January 1970, 20). Here the adjective "true" implies a critical or normative take on media. A letter to the editor congratulated the author of an op-ed piece in the *Times,* "for thereby he lifts this war crisis out of the streets and into the marketplace of ideas where judgments can be made rationally" (*NYT,* 10 June 1971, 42). The *Times* is here not only identified with the marketplace *tout court,* but the normative punch implicit in the notion of "ideas" is manifest. The marketplace of ideas is a more ethereal zone than the streets, filtering and refining debate—what one might call the Habermas effect. Oligopolistic patterns of media ownership raised the question in 1969: "What are the standards for judging 'monopoly' in the marketplace of ideas?" (*NYT,* 27 April 1969, 72). In 1978, former FCC commissioner Nicholas Johnson wrote, "We need for the marketplace of ideas something similar to what the antitrust laws do for the marketplace of business. . . . What could be more American than that?" (*NYT,* 19 November 1978, D37). A notice of a 1987 symposium on the "publishing industry's march to oligopoly" announced: "Panelists will discuss, among other matters, the effects of mergers on authors and editors and on the First Amendment marketplace of ideas" (*NYT,* 5 October 1987, C22). The term cuts both ways: for free marketeers it means no government regulation; for social democrats, ideological diversity.

By the 1980s, the center no longer held, and neoliberal and civil libertarian interpretations of the marketplace of ideas began to split apart. The deregulationist manifesto "A Marketplace Approach to Broadcast Regulation" (Fowler and Brenner 1982) was cowritten by Mark Fowler, the Reagan-appointed FCC commissioner who suspended the Fairness Doctrine in 1987. Though "marketplace of ideas" does not appear in this article, the friendly notion of "marketplace" eased the way to deregulation. A 1986 article on the legal status of corporate speech stated: "Traditional free market theory calls for getting Government out of the way and letting everyone speak or publish what they please, both to nurture freedom of conscience and keep the marketplace of ideas well stocked" (*NYT,* 4 May 1986, E8). This bizarre hybrid of neoliberalism and free speech shows the vulnerability of the term to free market logics, the way that it accommodates both social liberalism (diverse expression) and market liberalism (unfettered capitalism).

By the 1990s, the term loses steam as a new generation starts to abandon First Amendment absolutism in favor of restrictions on discourse damaging to women (pornography) and minorities (hate speech). As Cass Sunstein (1993, xviii) notes: "Above all, I suggest that there is a large difference between an 'marketplace of ideas'—a deregulated economic market—and a system of democratic deliberation." For Sunstein, neoliberal economics and politics were displacing vibrant public deliberation as the telos of the First Amendment. The left no longer embraces the First Amendment unequivocally as the banner of progress and is increasingly nervous about how defenses of the marketplace end up securing a corporate hold on public life. An ACLU affiliate noted that "racism has proved intransigent and we live in a real world, not an idealized marketplace of ideas" (*NYT,* 29 June 1990, B7). Observing the reign of commercial values in the TV industry, Todd Gitlin noted: "The maximization of box office is not conducive to what is euphemistically and nostalgically called the marketplace of ideas" (*NYT,* 14 June 1992, 58). Though the term lives on, enthusiasm for it today is patchy. Its history in large part is that of postwar liberalism in the United States. Just as people became post-Marxists and postfeminists in the 1980s and 1990s, so a new breed of postliberal emerged. Today it is rare to find people under fifty in the United States who call themselves "liberals," and the waning "marketplace of ideas" is one symptom of this slow change of opinion. By 1965, the term was already a cliché. As historian Christopher Lasch, always an acute observer of American intellectual politics, noted: "The anniversaries of *The Nation* and *New Republic,* so closely coinciding in time, have called forth the usual perfunctory statements, in official and semiofficial quarters, about the need for dissent, the importance of testing truth in the 'free market place of ideas,' and so forth. Such platitudes, of course, have become staples of public rhetoric in America" (*NYT,* 18 July 1965, E35). If it was a platitude in the 1960s, it at least attracted a large allegiance; by the turn of the millennium, it was an established bit of the lexicon, well past its ideological prime.

CONCLUSION

The "marketplace of ideas" is clearly a mixed bag of political and ideological tendencies whose contradictions mirror those of postwar liberal thought. For Bentham or Mill, supporting conformity and eccentricity in expression and lifestyle went together with supporting free markets. Market liberalism and civil libertarianism were cut from the same cloth. By the late twentieth century, liberalism broke into two halves (Keane 1991). Perhaps the enormous success and longevity of the "marketplace of ideas" stems from its marrying the two faces of liberalism, free speech and free markets, so characteristic of American political rhetoric.

What of the connection between markets and communication? There is an undeniable appeal in the marketplace as a metaphor: the ancient agora, whose name comes from the Greek word for speaking, posits a primordial link between speech and exchange. There is a romantic allure in the marketplace, the notion of an anarchic, diverse, creative place with many voices crying out at once. The marketplace presents itself as a utopia of loose coupling, an information bazaar, a milling place of promiscuous, anonymous circulation where there are no cartels or conspiracies and what you see is what you get. Free trade, moreover, always had the patina of cosmopolitanism and freedom from protectionism. The market metaphor evokes the efficiency of grounded intelligence, gaming the small gaps and adapting quickly to opportunity without a superintending paternal design. The market has always been one of the basic forms of human sociation—in which communication, in some form or another, will always be strongly implicated. Jevons, in his classic *Theory of Political Economy* (1911, 85) defined the market in communicative terms: "The traders may be spread over a whole town, or region of country, and yet make a market, if they are, by means of fairs, meetings, published prices, lists, the post office or otherwise, in close communication with each other." Information as the basic ingredient of the market has since become a fundamental of economic theory.

Don't worry; this is not an editorial for the *Economist.* To appreciate the utopian appeal of an idea does not mean to drop one's critical faculties. The market in some form will be a powerful agency in any complex social order: why let the capitalists monopolize this valuable intellectual property? But the utopia of the marketplace is often negated by the fact of the market. Most markets are not market*places:* they are not face-to-face affairs in the open air but abstractions operated by what Habermas calls "delinguistified steering media" such as money and power. Their form of communication is not agonistic or interactive, but fantastical and quantitative (advertising and spreadsheets). The "marketplace of ideas" drips with nostalgia for the town square. In an age of corporate gigantism, however chastened of late, it paints us a public place in which small producers wrangle about "ideas." It fudges profits and democracy, the freedoms to debate and to acquire. It extends the conviction in political-economic thought from Adam Smith and David Ricardo to Mill and Marshall that exchange is the most fundamental human act. It adds political surplus value to what Adam Smith (1952, 6) famously called the human "propensity to truck, barter, and exchange one thing for another." It sells short older visions of the human estate, for instance, the Aristotelian notion, refracted via Hegel, Marx, and Dewey, that economic activity is basic to our species not as barter (exchange) but as the creativity of labor (production), or the Platonic-Christian belief that renunciation of both private acquisition and public agonism can be honorable.

Perhaps the ultimate danger of the "marketplace of ideas" is not political but ethical. The notion offers a bogus reassurance, too easy a theodicy for truth, too facile an understanding of evil. The kind of thinking it encourages gives us little fortification against disappointment by hard structural facts or against the lotus lands of egotism and hedonism. The main sin of attributing the notion to Milton, Smith, Mill, or Holmes is missing their warnings about the kind of people and society we would become if marketplace values of getting and spending alone prevailed. Their doctrines are all harsh in some way. Each borrowed from moral sources richer than negative liberty. Milton's militancy for the cross, Smith's call for self-command and public spirit (as checks against self-love), Mill's stoic appreciation for self-discipline and romantic pride in nonconformity, or even Holmes's military valor all serve as counterweights to the well-marketed doctrine that public life's chief end is the "untrammeled pursuit of happiness" (Garnham 1992, 375).

REFERENCES

Altschull, J. Herbert. 1990. "John Milton and the Self-Righting Principle." In *From Milton to McLuhan: The Ideas behind American Journalism*. New York: Longman.

Austin, J. L. 1970. "A Plea for Excuses." In *Philosophical Papers*. 2d ed. London: Oxford University Press.

Bunker, Matthew D. 2001. *Critiquing Free Speech*. Mahwah, N.J.: Lawrence Erlbaum.

Coase, R. H. 1974. "The Market for Goods and the Market for Ideas." *American Economic Review* 64: 384–91.

Curran, James. 1996. "Mass Media and Democracy Revisited." In *Mass Media and Society*, edited by James Curran and Michael Gurevitch, 81–119. 2d ed. London: Arnold.

Fish, Stanley. 2001. *How Milton Works*. Cambridge: Harvard University Press.

Fowler, Mark S., and Daniel L. Brenner. 1982. "A Marketplace Approach to Broadcast Regulation." *Texas Law Review* 60: 207–57.

Garnham, Nicholas. 1992. "The Media and the Public Sphere." In *Habermas and the Public Sphere*, edited by Craig Calhoun, 359–76. Cambridge: MIT Press.

———. 2000. *Emancipation, the Media, and Modernity: Arguments about the Media and Social Theory*. New York: Oxford University Press.

Habermas, Jürgen. 1989. *The Structural Transformation of the Public Sphere: An Inquiry into a Category of Bourgeois Society*. Translated by Thomas Burger and Frederick Lawrence. Cambridge: MIT Press.

Horwitz, Robert Britt. 1989. *The Irony of Regulatory Reform*. New York: Oxford University Press.

Jevons, W. Stanley. 1911 [1871]. *The Theory of Political Economy*. 4th ed. London: Macmillan.

Keane, John. 1991. *The Media and Democracy*. Cambridge: Polity.

Magee, James. 2002. *Freedom of Expression*. Westport, Conn.: Greenwood.

McChesney, Robert W. 1992. "Labor and the Marketplace of Ideas: WCFL and the Battle for Labor Radio Broadcasting." *Journalism Monographs,* 134.

Menand, Louis. 2001a. *The Marketplace of Ideas*. New York: American Council of Learned Societies.

———. 2001b. *The Metaphysical Club*. New York: Farrar, Straus and Giroux.

Mill, John Stuart. 1975 [1859]. *On Liberty*. New York: Norton.

———. 1977 [1836]. "Civilization." In *Collected Works of John Stuart Mill*, edited by J. M. Robson, 18: 118–47. Toronto: University of Toronto Press.

Milton, John. 1957 [1644]. "Areopagitica: A Speech for the Liberty of Unlicensed Printing, to the Parliament of England." In *John Milton: Complete Poems and Major Prose*, edited by Merritt Y. Hughes, 717–49. New York: Odyssey.

Napoli, Philip M. 1999. "The Marketplace of Ideas Metaphor in Communications Regulation." *Journal of Communication* 49: 151–69.

Nerone, John C., ed. 1995. *Last Rights: Revisiting Four Theories of the Press*. Urbana: University of Illinois Press.

Schwarzlose, Richard A. 1989. "The Marketplace of Ideas: A Measure of Free Expression." *Journalism Monographs*, 118.

Smith, Adam. 1952 [1776]. *The Wealth of Nations*. Chicago: Encyclopedia Britannica.

Smith, Jeffery A. 1988. *Printers and Press Freedom: The Ideology of Early American Journalism*. New York: Oxford University Press.

Sunstein, Cass R. 1993. *Democracy and the Problem of Free Speech*. New York: Free Press.

Tedford, Thomas L. 1997. *Freedom of Speech in the United States*. 3d ed. State College, Pa.: Strata.

5

Capitalism and Communication

A New Era of Society or the Accentuation of Long-Term Tendencies?

Bernard Miège

Besides the important work of Vincent Mosco (1996), the contribution of the political economy of communication to the way we understand the relations between communication and contemporary societies has rarely been systematically analyzed. In the 1970s, its contribution was decisive. The work that was carried out at that time allowed us to elaborate a reasoned critique of dominant theoretical approaches, be they functionalist, cybernetic, or structuralist. At that time, political economy shook the foundations of fixed ideas and allowed us to adjust the perspective of our scientific work to the critical concerns of social movements and alternative movements. In several regions of the world, the dominance of North American academic work was contested and numerous authors risked suggesting analyses that represented communication in a less schematic manner that corresponded more closely to observations academics were able to make here and there.

At that time (at least until the mid-1980s), various authors, who were working in different parts of the world and who were not always aware of similar work going on in other countries, began working on texts that studied in depth the same question. In retrospect, the most striking thing is that this work centered around the following issues: the economic transformations of the sphere of communication (more specifically the growing importance of telecommunications and the home computer, as well as the takeoff of the culture industries); the ongoing concentration of capital and its centralization; the creation of multimedia groups; successive changes in communication policies; the development of relations between the state and the markets; and the development of consumption and audiences.

For those interested in "communicational thought," the following period was marked by an undeniable expansion in the number of issues. The majority of authors who adhered to the political economy of communication were no longer willing to furrow the same field; their concerns broadened out and they found themselves widening the scope of the epistemological investigations that had until then been generally accepted. Certain researchers embarked on work of a genealogic nature. Others concerned themselves with the adaptation of the public space or with changes to territorial boundaries. Yet others concerned themselves with information and communication techniques or with the question of consumption and the formation of social behavior patterns related to the new tools. Such researchers were motivated by a desire to find more adequate answers to the developments they were witnessing. The communication sector diversified and gradually assumed a central position in the restructuring of the dominant mode of production—with economies and political systems breaking down in states where "real socialism" existed. Additionally, the dominant mode of production was allowed to give free rein to its deeper tendencies and used globalization to establish uncontested domination throughout the planet. From then on, communication found itself at the center of the system of production, and it became fundamental for the way societies and cultures were managed via the means of mediation (which are linked to communication or which it organizes). The importance of this transformation should not be overestimated, but it should not be neglected; we can no longer approach communication as if it formed one field among others. Though it is a "field" (according to the specific definition given to the term by Bourdieu), it is much more than a field in that it extends throughout all fields.

For this reason, it seems to me necessary that we center our research and the public debate around three main aims: (1) reformulating the question of the media in the light of new investigations which take into account changes witnessed, (2) treating the place of communication in the context of the capitalist mode of production, (3) developing a reasoned critique of the idea of an information society.

THE QUESTION OF THE MEDIA

For all specialists of communication, it goes without saying that the media, information technology, and communication technology are at the heart of their concerns and their analyses, but this is not the only thing that is involved. For many people the question of the media has increasingly come to be emblematic; it has come to summarize in and of itself the major questions concerning the future development of contemporary societies, the way in which they are structured socially, their economic future, and above all the sociocultural development of those societies. From Marshall McLuhan on, many authors, essayists, and even theoreticians have adopted this view of communication. I am not sure that many specialists have defended this position for any great length of time. For my own part, I long remained skeptical about all approaches that tended to accord the media such a central position and such a structuring role. I do not feel obliged to revise this defiant position. The development of societies does not take place with the succession of one era after another, defined according to the development of the media or the emergence of new forms of media, as it is often presented by cultural anthropologists or a technocentric conception of societal development. However, we should now admit that the means of communication force us to face up to some of the most decisive issues related to the development of social relations:

- the relations between the sphere of professional activity and the private sphere;
- the increasing individualization of social practices;
- the trend for interpersonal social exchanges to include long-distance mediated exchanges;
- the necessity of being able to rapidly gain access to the most wide-ranging information and knowledge in order to organize one's everyday life;
- the indispensable arbitration between multiple and contradictory demands in one's social agenda;
- the coexistence of partially public spheres (not necessarily dedicated to the publication of opinions, but nevertheless playing a role in the organization of everyday life and social categories), the habitus of which are progressively diversifying;
- the fact that individuals must gain new communication skills to function in their daily life and in their work.

The social functions now attributed to the media (and more generally to communication technology) clearly differ from those that the first authors, notably the functionalists, attributed to them with such absolute assurance. Their certainties are not our own. Above all, the media today seem to affect all parts of social life and all dimensions of social activity. The most developed societies have now been conquered by communication (by its technological means and by the strategies and complex vocational methods adopted by organizations, state agencies and by associations). These societies are increasingly controlled by mediated communication that favors interpersonal exchanges or at any rate exchanges or activity in which the individual plays an essential role. This transformation, far from having reached an end, is taking place progressively and surreptitiously. The mass media are taking on more and more importance, transforming themselves and becoming more interactive, but the media are not alone in this. The most individualized technology (not based solely on preconceived programs) goes increasingly hand in hand with the transformation of the media. Different "communication models" are being superimposed and are interacting with one another and, contrary to what cyberspace thinkers used to claim, the latter do not replace the former but rather mix together and interpenetrate one another. New communication is merging with mass communication, something that was unimaginable a few years ago.

These trends are still emerging for the moment and should not be overestimated, but they are asserting themselves despite the unrelenting certainties of authors who stand by the ideals of modernity and postmodernity. In order to get a better understanding of this development, we should rethink the relationship between the media and societies. Nicholas Garnham invites us to do just that: "Once we see the media in this way it becomes obvious that questions about the media are questions about the kind of society we live in and vice versa. The study of the media is thus a part of, and must be grounded in, the human sciences more generally. We study them because they give us a way into the general questions of social theory. The questions we ask about the media and the answers we might give to those questions can be understood only within the context of social theory more generally" (Garnham 2000, 5). I find myself largely in accord with this analysis, but not with the theoretical foundations that Garnham puts forward. They take us back to Immanuel Kant (since for Kant reason is not functionalist) and to the contemporary developments of his thought that we find in the work of Hannah Arendt.

If it is impossible to understand communication without the aid of a theory of action, then which theory can be relied on? The responses vary on this point. They are not always clearly stated, and many authors refuse to present their approaches as theories or present their ideas in the form of methodologies. (The ethnomethodologists work in this way.) For some of these authors, their position can be explained by the fact that they do not consider communication to be a decisive paradigm for action. In any event, rather than list my oppositions to these authors and stressing my differences, I will try to outline some aspects of a possible approach.

To the extent that communication does not escape the confines of the "global social space" (*l'espace social global*) that Pierre Bourdieu demonstrated to be both the field of the interplay of forces and the field of struggle, I will follow him, though Bourdieu did not go on to envisage the question that concerns us here. I would concur with him that a theory of action is not the product of an intentional conscience ("most human actions have a very different principle than that of intention, that is to say, the acquired predispositions that mean that an action can and must be directed towards such and such an end without our being able to establish whether it was motivated by a conscious aims" [Bourdieu 1994, 187]). In this way, symbolic violence entails submissions that are understood as such and are in any case considered to be common beliefs. (Bourdieu suggests masculine domination in the couple as an example.) Is it sufficient to restore communicational action to its place within the framework of habitus and to stress the role of symbolic violence in the treatment of different forms of domination in modern societies?

In responding to this question, I will outline my differences with the premises of Pierre Bourdieu. He focuses too exclusively on bringing to light the mechanisms that powers impose (however relevant this most assuredly is). Acting with others takes place in a system of constraints, and communication can also invite us to envisage means of cooperation and opportunities that allow us to engage in singular actions, at times even free of constraint.

For this reason, it seems to me that communicational action (and more generally social action) is a heuristic perspective but entails the impossible condition that we place ourselves in the framework of a system of thought that (1) structures action and production and allows us within the economy-world to link up work and nonwork (in the direction of current changes in the organization of work and life at work, running parallel to changes in information and communication techniques), (2) strives to coordinate communicational action (both the lived worlds of those acting and the social exchanges in which they take part in the public spaces that have been broken up into segments and which can no longer be limited to spaces for debate and argument), and (3) refuses a priori to limit itself to the systemic evaluation of symbolic violence exercised by the means and systems of communication. This thought can be attributed in part to Jürgen Habermas (Habermas 1987), and in particular to his proposals on the publicizing opinions and debates and to those he put forward concerning communicative action. I differ from Habermas on certain points: the single nature of the public space, reduced de facto to a political space; the primarily systemic character of dominance exercised by the systems and apparatus of communication; and the all but exclusive dominance of language in intersubjective and social exchanges. This thought is yet to be elaborated, but we are not lacking in resources to contribute toward its elaboration. I suggest that we would greatly gain by allowing our work to diversify with each field of study (the organization of work, education, health, the governing of close territorial boundaries, etc.) and by stressing the multiple dimensions of communication instead of aiming a priori at a unified theory.

COMMUNICATION IN THE CAPITALIST MODE OF PRODUCTION

Next we turn our attention to the *mode of production,* more specifically, the importance that communication is presently gaining in the capitalist mode of production in the world economy in the context of globalization and liberalization. We all know the analyses of Nicholas Garnham on this subject, which he developed primarily in his well-argued critique of M. Castells's theses (Castells 2000): the failure to understand the role of competition in the present process of capital accumulation, the exaggeration of the importance of the role played by networks, the automation of the financial sphere (which is studied as though it is not linked to the processes of production and consumption), the stress laid on the structural logic of a faceless capitalism in which social parties do not intervene and in which the Schumpeter model reigns. Nicholas Garnham writes: "This theory of the rapid expansion of the network company goes on to contribute to the theory that class conflict between workers and those who possess capital has come to an end. The first argument put forward was . . . that the global financial networks had created a faceless collective capitalism and that there were, consequently, no more capitalists. The problem with this kind of logic is that it fails to take into account human intervention" (Garnham 2000b in *Réseaux* 101: 72–73).

This is a crucial criticism. Many contemporary analyses (and not only those of Castells) take on board the argument of the growth of information and communication technology in order to draw conclusions about society (which are more or less deterministic) without taking into account the mode of production itself. Castells's logic is even more tortuous because he is a sociologist who plays the economist and draws on economic research and references with an aim to determining social changes. This leads him to stress the importance of the "mode of development," a new concept that serves primarily to turn our attention away from the mode of production.

How should we analyze the role that communication is taking on in the mode of production? We should not underestimate the difficulty of the task. To simply add a communicational approach will in no way ensure that we go further than approaches that are "economistic," or culturally or sociologically oriented. This is why it would be wise to point out mistakes and possible dangers (Miège 2002).

We should make a special point of avoiding the following:

- All-embracing approaches which assume that the changes we are witnessing are following the same course throughout all of the regions of the world and throughout all of the branches of industry, and so on. It is because of this assumption that the very idea of the "information revolution," which is so often spoken of, can turn out to be not only a premature conceptualization but also a barrier to further reflection. Consequently, we cannot hope for more than partial studies or studies that limit themselves to specific sectors.
- Lumping together our ideas and concepts of the media and information and communication technology. In talking about the intervention of this technology we invariably confuse things that should be differentiated:

their nature as a new sellable product and their impact on the level of production and on exchanges;

their stimulating an increase in industrial services, available in material or nonmaterial form or, to put it another way, a form of products characteristic of emerging productions (Lacroix and Tremblay 1997);

their impact on productivity, both globally and in different sectors, primarily resulting from the reorganization of production in workshops and offices;

their relation to changes in both production and the acquisition and transmission of knowledge.

- Technocentric visions of technical developments. Computerization analyses (which prevail in the sociology of work and organizations) seem far too reductive because they do not take into account the essential point—the development of information flow and opportunities to communicate. "Informationalization" (Miège and Tremblay 1999) (which should be distinguished from "informationalism") is, for this reason, the right perspective to adopt.

By noting the approaches to be avoided we can gain an idea of the degree to which recent research does not respect indispensable methodological requirements.

How can we now understand the role of information-communication in the capitalist mode of production? Three elements must be highlighted. First, the fact that information-communication is developing in an exclusively market-oriented context that is also industrialized, as we shall see. Almost all of the innovations, whether they be tools, product-services, or connections, must be paid for by the final consumers at home or at work. A deregulation strategy was systematically introduced into the communication industries sector from the mid-1980s on; in Europe, for example, this strategy has been almost fully carried out. The entire public debate (which is not always very clear) has opposed liberalist supporters of the market and those who set themselves up as the defenders of "public services," often without taking into account the extent of changes taking place. Regulation cannot function in the same manner when faced with a dense and complex offer of new services. Throughout this period, even when the governments were dominated by social-democratic parties, a new state policy was rarely envisaged to cater to these changes, a policy that would, for example, deal with the production of content and egalitarian access to networks. Support for, and expansion of, "national champions" was the sole policy put into practice and no new regulation was adopted.

Second, communicational activity is increasing and becoming internationalized, a development that remains difficult to grasp. This increase varies according to the industrial branch and has not always followed the paths predicted. For example, the predicted spread of American audiovisual and telecommunication firms throughout Europe either did not take place or had less impact than expected. Instead, we witnessed (let's say in the 1990s) consolidated cooperation between European monopolistic groups, and it was intra-European exchanges that made the most progress. We saw a greater interpenetration between groups that were dominated by either North American or European capital, which had deeply penetrated the world markets. This is the trend that world trade agreements aim to facilitate, and it was against these agreements that the social movements rose up to support the right to remain an exception and the right to cultural diversity in 1993 and once again in 1999 in Seattle and in 2001 in Genoa. Throughout this period, the American multinationals were "riding high" on the crest of a wave and showed a renewed dynamic verve in almost all areas of the communication sector. Despite the bursting of the investment bubble in the so-called New Economy in 2001 and the loss of financial assets for the great groups in both 2001 and 2002 as a result of overinvestment, a relative balance has been struck between what is most dynamic and new in world capital on the one hand and the rise in the industrialization of communication on the other. This balance is perfectly attuned to the development of capital's control of the whole planet, or at least in the regions that it finds worthwhile.

In this way, the rising communication industries are taking part in capital's most dynamic and aggressive campaigns on the world's stage. But we cannot limit ourselves to this aspect. Communication goes hand in hand with globalization in stitching the planet together with more or less efficient networks, networks that are less accessible than predicted (the program for "information highways" is yet to be put into operation), by offering new and largely international product-services and by offering state politicians and directors of private concerns a whole series of techniques for managing societies and companies. These two developments should be held together but not confused; they are not superimposed one on the other automatically, and a gap often develops between the globalization of communication (as a technique for dealing with social questions and as an ideology) and the international development of communication industries.

Finally, there is the spread of a new "globalitarian" ideology. This ideology is necessary for the profound transformation of the capitalist mode of production and is implicit within it. Where does it come from? How is it formed? How does it spread? Who in particular is affected by it? Does it fuse with enrooted cultural identities or is it superimposed upon them? These questions could make up the research program for a renewed "cultural studies." We already possess important analyses, such as those carried out by my colleague Armand Mattelart (especially Mattelart 1994). The difficulty is how to carry out such analyses without losing touch with developments already stressed.

THE EVER NECESSARY CRITIQUE OF THE INFORMATION SOCIETY

It is necessary once more to question the usefulness of the expression "information society." This term has been strongly criticized over the past three to four decades by the works of thinkers such as Daniel Bell and Alain Touraine (though for very different reasons). The expression itself has, nevertheless, become more popular and political leaders and advertising executives have more or less succeeded in asserting it as a program of action and a descriptive term for the "new society" that has been emerging since the 1990s. Despite all the supposedly obvious facts used to justify its use, this expression (and other similar expressions such as the "computer age" and the "network era") is still just as inconceivable as it ever was, and should be removed from public speaking and critically reappraised. There are some good reasons to support this.

The expression "information society" is linked to the economistic approach just rejected. By placing information and communication technology at the heart of the revolution along with the reorganization of information, authors who advocate the use of this expression make technological development and economic reorganizations central to their arguments. Social, cultural, and political changes are inferred, and, despite the denials of certain authors who perform a juggler's trick by choosing to speak of a "conditioning" technique rather than a "determining" technique, their conceptions lead to the dominance of technological and economic elements.

Analyses waver between different ways of seeing things. The information society is sometimes seen as a society in which information and communication technology have become dominant or just abundantly available. Sometimes it is seen as a society in which this same technology is held to be a source of gains in productivity and thus a new means of producing value. Finally (though more rarely), it is seen as a society in which the paradigm of information has asserted itself throughout all social activities. That these meanings overlap is not insignificant. This reveals the difficulty, from the theoretical perspective, of establishing the heralded era as "new." This does not, however, stop the thinkers of this "new society" from finding themselves in agreement on one point they hold to be essential—the certainty that we have gone beyond the industrial society, following radical structural changes, particularly with regard to the education of the workforce, the organization of companies, work in networks, the intensification of educational investment, and the development of computer skills and skills related to the culture of virtuality.

At this point, we return to the recent works of Manuel Castells and more specifically to a sociological analysis in the strict sense of the term. Some of his analyses might be considered stimulating (e.g., the passages on new "megapoles"), but few of Castells's arguments are convincing despite the impressive research he brings to bear on the subject. What is most surprising is that this excessive amount of material (based on facts taken from managerial press and consulting studies) is taken seriously by the academic community, which doubtless sees Castells's work as a reasoned elaboration of their strongly held beliefs.

It is becoming increasingly clear that Castells's work shares errors found in other modernist discourses. Such works minimize the diversity of what is at stake and do not try to measure the complexity of the changes we are undergoing. They tend to see these changes as widespread and draw conclusions that available data do not allow us to verify except intermittently and with reference to social categories and areas that have been well identified. When we look closely at the facts used to support Castells's argument, we cannot fail to notice the gap between the trends that emerge and the conclusions that he draws. All of these discourses take emerging phenomena for established practices. Above all, such arguments are based on a theory of technological innovation that is founded on a simplified idea of diffusion and should be contested.

We should indeed accept that the question of technological innovation and the question of the "influence" of technology are among the most important questions that the communication sciences have to consider. This is not the place to pursue an in-depth discussion of these questions; I will have to limit myself to pointing to one major trend. Observation shows, more often than not, that information and communication technology accompanies social changes and can accelerate them, but it rarely provokes social changes. For this reason it is essential that the emergence of technology be considered in close relation to social activity.

Castells's approach to information is rather abstract and would not be out of place in the work of an author attached to a cybernetic vision of information. Furthermore, in chapter 5 of his first volume, "Culture and Virtual Reality," he expresses a certain affinity with the theses of Marshall McLuhan. He aims to adapt theses that McLuhan elaborated in his work on electronic mass media and attempts to reapply them to the new media. He also adopts McLuhan's theory of stages (or "eras") for the development of the media. We find in Castells's work, for example, the following sentence: [with multimedia] "a new symbolic environment is being created which is making a reality of virtuality" (Castells 2000, 1:424). "This new system of communication is radically transforming space and time, the fundamental dimensions of human experience. Places are even losing the substance of their cultural significance, their historical and geographical significance, to be integrated into the functional networks which produce a space of flux which is replacing the space of locations" (Castells 2000, 1:242). The space of locations is none other than the space in which social functions are concentrated.

If, to all of this, we add Castells's assurance that an information revolution has already taken place—is already in place and operational, not simply in its formative stages and of a character yet to be defined—and Castells's certainty that we have moved beyond the industrial society (for he never envisages the possibility that industrialized service products might be the mark of a "neoindustrial society"), then we cannot help doubting the theoretical force of the work of this sociologist from Berkeley; we fail to be convinced by his conviction that we have moved on to a new form of society, if we consider society in terms of the mode of its development and its mode of production. Where Castells asserts that radical transformations have taken place, a claim he makes based on material he himself has put together, it would be more reasonable to conclude that we are witnessing ongoing changes. Where he speaks of decisive thresholds that have been passed and structural changes that have taken place, I would list tendencies at work.

For this reason, I find myself in agreement with Frank Webster (2000) when he says: "There can be no doubt that, in advanced nations, information and communication technologies are now pervasive and that information has grown in economic significance, as the substance of much work, and in amounts of symbolic output. But the idea that all such might signal the shift toward a new society, an information society, is mistaken. Indeed, what is most striking are the continuities of the present age with previous social and economic arrangements, informational developments being heavily influenced by familiar constraints and priorities."

I therefore find myself in agreement with Nicholas Garnham when he sees the theory of the information society as the dominant ideology of the present historical period: "not content with being technologically deterministic, this theory is also structuralist: in the end, it is the logic of the structure which decides what happens, for the network constitutes a new social morphology" (Garnham 2000b, in *Réseaux* 100: 59). Nicholas Garnham does not neglect to point out that even for Castells himself "the 'network society' (is) characterized by the pre-eminence of social morphology over social action." This is where it becomes obvious that harnessing economic, sociological, communicational, and symbolic research is fully justified.

From these too rapid considerations, or rather from these essential considerations mentioned too briefly, one conclusion asserts itself more than ever. We cannot content ourselves with the simplifications that the leaders of dominant nations, fashionable essayists, or hurried thinkers try to force on us when they herald the emergence of a new society. Though it is at times hard to resist the overwhelming flow of what are presented as obvious facts, we must persevere in following patiently those changes that are taking place in the dominant mode of production (which is no longer contested by an alternative system). We should not be afraid to consider these changes as one stage in a longer period and should avoid falling prey to illusions of brutal ruptures, qualitative leaps, and structural upheavals that herald radical innovations. However decisive certain technological and information changes may seem, we should nevertheless beware of taking them for indications that a new era has come upon us. These changes merely serve to reaffirm the dominant mode of production by introducing communication into it in all its diverse forms all the more forcefully.

NOTE

Translated by James Underhill and revised by the editors.

REFERENCES

Bell, Daniel. 1973. *The Coming of Post-Industrial Society: A Venture in Social Forecasting*. Harmondsworth, U.K.: Penguin.

Bourdieu, Pierre. 1994. *Raisons pratiques: Sur la théorie de l'action*. Paris: Seuil.

Castells, Manuel. 2000. *The Rise of the Network Society*. 3 vols. 2d ed. Oxford: Blackwell.

Garnham, Nicholas. 1990. *Capitalism and Communication: Global Culture and the Economics of Information*. London: Sage.

———. 2000a. *Emancipation, the Media, and Modernity*. Oxford: Oxford University Press.

———. 2000b. "La théorie de la société de l'information en tant qu'idéologie." *Réseaux* 101: 53–59.

Habermas, Jürgen. 1987. *Théorie de l'agir communicationnel*. Vols. 1–2. Paris: Fayard.

Lacroix, Jean-Guy, and Gaëtan Tremblay. 1997. *The Information Society and Cultural Industries Theory*. London: Sage. Special issue of *Current Sociology* 45, no. 4, devoted to the work of these two authors.

Mattelart, Armand. 1994. *L'invention de la communication*. Paris: La Découverte.

Mattelart, Tristan, ed. 2002. *La mondialisation des médias contre la censure: Tiers monde et audiovisuel sans frontières*. Brussels: De Boeck.

Miège, Bernard. 1997. *La société conquise par la communication: La communication entre l'industrie et l'espace public*. Grenoble: PUG.

———. 2000. *Les industries du contenu face à l'ordre informationnel*. Grenoble: PUG.

———. 2002. "La société de l'information: Toujours aussi inconcevable." *Revue européenne des sciences sociales* 40, no. 123: 41–54.

Miège, Bernard, and Gaëtan Tremblay. 1999. "Pour une grille de lecture du développement des techniques de l'information et de la communication." *Sciences de la société*, May 1999, 9–22.

Mosco, Vincent. 1996. *The Political Economy of Communication*. London: Sage.

Touraine, Alain. 1969. *La société post-industrielle-naissance d'une société*. Paris: Denoël-Gonthier.

Webster, Frank. 2000. "The Information Society Revisited." In L. A. Lievrouw and S. M. Livingstone, eds., *The Handbook of New Media: Social Shaping and Consequences of ICTs*. London: Sage.

———. 2002. *Theories of the Information Society*. 2d ed. London: Routledge.

6

Kugai
The Lost Public Sphere in Japanese History

Tatsuro Hanada

The concept of the public sphere was constructed as an ideal type extracted from the historical process of Western European society. The concept has a distinct historical and social context (Habermas 1989). This does not mean, however, that the concept is of only particularistic value to the European context since there are so many different societies in the world. Instead, the concept has a universal applicability if we recognize and accept its basic value in other social contexts.

In the contemporary world, the concept of the public sphere should not be treated as an independent factor, but rather in its relationship to capitalism and nationalism. We need to consider the movement of the social formation as a whole consisting of three spaces: the public sphere, the capitalistic market, and the nation-state. This has become much clearer since the 1989 collapse of the communist regimes in Central and Eastern Europe than it was before.

Prior to these events or, better, amid the ongoing process toward them, Nicholas Garnham stressed the "importance for democratic politics of a sphere distinct from the economy and the State":

> In my view, the implications of current developments are better understood, and an escape from the bind of the state/market dichotomy and from the hold of free press theory and necessary accompanying re-evaluation of public service

is better provided, by looking at the problem from the perspective of theory of the Public Sphere. (Garnham 1986, 40; 1990, 106)

In this chapter, first, I sketch the structure of bourgeois and postbourgeois society in Western countries where the principle of property has been continuous and basic. This principle has the power to spread from its region of origin to other parts of the world, and in the process of its diffusion a dichotomy has developed between center and periphery, depending on the relative intensity of this principle in each locale.

After 1868, Japan entered this worldwide process in an effort to "catch up" with the formation of bourgeois society, the so-called process of modernization, which consisted of nation-state building, industrialization, and militarization. It was thus able to prevent itself from being colonized by Western countries. In this process, the "public" authority connected to the emperor system enclosed the "public" sphere, as an attempt was made to understand modernization as democratization. Contradictions and conflicts existed, since the meaning of "public" was still ambiguous in this social context.

Second, in order to realize the potential of the concept of the public sphere, I focus on the type of public sphere found in Japanese medieval history. It is essential to develop the concept of the public sphere specific to one's own historical tradition in order to put this concept into future perspective. The Japanese term for this public sphere is *kugai*. In the modern Japanese language this term has become obsolete, which suggests that *kugai* is a lost public sphere in Japanese history.

THE GENEALOGY OF A DUALISTIC COMPOSITION: "CAPITALISM AND COMMUNICATION"

The Ambivalence of the Bourgeoisie

Because the bourgeoisie opposed medieval "public" authority, the new rising class had two faces on one body. The bourgeoisie in the initial stages were bound to the moral economy economically and culturally. This ambivalent composition enabled it to alter the medieval power structure through two kinds of resources: private property and enlightenment education (literacy). They created a domain of private persons confronting that of public authority. Utilizing the two resources they possessed, they produced two separate spaces, which grew to become the marketplace and the public sphere respectively.

The ambivalence of the bourgeoisie originated in this dualism, which has been a consistent characteristic of the modern era, between materials and *Geist* (mind), or production and communication. This ambivalence not only provided a dynamic of social change but also split social life in modernity.

Dualism in Marx's Theory

Karl Marx's theories of political economy addressed the ambivalence of the bourgeoisie with the formula of base and superstructure, which correspond respectively to materials and consciousness. These two separate structures were connected by the concept of "ideology," in which he asserted that the social forms of consciousness reflect the material base. This means that the interests of keeping property in the material world define ideal institutions "politically."

To explain the superstructure he employed again a dualism. Both the forces of production and the relations of production were this time connected to the concept of the "mode of production."

In his dialectical materialism, the material base and property are crucial, but at the same time he suggested the importance of *Verkehr*, which can be translated not only as transport but also as communication (Marx 1974). Here we can see that he grasped the social formation as a whole through the dualistic composition of both production and communication.

Capitalism and Socialism

Capitalism is based on private ownership by the bourgeoisie who own and control the means of production. People who possessed no such means had no choice but to sell their labor power. Those whose working power was a commodity are called the proletariat. In the struggle between the two classes—the haves and have-nots—there arose the political idea of socialism or communism, which sought to abolish private property and to have it "socialized" or "communized." This meant establishing collective ownership of the means of production instead of private ownership.

The "actually existing socialism" that collapsed in 1989 was organized according to two principles: (1) a centrally planned economy controlled by the state through collective organizations and (2) policy formulation centrally decided by a single party that was equal to the state. This meant that both the mechanism of the marketplace and the process of the public sphere were foreclosed. The latter seems to have been the main reason for the dysfunction of the system, while the opening of the public sphere through glasnost led to the end of the system (Sparks 1998) and the arrival of new problems through the introduction of the "actually existing capitalistic system."

As a result of this process, private property has come to be taken for granted. There seems to be no alternative to private ownership. The market mechanism based on private ownership has globalized itself and finds no effective enemy.

Identity Politics and the Future of the Principle of Ownership

Having previously emphasized economic and political factors, modern history now finds itself in the midst of a "cultural turn." Thus cultural factors have gained greater significance in the processes of social formation than ever before. The relative weight of communication is increasing along with the rise in production. We cannot explain today's economic and political phenomena without taking cultural factors into account. Capitalism and the nation-state themselves are shaped by cultural practices and operations.

Identity politics is the symbolic issue governing this circumstance. In identity politics, we can see a dichotomy between equality and difference, universal discourses and personal experience, and universality and locality. Conflicts do not occur over the ownership of material property but over the question of who will own one's body in which location. In other words, the issues have shifted from material property to spatial property. This means that it is necessary to obtain lived space rather than material property in order to keep one's sense of identity.

For the people concerned, the acquisition of space seems to become more crucial than material property. The question is whether the principle of ownership should be perpetuated in any form in the globalized world of the twenty-first century.

AN ALTERNATIVE CONCEPT OF THE PUBLIC SPHERE: *KUGAI* IN JAPANESE MEDIEVAL HISTORY

Muen, *Kugai*, and *Raku* (Unboundness, Public Realm, and Fairground)

The origin of the public sphere seems strongly connected with the concept of the "urban." I focus on arguments by Japanese historian Amino Yoshihiko, which I then compare with those of Henri Lefebvre and Jürgen Harbermas. Amino's concept of "urban sites" corresponds to Lefebvre's "urban form" (Lefebvre 1970, 1996). Amino's concept clearly distinguishes "urban sites" from "cities." In his research on medieval towns, Amino argues that urban sites are spaces structured according to the principles of *muen* (unboundness), *kugai* (public realm), and *raku* (fairground or marketplace) (Amino 1978). For Amino, urban sites appear to have a double character:

> Urban sites have precisely this dualistic meaning of being unbound [muen] land. The original meaning of *muen* land included the riverbanks where inns and marketplaces were set up, and wilderness as well as barriers and harbors. In particular, the area in front of the gates of temples and shrines were lands that perhaps best fit the notion of *muen*. However, these urban sites were also known as "*chi*" which means grounds of the earth. Although in the case of Kyoto and Kamakura [the seats of central government in medieval Japan], the two elements of this dual pattern intricately overlapped with one another, I myself always thought of this "*chi*" as essentially *muen* land. (Amino 1996, 94)

"The dualistic meaning" he refers to is the interchange between owning and not owning, which thus indicates a dialectic contradiction. In the following quote, he refers to this intricate overlapping:

> Many of those barrier stations and harbors were controlled and guarded by local feudal authorities. The Kinai [Region of Kyoto] and surrounding areas were under the jurisdiction of the Emperor. It is clear that the urban sites in Kyoto as well as Kamakura were indeed under sovereign control. As previously mentioned however, those places were at the same time seen as unbound [*muen*] land. When considering the characteristics of a town, one must pay special attention to both sides of what I have called "*muen*" land. (Amino 1996, 105)

In this way, the correspondence between Lefebvre's urban form and Amino's urban sites becomes clear. They are not existing towns in the real world. They may be understood instead as latent objects, or problematics of the process of becoming urban, which can be discerned through the disaggregating of cities. One can argue then that what Amino sought to convey through his use of this formula formed by the linked concepts of *muen*, *kugai*, and *raku* was a notion of that which was becoming urban. For Amino, the difference between *muen* land and *kugai* places and the distinction among the three concepts are not necessarily clear. In a previous work, I interpreted *muen* (unboundness) as a relational concept, *kugai* (public realm) as a spatial concept, and *raku* (fairground) as a utopian concept. I see them as forming a coherent set. The concepts form a mutually interwoven, correlational set, but each concept also connotes a certain hypothesis and definition that makes it a concept of potentiality. Consequently, they are neither fully accomplished nor finally completed, but may allow the potential only to become actualized, latent, or transformed. This recalls Lefebvre's spatial triad (Lefebvre 1991, 33), which might be presuming too much but forms the following connections between Amino's and Lefebvre's concepts: *muen* (unboundness) is the encounter, *kugai* (public realm) is the assembly, and *raku* (fairground) is the simultaneity (Lefebvre 1996, 138).

From *Kugai* to Urban Town

In his book the *World of Medieval Towns in Japan*, Amino writes:

> What then is *kugai*? The first to address *kugai* was Kasamatsu Hiroshi. . . . In addition, Fujiki Hisashi, by focusing on "*kugai* wayfarers" and "*kugai* roads" mentioned in "The Law Book of Lord Ouchi," attempted to grasp the formation of daimyo [feudal lords] power by examining how the "public" within the public authority suppressed the "public" of *kugai*. (Amino 1996, 123)

The actualization and empowerment of the principles of *muen*, *kugai*, and *raku* in Japan's medieval warring states period (1467–1568) came with the construction of autonomous towns. The public authority of Oda Nobunaga and Toyotomi Hideyoshi in the late sixteenth century sought to bring these self-governing towns under their control. They established a new early modern system of rule by gutting these towns through superior military force and absorbing them into the daimyo's castle towns. The same notion of the public is cited in the quotation above but with different meanings. These two meanings of the public should be differentiated from each other. This difference is not confined to the Japanese language. At the dawning of the modern West, in a reversal of the Japanese case, the modern bourgeois state in Europe was established when the public of the public authority was overwhelmed by the public of the public sphere. In the German language, the term for public authority is *öffentliche Gewalt*, and the word for public sphere is *Öffentlichkeit*. Both terms use the same expression for public here too. As with the English terms "public authority" and "public sphere," there's no signifier to differentiate these two concepts. How did this come about? In the historical process, the meanings of words constantly undergo a process of permutation since the ambiguity and inaccuracy of the signified as well as the changeability of the relationship between the signifier and the signified creates disjunctions in the meaning of language. Therefore, it is necessary to precisely and boldly construct the archaeology of the complex layers in which words, meanings, and social relations are deeply interwoven.

Earlier I stated that Amino's triad of *muen, kugai,* and *raku* form a unified conceptual device, but the differences among the points of this triad are less than clear. For example, in relation to the market outside the gates of Entokuji temple in Mino region, Amino writes: "this market is precisely the *kugai*—a site of *muen.*" He continues: "the meaning of the *raku* is exactly the same as the *kugai* and *muen*" (Amino 1996, 125). However, if one carefully reads Amino's work, it is possible that these three points are not equal but a hierarchy exists among them. The *kugai* is a site of *muen*—a social space constructed by the relational principle of *muen.* The *raku* is the state of *muen*—the dreamlike social condition that the relational principle of *muen* must strive for and produce. The *kugai* is the space that *muen* brings life to, while the *raku* bears the markings of *muen.* Within these, one finds a corresponding notion of freedom and peace in medieval Japan. When seen from this perspective, *muen* is the foundational concept. What then is *muen*? According to Amino:

> In turning one's attention from the world of *yuen* (boundness) to sites of *muen* (unboundness), the first thing one notices is that *muen* is simply the severing of relations. It is not a passive loss of relations, but an active severing of relations and the rejection of boundness. Furthermore, the important point is that it does not simply depend on individual will, but is supported by deeply rooted customs, legal principles, and the social and collective power of regulation. (Amino 1996, 14–15)

The idea of *yuen* (boundness—the antonym of *muen*) includes the bond of vassalage, the relations of private property, the ties of debt and credit, and litigious relations. It also includes the bond of living in a community tied to the land. *Muen*, on the other hand, is the freedom from these forms of restrictive and fixed ties and a liberal approach toward the pleasure of exchange. The place where *muen* thrives is the *kugai* (public realm), which includes such places as cemeteries, roads, temples, and markets. It also encompasses the sacred lands of the gods such as the forests, mountains, wilderness, oceans, and rivers as well as riverbanks, midlands, beaches, and the borderland between the spiritual and mundane worlds. In these sites, markets were established, commerce was conducted, various entertainments were performed, and rituals were enacted. Amino writes:

> Solicitations for contributions for charity *(kanjin)* were also held at such places, and offerings or tolls called '*joubun*' were collected from passers-by and boats. Numerous temples were erected near outlying roads and harbors following the Muromachi period [1392-1573], markets grew to become towns, and cities were formed. This was the process by which the autonomous towns, which called themselves *kugai* (public realms), were organized. (Amino 1996, 55)

Here Amino describes how cities were formed from the public sites of *kugai* through the amassing of the public realm. Following Amino further, the agents producing the public space are not the farmer settlers but the itinerant nonagricultural people. Such *kugai-mono* (people of the public realm) included marginal nomads such as artisans and entertainers as well as diviners, itinerant monks, and charity organizers. They were able to secure freedom of passage from others because their skills and techniques qualified them for this privilege and were a valuable resource they could exchange for such favors. These kinds of people, who were affiliated with Shintoism, Buddhism, and the emperor, were seen as having connections to the sacred and spiritual world.

Can this *kugai* (public realm) be called the public? To the extent that the public of the *kugai* was in an oppositional relationship to the public authority, we may say that it is public; to the extent that it cast off ties of *yuen* (bound) relations in communities, we may also say that it is public. Even if *kugai* began to disintegrate in the transitional period between the Middle Ages and the early modern period, its potential was not extinguished but became scattered, submerged, and transformed in the inner cities awaiting the opportunity to arise again.

The Case of the Public Sphere: From Urban Town to Public Sphere

Habermas's concept of the public sphere, which he located at the dawn of the history of modern Europe, was formed from the conjunction of three

differing spaces. First is the inner space of the conjugal family of the bourgeois intellectual strata. Historically, the intimate sphere of the conjugal
family was the source of privateness in the modern sense of a saturated and
free interiority (Habermas 1989, 28). Second was the space of the court
and aristocratic society. Third were the towns that were becoming the marketplaces for cultural products. Between the last two, the court and the
towns, one finds the transference of space and the succession of functions,
where a certain moment of modernity began to develop. For seventeenth-
century France, Habermas depicts this as follows:

> With the Hôtel de Rambouillet, the great hall at court in which the prince staged
> his festivities and as patron gathered the artists about him was replaced by what
> later would be called the *salon*. The hôtel provided the model for the *ruelles*
> (morning receptions) of the *précieuses*, which maintained a certain indepen-
> dence from the court. Although one sees here the first signs of that combination
> of the economically unproductive and politically functionless urban aristocracy
> with eminent writers, artists, and scientists (who frequently were of bourgeois
> origin) typical of the *salon* of the eighteenth century, it was still impossible, in
> the prevailing climate of the *honnêteté*, for reason to shed its dependence on the
> authority of the aristocratic noble hosts and to acquire that autonomy that turns
> conversation into criticism and *bons mots* into arguments. Only with the reign
> of Philip of Orléans, who moved the royal residence from Versailles to Paris, did
> the court lose its central position in the public sphere, indeed its status *as* the
> public sphere. For inasmuch as the "town" took over its cultural functions,
> the public sphere itself was transformed. (Habermas 1989, 31)

This brief but detailed description suggests several points. The fact that the
central position of the public sphere shifts from the court to the towns means
that the agent in each of these two spaces takes turns at the central role while
there is no difference in the point that both spaces remain to achieve their
cultural function. Amid the replacement of spaces and successions of functions, there arose conflicts and negotiations among and over the various
modes of linguistic activity. This produced qualitatively new forms, which
created a newly established spatial structure. What it established was the
forerunner of the "political public sphere" called the "public sphere in
the world of letters." On this point, Habermas writes:

> The bourgeois avant-garde of the educated middle class learned the art of
> critical-rational public debate through its contact with the "elegant world." This
> courtly-noble society, to the extent that the modern state apparatus became in-
> dependent from the monarch's personal sphere, naturally separated itself,
> in turn, more and more from the court and became its counterpoise in the town.
> The "town" was the life center of civil society not only economically; in cultural-
> political contrast to the court, it designated especially an early public sphere
> in the world of letters whose institutions were the coffee houses, the *salons*, and
> the *Tischgesellschaften* (table societies). (Habermas 1989, 29–30)

In the relationship between the intimate sphere (which was in ascendance), the court (which was in decline), and the towns (which were substituting and succeeding the court functions), the town was the center, but the confluence of the three created the public sphere in the world of letters. The subsequent political public sphere may be considered the discovered form of that which was becoming urban. On this occasion, the town was the place for the accumulation of linguistic activity and social connections, which resultantly produced the accumulation and exchange of cultural commodities. When one considers towns as well as nonurban areas, the level of development was clearly unequal, and the towns themselves were the cause of this inequality. However, the cause of this inequality is not merely economic, the accumulation of surplus and surplus value of material products, but rather it was linguistic activity and culture, the accumulation of surplus value in the symbolic world, which caused cities to become cities. The transmission and transformation of this cultural and symbolic surplus value affected the centralization of towns and the structuring of their power in contrast to the periphery.

On this basis, the following observations can be made. First, cities are a concept that can be traced back to the premodern period. What occurred at the dawn of the modern West was that the premodern city acquired and expanded into a new dimension, beginning the construction of the public sphere as an invisible dimension of itself. The "urban" gave birth to a new space that produced the public sphere as an invisible city. While *kugai* in Japan produced towns, the public sphere in Europe was produced from towns. In this way, the public sphere was differentiated from the town as another space.

A Comparison between the Concept of the Public Sphere and *Kugai*

Although the historical context for the emergence of the modern European public sphere and the Japanese medieval concept of *kugai* is clearly different, thereby rendering any comparison doubtful at best, I believe that a comparison is meaningful insofar as within each context the public arises, takes shape, and then disintegrates.

First, I will compare the relationship of towns to the public sphere. Although towns were formed from or with *kugai* in the Japanese context, the public sphere was formed from towns in Europe. The relationship is the reverse, since *kugai* gave rise to towns in Japan, but towns gave rise to the public sphere in the Western context. Unlike the public sphere, *kugai* was after its birth neither conceptualized nor institutionalized and was thus unable to survive. This is perhaps a result of its failing to eliminate Eros. The public sphere, on the other hand, by "turning conversation into criticism and *bon mot* into arguments" (in the words of the above quote from Habermas), strengthened the Logos that led to conceptualization and institutionalization and promoted its development as a political entity.

Second, I will take up the question of private property. The historian Amino sees in the principle of *yuen* (boundness—the antonym of *muen*) the creation of private property and personal vassalage. *Muen* and *kugai* are realized through resistance to such developments. This begs the question of whether the Japanese medieval and European notions of private property are the same. By confronting state authority, the property-owning European bourgeoisie formed a consciousness of their own subjectivity. The material possession of private property and the spiritual possession of cultivation (including literacy) were the impetus for the realization of individuality and the acquisition of personal freedom from the ties of community or state. Since the bourgeoisie were the supporters of the public sphere, one wonders whether the public sphere would not have formed without property. Moreover, without their subjectivity invested in private property, would the bourgeoisie have supported the idea of the public? If that were the case, the contradictions inherent in property become apparent since the same conditions might afterward have caused the decline of the public sphere.

However, with its lack of ownership and property (nonownership or antiownership), the case of *kugai* appears to be the opposite. Still, by merely stating that it is the opposite, this does not put the issue to rest. The problem is with the notion of private property in the "principle of *muen* (unboundness)." Even though it is undoubtedly property, it is more communal property than private property. The unboundness and lack of property in the Japanese Middle Ages was a strategy for achieving freedom from the ties of community functioning as public authority through the breakup of communal property. For Europe on the eve of modernity, private property was a strategy for achieving freedom from the ties of community or state functioning as public authority through the assertion of private autonomy from communal property. In short, the form of property opposed to communal property in medieval Japan appeared as a renunciation of property, while the form of property opposed to communal property in Europe appeared as private property. Though at first glance *kugai* and the public sphere appear to have different relationships to property, when viewed from the perspective of power relations in terms of what they opposed and how they formed themselves, they share much in common. This difference in strategy gives rise to several questions: Would a path leading to institutionalization of the public sphere rooted in a lack of property have been impossible? Was the institutionalization of the public sphere first possible through the route of rationalizing private property?

These questions are also suggestive for the problems of today, namely the question of whether *muen* (unboundness) is possible in today's world. If the ownership of property was one path to the formation of subjectivity, then is the principal of nonownership also an alternate path to the formation of subjectivity in a form of intersubjectivity? Or is private ownership a prerequisite for the private sphere that is the necessary counterpart to the public sphere? In other words, is it impossible to imagine a form of intersubjectivity not premised on private property? Or should we consider that the issue of *muen* (unboundness) and/or *yuen* (boundness) is not limited to the institutional problem of the relations of property, but we must consider the possibility that since it is a question of the mode of social linkages, boundness is a problem separate from private property?

Third, I will consider the question of religious custom. *Kugai*, which first originated as sacred sites and then came to inherit and include them, has a strong connection to Buddhism, Shintoism, and the emperor. In terms of the modern Western context, it had not yet undergone desacralization. What *kugai* lacked was a logic that had cast away superstition, a means for secularization, and a mechanism for linking the sacred and the secular. In contrast, the cultivation that served as the impetus for the formation of the public sphere was the culture of the Enlightenment and the desacralization of the intellect. From this began the process of rationalization in modern Europe. However, at the same time, had not this rationalization eliminated Eros? One can contrast this perspective, as noted in my first point earlier, with the observation that the constellation of *muen, kugai,* and *raku* was unable to survive since it had not eliminated Eros, and thus did not become institutionalized.

Fourth, I want to consider the structural elements of the public sphere and *kugai.* As mentioned earlier, the public sphere's structure is composed of the intimate sphere of the small bourgeois family, aristocratic court society, and market towns of cultural capital. In forming the literary public sphere, these elements worked to foster enlightened cultivation, social conversation, and cultural commodities respectively. When examined from a different angle, communicative competency, sites of mediation, and mediators were also necessitated. For Amino, on the other hand, seigniorial rule, urban place, and entertainment form the three structural elements of *kugai*. Seignorial rule appears to contradict the idea of freedom associated with *kugai*, but Amino maintains that the "household" (known as the *ie* in Japanese) cannot be understood unless one "recognizes the dualistic nature of the coexistence of two potential logics" (Amino 1996, 25). The dualistic nature that permeated the "household" included its function as a sanctuary *(asylum)* as well as a domain of feudal authority. As for this dualistic nature, the same can be said of the intimate sphere of small bourgeois families. The intimate sphere was a sanctuary from royal and ecclesiastical authority and at the same time a breeding ground of patriarchic authority. Urban places were the sites of mediation, and itinerant players with artistic competency served as the mediators. Were they individuals, groups, associations, or communes? What kind of relationship did these members of *kugai* have with one another? What kind of relationship to the emperor did they have? Was their direct connection to the Emperor based on faith or was it a charade devised to seek freedom from worldly authority? Was this like the acquisition by the leader of the intimate sphere of a vernacular version of the Bible, and his use of his own resource of literacy employing the strategy of invoking his direct connection to God, or rather the word of God? If this was the case, the strategy had the effect of removing and diverting the structure of feudal worldly authority, which consisted of the agency of the church in an alliance with sacred kingship, the mediating place of the altar, and the agent of the priest. What else could be the meaning of the strategy of *kugai's* close connection to the emperor? What is a difference between the emperor at that time in the medieval age and the Emperor in the modern emperor system during the era of nation-state building after the Meiji Restoration in 1868?

Fifth, I will consider the question of the media. Together with the vernacular typographic print Bible of the intimate sphere, the coffee houses, salons, and dinner clubs of the literary public sphere, and the pamphlets and newspapers of the political public sphere are all forms of media. Media each have their moment for structuring space, and in each moment they created their own space. As for *kugai*, what media issues are shaping it? In Amino's theory of *kugai*, the media does not appear to be explicitly addressed. However, I doubt that the public can be considered without overtly addressing the problem of the media. For that reason, I want to further examine the media.

Kanjin-Hijiri (Charity Monks) as Mediators, *Sajiki* (Spectator Gallery) as a Media Space

Previously I touched on how charitable activities were conducted at the sites of *muen* and *kugai*, and organizers of entertainment were called *kugai-mono*. By focusing on the solicitation of contributions to charity, Higashijima Makato's argument is intriguing for what it suggests regarding the problem of the media that is encompassed within the problematic of *kugai*. In his argument on the transformation of the structure of public obligation in premodern Kyoto, Higashijima draws attention to the role of culture (media) as a channel forming a consciousness of obligations. He analyzes the urban structure of *kanjin* (medieval charity) conducted for public concerns such as bridge building and famine relief, and argues that *kanjin* ultimately changed its structure and character in early modern society. First, we will consider what were these channels of charity by looking at Higashijima's work: "The reason why *kanjin* took the form of charitable performances was to create a common site of the high and the low to solicit widely contributions and alms. Its logic was like that of 'concert aid' where contributions are made in exchange for public entertainment" (Higashijima 1993, 3; 2000, 35).

The structure of obligations changed, from the perspective of the city's residents, from a compulsory levy to a contribution mediated by public entertainment. Charity was designed as a mediator between government authority and urban residents. Unlike earlier methods, it concealed the directness of government authority and aroused the voluntarism of urban residents. In short, charity may be considered here a device for resolving issues of public concern by soliciting the participation of urban residents. For government authorities, it was an effective and valid means of achieving its goals. For the city's residents, it created a heightened sense of public obligation and the fulfillment of voluntarism. The media device of charity was embodied through the space of the *sajiki* (spectator gallery), which Higashijima sees as being characterized by the cohabitation of the wealthy and the poor and also by comity between high-status and low-status people. In other words, the emperor, shogun, wealthy people, and beggars all share the same physical space and coexist in the same location. Furthermore, he raises the principle of the openness of spectatorship to argue that charity established channels outside the ties of community *(muen)*.

> The obligation mediated by charity entertainment does not function to maintain a closed community, but is based on the principle of the openness of the *sajiki* space and is established at a level that transcends distinct communities. It can be ranked as a completely new method of procurement through private, individual wealth. (Higashijima 1993, 7–9; 2000, 47)

In its autonomy from government authority and its self-assertion of private, personal wealth issuing from *muen* (unboundness), one can glimpse the potential for the formation of a private realm. However, the structure of charity contains a contradiction. In the case of charity for a bridge, the providers and beneficiaries of charitable events are fundamentally the same, since the benefit of restoring bridges accrues directly to the urban residents who contributed. As opposed to those who have passed through these channels of benefits, the beneficiaries in the case of famine relief, on the other hand, who have migrated to the city, are different from the providers of charity. According to Higashijima, in this instance, the advantage for the urban residents who are providing the charitable benefits is that they can directly avoid beggars during periods of famine. In this way, it is a voluntary public obligation that forms an indirect channel of refuge from beggars. However, these channels of charity began to deteriorate during the early modern period. According to Higashijima's view, the voluntarism of the bridge building drives that were structured around channels of benefits adapted to private interests become subsumed under public works based on bids. As for famines, virtuous townsmen organized relief through the formation of an open consensus mediated by printed works that contributed to the elimination of the principle of the *sajiki* (spectator gallery) of all urban residents. The structure of obligation mediated by charity was replaced as a consequence of a structural transformation in government authority. With the establishment of urban communities during the warring states period (1467–1568), authority used these communities as local organizations for exclusion and control. This system of exclusion and control became institutionalized through the exercise of power, which excluded the charitable activities of *kanjin-hijiri* (charity monks) and severed the channels of charity. In its place, Higashijima suggests that the construction of a new channel of public obligations was necessitated.

The space of the *sajiki*, which mediated between the exercise of government authority and the urban residents' sense of obligation, was a physical as well as a symbolic space. But its complex layering was first formed from the operation of the principle of *muen* and the *kugai-mono* (*kanjin-hijiri*—charity monks as people of the public realm). It was established as something that was not continuous or permanent. At such a site two phases united, and under these conditions the urban residents' sense of obligation nourished and produced (among other things) a consciousness of that which was becoming public. However, the process of reconstructing government authority in the beginning of the early modern period, together with the formation of urban communities, undermined the social unity of the *sajiki* (spectator gallery). Consequently, the channels within the consciousness of the urban residents and the channels of government authority were severed and broken. For Higashijima, this represents the transition from a model in which obligations are mediated directly by participation in charitable activities to a model in which obligations are mediated indirectly by the printed word.

What is of most interest in this is the shift from the *sajiki* to the printed word. For evidence, Higashijima points to the manuscript *Inu Houjouki* published in Kyoto by Yamamoto Shichirobei in 1682. This work praises contemporary famine relief in comparison to earlier periods and has an enlightened and moral character for having made this known to the world. This record has been judged to be not merely the record of one man, but a publication premised on the demands of society. Furthermore, several texts appear following the *Inu Houjouki* that are critical of its perspective. This is confirmed through the text and its reception, as there arose a debate on the methods of famine relief and the formation of an open domain for addressing this issue. As such, after the channels of *kanjin* and *sajiki* that functioned as a form outside of the ties of community were abolished, the (internal) community of the city's residents was forced to carry this burden instead. At that time, what is most significant is that despite the fact that such charities vanished during the transition from the direct charity-mediated model to the indirectly mediated model of obligations, the meaning spaces produced by these charitable activities remained. These sites of meaning were inherited in the early modern period by published works and writings. Finally, according to Higashijima's perspective, this sphere forms the prehistory for the thriving of the literary public sphere in the *bakumatsu* (late Tokugawa period), represented for example by *fusetsuryu* (pamphlets containing gossip and rumor). One can argue that amid the reassertion of government authority, the communication media was remaking the potential of the public. Why is this important? Because one can observe here the appearances, disappearances, and transformations of mediated spaces in the Japanese historical process. This long, selective summary of Higashijima's work is intended to illuminate the connections to the problematic of the media.

CONCLUSION

The Potential of a Lost History of Publicness

In this chapter I have brought together material from a number of apparently unrelated fields in an attempt to demonstrate the multilayered relations linking the city, public sphere, and media, or, to be more precise, the multilayered relations linking "the urban," "the public," and "the mediated" as potentialities undergoing continuous transformation. In order to provide a mooring for these complex relations I have employed Lefebvre's methodology of "postulating latent objects, or possible objects, and demonstrating their birth and development in relation to process and practice." The city, public sphere, and media should all be understood as concepts moving in a duality between actuality and potentiality.

Spatial differentiation comes about amid the overlapping of urban social relations with the social relations of mediation. From this, public social relations are constructed, and the public sphere emerges as a social space. Only when one adopts the perspective of a duality between actuality and potentiality does one gain the ability to speak of universality expressed only in potential form. The universal emerges in the explosion and implosion of particular actualities. From such a perspective it becomes possible to construct a problematic for the three potentialities listed above, transcending the limitations of the capitalist period and irrespective of the differences between East and West.

Potentialities exist continuously, sometimes emerging on the surface, sometimes becoming submerged (latent) and undergoing transformation, depending on social actions and social relations in the historical process.

The Possibility of Nonownership

In the sphere of production, following the failure of the socialist system of collective ownership, there seems to be no existing alternative to the principle of market economics based on private ownership. What kind of alternative might potentially be constructed in the future? Seen from the perspective of a duality between the sphere of production and the sphere of communication, would it not be possible to construct a principle of nonownership in the sphere of communication or the life world? One possibility would seem to be the construction of a social space in the form of *kugai* (public realm) based on the concept of *muen* (unboundness), which was active in medieval Japan. The method of acquiring freedom on the basis of ownership seems to contain within it the logic of excluding others, reducing other people to the status of mere tools. How might freedom be attained without being founded on ownership? Perhaps we can find such a potentiality underlying the current trend known as the "cultural turn."

NOTE

The author wishes to thank Jason Karlin and David Buist for editing the manuscript version of this chapter.

REFERENCES

Amino, Yoshihiko. 1978. *Zoho muen/kugai/raku: Nihon-chusei no juyu to heiwa* [Unboundness/public realm/fairground: Freedom and peace in medieval Japan]. Tokyo: Heibon-sha. In Japanese.

———. 1996. *Nihon-chusei-toshi no sekai* [The world of medieval towns in Japan]. Tokyo: Chikuma-shobou. In Japanese.

Garnham, Nicholas. 1986. "The Media and the Public Sphere." In Peter Golding, Graham Murdock, and Philip Schlesinger, eds., *Communicating Politics: Mass Communications and the Political Process,* 37–53. Leicester, U.K.: Leicester University Press.

———. 1990. *Capitalism and Communication: Global Culture and Economics of Information.* London: Sage.

Habermas, Jürgen. 1989. *The Structural Transformation of the Public Sphere: An Inquiry into a Category of Bourgeois Society.* Cambridge: Polity.

Hanada, Tatsuro. 1996a. *Kokyoken toiu na no shakai kukan: Kokyoken, media, shimin shakai* [A social space named the public sphere: The public sphere, the media and civil society]. Tokyo: Bokutaku-sha. In Japanese.

———. 1996b. "Toshi, kokyoken, media no triplex: Kanotai no rekishi" [The triplex of city, the public sphere, and media: The history of potential form]. In Yasunao Ojita et al., eds., *Toshi to gengo* [City and language], 17–50. Tokyo: Aoki-shoten. In Japanese.

———. 1999. *Media to kokyoken no politics* [The politics of media and the public sphere]. Tokyo: University of Tokyo Press. In Japanese.

Higashijima, Makoto. 1993. "Zenkindai-Kyoto niokeru kokyofutankozo no kenkyu" [The transformation in the structure of public obligation in premodern Kyoto]. *Rekishigaku-kenkyu* [Studies of history] 6, no. 49: 1–18. In Japanese.

———. 2000. *Kokyoken no rekishiteki sozo: Goko no shiso e* [The historical creation of the public sphere: Toward the concept of the heterosphere]. Tokyo: University of Tokyo Press. In Japanese.

Lefebvre, Henri. 1970. *La revolution urbaine.* Paris: Gallimard. Japanese translation: Tokyo: Shobun-sha, 1974.

———. 1991. *The Production of Space.* Oxford: Blackwell.

———. 1996. *Writing on Cities/Henri Lefebvre.* Oxford: Blackwell.

Marx, Karl. 1974. *Grundrisse der Kritik der politischen Ökonomie.* Berlin: Dietz.

Sparks, Colin. 1998. *Communication, Capitalism, and the Mass Media.* London: Sage.

7

Truth Commissions, Nation Building, and International Human Rights

The South African Experience and the Politics of Human Rights Post-9/11

Robert Horwitz

One of the key features of transitions to democracy over the past fifteen years or so is the "truth commission." Designed to construct a record of the human rights abuses that took place during the prior period of state authoritarianism and internal violent conflict, the truth commission in an important respect represents the triumph of the human rights movement that began in the aftermath of World War II with the Nuremberg trials and the 1948 Universal Declaration of Human Rights. Truth commissions bring into the orbit of the nation-state a set of standards of human rights that, in their expansive version, claim to be rooted in universal values of human life and the inherent dignity of the individual. In their more modest guise, they call on the concept of "negative liberty" of protection of human agents against abuse and oppression, as found in the Universal Declaration of Human Rights (United Nations General Assembly 1948; Berlin 1970; Ignatieff 2001). Versions of truth commissions have accompanied the transition from authoritarianism to democracy in more than twenty countries, primarily in Latin America and Africa, and more seem to be announced monthly, most recently in Asia. These commissions have been dedicated—differentially, to be sure—to uncovering the hidden history of violence, rape, torture, and murder perpetrated primarily by the old regime and its military, but also, in recognition of the implicit universalism of human rights principles and/ or the political necessity of the appearance of evenhandedness, toward violations of human rights perpetrated by the political opposition/liberation movement, as well.

Although the pedigree of truth commissions in the historic human rights movement is unimpeachable, and the very formation of truth commissions is testament to the growing moral authority of human rights principles, the commissions may not represent the victory of the human rights agenda in contemporary global politics. Rather, the proliferation of truth commissions underscores two sets of weakness. First, at the international level, the need for such commissions in so many countries indicates the weakness of the international human rights agenda in the face of *Realpolitik* and the doctrine of nonintervention in the domestic affairs of other countries that followed from the 1648 Treaty of Westphalia. After all, the states now instituting truth commissions were earlier engulfed in internal conflict and years, if not decades, of human rights violations, and the international community did little or nothing to stop them. Under the Westphalian doctrine of state sovereignty, rights-abusing regimes correctly claimed that international organizations and concerned states had no jurisdiction over their domestic affairs. And even if other states raised an occasional admonition about human rights abuses, many states sided with rights-violating regimes because of those regimes' strategic position in Cold War conflicts. Second, at the domestic level, the establishment of truth commissions reflects a weakness in a newly democratic government's ability to bring to justice the authoritarian violators of human rights through the normal channels of the judicial system. Because truth commissions often operate with incomplete or no publicness, have no judicial function, and/or are bound to predetermined amnesty agreements, they may institutionally abet the escape from justice (see Hayner 1994; Truth Commissions: A Comparative Assessment 1996). The Guatemalan truth commission, for instance, failed to promise any sort of reparations for victims and, as mandated, lacked the authority to name, much less punish, perpetrators.

Because of this possible paradoxical role of truth commissions in thwarting the punishment of perpetrators, many participants in truth commissions and the many scholars who have studied them have wondered whether the commissions present a juxtaposition of "truth *versus* justice" (see, among others, Minow 1998; Tutu 1999; Jeffery 1999; Rotberg and Thompson 2000; Boraine 2000; Hayner 2001). In this chapter I suggest that the specific way truth commissions are organized and how they go about their business largely determine whether truth is seen to compromise justice or, rather, implement it. A key factor is the communicative function of truth commissions. I explore this through some observations about the Truth and Reconciliation Commission, the South African variation of the truth commission. The second orientation of the chapter follows from the weakness identified above in terms of when and whether the international community is willing to intervene in a human rights crisis internal to a sovereign state. In this, the chapter briefly follows the new politics of human rights and begins to explore how the attacks of September 11, 2001, may have altered the way the international community, and especially the United States, approaches the question of human rights.

SOUTH AFRICA'S TRC: TRUTH VERSUS JUSTICE OR JUSTICE THROUGH THE COMMUNICATION OF TRUTH?

Truth commissions are clearly focused on the violation of human rights, but this in no way exhausts their role. Truth commissions are complicated political bodies charged, implicitly or explicitly, with multiple, often contradictory agendas and expectations, from uncovering previously hidden crimes to facilitating catharsis to achieving justice and retribution to fostering nation building. Their mandates inevitably reflect the relative political strength of the parties in conflict that create them. In South Africa, the Truth and Reconciliation Commission was born of the agreement between the National Party, the white party of apartheid, and the African National Congress, the primary anti-apartheid liberation organization, that there would be no Nuremberg-type tribunal and that some kind of amnesty must prevail in the post-apartheid dispensation. In the remarkable South African transition from apartheid authoritarianism to nonracial democracy, amnesty was one of the key conditions of the transition that the National Party was able to impose on the ANC, along with the protection of property rights and the security of tenure in posts for civil servants (including the payment of pensions), and the nearly complete independence of the central bank. Whereas in many respects the transition to democracy in South Africa was distinguished by an unusual profusion of open participatory structures oriented toward recasting all manner of social, economic, political, and cultural institutions to divest them of their apartheid lineage and make them accountable to the new democratic polity, the key issues mentioned above—property rights, civil service, central bank, and amnesty—were off limits to negotiation outside the closed confines of the elite pact between the leaderships of the ANC and the National Party (see Record of Understanding 1992; Shubane and Madiba 1992; Shubane and Shaw 1993; Horwitz 2001). The final clauses of the Interim Constitution of 1993, the document that encoded the essential agreements of the transition, stated that:

> The adoption of this Constitution lays the secure foundation for the people of South Africa to transcend the divisions and strife of the past, which generated gross violations of human rights, the transgression of humanitarian principles in violent conflicts and a legacy of hatred, fear, guilt and revenge.

> These can now be addressed on the basis that there is a need for understanding but not for vengeance, a need for reparation but not for retaliation, a need for *ubuntu* but not for victimization.

In order to advance such reconciliation and reconstruction, amnesty shall be granted in respect of acts, omissions and offences associated with political objectives and committed in the course of the conflicts of the past.

To this end, Parliament under this Constitution shall adopt a law determining a firm cut-off date which shall be a date after 8 October 1990 and before 6 December 1993 and providing for mechanisms, criteria and procedures, including tribunals, if any, through which such amnesty shall be dealt with at any time after the law has been passed (Republic of South Africa 1993).

The TRC was thus born of the reality of political stalemate between two powerful, opposed parties, and amnesty was necessary to move beyond the violent deadlock. In this regard, South Africa fits the pattern of the many transitions from authoritarianism in which the political and military strength of the outgoing regime is able to counter strong public demand for justice in the form of criminal trials. According to this pattern, the new democratic government, worried about a military coup or sabotage by ancien régime security forces, opts to establish a truth commission as a compromise position (see O'Donnell and Schmitter 1986; Kritz 1995). In South Africa's case, the decision to institute a truth commission rather than a war crimes tribunal was couched by the ANC not in the terms of the reality of power politics, but rather in the quasi-spiritual language of the concept of *ubuntu*. A word in the Nguni languages (the linguistic root of Xhosa and Zulu, among others), *ubuntu*, is said to express the high value on human worth found in traditional African societies. *Ubuntu* conveys a humanism rooted not in Western individualism but in a communal context—a concept expressive of a culture that emphasizes communality and the interdependence of the members of a community; a concept which conveys the belief that each individual's humanity is ideally expressed through his or her relationship with others and theirs in turn through a recognition of his or her humanity. In Xhosa, *ubuntu* means humanity; in Zulu it means human nature. *Ubuntu* expresses the quality of being human manifested in sharing, charitableness, and cooperation (Sparks 1990). Archbishop Desmond Tutu, the chairman of the TRC, regularly invoked the concept of *ubuntu* as fostering an African form of restorative justice in contrast to a retributive Western one (Tutu 1999). It should be noted that the ANC had earlier instituted a truth commission process with respect to its own human rights violations in its training camps in Tanzania and other parts of southern Africa (see African National Congress 1996).

The TRC began operating in December 1995 under the leadership of Archbishop Tutu. A national body created by an act of parliament (as opposed to some truth commissions, like El Salvador's, that were supranational bodies under the aegis of the United Nations), South Africa's TRC was charged with uncovering human rights violations, providing a process for the identification of victims eligible for reparations, and determining the conditions of amnesty for perpetrators. The TRC was also charged with fostering reconciliation generally. The commission was independent of government and political parties. Unlike earlier truth commissions, the TRC would take testimony *publicly*, and amnesty would be determined on an individualized basis. Unlike many other truth commissions, there would be no blanket amnesty under the TRC. Individual perpetrators of human rights violations would be granted immunity from criminal and civil penalties only if they came clean and made full public confession of their offenses. If they did not make full confession, or if the crimes were deemed not to be political in motivation (one could not claim amnesty for ordinary criminal acts), perpetrators could be subject to prosecution before the courts. The TRC was able to function in this manner because it was better supported than previous truth commissions, and was given quasi-judicial powers, including subpoena and search-and-seizure powers. Unlike many or perhaps most truth commissions, the South African TRC was strong and well resourced.

A central feature, perhaps the most important feature, of the TRC was its communicative purpose and function. The TRC gave victims voice. The stories of people who had been injured by the apartheid state apparatuses, whose husbands, brothers, wives, sons, and daughters were tortured and killed, were heard by the commission in a process that can only be described as public bearing of witness. The TRC took more than 21,000 statements from survivors and families of political violence and held more than fifty public hearings, which took place all around the country. The geographical decentralization of the hearings made it possible for poor and disabled people to appear and give evidence. Openness also applied to the amnesty hearings. An early provision of the National Unity and Reconciliation Bill, the legislation that officially established the TRC, had amnesty hearings to be conducted in camera. This was of great concern to many organizations in civil society, and their opposition prompted the principles of openness and transparency to apply to all TRC hearings (Boraine 2000, 64–70). Of critical importance, the hearings were amplified by being broadcast to the public on the radio and television outlets of the South African Broadcast Corporation. The SABC, having for decades served as essentially a state broadcaster, the mouthpiece of the apartheid government, was earlier recast as a public service broadcaster in one of the many participatory reform processes that were part and parcel of the South African transition to democracy. The reform of the SABC represented another aspect of giving the previously disenfranchised voice and of establishing broadcasting as a key institution of the newly constituted democratic public sphere (Horwitz 2001; also see Garnham 1986). The extraordinary scope of media coverage of the TRC may have been a means for the South African media, especially the SABC, to display their own transformation and ideological commitment to a new South Africa. The relationship between the SABC and the TRC, described as symbiotic by some observers (see Krabill 2001), transformed the commission into a long-running media event (Dayan and Katz 1992). The pain and catharsis of the victims, predominantly but hardly exclusively black, were on vivid media display day after day, week after week, month after month, for 224 days. Approximately 90 percent of the statements came from black people, mostly from women (Truth and Reconciliation Commission South Africa 1998, vol. 1, chap. 6, para. 29). Their accounts of apartheid abuses saturated the media and public consciousness. Those amplified stories served both to authenticate the victims' trauma and suffering (as opposed to rather simplistic notions of the therapeutic), and to flood a skeptical white public with irrefutable evidence of apartheid crimes. As the South African journalist Antjie Krog (1998) shows in her extraordinary account of the TRC and its reception, *Country of My Skull,* even as the white and especially Afrikaner public criticized the TRC for bias or unfair treatment, it had to acknowledge critical facts. The virtually inescapable descriptions of apartheid crimes facilitated a public discussion of recent South African history.

In this act of displaying and amplifying victim testimony publicly, the TRC was perhaps more akin to successful war crimes tribunals than to other truth commissions, which sometimes were not public, or did not allow widespread and extensive victim testimony, or kept the publication of a final report rather quiet (Hayner 1994). Gary Jonathan Bass (2000) argues in *Stay the Hand of Vengeance,* a history of international war crimes tribunals, that the consequentialist claims for the liberal legalism of war crimes tribunals are often oversold. Supporters of international war crimes tribunals argue that they build up a sturdy peace by: purging threatening enemy leaders; deterring future war criminals; rehabilitating former enemy countries; placing the blame for atrocities on individuals rather than on whole ethnic groups; and establishing the truth about wartime atrocities. Bass argues that but for the last, evidence for the claims is equivocal—apparent enough in some cases but not in others. The most successful war crimes tribunal in history, Nuremberg, clearly has not had much deterring effect. As for rehabilitation, the Nuremberg trials may have been an important element in the rehabilitation of Germany, but the Tokyo war crimes trials surely did not have such an outcome in Japan, which is only now, more than fifty years later, beginning to reckon with its horrific wartime behavior (see Dower 1999). The one unambiguous benefit of war crimes tribunals in Bass's view is that tribunals document the history of abuse and set the record straight. This is in fact the hallmark of the strong truth commissions such as the TRC. Like war crimes tribunals, the consequences of truth commissions may also be oversold, especially their purported function in fostering reconciliation. Like war crimes tribunals, it is the communicative function of truth commissions in establishing a record that is crucial—perhaps more for negative reasons than positive ones. The *failure* to bring out the truth of official widespread human rights abuses makes it much easier for countries or groups to avoid the difficult task of confronting that history. The failure of the Constantinople war crimes process after World War I, for example, beset by weak evidence gathering and a flagging of political will on the part of the Allied powers, made it possible for the Turks to avoid confronting the reality of the 1915 Armenian holocaust, a denial that continues to this day (Bass 2000, 284–310). Likewise, the failure of some Latin American truth commissions to document and communicate human rights abuses publicly has permitted the perpetrators (and groups that indirectly benefited from the abuses) to ignore or disavow those crimes (Hayner 1994).

This is not to say that South Africa's TRC process was unproblematic, that truth unambiguously served justice. We need not be postmodernists to acknowledge the disputatious category of "truth," the constructed nature of personal narrative, and the difficulty determining objective facts. The TRC employed four different kinds of truth—"factual or forensic," "personal and narrative," "social," and "healing or restorative" (Truth and Reconciliation Commission South Africa 1998, vol. 1, chap. 2, para. 30–44). Yet it was the *focus* of the TRC's attention that raised the most questions about whether truth was serving justice. The TRC concentrated primarily on individual violent *acts*, and hence seriously downplayed the historical ongoing *state* of violence inherent to the apartheid system. The TRC's focus on illegal acts such as detention, torture, and murder excluded as beyond the commission's mandate the range of violent and unjust *policies* that were legal under apartheid. Indeed, the TRC's effective mandate was not to determine the legality of apartheid itself, but rather of actions that were illegal even under the laws of the apartheid system. The commission addressed aspects of the institutional context in which apartheid operated by holding hearings on various institutions, including business and labor, the media, the religious community, the legal community, prisons, and health care. But these "institutional" hearings felt disembodied to many TRC detractors. In the view of critics such as Mahmood Mamdani (1996), the TRC's narrow, individualistic, and legalistic orientation meant the commission refused to see apartheid as a system dedicated to the dispossession of Africans of their land and exploitation of their labor. It meant that apartheid's victims were only those thousands who were physically abused, rather than the millions who suffered economically as a result of the day-to-day workings of the exploitative system. The orientation also meant that the TRC's final report was bereft of a coherent historical context or overview.

Notwithstanding this criticism, the TRC did largely succeed in presenting a national history lesson, albeit without an overriding principal narrative—a grievous lacuna for some commentators (e.g., Wilson 2001), the intelligent avoidance of a hegemonic reading for others (e.g., Jeffery 1999). The dramaturgical thrust of the TRC's public hearings, whether intentional or not, had some of the impact of what Mark Osiel (1997) has urged as "liberal show trials," in which a spectacularly public process of storytelling displaces the typically dry, procedure-bound nature of legal trials (features that make trials largely impenetrable to popular consciousness). The public history lesson is of no small moment, because acknowledgment, or the moral reckoning with atrocities, not only validates the suffering and the humanity of the victims, it also forms the basis for a process of moral reconstruction and the possibility of laying the foundations for a reconstructed political order and political culture (see Truth Commissions: A Comparative Assessment 1996; Allen 1999). Truth commissions have evolved to secure three essential functions or goals: knowledge, acknowledgment, and transformation. In the case of South Africa, reconciliation is the nub of transformation. The TRC wasn't simply a truth commission; it was a body whose name and mandate required it to seek reconciliation.

Was the TRC successful in the latter? Is reconciliation even a legitimate goal of a truth commission? The TRC was divided into three committees: the Human Rights Violations Committee, the Reparations and Rehabilitation Committee, and the Amnesty Committee. The Amnesty Committee received over 7,000 amnesty applications, but most came from prisoners who had a built-in interest in confessing to their crimes. Fewer than 600 were granted. Despite Archbishop Tutu's appeals, whites did not come forward to testify in significant numbers. A large number of white generals and Inkatha Freedom Party warlords, as well as some ANC politicians, did not come forward. Those who did provided some extraordinary testimony, but many observers and black victims objected to the fact that these violators of human rights (such as the notorious apartheid-era defense minister, Magnus Malan) received amnesty rather than justice (see James and Vijver 2000; Wilson 2001). The public confession that secured amnesty felt hollow to these observers, perhaps because, unlike in Catholic countries where confession is a meaningful part of religious life, the practice does not resonate among the predominantly Calvinist Afrikaners (MacDonald 1996). In a non-Catholic milieu, confession may be an ineffective cultural tool, an empty sign. After all, one could receive amnesty just by the act of confession; one did not have to express contrition or remorse. Addressing the question of how successful the TRC was, Antjie Krog reflects that while the TRC established factual truth of what happened and bore witness to the suffering of victims, it was less successful in convincing South Africans of the moral truth in answering the question, Who was responsible? In this vein, few believe the TRC process achieved reconciliation in a deep moral sense. Some critics, like Richard Wilson (2001, 21), whose *The Politics of Truth and Reconciliation in South Africa: Legitimizing the Post-Apartheid State* offers a trenchant critique of the TRC, argue that the invocation of human rights embodied in the TRC process and its calculated, even duplicitous, incantation of the African concept of *ubuntu* sacrificed even a moderate notion of justice as retribution to the ANC's goal of nation building and state formation. Wilson argues that the truth commission was part of a general, long-term orientation within state institutions that asserted the state's ability to rein in and control the informal adjudicative and policing structures in civil society.

But these criticisms might be too harsh. The TRC process in principle permitted South Africa to address its horrific past without, in Archbishop Tutu's (1999, 63) phrase, being "held ransom to it." This "third way" (Tutu's phrase) between the extreme of the Nuremberg trials and the national amnesia associated with the blanket amnesty found in several of the Latin American truth commission processes, brings to mind Ernest Renan's famous 1882 essay, "What Is a Nation?" A country with South Africa's dreadful history must bear witness, but it needs to forget a little bit as well, so that the past does not utterly tie the hands of the future. Renan writes:

> Forgetting, I would even go so far as to say historical error, is a crucial factor in the creation of a nation, which is why progress in historical studies often constitutes a danger for [the principle of] nationality. Indeed, historical enquiry brings to light deeds of violence which took place at the origin of all political formations, even of those whose consequences have been altogether beneficial. . . . the essence of a nation is that all individuals have many things in common, and also that they have forgotten many things. . . . It is good for everyone to know how to forget. (Renan 1990; see also Kundera 1980)

Antjie Krog suggests that the TRC was/is an important part of the consolidation of democracy as the new South Africa engages in the incremental, day-to-day processes of negotiation that ensure the survival of the society. Reconciliation isn't people of different races hanging out, sharing confidences, and laughing together as in the attractive and ubiquitous Castle Beer advertisements. Reconciliation is less grand and more profound; it is the setting in motion of a set of expectations and processes for negotiating day-to-day existence without the resort to violence.

Even though the ANC almost refused to endorse the final TRC report (because in its evenhandedness, the TRC condemned some of the actions of the ANC in addition to its rebuke of apartheid crimes), the TRC must be understood as part of the broader ANC nation-building move to transform South Africa's race and ethnic-based nationalisms for a more broadly based civic nationalism in a post-apartheid human rights constitutionalism. In this regard, I largely agree with Richard Wilson's evaluation but do not share his condemnation of the sacrifice of individual victims' retributive justice for the country's future. Wilson's argument that the absence of retributive justice is responsible for the high levels of criminality in post-apartheid South Africa is suggestive, but in view of the complex sources of crime, including the historic damage of apartheid and continued high levels of poverty and unemployment, such a suggestion is highly speculative. It is also telling that, for all of the crime and violence in post-apartheid South Africa, there have been virtually no political vengeance killings. As for the criticism that the TRC sacrificed justice in the name of a pseudo reconciliation and a hidden nation-building program, it is instructive to turn again to the historical example of war crimes trials. Presumably the alternative to a truth commission was a Nuremberg-style process of criminal justice. (No one in South Africa credibly offered the solution of summary executions and/or forcible confiscation of property of National Party leaders and apartheid's beneficiaries, the other alternative to war crimes trials.) Yet the justice secured even by war crimes trials is primarily symbolic. Such trials go after the big fish and some particularly ghastly underlings, but pursue only a fraction of the alleged perpetrators (Bass 2000, 295–96). Apart from reparations to victims (an act of real, tangible benefit to victims and not to be devalued), the actual retributive justice that war crimes trials achieve is itself primarily symbolic. With this in mind, when assessing the success or failure of the TRC, perhaps it is better to separate the truth function from the reconciliation function and not assume they are inextricably linked, or, at least, inextricably linked in time. Whether in terms of war crimes tribunals or truth commissions, justice cannot be simply *performed*; justice is not a one-time event. Rather, achieving justice—or reconciliation—must be seen as a long *project*, which can only be set in motion by the process of publicly communicating the truth of human rights abuses. In this sense, the rhetorical construction is not simply one of truth *versus* justice, but truth as reasonable prelude to justice and, perhaps, reconciliation. Just as the Nuremberg war crimes tribunal was not a quick fix for the rehabilitation of Nazi Germany but rather part of a much more ambitious and time-consuming project of education and social engineering, so too should the South African TRC be understood as a process of establishing the truth and of setting in motion the process of reconciliation within a project of nation building. It might even be argued that reconciliation is a synonym for nation building (Tepperman 2002, 142).

TRANSNATIONAL HUMAN RIGHTS AND
THE QUESTION OF STATE SOVEREIGNTY

It is to the problem of nations, human rights, and nation building that I now turn. I suggested at the beginning of the chapter that the ascendance of human rights on the international agenda may signal a shift from the traditional doctrine of state sovereignty, of nonintervention in the domestic affairs of other countries. As Henry Kissinger (2001, 237), of all people, reminds us, the doctrine of state sovereignty and its corollary, domestic jurisdiction, was the human rights slogan of the seventeenth century. In the aftermath of the horrendous Thirty Years War in Europe between Protestant and Catholic principalities, the doctrine sought to prevent rulers of one faith from inciting uprisings of their coreligionists ruled by a prince of a different faith. The international system based on the Treaty of Westphalia had an answer for the problem of violence *between* states—recourse to war—but it offered no solution to violence *within* states arising from civil wars and ethnic conflicts. It dealt with the problem of peace and left justice to the domestic institutions. International law became defined as that law governing relations between nation-states alone; individual human beings within nation-states had no standing in international law. The doctrine of state sovereignty has meant that the state is subject to no other state, and has full and exclusive powers within its jurisdiction (Hoffmann 1966). The contemporary human rights agenda argues the opposite. Peace flows from justice, and the nation-state cannot be relied on to deliver justice; the state must be put under some kind of supranational authority entitled to use force to make its writ run.

Although most historians date the international human rights initiative to nineteenth-century opposition to the slave trade, and root the idea of individual human rights in the philosophy of the European Enlightenment, the *politics* of human rights as we know it today could be said to be the legacy of Woodrow Wilson (see Lauren 1998). I should say Wilson in theory, not Wilson in deed. In the realm of theory, Wilson justified American intervention in the international arena not on the traditional basis of the pursuance of national interest (the core of *Realpolitik*, or realism), but on the basis of universal values, of self-determination, democracy, and international law and organizations. Those who support and rely on international law and international organizations are known as liberal legalists. Realists, in contrast, argue that international relations differ from domestic politics in the lack of a common ruler among self-interested states. To survive in such conditions of anarchy, states must rely on self-help for their own security. If, nationally, the force of a government is exercised in the name of right and justice, writes neorealist Kenneth Waltz (1979, 112–13), internationally the force of a state is employed for the sake of its own protection and advantage. Realists insist that international norms and institutions are mere veils over state power. Most of the twentieth century witnessed a seesaw battle in American foreign policy between the liberal legalists (the Wilsonians) and the realists (labeled by Kissinger "Jacksonians," after the policies of President Andrew Jackson), who would essentially ignore international affairs unless the security of the United States were threatened. This Kissingerian account is, of course, grossly tendentious. Andrew Jackson's isolationism did have a "foreign policy": Indian removal; Woodrow Wilson's invasion of Russia in 1918 was just one example of the imperialism that gave lie to his sponsorship of the doctrine of self-determination and democracy. Any discussion of American foreign policy that fails to take into account the history of U.S. imperialism both internally and internationally is flawed. Nonetheless, there were and are real differences within the American foreign policy elite, and American foreign policy cannot be reduced to some imperialist essence. American foreign policy reflects many tendencies: realism and liberal legalism, imperialism and support for self-determination. For example, at the peak of its power as the lone major nation not devastated by World War II, the United States helped launch the international organizations of the postwar world, establishing the

United Nations and myriad measures that institutionalized international co-operation on a variety of global issues. Yet, contrary to a common assumption that the ascendance of international human rights principles is inseparable from the rise of American global hegemony, American policy makers were deeply wary about human rights. Like the other major powers at the end of World War II, the United States worried that the international recognition of human rights would weaken the doctrine of state sovereignty, and pushed for the inclusion of article 2 (7) of the United Nations Charter to safeguard the traditional doctrine.[1] In Paul Gordon Lauren's (1998) history of the evolution of human rights, it was the tireless efforts of the nongovernmental organizations and the small nations that overcame the major powers' reticence in establishing the Universal Declaration of Human Rights. Moreover, the European Convention on Human Rights, which came into force in 1953, was put together largely without the help of the United States.[2]

Wilsonian liberal legalists and Jacksonian realists made common cause against the Axis powers in World War II and against communism. With the end of the Cold War they again parted company. Kissinger argues that the Clinton administration represented the triumph of extreme Wilsonianism. Clinton did little when Iraq evicted U.N. weapons inspectors in 1998—which realists saw as a classic threat to American interests. In contrast, his administration deployed the military in Somalia, Haiti, Bosnia, and Kosovo, conflicts that reflected a commitment to international human rights but no traditional notion of American national interest (Kissinger 2001, 255). We should note, of course, that this is Henry Kissinger, master of *Realpolitik*, possible war criminal in the eyes of some, speaking. In sharp contrast to his analysis, many in the human rights community are deeply critical of the United States and the European democracies, in spite of those states' professed commitment to human rights. The critics find the commitment rather shallow, hardly Wilsonian, the equivalent of an inversion of Theodore Roosevelt's old maxim: "Speak loudly and carry a small stick." After all, the great democratic powers did nothing to halt the Rwandan genocide, or Iraq's slaughter of its Kurds, or, earlier, Pol Pot's reign of terror in Cambodia. During the Cold War, much of the time the United States found it rather easy to condone the dismal human rights records of its anticommunist puppet regimes. Many of the Latin American military officers whom truth commissions found responsible for human rights abuses had received their training in the United States. Samantha Power (2002), executive director of the Carr Center for Human Rights Policy at Harvard's Kennedy School of Government, and fairly representative of the critics of U.S. commitment to human rights, argues that the United States did not do what it could and should have done to stop genocide because it wanted to avoid engagement in conflicts that posed little threat to American interests. At the same time, policy makers hoped to contain the political costs and avoid the moral stigma associated with allowing genocide. In other words, in the critics' view, the United

States may give lip service to human rights, but it will commit to action only when its traditional national interests are threatened.

Ultimately the Clinton administration intervened in Somalia, Haiti, Bosnia, and Kosovo, for no clear purpose of national interest, however desultorily. In this respect, Kissinger is correct. Part of what underlay these reluctant interventions is the growing inability of democratic states to resist a human rights agenda pushed by an effective transnational human rights advocacy network. As Margaret E. Keck and Kathryn Sikkink (1998) argue, particularly in the human rights arena a transnational network consisting of the U.N. Commission on Human Rights, Amnesty International, Human Rights Watch, Freedom House, and scores of other often well-funded transnational and local groups is helping to transform the practice of national sovereignty by creating new issues and pressuring more powerful actors to take positions. In Keck and Sikkink's view, the currency of the advocacy network is information, strategically mobilized for use as leverage and to hold governments accountable. But what is the basis for such leverage? In a word, norms, the conflicts over which are played out in an increasingly international public sphere. The transnational human rights advocacy network reflects a broad, if sometimes amorphous public commitment to human rights and in turn has influenced key portions of democratic publics in many countries to adopt the conception of individual human rights as part of their core beliefs (see Anheier, Glasius, and Kaldor 2001; Laber 2002; Khagram, Riker, and Sikkink 2002). Those human rights norms have been institutionalized in the establishment of U.N. and regional organizations dedicated to them. Indeed, an international social structure of human rights norms and institutions developed between 1973 and 1985 (see Risse, Ropp, and Sikkink 1999). It seems reasonable to assume that media, particularly visual media, play some significant role in rendering human rights information symbolically meaningful to distant democratic polities. This is not an argument about the unmediated influence of global news on public opinion; it is to suggest rather that global media and the transnational human rights advocacy network work in tandem to lessen the psychological distance between peoples, at least in the particular register of human rights. The historian Thomas Laqueur (2001) has noted what Adam Smith and other eighteenth-century moralists discerned as the natural sense of immediate *local* sympathy with suffering. In our age of global media, rights talk, and transnational advocacy networks, all of humanity potentially and at certain moments has been brought within the fold of our compassion. This compassion needs to be directed to have consequences, and the existence of international organizations, including U.N. agencies and the International Court, and, increasingly, national courts willing to assert jurisdiction over lawsuits that have international dimensions, are the settings wherein that compassion—and hard-nosed coercion—are mobilized. The recent successful effort at securing reparations from European corporations and banks for their use of slave and forced laborers during World

War II is the latest manifestation of the human rights agenda. Stuart Eizenstat (2002), who guided the class-action lawsuits on behalf of the Clinton administration, calls this development the "civil version of Nuremberg" and points to the possibility of its precedential value for further efforts at obtaining historical apology and reparations, for example, to Korean comfort women and the descendents of African American slaves. These developments would indicate that the human rights agenda has begun to nibble away at the doctrine of state sovereignty. This emerging system of human rights institutions, mass media publics, and organized advocacy networks also suggests the fragile success of a new international regime of communicative rationality over, or at least in complex conjunction with, the power politics of state sovereignty (see Habermas 1996). The international social structure of human rights norms and institutions sometimes goads Western government to act. And, as Thomas Risse and Kathryn Sikkink (1999) suggest, a repressive state can enter into a spiral of human rights socialization that moves from external coercion and tactical concessions to a stage where the state engages in moral discourse and accepts the international norm.

Kissinger, representing hard-nosed *Realpolitik*, attacked Clinton's interventions as foolish, misconceived, and counterproductive, not simply because they had no foundation in American national interest, but because they occurred without reference to their historical contexts. The crux of this latter criticism is that these interventions were undertaken in places and contexts essentially characterized by "failed states." Failed states is the new term for those countries so wracked by internal violent conflicts that they are without functioning governmental institutions, and seemingly without prospects of any national accommodation. Somalia was an anarchic cauldron of vicious warlords, "not a country but a collection of warring tribes" (Kissinger 2001, 265); Haiti, ruled by a series of autocratic and deeply corrupt leaders, has been dysfunctional for a century; Bosnia, a "bottomless pit of Balkan passions" (Kissinger 2001, 267), was an impossible multiethnic state, as was, in different ways, Kosovo. Because these involve failed states, or, in Samuel Huntington's (1996) parallel realist view, conflicts that involve "clashes of civilization" and are hence intractable, intervention in their affairs has no so-called exit strategy. After stopping the killing, the interveners must remain in these countries indefinitely, engaging in peacekeeping and "nation building." The debate about exit strategy, a practical concern, may be a stand-in for a theoretical debate about defining the limits of the universality of interventions on behalf of human rights.

This nation-building role, this unworkable "overextension" of American power in the name of protecting human rights, is what the new Bush administration denounced—at least prior to September 11. Bush's unilateralism on almost all fronts signaled a fervent return to realist principles and a rejection of international organizations. The litany by now is well rehearsed: backing out of the Kyoto global climate protocols; the expressed intention to skirt the ABM treaty; calling a halt to negotiations with North Korea; the go-ahead for deployment of a missile defense system; the adamant refusal to sign on to the International Criminal Court. Then came the attacks of September 11. The attacks were understood by the Bush administration to show that "failed states," which are found mostly in postcolonial border zones, because they foster and harbor long-suffering and enraged people whose resentments of the prosperous west can eventuate in terrorist assaults against it, can no longer be seen outside the prism of human rights and American national interest (National Security Strategy of the United States of America 2002). In the eyes of nearly all policy makers and commentators, Afghanistan demonstrated the price of neglect of failed and failing states. After earlier denouncing Clinton's efforts at nation building, following September 11 the Bush administration pledged to stay the course in rebuilding a stable state in Afghanistan and shoring up a weak, deficient Pakistan.

As Michael Ignatieff (2002a) has written, while a new international order is emerging, it is a different picture of the world from the one entertained by liberal international lawyers and human rights activists, who had hoped to see American power integrated into a transnational legal and economic order, organized around the United Nations, the World Trade Organization, and the International Criminal Court. The emerging international order is being crafted to suit American imperial objectives. September 11 seems to have made visible a new divide in American foreign policy circles, illustrated most clearly by the fall 2002 debate over whether to go to war against Iraq. Those winning the debates inside the Bush administration are *not* the realists; the realists (including prominent scholars Kenneth Waltz, John Mearsheimer, Barry Posen, Stephen Walt, and twenty-nine others who signed a *New York Times* editorial advertisement in September) have largely counseled against war with Iraq as not meeting the standard of advancing U.S. national interests (see Scowcroft 2002; War with Iraq Is *Not* in America's National Interest 2002). Rather, those winning the debate—led by Vice President Dick Cheney, Secretary of Defense Donald Rumsfeld, and the coterie of former students of Albert Wohlstetter, many of whom populate the influential national security advisory group known as the Defense Policy Board—are a new breed of hawkish interventionists. They hold a deep-seated mistrust of international treaties and organizations and advocate as the national security policy of the United States the suppression of any potential adversary that would pursue a military buildup and unilateral preemptive military action against such adversaries (The National Security Strategy of the United States of America 2002; FitzGerald 2002; Lemann 2002). They constitute a third position in foreign policy analysis, neither realist nor liberal legalist. The rhetoric of the new American hegemony, as seen in the National Security Strategy document, is in part the traditional language of American exceptionalism and the United States as the city on the hill. But it also reflects the rhetoric of international human rights. In parallel, the language of the new interventionism implicitly recognizes the inadequacy of the old Westphalian doctrine of state sovereignty. Paradoxically, human rights and nation building now matter, but only because *not* paying attention to them is seen to threaten American security. As the essayist Hendrik Hertzberg (2002) has observed, the contradiction at the heart of the Bush administration's foreign policy is that it recognizes that state sovereignty is in many ways an outdated doctrine, but it essentially rejects international law and organizations in favor of presumably benevolent American dictatorship.

TOWARD A CONCLUSION: THE PARADOX OF HUMANITARIAN INTERVENTIONISM AS LEGITIMATION FOR THE NEW AMERICAN IMPERIALISM

Historically, the human rights movement was built to challenge tyranny by strong states and to defend the civil and political rights of dissidents within them. The movement has been very successful at the level of establishing a rights-oriented political and discursive agenda, if less successful in actually protecting human rights. Institutions dedicated to human rights have been established; human rights talk is everywhere; rights-oriented nongovernmental organizations (NGOs) seem to be found everywhere. This international social structure of human rights norms and institutions is in part what lies behind the phenomenon of truth commissions. Truth commissions grew as a compromise mechanism to address human rights and justice in states that had made a transition from authoritarianism to democracy. The human rights agenda has begun to challenge the old doctrine of state sovereignty, augmenting, if not replacing, power politics with international organizations, norms, and even, perhaps, a communicative process of moral discourse. But the strong state orientation of the historic human rights movement may now be anachronistic. If scholars like Michael Ignatieff (2002b) are correct, the human rights movement now faces a world where many of the most urgent human rights challenges come not from strong states, but from disintegrating, "failed" states. The main problem now is often not the civil and political repression of individuals, but the genocide, ethnic cleansing, and massacre of entire communities. To the extent that the mechanisms of diffusion of international norms in the human rights arena have been successful, it is with established, if authoritarian and repressive, states. That diffusion does not work in the context of failed states. In this world, especially post-9/11, stability seems to be increasingly understood as a prerequisite to human rights, and the lack of stability as legitimate pretext for outside military intervention. It is probably true that some degree of stability *is* a prerequisite for human rights. In their own way the truth commissions reflected a balance between rights and stability. Their "compromised" nature reflected the fact that individual retributive justice was traded for the public revelation of misdeeds, some abstract notion of reconciliation, and the pragmatic need for nation building in the face of the threat of reversal of the democratic political transition. But the new geopolitical situation and the post-9/11 interventionism seem quite distant from the vision of the world championed by human rights activists. It is a world where the sole remaining superpower, having experienced terrorism on its turf and whose foreign policy is now controlled by hawkish interventionists, deploys the language of human rights to announce its own right to ignore international organizations and norms in favor of unilateral intervention.

NOTES

The author wishes to thank Lew Friedland, Val Hartouni, Vicente Rafael, Michael Schudson, and Elana Zilberg for their valuable conceptual and editorial suggestions.

1. "Nothing contained in the present Charter shall authorize the United Nations to intervene in matters which are essentially within the domestic jurisdiction of any state or shall require Members to submit such matters to settlement." See Lauren 1998, 172–204.

2. American attention to human rights in the 1950s and 1960s was intimately bound up with the attention that policy makers were forced to pay to the links between foreign and domestic policy. The propaganda value of attacking the Soviet bloc for its unfreedoms was rather diminished when the United States was confronted with the abysmal treatment and status of its own African American citizens. Some policy makers legitimated the efforts of the black civil rights movement because of foreign policy concerns. See, among others, Lauren 1996.

REFERENCES

African Nation Congress. 1996. ANC Submission to the Truth and Reconciliation Commission. Available at www.geocities.com/CapitolHill/5013/trcall.html.

Allen, Jonathan. 1999. "Balancing Justice and Social Unity: Political Theory and the Idea of a Truth and Reconciliation Commission." *University of Toronto Law Journal* 49: 315–53.

Anheier, Helmut, Marlies Glasius, and Mary Kaldor, eds. 2001. *Global Civil Society 2001*. Oxford: Oxford University Press.

Bass, Gary Jonathan. 2000. *Stay the Hand of Vengeance: The Politics of War Crimes Tribunals*. Princeton: Princeton University Press.

Berlin, Isaiah. 1970. "Two Concepts of Liberty." In *Four Essays on Liberty*. Oxford: Oxford University Press.

Boraine, Alex. 2000. *A Country Unmasked*. New York: Oxford University Press.

Dayan, Daniel, and Elihu Katz. 1992. *Media Events: The Live Broadcasting of History*. Cambridge: Harvard University Press.

Dower, John W. 1999. *Embracing Defeat: Japan in the Wake of World War II*. New York: Norton.

Eizenstat, Stuart. 2002. Address to the University of California, San Diego Thurgood Marshall College, April 15.

FitzGerald, Frances. 2002. "George Bush and the World." *New York Review of Books*, September 26, 80–86.

Garnham, Nicholas. 1986. "The Media and the Public Sphere." In *Communicating Politics*, edited by Peter Golding et al., 37–55. Leicester, U.K.: Leicester University Press.

Habermas, Jürgen. 1996. *Between Facts and Norms: Contributions to a Discourse Theory of Law and Democracy*. Translated by William Rehg. Cambridge: MIT Press.

Hayner, Patricia B. 1994. "Fifteen Truth Commissions—1974 to 1994: A Comparative Study." *Human Rights Quarterly* 16: 587–655.

———. 2001. *Unspeakable Truths: Confronting State Terror and Atrocity*. New York: Routledge.

Hertzberg, Hendrik. 2002. "Manifesto." *New Yorker*, October 14, 21, 63–66.

Hoffmann, Stanley. 1966. "International Systems and International Law." In *The Strategy of World Order*. Vol. 2, *International*, edited by Richard A. Falk and Saul H. Mendlovitz, 134–66. New York: World Law Fund.

Horwitz, Robert B. 2001. *Communication and Democratic Reform in South Africa*. New York: Cambridge University Press.

Huntington, Samuel P. 1996. *The Clash of Civilizations and the Remaking of World Order*. New York: Simon & Schuster.

Ignatieff, Michael. 2001. *Human Rights as Politics and Idolatry*. Princeton: Princeton University Press.

———. 2002a. "Barbarians at the Gate?" *New York Review of Books*, February 28, 4–6.

———. 2002b. "The Rights Stuff." *New York Review of Books*, June 13, 18–20.

James, Wilmot, and Linda van de Vijver. 2000. *After the TRC: Reflections on Truth and Reconciliation in South Africa*. Cape Town: David Philip.

Jeffery, Anthea. 1999. *The Truth about the Truth Commission*. Johannesburg: South African Institute of Race Relations.

Keck, Margaret E., and Kathryn Sikkink. 1998. *Activists beyond Borders: Advocacy Networks in International Politics*. Ithaca, N.Y.: Cornell University Press.

Khagram, Sanjeev, James V. Riker, and Kathryn Sikkink, eds. 2002. *Restructuring World Politics: Transnational Social Movements, Networks, and Norms*. Minneapolis: University of Minnesota Press.

Kissinger, Henry. 2001. *Does America Need a Foreign Policy? Toward a Diplomacy for the Twenty-first Century*. New York: Simon & Schuster, 2001.

Krabill, Ron. 2001. "Symbiosis: Mass Media and the Truth and Reconciliation Commission of South Africa." *Media, Culture, and Society* 23: 567–85.

Kritz, Neil J., ed. 1995. *Transitional Justice: How Emerging Democracies Reckon with Former Regimes*. Washington, D.C.: United States Institute of Peace Press.

Krog, Antjie. 1998. *Country of My Skull: Guilt, Sorrow, and the Limits of Forgiveness in the New South Africa*. New York: Three Rivers.

Kundera, Milan. 1980. *The Book of Laughter and Forgetting*. Translated by Michael Henry Heim. New York: Knopf.

Laber, Jeri. 2002. *The Courage of Strangers: Coming of Age with the Human Rights Movement*. New York: Public Affairs.

Laqueur, Thomas W. 2001. Comment. In Michael Ignatieff, *Human Rights as Politics and Idolatry*, 127–39. Princeton: Princeton University Press.

Lauren, Paul Gordon. 1996. *Power and Prejudice: The Politics and Diplomacy of Racial Discrimination*. 2d ed. Boulder: Westview.

———. 1998. *The Evolution of International Human Rights: Visions Seen.* Philadelphia: University of Pennsylvania Press.

Lemann, Nicholas. 2002. "The War on What?" *New Yorker*, September 16, 36–44.

MacDonald, Michael. 1996. Conversation with author.

Mamdani, Mahmood. 1996. "Reconciliation without Justice." *South African Review of Books*, 46. Available at www.uni-ulm.de/~rturrell/antho3html/Mamdani.html.

Minow, Martha. 1998. *Between Vengeance and Forgiveness: Facing History after Genocide and Mass Violence.* Boston: Beacon.

National Security Strategy of the United States of America. 2002. September 17. Available at www.whitehouse.gov/nsc/nssall.html.

O'Donnell, Guillermo, and Philippe C. Schmitter. 1986. *Transitions from Authoritarian Rule: Tentative Conclusions about Uncertain Democracies.* Baltimore: Johns Hopkins University Press.

Osiel, Mark. 1997. *Mass Atrocity, Collective Memory, and the Law.* New Brunswick, N.J.: Transaction.

Power, Samantha. 2002. "Genocide and America." *New York Review of Books*, March 14, 15–18.

Record of Understanding. 1992. Meeting between the state president of the Republic of South Africa and the president of the African National Congress, World Trade Center, September 26. Available at www.anc.org.za/ancdocs/history/transition/record.html.

Renan, Ernest. 1990 [1882]. "What Is a Nation?" In *Nation and Narration*, edited by Homi K. Bhabha, 8–22. London: Routledge.

Republic of South Africa. Constitution of the Republic of South Africa, Act 200 of 1993. Available at www.polity.org.za/govdocs/legislation/1993/constit0.html.

Risse, Thomas, Stephen C. Ropp, and Kathryn Sikkink, eds. 1999. *The Power of Human Rights: International Norms and Domestic Change.* New York: Cambridge University Press.

Risse, Thomas, and Kathryn Sikkink. 1999. "The Socialization of International Human Rights Norms into Domestic Practices: Introduction." In *The Power of Human Rights: International Norms and Domestic Change*, edited by Thomas Risse, Stephen C. Ropp, and Kathryn Sikkink, 1–38. New York: Cambridge University Press.

Rotberg, Robert I., and Dennis Thompson, eds. 2000. *Truth v. Justice: The Morality of Truth Commissions.* Princeton: Princeton University Press.

Scowcroft, Brent. 2002. "Don't Attack Saddam." *Wall Street Journal*, August 15.

Shubane, Khehla, and Pumla Madiba. 1992. *The Struggle Continues? Civic Associations in the Transition.* Johannesburg: Centre for Policy Studies.

Shubane, Khehla, and Mark Shaw. 1993. *Tomorrow's Foundations? Forums as the Second Level of a Negotiated Transition in South Africa.* Johannesburg: Centre for Policy Studies.

Sparks, Allister. 1990. *The Mind of South Africa: The Story of the Rise and Fall of Apartheid.* London: Mandarin.

Tepperman, Jonathan D. 2002. "Truth and Consequences." *Foreign Affairs* 81: 128–45.

Truth and Reconciliation Commission South Africa. 1998. *Report.* Cape Town: Juta. Available at www.doj.gov.za/trc/index.html.

Truth Commissions. 1996. A Comparative Assessment: An Interdisciplinary Discussion Held at Harvard Law School. Available at www.law.Harvard.edu/programs/HRP/Publications/truth1.html.

Tutu, Desmond Mpilo. 1999. *No Future without Forgiveness*. New York: Doubleday.
United Nations General Assembly. 1948. Resolution 217A (III), Universal Declaration of Human Rights, December 10.
Waltz, Kenneth. 1979. *Theory of International Politics*. Lexington, Mass.: Addison-Wesley.
"War with Iraq Is *Not* in America's National Interest." 2002. *New York Times*, September 26, A29.
Wilson, Richard A. 2001. *The Politics of Truth and Reconciliation in South Africa: Legitimizing the Post-Apartheid State*. Cambridge: Cambridge University Press.

8

Show Me the Money
Challenging Hollywood Economics

Janet Wasko

Over the past few decades, Hollywood economics has attracted a good deal of attention from the media as well as from academics in various disciplines.[1] Many of these Hollywood analysts stress that the U.S. commercial film industry is different, with a set of unique characteristics that sometimes defies typical economic analysis.[2] It is commonly assumed that the film business is not only unique, but risky, uncertain, and even chaotic. The industry's key trade association, the Motion Picture Association of America (MPAA), explains this point on its website:

> Moviemaking is an inherently risky business. Contrary to popular belief that moviemaking is always profitable, in actuality, only one in ten films ever retrieves its investment from domestic exhibition. In fact, four out of ten movies never recoup the original investment. In 2000, the average major studio film cost $55 million to produce with an extra $27 million to advertise and market, a total cost of over $80 million per film. No other nation in the world risks such immense capital to make, finance, produce and market their films. (www. mpaa.org/anti-piracy)

This chapter challenges a few of the assumptions of Hollywood economics by considering the film industry from a political economic perspective. The first section will discuss how film has been studied from this perspective and the second section will consider the issue of film as a risky business, as well as why the major Hollywood companies dominate the film industry.

THE POLITICAL ECONOMY OF MOTION PICTURES

Analysis of the U.S. film industry has been the focus of ongoing research in the political economy of communication. Fundamentally, the political economy of film analyzes motion pictures as commodities produced and distributed within a capitalist industrial structure. As Pendakur notes, film as a commodity must be seen as a "tangible product and intangible service" (Pendakur 1990, 39–40). Similar to other industry analysis, the approach is interested in questions pertaining to market structure and performance. However, political economists analyze these issues as part of the larger communication and media industry and within a wider social context. Most importantly, the political and ideological implications of these economic arrangements are relevant, as film must also be placed in an entire social, economic, and political context and critiqued in terms of the contribution to maintaining and reproducing structures of power.

For instance, when looking at the international popularity of U.S. films, rather than celebrating Hollywood's success, political economists are interested in how U.S. films came to dominate international film markets, what mechanisms are in place to sustain such market dominance, how the state becomes involved, how the export of film is related to marketing of other media products, the consequences for indigenous film industries in other countries, and the political/cultural implications.

The focus on one medium or industry such as film may be seen as antithetical to political economy's attempt to go beyond merely describing the economic organization of the media industries. The political economic study of film must incorporate not only a description of the industry, but, as Mosco explains, "a theoretical understanding of these developments, situating them within a wider capitalist totality encompassing class and other social relations (offering a) sustained critique from a moral evaluative position" (Mosco 1996, 115). Consequently, political economists recognize and critique the uneven distribution of power and wealth represented by the film industry, directing specific attention to labor issues, as well as alternatives to commercial film. In other words, the approach attempts to challenge the industry rather than accept the status quo.

While perhaps not as recognized as other cinema studies approaches, the political economy of film is represented in a wide range of research. Some classic economic studies fit the above description but were not explicitly identified with political economy. For instance, Klingender and Legg's *Money behind the Screen* examined finance capital in the film industry in 1937, tracing studio owners and their capitalist backers (Klingender and Legg

1937), while Mae Huettig's study of the film industry in the 1930s documented the power inherent in the various sectors of the industry (Huettig 1944).

More recently, Thomas Guback's work represents an ideal example of political economy of film. *The International Film Industry* presented primary documentation about how the U.S. domination of European film industries intensified after 1945, with the direct assistance of the U.S. government (Guback 1969). He followed this classic study with several articles documenting the international extension of U.S. film companies in the 1970s and '80s, especially emphasizing the role of the state in these activities (in Balio 1976). In another article, Guback defended a nation's right to resist Hollywood's domination and develop its own film industry based on economic and cultural factors (Guback 1989). And finally, in an in-depth analysis of the U.S. film industry in *Who Owns the Media?* Guback presented a strong critique of Hollywood's structure and practices, as opposed to the other industrially oriented articles in the same volume (Compaine 1982)

Pendakur's study of the Canadian film industry employs a radical political economy of film, but also incorporates industrial organization theory to examine the market structure of Canadian film (Pendakur 1990). "Marxian political economy's concern with power in class societies and its emphasis on a dialectical view of history help explain how the battle to create an indigenous film industry has been fought in Canada, in whose interests, and with what outcome" (39). Pendakur (1998) also examined labor issues in film, adding to the growing literature documenting the history of labor organizations and workers in the U.S. film industry.

Meanwhile, many other scholars have taken a political economic approach in looking at various aspects of film. Nicholas Garnham incorporated an analysis of the "Economics of the U.S. Motion Picture Industry" to exemplify the production of culture in his collection, *Capitalism and Communication* (Garnham 1990). Aksoy and Robins's more recent study of the motion picture industry focuses on issues of concentration and globalization, and draws fundamentally on political economy (Aksoy and Robins 1992). Another example is Prindle's *Risky Business: The Political Economy of Hollywood,* which especially emphasizes the social and political implications of Hollywood's unique industrial structure (Prindle 1993). Most recently, Miller et al. (2001) have presented an overview of global Hollywood, relying strongly on a critical political economic approach and emphasizing the role of film workers.

In my own work, I have examined capital, technology, and labor as they pertain to Hollywood. *Movies and Money* (Wasko 1982) presented the historical development of relationships between Hollywood and financial institutions, while *Hollywood in the Information Age* (Wasko 1994) examined continuity and change in the U.S. film industry relating the introduction of new technologies during the 1980s and early 1990s. In addition, "Hollywood

Meets Madison Avenue" considered the ongoing commercialization of film by focusing on the growth of product placement, tie-ins, and merchandising activities in film marketing (Wasko, Phillips, and Purdie 1993), while an overview of Hollywood labor unions was presented in a collection on global media production (Wasko 1998).

Despite these various studies, it is clear that a political economic approach is much less common in film studies than in communication research. Guback's explanation (Guback 1978) was that most film analysis relies on the relatively easy access to film texts. Scholars depend on the material that is available for study, whether film texts or industry-supplied information. Consequently, analysis is mostly based on material generated by the industry itself and is hardly ever critical of the industry.

On the other hand, why is film included less often in much of the work in political economy of communication? While film appears in general overviews of communication or media industries, it seems to receive less careful analysis than other forms of media or communication (Jowett and Linton 1980). One reason may be the academic fragmentation that often separates film studies from media and communication studies in university organizational charts, professional organizations, and scholarly journals. Another explanation is that film studies typically has been based in the humanities, while communication and media studies tend to draw more on the social sciences. Beyond this fragmentation, though, there also may be different perceptions of film's significance for communication scholars. Motion pictures often represent entertainment and thus are not as worthy of scholarly attention as news and information programming, or computer and information technologies.

These oversights need to be addressed if we are to understand film in its actual social context. These days, film must be considered part of the larger communications and media industry. More than ever before, distribution outlets such as cable and satellite services link news, information, and entertainment programs. Sometime in the future, it seems likely that there will be further links via new digital and multimedia forms. It is no longer novel to observe that news is looking more like entertainment, with new forms evolving, such as infotainment, docudramas, and so on.

But of importance, these activities are, more than ever, under the same corporate ownership. Films are produced by the same companies that are involved with other media and communications outlets, and it is no secret that fewer and fewer giant corporations control these activities. These transnational corporations have diversified into all areas of the media, sometimes attempting to maximize profitability by building synergy between their corporate divisions. For some companies, film plays a key role in these synergistic efforts, as corporations such as the Walt Disney Company build product lines that begin with a film but continue through television, cable, publishing, theme parks, merchandising, and so on. Companies like Disney not only distribute products to these outlets but also own the distribution outlets.

Communication scholars may find it useful to look more closely at the international expansion of the U.S. film industry to better understand the historical evolution of current globalization trends. While the expansion of global markets may be relatively new for some media, the U.S. film industry developed global marketing techniques as early as the 1920s and maintains its dominant position in international media markets. As the film industry and its wealth become ever more concentrated, it is increasingly difficult to avoid the issues and analysis that a political economy of film presents.

HOLLYWOOD AS A RISKY BUSINESS

As already noted, moviemaking has been described as an "inherently risky business." Yet, when Hollywood is considered from a political economic perspective, any number of issues are suggested, which makes the risky nature of the business much less obvious. Some of the issues that need to be considered (and will be discussed further in this section) include the availability of data, distribution arrangements, definitions of profit, sources of revenue, and the level of analysis. In addition, the distribution sector of the industry (also known as the Hollywood majors or the studios) must be examined more carefully to make any sense of the reputed risky nature of Hollywood filmmaking.

A Dearth of Data

It is a challenge to generalize about economic aspects of the motion picture industry because of the dearth of reliable data. Assessments of costs and profits for Hollywood films depend mostly on inconsistent trade press reports and unsystematic data from lawsuits and other sources. Practically every film industry researcher has acknowledged the problems of securing basic industry data and reliable information on deals and relationships. Outsiders analyzing the film industry, as well as some Hollywood insiders, often express frustration at the difficulties of understanding the complexities of the industry, as well as finding reliable information. As media analyst Harold Vogel observes: "The lack of access to real numbers in this industry is astounding and it's getting worse all the time. We have no way to judge Hollywood's actual return on equity, nor can we accurately assess the year-to-year health of the film business."[3]

Production Excess

Very often, the riskiness of filmmaking is attributed to the high cost of production and marketing. Negative costs for the average Hollywood film in 2002 were reported to be $58.8 million, with additional marketing expenses averaging $30.6 million. High production costs often are blamed on demanding stars who receive multi-million-dollar contracts, in addition to profit-sharing deals. Some have argued that the power in the industry actually resides with a handful of these well-compensated stars.

A few Hollywood economists argue that the moviemaking business is out of control with inflated production budgets and outrageous marketing expenses. It might be argued very simply that film production doesn't need to be so costly, doesn't require extravagantly paid stars, and doesn't demand huge amounts to be spent on advertising and marketing. While some people in the industry would agree with these points, this begs the question of whether prevailing film industry practices are inherently risky. Even though reliable information is not always available, it is important to try to account for production costs and distribution revenues related to current Hollywood patterns to understand their supposedly risky nature.

Production/Distribution Deals

To begin to understand the allocation of costs and revenues, different types of deals commonly used in the industry need to be clarified. The major distribution companies (also called the studios) develop, produce, and distribute a slate of "in-house" films each year. However, many production/distribution deals also are arranged with separate production companies. Some of these production companies are truly independent from the major distributors. The most successful production companies have ongoing arrangements (PACTS) with the studios, which provide varying levels of financial support in addition to distribution deals.

The majors also distribute films without any financial involvement in a film's production. These agreements are called negative pickups, and they are typically arranged before a film's completion. In this type of deal, the distributor may provide an advance to the producer and finance releasing costs; the distributor and producer then share the profits. The producer provides the production capital, limiting the studio's risk to distribution.

Coproduction/distribution deals are also possible between major distributors, as is the presale of distribution rights to foreign distributors. The important point here is that the Hollywood majors don't always "risk" the capital to finance the production of the films that they distribute.

Furthermore, when one of the Hollywood majors agrees to distribute a film, it usually has the power to negotiate a favorable distribution deal. First, the distributor receives a distribution fee that is intended to cover the distributor's operations or "fixed-distribution overhead costs." The fee is charged for the distributor's efforts in soliciting play dates, booking the picture, collecting rentals, and so on. How and when distribution fees are charged, as well as what expenses are included in this fee, are highly disputable issues. Distribution fees are typically paid before any distribution expenses, production costs, or other charges. The fee is a nonnegotiable percentage of revenue from a specific source and varies according to geographic area and market. For instance, distribution fees are 25 percent for network television revenues and 30–40 percent for syndication revenues (although independent distributors may charge as much as 50 percent).

While many observers consider the distribution fee relatively high, it is defended because of the assumed high risk of film distribution, where it is claimed that distributors often do not recoup distribution expenses. It is important to understand that distribution expenses are different from, and paid after, the distribution fee.

Determining how distribution expenses should be covered and whether they are appropriate remains one of the most controversial issues in motion picture accounting. A few of these charges are particularly contentious. For instance, a film's distribution expenses typically include an allocation to cover the company's annual dues to the distributors' trade organization (the MPAA), bad debts or uncollectable rentals, and charitable contributions and legal fees. In addition, a 10 percent overhead charge is included in distribution expenses for the fixed costs of the distributor's marketing department, as well as a production overhead charge—anywhere from 12 to 25 percent, but usually 15 percent of the direct production costs, no matter where the film is produced.

Although the actual expense of production for Hollywood films continues to rise, distribution expenses also continue to push up the cost of a film. However, it might be argued that because of high distribution fees and carefully structured distribution deals, the risk to distributors is often negligible.

Determining Profits

Who takes risks and who receives profits? Hollywood's notorious creative accounting makes it difficult, if not impossible, to answer this question. Nevertheless, a more careful look at the way that profits are determined is necessary.

After all fees and expenses are paid, a film is said to "break even" or begins to produce "net profits." However, break even is incredibly complex, having been described as a "magical number with a myriad of definitions." Some accountants claim that three and a half to four times the negative cost must be taken in at the box office for a film to reach net profit, and most pictures never generate a net profit. For instance, witnesses in one lawsuit testified that "twenty-nine of the motion pictures released by Paramount from 1975 to 1988 achieved significant net profits—an annual average of more than two of the studio's fifteen releases" (cited in Daniels et al. 1998, 226).

But, profits for whom? While each film is different, various types of profit participations are possible. Gross participants are those few stars or "players" who have the power to arrange deals that involve a percentage of a film's gross receipts. Even more complex are the arrangements for net profit participations. Studio accountants explain that the "participation in net profits is a *contractually defined* formula by which a participant might obtain additional compensation if various criteria are met" (emphasis added) (Daniels et al. 1998, 225). In other words, every profit participation is differently defined. For instance, the Paramount films mentioned above paid more than $155 million to over eighty-four profit participants. However, in recent years, net profit participants reportedly have received much less because stronger players have been taking larger gross profit shares.

A film's producer also expects to receive a share of the film's revenues; however, the amount is determined differently from these other participants. Often, a producer splits 50 percent of what is left of net profits with the distributor (the distributor already having received distribution fees and covered distribution expenses, which may include numerous overhead and other charges). The producer also may have assumed the risk of providing or arranging production costs. In addition, the producer may have to wait until other participants are compensated, as it is claimed that the producer is responsible for the production of the film and thus the cost of talent.

Another problem in determining profits involves Hollywood's highly controversial accounting methods. The industry is known for using unusual procedures including reporting accounts differently for profit participation and for other purposes (tax accounting, etc.). Other problems involve the definition of terms that change from contract to contract. Potential problems involve allocation, reporting, and timing of revenues and expenses, or arbitrary price allocations; the timing of reporting revenues; the classification of revenue; and the amount of revenue.

One lawsuit claimed that "the entire participation system amounts to nothing more than a price-fixing conspiracy by the major powers in a company town."[4] The most widely publicized case involving profit participants was Art Buchwald's widely covered suit against Paramount in 1988, when he claimed that the film *Coming to America* earned a sizable profit and he deserved to participate in those funds (Cones 1992; O'Donnell and McDougal 1992).

Sources of Revenues

As noted above, it is claimed that the majority of Hollywood films are risky because they do not recoup their costs. However, most of these claims focus only on the revenues received during a film's theatrical release. It is obvious that motion pictures are sold in many retail markets, or "windows of exhibition," including home video, cable, and television. (In the future, this may include the Internet and video on demand.) Other products and merchandise related to Hollywood films may contribute additional revenues. Hollywood films continue to make money for the major studios in various platforms and in various ways years after their initial theatrical release.

Because of the significance of these sources of revenue, a brief overview of each market will be presented in the following section. It is important to note that these markets operate differently. For instance, the domestic theatrical market has different business practices than foreign theatrical markets, and so on.

Theatrical Exhibition

Although box office receipts are only one source of revenue for a Hollywood film, theatrical release usually comes first and sets the value for the markets that follow. Other windows may represent higher earnings, but theatrical revenue is still substantial. The motion picture industry reported $9.5 billion in domestic box office revenue for 2002, representing the biggest year-to-year increase in twenty years. Admissions for the same year rose to $1.64 billion—the largest increase in forty-five years (MPAA 2003).

The distributor's share of the total box office receipts (the gross) is called the film rental. While the film rental can be as high as 90 percent of the box office gross after exhibitor's expenses, exhibition deals are usually much more complex. It is often claimed that distributors receive 50 percent of the overall box receipts; however, in reality, distribution's share of the box office is probably underestimated.

Home Video (VHS/DVD)

The home video market is an extremely important source of revenue for Hollywood but is often overlooked in assessments of the risky nature of the film business. By 1986 it was claimed that 45 percent of all revenue received was from the video marketplace. By 1990, U.S. and foreign video revenues accounted for 35–50 percent of a typical film's total income. By the end of the twentieth century, it was even higher.

The home video industry experienced its best year ever in 2001 with U.S. spending totaling $18.7 billion. Home video consumers spent $7 billion renting VHS tapes and $4.9 billion purchasing VHS tapes.

The significance of the home video business has been accentuated with the rapid growth of DVDs (or digital versatile disc). Video consumers in the United States spent an unprecedented $1.4 billion renting DVDs in 2001, and $6 billion in sales and rentals together. DVDs in some cases account for 30 percent of a studio's retail revenue from home video sales and rentals. The discs wholesale for only $10–$15 each (compared to $45–$65 for videocassettes) and are sold to consumers at $18–$30. One studio head explains that the studios make $15 in profit on the sale of one DVD.

Again, the sale of videocassettes and DVDs often represents larger revenues than the theatrical box office. Previously distributors did not receive revenues from video rentals, but a direct revenue-sharing model has been adopted since the late 1990s, with tapes sold at a lower cost to retailers (around $8–$10) for 45–50 percent of the rental fees. The major studios have made such arrangements with the leading U.S. retail chains, Blockbuster and Hollywood Entertainment.

Home video rights are typically arranged as part of the initial distribution deal and the studios often insist on these rights as part of the deal. It also is relevant that, for purposes of calculating profit participations and producers' share of revenues, home video revenue is reported as a standard 20 percent royalty on wholesale sales. In other words, the "studio includes only 20 percent of videocassette revenue in gross receipts and puts most of the remaining 80 percent in its pocket" (Baumgarten et al. 1992, 53). In addition to counting only 20 percent of the wholesale revenues, distribution fees and other expenses are extracted from this amount. From the 20 percent reported, the studio takes a distribution fee (typically 30 percent in domestic markets and 40 percent in foreign markets), plus additional expenses. While the reason for this dubious practice may be historical, the practice is one of the most controversial in motion picture accounting.

Cable Television

Another important market for Hollywood films is cable television, including pay cable and pay per view (PPV).

After the exclusive home video window closes, studio films may be made available for pay-per-view venues, on both cable and satellite TV systems. At this stage, the movie is available exclusively for two to six weeks on PPV. (The film will always be available on video after its initial availability, so subsequent discussions of "exclusivity" do not take into account the home video window.) Generally, studios get anywhere from 45 to 55 percent of the revenues generated from PPV, depending on the individual movie and the number of PPV channels on which it can be exhibited.

Pay cable release of major motion pictures usually follows home video and PPV release. Cable systems arrange to carry pay services through contracts (usually 3–5 years in length) which specify fees paid by the operator plus other provisions. Typically, the cable operator keeps 50 percent of pay revenues, while the remainder goes to the program supplier. The major studios have "output deals" with the major pay-TV channels (HBO/Cinemax and Showtime/Movie Channel), thus every major feature film eventually airs on one of these channels. Also, remember that the same companies that own these pay-TV outlets own the major distributors. Output deals specify base license fees paid by pay-TV services according to the box office gross of a film. For instance, if a film received $5 million at the box office, the base license fee might be 50 percent, or $2.5 million. The average is claimed to be approximately $6 million to $8 million per picture, but for wildly successful films, the fee is considerably higher. For instance, *Batman* received over

$200 million at the box office and its pay cable license fee was reported to be around $15 million. Foreign pay-TV deals are even more varied but are important outlets for Hollywood films.

Thus film companies generate additional income from selling their films to pay cable. In 1984 it was estimated that the film business received $600 million from the pay cable market. Around the same time, pay cable revenues were said to contribute about $3 million to an average Hollywood film's revenues. These revenues have increased considerably since that time.

Television

Since the mid-1950s, television has provided an important market for Hollywood films. This area includes broadcast TV and advertiser-supported cable. Although the industry sometimes refers to advertising-supported television as "free," the term is misleading, since advertising represents a form of financing television that is not entirely "free." Consumers ultimately pay higher prices for products and services, to which advertising expenses have been added. Be that as it may, when reporting revenues from television, the industry usually refers to network, syndicated and cable television, and foreign television.

After a film reaches the premium cable or pay-TV market, it may appear on network television twelve to eighteen months later, for one or two runs. Increasingly, the top-rated cable channels—USA Network, TBS, TNT—have been able to outbid the networks to obtain rights to broadcast movies. In some cases, the network or cable channel may even buy future runs at five- or ten-year intervals.

The network or cable channel negotiates with the studio for each movie, typically paying the studio a fixed amount ranging from $3 million to $15 million, depending on the movie and the number of runs.

Following the broadcast premiere and second run (or however many runs the network or cable channel has bought the rights to broadcast), the movie then goes into syndication, again either on network television or a cable network, or even both. In the syndication market, films are sold in packages of fifteen to twenty films to individual stations, groups of stations, and advertiser-supported cable channels, usually two to three years after theatrical release. Films are licensed to the highest bidder on a title-by-title basis, and a single license fee is paid for the package.

Generally, then, television is still a viable market for Hollywood films and at least offers the potential of generating revenues for a motion picture over a relatively long period of time.

Foreign Markets

Hollywood features also attract revenues from theatrical, television, and home video markets in international markets. In foreign theatrical markets, distributors may use their own subsidiaries, a foreign affiliate or a subdistributor. Even though various expenses are deducted before a studio receives foreign revenues, the U.S. distributor usually reports 100 percent of the film rental as revenue in calculating profit participants' and producers' shares. In other words, the studio is reporting more revenue than it actually receives so that a larger distribution fee can be charged. Foreign television markets are similar to syndicated television, where films are sold in packages and the license fees allocated among various films in the package.

The foreign market has grown substantially in the past years, with estimates of 50 percent of Hollywood's overall revenues coming from international markets. An important point to note here is that the distribution of films to foreign markets requires little by way of additional costs. Film's "infinitely exportable" nature, as discussed by Guback and others, translates to additional nearly pure profits in constantly expanding foreign markets.

Nontheatrical Markets

A variety of additional nontheatrical markets may attract even further revenue. The largest is the airlines, although Hollywood films are also licensed to the military, schools, hospitals, prisons, colleges, public libraries, railroads, churches, oil companies, and so on. Nontheatrical sales are typically negotiated for flat fees or a specific amount per viewer, and represent a relatively minor source of revenue compared to the previously discussed markets. For instance, annual airline expenditures on in-flight entertainment and communication were $2.1 million in 2000 and were estimated at $1.9 million for 2001. Nevertheless, the airline business represents additional revenue for Hollywood films.

Merchandising, Video Games, Music, Publishing

Although not all films generate additional revenue from these sources, some box office hits profit handsomely from additional commodities that flow from the film commodity. These additional revenues may lessen the risk of films overall, at least for the major players involved. Many different kinds of deals are involved in the licensing of rights to characters, stories, and music that flow from the initial film product. It may come as no surprise that distributors demand additional fees to manage these markets.

Other Sources of Distributor Revenues

Distributors sometimes collect interest from revenue sources that are slow to pay (exhibitors, airlines, etc.). How and whether this interest income is shared with outside participants is another potential area of dispute.

A wide variety of additional revenues are possible from the marketing opportunities created by a Hollywood film. For instance, the sale of advertising materials (posters) may bring in additional funds, as well as the sale of the making-of-the-movie programming created for television outlets.

New Outlets

It is too early to include revenues from Internet and video-on-demand outlets, as these venues are just emerging as possible markets and sources of revenue for Hollywood films. It seems likely that the major distribution companies will do everything in their power to maintain their control over these new outlets. However, huge problems still loom, especially those pertaining to piracy and appropriate business models (see Harries 2002).

DIVERSIFIED REVENUES, OR WHY THE MAJORS ARE STILL MAJOR

Statements such as the MPAA quote at the beginning of this chapter focus on individual films rather than on the overall activities of film companies and the U.S. film industry. Almost always, claims about the riskiness of the film business ignore or at least downplay the ongoing power and strength of the dominant distribution companies in the industry, as well as their diversified and global organizations.

From the 1950s on, the Hollywood majors became part of diversified conglomerates, no longer depending on movies as their only source of income but becoming involved in a wide range of cultural production, from audiovisual products to theme park operations. But interest in Hollywood firms became especially intense at the end of the 1980s with a flurry of mergers and consolidation. Deregulation, privatization, technological developments, and the opening of new international markets contributed to this concentrated growth. Interestingly, foreign interests were attracted to Hollywood conglomerates for many of the same reasons that Hollywood increasingly was looking to international markets. At the end of the twentieth century, several of the Hollywood majors were owned by foreign companies—Columbia/Tri-Star by Sony, Universal by Vivendi, and Fox by News Corp.

Hollywood is dominated by a handful of companies that draw much of their power from film distribution, which is central to the film business. Despite the presumed risk involved, the major distribution companies manage to survive and (usually) profit.

Clearly the distribution process is designed to benefit the distributors but not necessarily production companies. In addition to their positions in diversified conglomerates, the majors have distinct advantages that include distribution profits, enormous film libraries, and access to capital. As industry insiders Daniels, Leedy, and Sills (1998, 5) observe, "The studios have Oz-like power over the motion picture industry and cash in abundance. Or perhaps more properly, access to abundant capital."

The majors claim to encounter intense competition in the film industry, as well as in other activities. But many companies have attempted to enter the distribution business over the years and have failed. Examples included the so-called instant majors of the 1970s and 1980s (National General, Cinerama) and more recently Orion, DEG, Lorimar, Embassy, and Allied Artists. The major distributors still dominate, as indicated by the fact that eight companies received 95 percent of the box office revenues in the United States and Canada in 2000.

At one time, Hollywood could be depicted as a "three-tier society." At the top were the big studios or the majors—Paramount, Twentieth Century Fox, Warner, Universal, Disney, and Columbia. The second tier included a handful of smaller or less influential production and/or distribution companies, or minor majors, including MGM/UA, Orion, Carolco, and New Line Cinema. And at the bottom were the much smaller and often struggling "independent" distributors and production companies. Although the majors still dominate the top tier, there are far fewer second-tier companies, and some have been taken over by the majors (Miramax, New Line, etc.). Others have faded into oblivion (Orion). The only new company on the scene that has significant clout is Dreamworks.

Despite the risky nature of the film business and the "inflated" demands of stars and others to share in profits, the major distributors remain in control. They often set the terms of deals and occupy dominant positions. An industry insider explains it this way: "the pervasive market power of the major studio/distributors in the U.S. (the MPAA companies, generally) has been gained and is maintained by engaging in numerous questionable, unethical, unfair, unconscionable, anti-competitive, predatory and/or illegal business practices" (Cones 1997).

Again, the distributors argue that the film business is risky. It is estimated that about 5 percent of the films released by Hollywood companies earned about 80 percent of the industry's total profit over the past decade (De Vany and Walls 2001). Thus success propels more success and a few movies, mostly the major studios' movies, make most of the profit.

Nevertheless, the context of the distribution business needs to be understood. As Larry Gerbrandt, chief content officer and senior analyst for Kagan World Media, explains:

> it's not unusual for a studio to have invested a billion dollars and to generate less than a 10 percent return on that. So on a stand-alone basis, it's not a very good business. However, if they didn't make movies, you wouldn't be able to run theme parks. You wouldn't be able to run or create TV networks. You wouldn't have libraries against which you can create cable networks. The movies really provide the economic foundation and much of the leverage that these companies have in terms of being able to do other businesses.
>   . . . Having a blockbuster film allows you to charge more for almost everything else you do that year, because of the way movies are packaged in with

other business deals and other films. So the hits are really the locomotives that drag the rest of the train down the tracks. (PBS/Frontline 2000)

As discussed above, film distribution involves a number of different markets in which revenues are gleaned for the lease or sale of motion pictures, as well as other related products. One estimate is that global distributor revenues of U.S. films in 2000 totaled $29.8 billion. This included revenues from theatrical, home video, television and other outlets in the U.S. and foreign markets. As a research report recently concluded:

> Most of these revenues, wherever they are earnt, accrue to the major American film distributors, whose attractive flow of product gives them an adequate revenue base on which to support worldwide distribution networks serving theatrical, home video and television markets. Although the practice of selling some foreign rights to subsidise film budget means that the studios' share of the international market is lower than in North America, studio-owned distributors almost certainly command 90 percent of the world market for American films. (Dodona Report 2001, 9)

To consider only the domestic market—which Hollywood considers to be the United States and Canada—in any year, the major distribution companies receive at least 80 percent of the domestic box office and often considerably more. One of the factors that help the majors dominate is the concentration of the market on a small number of films. In the past three years the top forty films have consistently received more than 60 percent of the (North) American box office—and about two-thirds of this amount was received by the top twenty films each year (Dodona Report 2001, 9). As a recent report concludes, "The highly concentrated nature of the market not only contributes to the studios' ability to continue to dominate it, as their superior resources enable them to attract the best projects and creative talent" (Dodona Report 2001).

An oligopoly in motion picture distribution has existed for decades and continues to this day. In typical fashion, the Hollywood oligopoly represents a relatively few large companies that dominate an industry where entry is relatively difficult and collaborative behavior is typical. The majors' dominance is indisputable and often defended as necessary for the industry to succeed.

Despite some concerns over the limitations of companies actually becoming too big, there are still some clear advantages to large, strong, diversified companies. A recent PBS special (2001) focused on the film industry's role in the large, diversified conglomerates which own them. The program's producers contrasted studio revenues with the operating income of the parent companies' business segments. (Operating income is essentially revenues minus expenses, excluding interest and taxes; net income, on the other hand, is what is commonly referred to as the "bottom line.") For instance, Disney's "studio entertainment"—including Walt Disney Pictures, Touchstone Pictures, and Miramax—generated almost $6 billion in revenue for Walt Disney Corp. But after the costs are tallied, the operating income for that segment of the business was only $110 million. Other companies posted much higher operating revenues. Note, however, that the companies' definitions of the business segments that house their studios may include other operations, such as television studios and theme parks, making it difficult in those cases to isolate the studios' contributions.

Studio Entertainment accounts for 23.6 percent of the revenue that Disney's top business segments generate, and only 2.7 percent of its operating income. Filmed Entertainment accounts for 21.7 percent of the revenue that AOL Time Warner's top business segments generate, and only 9.1 percent of its operating income. Entertainment accounts for 13.5 percent of the revenue that Viacom's top business segments generate, and 8.9 percent of operating income. Filmed Entertainment accounts for 27 percent of the sales revenue that News Corp.'s top business segments generate, and 15.5 percent of operating income. Pictures account for 7.7 percent of the sales and operating revenue that Sony's top business segments generate, and only 1.8 percent of operating income. TV/Film accounts for 31.2 percent of the revenue that Vivendi's top business segments generate, and only 23.6 percent of operating income.

Generally, then, the role of film for conglomerate ownership is mixed. Nevertheless, the major distribution companies are embedded in these larger structures. As Peter Bart, editor of *Variety,* has quipped:

> It's hypocritical for any of the studios to say, or networks to say, [they're] on the brink of bankruptcy, because obviously they live under the very handsome corporate umbrella of gigantically rich companies. I mean, they're not even companies. They're sort of nation-states. AOL Time Warner is a nation-state. So is Vivendi. (PBS/Frontline 2000)

It is important to note that the dominant film corporations are not omnipotent or infallible and are susceptible to economic ups and downs, recessions, depression, and other problems. The Hollywood companies in particular have continually encountered criticism for escalating costs, inefficient and unstable management, and luxurious habits and lifestyles. Nevertheless, the majors remain major.

THERE'S NO BUSINESS LIKE SHOW BUSINESS?

Maybe Hollywood is a unique industry. And maybe individual films represent risky enterprises. However, through a political economic lens, it is possible to question these assumptions. If indeed the industry is risky, it still manages to survive and companies—especially the major distribution companies that are connected to larger entertainment conglomerates—continue to thrive, having adapted various organizational and policy responses to such risks.

Despite the unique and cyclical nature of the industry, there are general, ongoing tendencies and characteristics that do not change. From a political economic perspective, it is important to emphasize that the basic motivation of the industry has not changed. Motion pictures developed in the United States as an industry and continued to operate in this mode for over a century. The primary driving force and guiding principle for the industry is profit, and capital is used in different ways to achieve that goal. Inevitably, individuals and companies come and go as companies move from one project to another, to other businesses, to new or more profitable technologies. Nothing is "sacred"—not even film. As Thomas Guback pointed out many years ago, "The ultimate product of the motion picture business is profit; motion pictures are but a means to that end" (Guback 1978). A Hollywood executive explained it this way: "Studios exist to make money. If they don't make a lot of money producing movies, there's no reason for them to exist, because they don't offer anything else. They offer entertainment, but you don't need studios to make entertainment. You don't need studios to make movies. The reason they exist is to make money" (Taylor 1999, 59).

The profit motive and the commodity nature of film have implications for the kind of films that are produced (and not produced), who makes them, how they are distributed, and where/when they are viewed. While it is common to call film an art form, Hollywood film, at least, cannot be understood without the context in which it is actually produced and distributed—an industrial, capitalist structure.

NOTES

This chapter is based on material included in Janet Wasko 2003, *How Hollywood Works* (London: Sage)

1. The U.S. film industry is regularly featured on television programs and magazines such as *Entertainment Tonight, Access Hollywood,* and *Entertainment Weekly,* although these sources focus mostly on celebrities and stars. Recent special programs on PBS *Frontline* in the United States and ITV in Britain have looked in depth at the U.S. film industry. Meanwhile, a plethora of books by industry insiders explore Hollywood economics, primarily for industry wannabes or investors. Examples include Cones 1992, 1997; Daniels, Leedy, and Sills 1998; Harmon 1994; Leedy 1980; Litwak 2000; Lukk 1997; Moore 2000; Sherman 1999; Vogel 2001; Wiese 1989. A few economists and business experts continue to focus on Hollywood economics (see De Vany and Walls 2001; Litman 1998; Borcherding and Filson 2000; Storper and Christopherson 1987). Within media studies, a branch of research called media economics has emerged, which sometimes includes the motion picture industry (see Gomery 1989; Albarron 1996; Picard 1989). Growing numbers of film scholars are examining film economics from a media economics or industrial perspective. For example, see Kindem 1982; Kawin 1992; Wyatt 1994.

2. Some of these analysts even argue that the conventional measures of concentration and competition are not applicable to the film industry. See Prindle 1993; De Vany and Walls 2001; Borcherding and Filson 2000.

3. Cited in Meredith Amdur, "H'w'd Burns as Feds Fiddle," *Variety,* 29 July 2002, 1, 51.

4. Garrison v. Warner Bros., Inc., et al., U.S. District Court, Central District of California, Case No. CV-95-8328, filed January 18 1996. Cited in Daniels et al. 1998, XXI.

REFERENCES

Aksoy, A., and Kevin Robins. 1992. "Hollywood for the Twenty-First Century: Global Competition for Critical Mass in Image Markets." *Cambridge Journal of Economics* 16, no. 1: 1–22.

Albarron, Alan B. 1996. *Media Economics: Understanding Markets, Industries, and Concepts.* Ames: Iowa State University Press.

Allen, Robert, and Douglas Gomery. 1985. *Film History: Theory and Practice.* New York: Knopf.

Amdur, Meredith. 2002. "H'w'd Burns as Feds Fiddle." *Variety* (29 July).

Balio, Tino, ed. 1976. *The American Film Industry.* Madison: University of Wisconsin Press.

Bart, Peter. 1999. *The Gross: The Hits, the Flops—The Summer That Ate Hollywood.* New York: St. Martin's.

Baumgarten, Paul A., Donald C. Farber, and Mark Fleischer. 1992. *Producing, Financing, and Distributing Film: A Comprehensive Legal and Business Guide.* 2d ed. New York: Limelight.

Borcherding, Thomas E., and Darren Filson. 2000. "Coming to America: Tales from the Casting Couch, Gross and Net, in a Risky Business." Independent Institute Working Paper, no. 22. www.independent.org/tii/WorkingPapers/Hollywood.pdf.

Compaine, Benjamin, ed. 1982. *Who Owns the Media? Concentration of Ownership in the Mass Communications Industry.* White Plains, N.Y.: Knowledge Industry Publications.

Cones, John W. 1992. *Film Finance and Distribution: A Dictionary of Terms.* Los Angeles: Silman-James.

———. 1997. *The Feature Film Distribution Deal: A Critical Analysis of the Single Most Important Film Industry Agreement.* Carbondale: Southern Illinois Press.

Daniels, Bill, David Leedy, and Steven D. Sills. 1998. *Movie Money: Understanding Hollywood's Creative Accounting Practices.* Los Angeles: Silman-James.

De Vany, Arthur, and David Walls. 2001. "How Can Motion Picture Profits Be So Large and Yet So Elusive? The Alpha-Stable Distribution." Proceedings of the Third Business and Economics Scholars Workshop in Motion Picture Industry Studies.

Dodona Report. 2001.

Garnham, Nicholas. 1990. *Capitalism and Communication: Global Culture and the Economics of Information.* London: Sage.

Gomery, Douglas. 1989. "Media Economics: Terms of Analysis." *Critical Studies in Mass Communication* 6, no. 1: 43–60.

Guback, Thomas H. 1969. *The International Film Industry: Western Europe and America since 1945.* Bloomington: Indiana University Press.

———. 1978. *Are We Looking at the Right Things in Film?* Philadelphia: Society for Cinema Studies.

———. 1989. "Should a Nation Have Its Own Film Industry?" *Directions* 3, no. 1.: 489–92.

Harmon, Renée. 1994. *The Beginning Filmmaker's Business Guide: Financial, Legal, Marketing, and Distribution Basics of Making Movies.* New York: Walker.

Harries, Dan, ed. 2002. *The New Media Book.* London: BFI Publishing.

Huettig, Mae D. 1944. *Economic Control of the Motion Picture Industry.* Philadelphia: University of Pennsylvania Press.

Jowett, G., and J. M. Linton. 1980. *Movies as Mass Communication.* Beverly Hills, Calif.: Sage.

Kawin, Bruce F. 1992. *How Movies Work.* Berkeley: University of California Press.

Kindem, Gorham, ed. 1982. *The American Movie Industry: The Business of Motion Pictures.* Carbondale: Southern Illinois Press.

Klingender, F. D., and S. Legg. 1937. *Money behind the Screen.* London: Lawrence & Wishart.

Leedy, David J. 1980. *Motion Picture Distribution: An Accountant's Perspective.* Self-published booklet.

Levy, Frederick. 2000. *Hollywood 101: The Film Industry.* Los Angeles, Calif.: Renaissance.

Litman, Barry L. 1998. *The Motion Picture Mega-Industry.* Boston: Allyn & Bacon.

Litwak, Mark. 1986. *Reel Power: The Struggle for Influence and Success in the New Hollywood.* New York: New American Library.

Lukk, Tiiu. 1997. *Movie Marketing: Opening the Picture and Giving It Legs.* Los Angeles: Silman-James.

Miller, Toby, Nitin Govil, John McMurria, and Richard Maxwell. 2001. *Global Hollywood.* London: BFI Publishing.

Moore, Schuyler M. 2000. *The Biz: The Basic Business, Legal, and Financial Aspects of the Film Industry.* Los Angeles. Silman-James.

Mosco, Vincent. 1996. *The Political Economy of Communication: Rethinking and Renewal.* London: Sage.

MPAA Website. 2003. www.mpaa.org.

O'Donnell, Pierce, and Dennis McDougal. 1992. *Fatal Subtraction: How Hollywood Really Does Business.* New York: Doubleday.

PBS/Frontline. 2000. "The Monster That Ate Hollywood." www.pbs.org/wgbh/pages/frontline/shows/hollywood/interviews/gerbrandt.html.

Pendakur, Manjunath. 1990. *Canadian Dreams and American Control: The Political Economy of the Canadian Film Industry.* Detroit: Wayne State University Press.

———. 1993. "Political Economy and Ethnography: Transformations in an Indian Village." In *Illuminating the Blindspots: Essays Honoring Dallas W. Smythe.* Norwood, N.J.: Ablex.

———. 1998. "Hollywood North: Film and TV Production in Canada." In *Global Productions: Labor in the Making of the "Information Society."* Cresskill, N.J.: Hampton.

Picard, Robert. 1989. *Media Economics: Concepts and Issues.* Newbury Park, Calif.: Sage.

Prindle, D. F. 1993. *Risky Business: The Political Economy of Hollywood.* Boulder: Westview.

Sherman, Eric. 1999. *Selling Your Film: A Guide to the Contemporary Marketplace.* 2d ed. Los Angeles: Acrobat.

Squire, Jason E., ed. 1992. *The Movie Business Book.* 2d ed. New York: Simon & Schuster.

Storper, M., and S. Christopherson. 1987. "Flexible Specialization and Regional Industrial Agglomerations: The Case of the U.S. Motion Picture Industry." *Annals of the Association of American Geographers* 77, no. 1.

Taylor, Thom. 1999. *The Big Deal: Hollywood's Million-Dollar Spec Script Market.* New York: William Morrow.

Vogel, Harold L. 2001. *Entertainment Industry Economics: A Guide for Financial Analysis.* 5th ed. New York: Cambridge University Press.

Wasko, Janet. 1982. *Movies and Money: Financing the American Film Industry.* Norwood, N.J.: Ablex.

———. 1994. *Hollywood in the Information Age: Beyond the Silver Screen.* Cambridge: Polity.

———. 2001. *Understanding Disney: The Manufacture of Fantasy.* Cambridge: Polity.

Wasko, Janet, Mark Phillips, and Christopher Purdie. 1993. "Hollywood Meets Madison Ave.: The Commercialization of U.S. Films." *Media, Culture, and Society* 15, no. 2.

Wiese, Michael. 1989. *Film and Video Marketing.* Studio City, Calif.: Michael Wiese Productions.

Wyatt, Justin. 1994. *High Concept: Movies and Marketing in Hollywood.* Austin: University of Texas Press.

9

The Fight for Proportionality in Broadcasting

Richard Collins

Clearly the nub of public service broadcasting is the extent to which it serves the public interest and, in so doing, forecloses the market or makes it difficult for others to supply services. This will be one of the nubs of Ofcom's (Office of Communications) responsibilities and it will be the absolute core of the judgments it will have to make at the highest level (Patricia Hodgson, chief executive of the Independent Television Commission (ITC) to the Joint Parliamentary Scrutiny Committee on the Draft Communications Bill, 23 May 2002).

BROADCASTING POLICY IN 2002

The year 2002 saw the United Kingdom drawing to the close of a broadcasting policy cycle. The government published its draft communications bill (DTI/DCMS, 2002a) proposing, at least formally, an end to a specific broadcasting policy and the beginning of policy and institutions for a "converged" and unified world of electronic communications. The Joint Parliamentary Scrutiny Committee (chaired by Lord Puttnam and henceforth referred to as the Puttnam Committee) was established to consider the government's draft reported on July 31. In turn, the secretaries of state responsible for the bill, perhaps thinking of the long grass, undertook to "look long and hard at the committee's recommendations" (quoted in the *Financial Times,* 1 August

2002, 2). The most important change foreshadowed in the bill is the integration of five established regulators, Oftel, the three broadcasting regulators——the Independent Television Commission, the Broadcasting Standards Commission, the Radio Authority—and the Radiocommunications Agency, into a new agency known as Ofcom. The measures proposed in the draft bill are, the government claims, intended to "keep pace with the rapid and revolutionary changes that have occurred" (DTI/DCMS 2002b, 3). Apart from a formal integration of regulators into Ofcom, what seems most striking about the draft bill is the number of provisions for broadcasting that reflect a simple rolling forward of established arrangements rather than restructuring of a kind commensurate with "revolutionary changes." Nowhere is the strength of the status quo more apparent than in the treatment of the British Broadcasting Corporation (BBC), which, although the United Kingdom's largest single broadcaster, remains substantially outside Ofcom's remit. True, as currently drafted, the bill gives Ofcom some jurisdiction over the BBC, but only in respect of most, but not all, the provisions of the so-called tiers 1-2 of content regulation and also of tasks now exercised by the Office of Fair Trading (independent production quota, competition law), the Broadcasting Standards Commission (privacy and fairness), and the ITC (licensing of the BBC's commercial services). The most important provisions of the regulatory regime, which will apply to the BBC, remain outside the draft bill and are to be embodied in the new agreement between the BBC and the Secretary of State for Culture, Media, and Sport. The draft agreement (published 31 May 2002) mirrors content regulation provisions in the draft bill but instead of the line of regulatory accountability running from the broadcaster to Ofcom, as is the case for Channel 4, ITV, and Channel 5 (all, formally at least, public service broadcasters), the BBC will be responsible to its own governors for matters that, for other broadcasters, are Ofcom responsibilities. In this respect the BBC is unique. It will be the only public sector communications undertaking outside the formal jurisdiction (for most of its activities) of a sectoral regulator.

EARLIER BROADCASTING POLICY CYCLES

Remaining outside Ofcom's jurisdiction is but one instance of the BBC's striking contemporary successes. Whether measured in terms of audience share, broadcasting revenues, or government support, the contemporary BBC rides high, particularly when compared to the corporation's position at the end of the two previous policy cycles. Each of these cycles (in 1987 and 1994) was marked by discussion of the BBC's status in a leading U.K. policy journal, *Political Quarterly*. Common to each earlier cycle was contributors' alarm at the threatened status of public service broadcasting[1] and the BBC's in particular. Indeed, two contributors to *Political Quarterly* in 1994 referred to a "sustained ideological assault on the ethos and organisation of public service broadcasting as a whole" (Kuhn and Wheeler 1994, 434). Such concern is easy to understand in a longer-run historical context. The policy debate in 1987 focused on the impact of the Peacock Report *(Report of the Committee on Financing the BBC)* published the previous year. Peacock (1986) had proposed breaking up the BBC (by privatizing Radios 1 and 2), opening up U.K. broadcasting markets, and fostering competition. The year 1994, though not marked by publication of so weighty a policy document as the Peacock Report, nonetheless saw contributors grappling with both the legacy of Peacock and the consequences of technical change that had made possible the powerful novel presence of BSkyB in the U.K. broadcasting market (following the introduction of direct-to-home satellite television to the United Kingdom in 1990). Commentators on the two previous policy cycles thus addressed a U.K. broadcasting regime in which the BBC would have, at best, a marginal presence and where government had lost its ability to control entry to the U.K. broadcasting market. Both developments, intellectual and technical, threw into question time-honored arrangements and assumptions—particularly about public service broadcasting.

In contrast, the dominant voices in earlier policy cycles strongly supported the BBC. Publication of the Annan Report in 1977, for example, resulted in a signal strengthening of public service broadcasting with the establishment in 1982 of Channel 4 and S4C. Annan also provided a ringing endorsement of the BBC as the "most important cultural organisation in the nation" (Annan 1977, para. 8.1) and recommended that the "BBC should continue to be the main national instrument of broadcasting in the United Kingdom" (Annan 1977, 476). This proposal echoed, almost verbatim, the 1960 finding of the Pilkington Committee that the BBC should "remain the main instrument of broadcasting in the United Kingdom" (Pilkington 1962, 288). Pilkington had awarded the third U.K. television service to the BBC (BBC 2 began transmissions in 1964). The Annan and Pilkington broadcasting policy cycles thus acknowledged the BBC's preeminence. In the 1980s and 1990s, rather than the expansion of public service broadcasting recommended by Pilkington and Annan, public service broadcasting was embattled.

The majority of the Peacock Committee had recommended that BBC Radio 1 and 2 be privatized, that 40 percent of BBC programs be supplied by independent producers, and that "well before the end of the [twentieth] century subscription should replace the licence fee" (Peacock 1986, para. 673). So too in 1994 was the BBC seen to operate in a hostile environment. Government had pressured the BBC to improve its internal efficiency and sanitize its news and current affairs coverage. It kept the BBC on a tight financial rein and secured the early resignation of an incumbent director general. The commercial context was no friendlier to public service broadcasting than was the political. The financial power of pay-TV was growing, denuding the BBC of programming (notably sports rights) it had once taken for granted. Advertising-financed radio and television was similarly resurgent. Classic FM had broken into the BBC's serious music fiefdom, and ITV enjoyed program funding considerably more generous than the BBC's. The measure of the BBC's retreat and decline from the sanctified eminence enjoyed by the "main national instrument of broadcasting" was the BBC's self-definition as a "complement [to] the enlarged commercial sector" (BBC 1992, 19).

THE BBC IN 2002

But in 2002, the BBC regained its former preeminence. The ITC awarded the BBC the task of reinvigorating, and reinventing, digital terrestrial television in July 2002.[2] The secretary of state for culture, media, and sport, Tessa Jowell, seemed to anticipate the outcome of the forthcoming review of the BBC's role, and the terms of a new Royal Charter (the current charter expires in 2006), when she expressed her pride in the BBC indicating that privatization was "highly unlikely" (quoted in the *Financial Times*, 5 June 2002, 4).[3] The secretary of state's support for the BBC has been echoed widely. Lord McNally, Liberal Democrat and a key member of the Puttnam Committee, was no less effusive in his support and stated (in the Joint Parliamentary Scrutiny Committee on the Draft Communications Bill, 23 May 2002) that "it is neither the British people's wish nor Parliament's intention to create a level playing field between the BBC and the commercial sector. The BBC is our broadcasting flagship and it is going to rightly have certain protections from the marketplace that are the way of delivering a robust public service broadcaster for this country."

The BBC currently enjoys a very favorable funding regime whereby the annual license fee is set to rise at RPI+1.5 percent (RPI = Retail Price Index) until 2006. McKinsey concluded that (ITC 2002a, 26) U.K. public funding per head for broadcasting was the highest of the thirteen countries[4] surveyed (and estimated total U.K. funding per head for broadcasting to be second only to that of the United States).[5] Public attitudes to public service broadcasting, revealed by BBC (1999) and ITC (2001) research, also appear highly positive and echo other positive performance indices. In 2001, BBC television accounted for 38 percent of U.K. television viewing and BBC radio for 53 percent of U.K. radio listening (ITC 2002; www.rajar.co.uk). Far from the current policy cycle threatening a "sustained ideological assault on the ethos and organisation of public service broadcasting as a whole" the most salient theme in the 2002 cycle seems, as the *Financial Times* (1 August 2002, 14) put it, to be maintaining "the present cosy arrangements." Arrangements that favor the BBC and scarcely resemble the pay-TV-based "sophisticated market system based on consumer sovereignty" (Peacock 1986, para. 592) envisaged by the Peacock Committee.

THE POLITICAL QUARTERLY DEBATE

The strength of the BBC's contemporary position is owed partly to supporters of public service broadcasting's success in wresting back the intellectual high ground of broadcasting policy from proponents of markets who, following publication of the Peacock Report, formerly mobilized the dominant ideas, which have proved to be strikingly fallible—such as the Peacockian predications that technological change would radically restructure broadcasting. Samuel Brittan's and Nicholas Garnham's articles in *Political Quarterly* (Brittan 1987; Garnham 1994) conveniently represent the positions of the rival proponents of markets and public broadcasting.

Brittan had been a leading member of the Peacock Committee, which concluded that technical change would both eliminate scarcity in the radio frequency spectrum and enable broadcasters to price access to broadcasting content and services through pay, or subscription, television. Broadcasting would thus become more responsive to demand, and consequentially the need for state intervention in broadcasting would decline, perhaps to extinction. Brittan summarized, "There may in future no longer be any physical need to limit broadcasting to a small number of channels. Instead there could be an infinite number of services which customers could select and pay for directly. The distinction between publishing and broadcasting would then largely disappear with a consequent extension of cultural diversity and freedom" (Brittan 1987, 20). Such an emancipation of broadcasting would have obvious adverse consequences for the BBC (as well as other incumbent broadcasters).

U.K. BROADCASTING IN 2002

Fifteen years on, Brittan's vision is far from realization. Technological change has introduced a new force into U.K. broadcasting: direct-to-home satellite television. But this new force does not obviously exemplify the "extension of cultural diversity and freedom" anticipated by Brittan. Broadcasting is a complex sector with a long supply chain, and at many points supply is constrained. For example, broadcasting is still channeled through a limited number of transmission infrastructures, and the broadcasting market (or markets) is dominated by very few suppliers. Supply to the final consumption market is constrained by restricted access to each of four main transmission infrastructures: analog terrestrial, digital terrestrial, cable, satellite.

Of these, analog terrestrial and satellite services have a potentially universal reach. However, digital terrestrial and cable, because of the high cost of extending service to remote communities, are unlikely ever to approach the levels of availability of analog terrestrial and satellite services. More than 99 percent of U.K. homes are currently served by analog terrestrial services.[6]

But only 24 percent of U.K. TV homes have satellite receiving equipment (virtually 100 percent of which is digital), only 14 percent (3.5 million) of TV homes subscribe to cable (these homes represent between 25 percent and 30 percent of those able to subscribe to cable because their homes are passed by cable networks), and of these 2 million have access to digital cable. Only 5 percent of U.K. TV homes have digital terrestrial television (ITC 2002).[7] Even the television program supply market, which the Peacock Committee proposed to open up through a 40 percent quota for programs made by independent producers, remains dominated by vertically integrated broadcasters, not least the BBC, which accounted for an estimated 50 percent of the 2001 television program market of £3.12 billion (Merrill Lynch 2002, 25).[8]

Constraints in supply are echoed in consumption patterns. In the year ending 31 December 2001 the five main public service television channels accounted for 80 percent of U.K. television viewing. The remaining 19 percent of consumption was accounted for by cable and satellite services (of which BSkyB services accounted for 6.1 percent of consumption).

BBC	38 percent
ITV (16 ITV companies including GMTV)	27 percent
Channel 4/S4C	10 percent
Channel 5	6 percent

If the free-to-air television market is regarded as a separate market to the subscription television market, the BBC accounted for 46 percent of television consumption in that market. Rebasing viewing shares to take account only of the free-to-air market, individual broadcasters' shares approximate as follows:

BBC	46 percent[9]
ITV (16 ITV companies including GMTV)	32 percent
Channel 4/S4C	12 percent
Channel 5	7 percent

Source: ITC 2002. NB percentages rounded.

If revenues are considered, a different picture emerges. Public service broadcasters accounted for the following percentages of overall 2001 U.K. television revenues of £7.770 billion:

BBC	21 percent
ITV	24 percent
Channel 4/S4C	8 percent
Channel 5	3 percent

The bulk of the remaining 44 percent of revenues is accounted for by cable and satellite at 40 percent with digital and other services representing the residue. If the free-to-air television market is regarded as a separate market from the subscription television market, and cable and satellite revenues are excluded, the BBC accounts for 38 percent of free-to-air analog television revenues (all of which is formally regarded as public service broadcasting revenue).[10]

A picture of a U.K. television market which echoes Garnham's (1994, 17) prediction of a "UK broadcasting market [split] into three roughly equal parts," the BBC, ITV (itself dominated by two firms, Carlton and Granada), and BSkyB. Each is funded by revenue streams that are not subject to serious levels of competition (with the qualified exception of ITV's advertising funding). A far cry from the expectation of a burgeoning pluralized market which led the Peacock Committee to envisage that broadcasting would change profoundly and quickly, with stage 2 of the transition to "a sophisticated market system based on consumer sovereignty" (Peacock 1986, para. 592) beginning "well before the end of the century" (Peacock 1986, para. 673). The current shape of contemporary U.K. broadcasting suggests that the "idea of a broadcasting market akin to publishing," to which Brittan (1987, 4) looked forward, is likely to be a very late-blooming flower.

FAILURE IN THE BROADCASTING MARKET

Garnham argued, in contrast to Brittan's confidence that technological change and reregulation would enable competition and pluralism to blossom, that the economic characteristics of broadcasting indicated an intrinsic tendency toward oligopoly in broadcasting. This tendency to oligopoly, rather than the pluralized electronic publishing type of regime envisaged by Brittan, would prevail. History seems to bear out Garnham's judgment that reduction of spectrum scarcity would do little to promote the diversity and freedom anticipated by Brittan.[11] History also bears out Garnham's prediction that economies of scope and scale would lead to an oligopolistic broadcasting market which would in turn demand government intervention to sustain broadcasting as an "arena for democratic argument . . . support for dramatic presentations of distinctly British issues, problems and experiences . . . the sense of social solidarity which the provision of a shared national or regional cultural space makes possible" (Garnham 1994, 18).

However, Garnham and other proponents of public service broadcasting did not consider two questions, each of which arises insistently in the current policy cycle. First, how do the putatively oligarchic tendencies of broadcasting economics play out in a public service context? Might not a public service broadcaster act in oligopolistic fashion, as Tim Yeo, MP, suggested (when he was shadow secretary of state for culture, media, and sport)? Yeo bracketed the BBC and BSkyB together as possibly abusively dominant broadcasters: "British television is now dominated by the BBC and Sky, both of whom are more eager to exploit their power than they care to admit" (Yeo 2002, 16). Second, if intervention is necessary to secure the diversity and pluralism necessary for broadcasting to act as a forum for democratic debate, how are we to know how much intervention is required? How do we know whether intervention is proportionate? And what answer should we give to the three-bears question of broadcasting policy—is the BBC overfunded, underfunded, or is public broadcasting finance just right?

In 1999, the Independent Review Panel on the Future Funding of the BBC (henceforth, the Davies Panel), chaired by Gavyn Davies (now chairman of the BBC governors), acknowledged the importance, and difficulty, of the question of proportionality when referring to BBC funding.

> Rather than funding the maximum amount that the BBC can usefully spend (a sum almost without limit) we aim to fund the minimum level of BBC output which is needed to maintain a critical mass of public service broadcasting in the changing marketplace. . . . Defining that minimum is no easy task. (Davies 1999, 9)

The Davies Panel referred obliquely but pertinently to the drive to over-maximize output which, it is often argued, is characteristic of nonprofit distributing undertakings such as the BBC. If "normal" commercial firms are driven to maximize profit as their key performance indicator, then public, nonprofit distributing firms are driven to maximize output and size as theirs. Output maximization may be seen as good (more output is better than less). But output may not be well matched to demand, may use resources wastefully (e.g., by entering markets prematurely or through overinvestment), and may lead a public firm to behave aggressively and anticompetitively, for example, by excluding rivals from markets.[12]

TOO MUCH, TOO LITTLE, OR JUST RIGHT?

Over the last two policy cycles, proponents of public service broadcasting have generally argued that the BBC has too little public funding.[13] Now, increasingly, voices are raised which suggest the BBC has too much, does too much, and too much of what it does is mimicry of commercial broadcasters' behavior. The *Financial Times*, for example, claimed that "the biggest threat to diversity is the BBC, which is moving into all sorts of new sectors" (1 August 2002, 14).[14] How may one judge whether the BBC has too much, too little, or just the right amount? The arguments deployed by Garnham, Graham, and others (that the broadcasting market fails, is likely to continue failing, and that a public sector presence is likely to serve the public interest) do not help establish *how much* the market fails and what level of intervention in the U.K. broadcasting market is proportionate to the extent of market failure.

If the level of intervention is a guide to the level of failure, prima facie, the U.K. broadcasting market fails comprehensively. The United Kingdom spends more per head on public service broadcasting than does any other country. Or, put another way, 56 percent of U.K. expenditure on television is spent on public service television (not counting the unpriced radio spectrum assigned to the BBC and Channel 4 and the discounted price for spectrum paid by Channels 3 and 5 in recognition of their public service mandates). Whether that level of resourcing is proportionate to the scale of market failure is difficult to determine. As the ITC acknowledged in its acerbic comment to the Joint Parliamentary Scrutiny Committee on the Draft Communications Bill, no clear definition of public service broadcasting exists against which to measure performance or allocate resources. The ITC judged that the draft remits for public service broadcasters proposed by government were "at such a general level that it is impossible to assess sensibly what Parliament could expect each to contribute" (ITC 2002b, 8).[15]

PUBLIC SERVICE BROADCASTING

Accordingly, public service broadcasting has often been defined performatively—as what public service broadcasters do. Again, the Davies Panel identified the issue succinctly: "Too often the BBC in effect behaves as if public service broadcasting is everything the BBC chooses to put out" (Davies 1999, 139). But neither a performative definition nor the time-honored British recourse to the sound judgments of sound chaps for a definition—recently memorably exemplified in the Davies Panel's confident statement that though the panel could not "offer a tight new definition of PSB" members were confident they "knew it when we saw it" (Davies 1999, 10)—can be a satisfactory guide to the conduct, funding, and governance of public service broadcasting.

The absence of defined broadcasting policy goals, coupled with an analysis of the extent to which the commercial market fails to achieve such goals, causes the proper scope and extent of public service broadcasting to remain mysterious. Too little has been defined for us to know whether the U.K. has too much, too little, or just the right amount of public service broadcasting. Indeed, one of the most striking of the opportunities missed in the current broadcasting cycle has been to (re)define public service broadcasting. There is, for example, no obvious reason why Channel 5 should be classified as a public service broadcaster, thereby enjoying a host of privileges including "must carry" status, and channels such as Artsworld, Discovery, and the History Channel should be denied this status.

If there is no satisfactory definition of public service broadcasting against which to calibrate financial allocations and benchmark the BBC's performance, how far does BBC programming differ from that of other broadcasters?

Does it deliver the "arena for democratic argument . . . and shared national or regional cultural space" that Garnham argued was public service broadcasting's raison d'être? Here we also encounter some difficulty, for there is no corpus of research and analysis that addresses sufficiently the program content and schedule composition of commercial and public broadcasters in the U.K. over a sufficiently long period for us to draw conclusions with confidence. A critic of the BBC might refer to a day when the BBC2 schedule was choked with billiards, and BBC1's was filled with soaps and "Diet or Die" programming (see Collins 2002), to substantiate the contention that the BBC preemptively mimics commercial broadcasters' programming and scheduling. But against such an argument, sustained by evidence drawn from analysis of all of 1/365 of one year of BBC output, a BBC proponent might adduce (as did Greg Dyke to the Joint Parliamentary Scrutiny Committee on 20 June 2002) the *History of Britain,* a Panorama program on Ireland in the 1970s, and a BBC2 series on pedophilia as exemplars of the distinctive public service character of BBC programming. More research is needed to establish how far the BBC's television output differs from that a profit maximizing broadcaster has transmitted or might reasonably transmit. In the absence of a decent-sized corpus of research on television content that would enable us to adjudicate between rival views on whether the BBC discharges its public service mandate, what other evidence may we consider?

DUMBING DOWN?

First, consider Merrill Lynch's recent study of U.K. free-to-air television (8 March 2002). This compared the channels' programming expenditure to their share of viewing in order to construct a measure of commercial effectiveness. Merrill Lynch identified (using 2001 data) a "viewership power" ratio of 1.07 for ITV, 0.81 for Channel 4, 1.00 for BBC1, and 0.89 for BBC2 and commented (2002, 25), "as a public service broadcaster, the BBC might be expected to have a materially lower viewership/programme spend ratio than the commercial sector. Interestingly, BBC1 has only a slightly lower Viewership Power Ratio than ITV at 1.00 compared to 1.07 for ITV. No other Public Service Broadcaster in Europe has such a high Power Ratio, which indicates that the BBC is either very commercial in its approach, or very successful at commissioning programming, or both." Merrill Lynch's comparison of relative efficiencies, measured by turnover per employee, of U.K. broadcasters found the BBC to be less efficient than Channels 4 and 5 and the two principal ITV companies, Carlton and Granada. The BBC achieved less than £200,000 turnover per employee whereas Channel 4 and 5 scored more than £800,000 per employee and Carlton and Granada scored £290,000 per employee.[16] These two fragments of evidence are not sufficient to draw a very firm conclusion, but the balance of probabilities suggests that the BBC is more likely to be very commercial in its approach than very efficient at commissioning programming.

Second, consider Mark Thompson's view that the BBC's success in securing a high audience share and public support may have been achieved by "dumbing down" the schedule or, as Merrill Lynch put it, by adopting a very commercial approach. Thompson, formerly head of BBC Television and now chief executive of Channel 4, in his celebrated speech at the Banff Television Festival 2000, acknowledged the justice of the charge of dumbing down. Thompson stated that the "charge [that the BBC has seriously weakened its scheduling of classical music] that these critics make, which is that there's much less than there once was, fewer hours, less impact, fewer risks. And they're right" (Thompson 2000, 6).

Thompson's choice of music as an example was particularly telling. The Annan Committee had claimed that "more than any other single influence the BBC has transformed Britain from a *Land ohne Musik* to a great centre of music making" (Annan 1977, para. 8.2). If there is too little to distinguish BBC programming and scheduling from that of commercial broadcasters, there is room to speculate about why this may be so.

Proponents of public service broadcasting (I among them) have argued that a successful public broadcaster must transmit popular programming for both pragmatic and principled reasons. Pragmatic, because if too few of those who pay license fees consume too little of the output they fund, then the legitimacy of public funding erodes. Principled, because viewers and listeners in general will consume the "merit goods" that are the core of public broadcasters' raison d'être only if they habitually use public broadcasting services. However, the Davies Panel proposed a third possible explanation— expansion and extension of its commercial activities might compromise the BBC's public service vocation. Davies stated that "as commercial activities expand, there is a danger of an unintended feedback into the type of programs which are made throughout the BBC. To put it simply, BBC producers may find it more attractive to make programs with obvious commercial potential than to make programs of a public service character" (Davies 1999, 90). If so, the BBC may reasonably plead that the commercialization of its values echoes the secretary of state's mandate, as part of RPI+1.5 percent license fee settlement, to raise £1.1 billion between 2000–2007 through cost savings (hence the Dyke jihad against "cabs, croissants, and consultants") and commercial exploitation of BBC assets.

PUBLIC SERVICE, THE PUBLIC SECTOR, AND COMPETITION

Perhaps the BBC should not be considered a public service broadcaster but rather a public sector broadcaster. If much of the programming it schedules differs little from what commercial broadcasters might provide, so what? There is little public dissatisfaction with public service broadcasting (e.g., ITC 2000). Why should programs that provide cost-effective gratification to viewers not be provided by a public sector body? But even a high level of satisfaction with the BBC does not mean all is well. If BBC schedules mimic commercial broadcasters' the BBC license fee is a form of compulsory pay television service paid for by all viewers whether or not they use BBC services. One might acknowledge (as did both Garnham and the Peacock Committee) that a public service table d'hote may provide license fee payers with good value for money, but few restaurants require diners to pay whether or not they eat.

There is then a case for the prosecution: A growing BBC with a tendency to exercise its market power and with too little to distinguish its programming from commercial rivals—rivals who, moreover, are disadvantaged by being denied the BBC's access to unpriced spectrum and funding via a compulsory levy on viewers. The case for the defense is that failure of the U.K. broadcasting market necessitates intervention, intervention to ensure universal provision of a portfolio of services, at affordable prices, superior in diversity, quality, and independence to what would be provided by commercial broadcasters. So far so familiar. What is new in the current policy cycle is the scope and scale of the BBC's move into commercial activities, its diversification from its core radio and television broadcasting portfolio, and the disparity between its secure access to real resources, guaranteed to grow at compound rate, and its rivals' dependence on the vicissitudes of the advertising and subscription markets.

COMPETITION POLICY AND THE BBC

Proponents of public service broadcasting have often (mea culpa) argued for the positive effect of public broadcasting on commercial broadcasters' performance and behavior. How could services of the scale of U.K. public service broadcasting, with a single supplier, the BBC, responsible for 53 percent of final consumption in radio; public broadcasters as a whole responsible for more than 80 percent of final consumption in television; and a single supplier, the BBC, responsible for 38 percent of final consumption (and 50 percent of the television program market) *not* influence the market as a whole? Latterly the argument has shifted, and increasingly it's argued that the BBC's influence has ceased to be positive. Here Garnham's argument about oligopoly is relevant. A firm (or group of firms) with market power is potentially able to exploit economies of scope and scale, lever significant market power in one market to affect outcomes in neighboring markets, for example, set prices at predatory levels, cross-subsidize, refuse to supply potential customers, and otherwise trade unfairly. The director general of fair trading, John Vickers (Vickers 2002, 4), referred to this distinctive, and general, characteristic of the broadcasting sector, stating that "broadcasting is a multi-layered industry, in which market power at one level of the supply chain may have far reaching effects at other levels. All this is relevant for analysis of competition in the sector" before making specific observations about the BBC referring to "the increasing tendency of the BBC to launch services on markets beyond its traditional public service broadcasting remit, such as web searching, has aroused considerable public interest and could raise difficult competition issues."

The theoretical concerns acknowledged by the director general echo complaints about the BBC expressed by, among others, Producers' Alliance for Cinema and Television (PACT), International Publishing Corporation (IPC) magazines, and Independent Television News (ITN).[17] Here it's important to acknowledge that there is no warm smoking gun. The BBC has weathered successfully all competition cases thus far brought against it. Nonetheless, prima facie, the BBC is at or close to dominance in a number of markets,[18] not just in final consumption markets but in neighboring markets further up the supply chain. It is sometimes forgotten that the BBC provides programs to its channels (in contrast to the separation of program supply from channel scheduling and broadcasting of C4 and ITV), inputs to program production (facilities, subtitling, orchestras), and that in many of these markets it also supplies to third parties. For example, the BBC has established a number of wholly owned subsidiary trading companies[19] including BBC Resources,[20] which provide services to the BBC and, on commercial terms, to third parties along the whole broadcasting supply chain from inputs to programs (facilities, outside broadcasts, BBC orchestras, etc.) thorough sale of programs to provision of channels to final consumers. These factors have led to claims that the Competition Act is insufficient to deal with the BBC's dominance.

The Puttnam Committee, in a delphic drafting of consummate skill, referred to "a number of unanswered questions about the precise extent to which the BBC's public service broadcasting functions justify market behaviour which might otherwise be subject to examination under competition law" (Puttnam 2002, para. 215). The director general of fair trading has also referred specifically to the BBC in his speech "Competition Policy and Broadcasting" (24 June 2002) and observed, "Should some broadcaster(s) have special immunity from competition law, perhaps on grounds of having a 'public service' remit? Not in my view. It is clear that some socially desirable services need subsidy to be provided. However, the provision of such services should not result in undue distortion of competition on the wider market place" (Vickers 2002, 3).[21]

Reviewing the distinctive features of broadcasting, which make competition regulation less straightforward than in some other sectors, Vickers identified four relevant issues: the relationship of high fixed and low variable costs, the stratification of broadcasting markets in virtue of different methods of revenue generation (but where there is no direct financial nexus linking broadcasters to most viewers), the multilayered character of broadcasting (which permits the leverage of market power in one sector of the supply chain to others), and the status of the BBC. Vickers hinted that he would favor Ofcom regulation of the BBC in the same way as other broadcasters. Not only was the effect of the BBC's public services on the U.K. broadcasting market likely to be considerable—in each of the final consumption markets of radio and television the BBC is the largest single player, accounting for 53 percent of radio consumption and 38 percent of television consumption—but the scale of the BBC's commercial activities is also significant. The BBC's accounts (at www.bbc.co.uk) for 2001–2002 show that BBC Worldwide's turnover was £660 million, BBC Technology and Resources' £357 million (of which £331 million was accounted for by intra-BBC trading). The BBC's commercial activities, depending on how intragroup trading is to be treated, can plausibly be stated to exceed £1 billion a year. Referencing this sum against a convenient commercial benchmark, the BBC's commercial activities approximate to three to five Channel 5s!

Moreover, there are prima facie grounds for concluding that the BBC is dominant (or close to dominant)[22] in more than one relevant market. For example, as already stated, the BBC accounts for 50 percent of the U.K. market for television programs. It is required to source 25 percent of programs in qualifying categories from independent producers, but PACT[23] has claimed that the 25 percent quota is a ceiling rather than a floor and that the BBC treats the 75 percent of the program market that is, in theory, open both to in-house and independent producers, as a guaranteed market for in-house production from which independent producers are effectively excluded.[24] PACT points out that the BBC's fair trading guidelines do not cover program supply and unfavorably contrasts the BBC's trading terms with those which obtain with the ITV network (where program acquisition and network scheduling is decoupled from the direct influence of the program-producing ITV companies). The BBC did not meet its independent production quota in the financial year 2001–2002.[25]

Formally, the BBC is required to secure approval from the secretary of state for new public services whereas new commercial services, ones which are neither novel or contentious, are permitted under the "umbrella" consent granted to the BBC for its BBC Worldwide commercial arm by the secretary of state. The BBC has made a broad distinction between broadcast services to many potential viewers and listeners, which it regards as public services, and those for specific targeted audiences (e.g., its joint ventures with Flextech), which it has deemed to be commercial services. But defining whether a service is a public service is the BBC's decision. To grant approval, the secretary of state must be satisfied that the proposed new service will not have a significant adverse effect on the market in question and, since 1999, public consultation (but not with competition authorities) has been required before the secretary of state's decision. Consents granted by the secretary of state have often been widely drawn and have permitted the BBC to introduce services (such as a search engine on the BBC website) that are unlikely to have been envisaged when consent was granted.

So that the BBC's commercial services are not unfairly advantaged (by drawing on resources provided to sustain its public services), the BBC has formulated its own commercial policy guidelines. Compliance is audited annually but audit (unless specifically requested by the BBC) customarily considers the compliance *process* rather than substantive issues. The aim of the BBC's fair trading commitment and its implementation through the guidelines is, of course, to ensure that the BBC's commercial subsidiaries operate at arm's length from publicly funded activities and are not unfairly advantaged by access to resources primarily funded for the BBC's public service objectives. There are obvious difficulties in ensuring fair trading in these circumstances. Benchmarks for the allocation of common costs between public and commercial activities are not always available, pricing intergroup transfers may not always be susceptible to referencing against objective norms, commercial arms of the BBC may benefit from information not available to third parties, and the distinction between commercial and public service activities may not always be easy to draw. The absence of a clear definition of the BBC's public service mandate is one relevant consideration, but the BBC's news-to-mobile-phone service provides a concrete example of the potential for such distinctions to be made in ways that may appear somewhat subjective. The service was launched first on a commercial basis but when found to be unviable commercially was reclassified as a public service.[26] There are, therefore, grounds to suppose that the BBC behaves as an output maximizer and is less constrained by financial incentives than a commercial broadcaster might be. These are, of course, characteristics that might be regarded favorably. But, being an output maximizer, the BBC has both power and incentive to abuse its dominance and thereby drive out diversity and competition—perversely reinforcing the need for public service broadcasting through a self-fulfilling prophecy.

CROWDING OUT

The impact of BBC entry into established markets (e.g., for facilities, program supply, etc.) is not the only relevant consideration. It is also worth considering the potential for core elements of public service broadcasting to "crowd out" actual, or potential, provision by other suppliers with a potential adverse impact on diversity and pluralism. Crowding out is a difficult argument to substantiate for it turns on a hypothetical question—would *y* have happened had not *x* happened? The Davies Panel took the problem sufficiently seriously to consider the matter (see its discussion "Fair Trading or Foul?" 91–94) through discussion of three worked examples. In one of the three cases the panel identified the possibility of using "licence fee money . . . to make programs of a type which could perfectly well be left to the private sector" (Davies 1999, 92). The panel clearly deprecated such behavior by the hypothetical public service broadcaster but acknowledged the difficulty in distinguishing between illegitimate crowding out and fair and appropriate competition.

Crowding out, if a reality, has the obvious potential for public service broadcasting to create the market failure (undersupply of merit goods by the private sector) that public broadcasting exists to redress. It is a form of self-fulfilling prophecy to which an output maximizing regime of public provision is potentially vulnerable. John Hambley, chief executive of Artsworld,[27] testified to the difficulty Artsworld, and other similar channels, experienced as a consequence of the mutually reinforcing advantages enjoyed by the BBC. The effect of these advantages was, he claimed, for the "dominance of the BBC to lead to a closed circle of types of programs made by the same program makers working within a commissioning structure which narrowed choices for consumers." Among the BBC's advantages Hambley instanced, among others,

- The privileged regulatory status of public service broadcasting whereby BBC channels enjoyed "must carry" status, making it more difficult for competing commercial services to secure access to transport infrastructures of limited capacity;
- The extent to which policy makers, e.g., in Data Creation and Maintenance System (DCMS), relied on the BBC for expert advice (a relationship which he described as "uncritical");
- The effect of the BBC's presence in a series of complementary neighboring markets;[28]
- Concern over BBC terms of trade in program supply;[29]
- The BBC's ability to cross market and promote its activities;
- The scale of the BBC's marketing spend (two interviewees separately mentioned the scale of the BBC's launch for BBC4, one estimating the BBC's expenditure to have exceeded £1 million).

Hambley testified to the chilling effect of the BBC presence on market entry and the impact of the BBC's expansion into digital services on Artsworld. He referred specifically to the crisis earlier in 2002 when closure of the channel was thought to be imminent and one of Artsworld's principal investors, the Guardian Media Group (GMG), withdrew from Artsworld. Hambley said, "If BBC4 hadn't come along GMG would have hung in there. They decided they couldn't face the might of the BBC." He continued, "I think BBC funding and size is disproportionate and will go on being so. One doesn't know what will come next." Hambley instanced another case of crowding out known to him, where investors decided not to proceed with a new U.K. television nature channel for fear of competition by the BBC. Geoff Metzger, managing director of the History Channel,[30] stated that he was "very concerned about the launch of the BBC's commercial service, "UK History," and referred to the aggressive business plans foreshadowed by the director of U.K. History, Matt Tombs.[31] Metzger further stated that "anyone entering the market now[32] does so with knowledge of much greater risk." The chief executive of Digital Classics,[33] Chris Hunt,[34] made the most powerful criticism of the BBC and stated that it "had the market power and the will to take out the opposition." Hunt further stated that "we would still be running were it not for BBC4."

Overall, Hambley deprecated the narrowing and commercialization of the BBC's program offer[35] and argued that "the dominance of the BBC leads to a narrowing of choices for consumers and to a lack of diversity in the voices available on television and radio." Perhaps this is special pleading, to which one might respond by echoing Mandy Rice-Davies's immortal words, "he would say that wouldn't he?" Perhaps. But proponents of a broadcasting policy seeking to foster diversity and pluralism and to ensure that viewers enjoy high-quality, merit-good programming must surely see the fragility of Artsworld and testimony to perceptions of the BBC's market power, whether exercised in a formally anticompetitive way or not, as chilling market entry as matters of concern. It is one of the many ironies in contemporary U.K. broadcasting that Artsworld's lifeline to survival came from BSkyB. Sky's support stemmed from its perception that subscriptions to its film and sports channels had plateaued and the consequential need, if Sky is to extend its subscriber base, to secure customers for different types of television, such as the arts programs screened by Artsworld.[36]

From the perspective of competition policy, there are thus several areas of potential concern arising from the BBC's activities. At the most general level there is the potential for a public firm to act more aggressively than a for-profit, investor-owned firm in excluding potential competitors from markets and maximizing output rather than returns. This, added to the tendency toward an oligopolistic structure to broadcasting markets identified by Garnham, suggests a greater potentiality for anticompetitive behavior by a public broadcasting undertaking than that of a private undertaking. To balance such potentialities, there are countervailing forces, including the fair trading requirements of the Competition Act 1998 (except insofar as the BBC undertakes specific public service obligations imposed by government); the compliance procedures established by the BBC; and the approval regime for new BBC services established by the secretary of state. Resolving whether there are actual, not solely potential, grounds for concern is a complicated matter. First, the markets would have to be defined and analyzed; second, assessment of the extent to which the requirements of the Competition Act were satisfied; and third, assessment of the adequacy of the act's provisions are sufficient and, if they were not, what sector-specific ex ante regulation (i.e., regulation beyond the bounds of the generic provisions of competition law) might be required. This too lies beyond the scope of this chapter.

EX ANTE REGULATION AND THE BBC

The director general of fair trading identified the scale of intervention represented by the BBC, "which provides services that are primarily free at the point of delivery in return for about £2.5billion per annum in taxpayers' money—not far off one day's gross domestic product for the UK" (Vickers 2002, 4). He asked, "Is general competition law, and the rules on mergers in particular, enough to constrain power and protect diversity and choice in broadcasting?" Vickers answered his own question by acknowledging that competition regulation is not always sufficient to secure public policy goals in broadcasting: "Given the inevitable imperfections of prescriptive conduct regulation in such a fast moving sector, there is a case for a degree of structural limitation, beyond general merger control rules, on some potential patterns of ownership of media assets. There may also be scope for specific regulations covering access to bottlenecks" (Vickers 2002, 3). The need for ex ante regulation in broadcasting has long been recognized, notably in regulation governing ownership, in order to foster and secure pluralism.

There is, I propose, a strong prima facie case for supposing that the scale of BBC activities and the mix between public and commercial activities constitute an instance (and certainly not the only one) of one of the "patterns of ownership of media assets" that the director general of fair trading identified and that, accordingly, ex ante regulation should apply to the BBC. It is not necessary for the BBC (or any other broadcaster with significant market power) to behave anticompetitively for market entry, with its potential to extend pluralism, enhance diversity, intensify competition, and foster innovation, to be chilled. All that is required is for potential entrants to apprehend the vulnerability of their nascent businesses to anticompetitive behavior by one or more incumbents with significant market power.

It may seem paradoxical to argue for ex ante regulation to redress the potential for abuse of market power by a public service broadcaster when public service broadcasting has itself been advocated as a form of ex ante regulation designed to countervail the inherently oligopolistic character of the broadcasting market. Although Garnham did not envisage public service broadcasting as potentially oligopolistic, there is no reason to suppose that publicly owned broadcasters are not as subject to the inherent economic properties of the broadcasting commodity as are privately owned broadcasters.

Ex ante regulation, following the formulation in the European Union Framework Directive,[37] may appropriately be imposed when "there are one or more undertakings with significant market power and where national and community competition law remedies are not sufficient" (European Parliament and the Council 2002, OJ L 108/33 recital 27). The BBC has significant market power and its capacity to move activities to and fro across the boundary between its public service and commercial roles suggests that competition law is insufficient to still apprehensions that it may use its market power anticompetitively. Of course, a regulator implementing ex ante provisions would still have to define markets and establish dominance (as it would if implementing the provisions of the Competition Act). But ex ante regulation would signal clearly what behavior is likely to occasion concern and potentially provides a quicker means of constraining anticompetitive behavior than would recourse to the Competition Act.

Ex ante regulation of the BBC might take any of a number of forms from structural separation to bringing the BBC under a strengthened Ofcom. The merits of structural separation have been widely rehearsed in the context of telecommunications, and both the Peacock and Davies enquiries canvassed some forms of structural separation of the BBC. David Liddiment (formerly ITV director of programming) has also recently argued for separation of BBC program production and supply from channel control: "Cut the umbilical cord between the BBC and its production arm" (Liddiment 2002, 5). Each recommendation identifies different parts of the BBC as suitable for separation but each advocates some form of separation.

An obvious possibility would be to reinforce the separation of BBC Resources enjoined by the Davies Panel (and not yet fully implemented) with a separation of schedule and channel management from program production. Bringing the BBC unequivocally under independent scrutiny and the jurisdiction of an Ofcom endowed with powers to regulate broadcasting akin to those currently exercised by Oftel in telecommunication licensing (e.g., to demand information, to prohibit undue preference and cross subsidy, and to impose penalties) provide another option. PACT and others have made highly specific suggestions, for example, that Ofcom be charged with promoting competition in content provision and distribution and that a code of practice be formulated based on the existing ITV networking arrangements but applying to all public service broadcasters. PACT has also proposed that the BBC, and Channel 4, be required to adhere to a "best value" procurement regime akin to that which applies to local authorities.

A clear definition of the BBC's public service remit will also be necessary—the ease with which the BBC's news-to-mobile service was redesignated from its initial status as a commercial service to its subsequent status as a public service testifies to how flexible the interpretation of public service may be. Without a clear definition of public service broadcasting there can be no sensible assessment of the extent to which U.K. public service broadcasters have discharged their mandates and whether the public resources they receive are proportionate to their public service tasks.

THE DRAFT COMMUNICATIONS BILL

Government has defined three headline objectives for U.K. media and communications. It aims for a "dynamic, competitive communications industry" for "universal access to a choice of diverse services of the highest quality" and to ensure that "citizens and consumers are safeguarded" (DTI/DCMS 2002, 3). The government has also undertaken that "Ofcom will have the powers necessary to prevent unfair competition" (DTI/DCMS 2002b, 5). But it is not clear that the draft bill provides Ofcom with the powers required to address the potential competition questions that might be posed by the BBC. Ofcom will have power to implement the Competition Act 1998 concurrently with the Office of Fair Trading and will also dispose of some ex ante powers when European directives on electronic communication services are transposed into the U.K. Communications Act. However, there are two areas where problems may arise from these arrangements. First, while Ofcom is responsible for reporting on the performance of public service broadcasters taken as a whole, it will lack jurisdiction over most BBC activities. Second, while the BBC's commercial activities will be subject to Ofcom regulation (in virtue of the concurrent competition powers shared by Ofcom and the Office of Fair Trading), Ofcom lacks power to regulate key areas of BBC activity such as broadcast content, educational publishing, web portal, and so on. Moreover, the distinction between commercial and public service activities has been defined (and is and may be redefined) by the BBC. Experience in U.K. regulation of telecommunications has vindicated the model of "asymmetrical" regulation, which has applied more exacting regulation to incumbents (chiefly British Telecom but also Hull Telephones/Kingston Communications where relevant) than to market entrants. Yet the "asymmetrical" regulatory model for broadcasting foreshadowed by the draft bill is one of *less* demanding Ofcom regulation for the incumbent BBC.

THE ROLE OF COMPETITION

Competition, though a headline objective for government and high among the duties prescribed for Ofcom, is a means to an end, not a value in itself. But competition, at best, establishes a self-regulating structure to markets. Well-functioning competition promotes innovation and efficiency in use of resources. A price system enables consumers to signal preferences. The scale and complexity of communications markets make planned development and detailed regulation either inconceivable or excessively costly or both— hence the government's advocacy of competition-based regulation. These are familiar arguments, and the realities of U.K. electronic communications, not least for the reasons given by Nicholas Garnham in 1994, fall far short of these theoretical ideals. Moreover, the U.K. experience of competition-based regulation is spotty. The case of telecommunications regulation suggests that the model has been made to work well enough by Oftel, using clear rules oriented to the consumers' interests. But the specter of Railtrack enjoins advocates of competition and structural separation to exercise considerable caution. Competition in supply of outsourced factors of production may well lead to an excessive emphasis on price, rather than quality, as the decisive selection criterion. But such risks must be balanced against others—notably the risk of the threat to pluralism posed by the exercise of market power by a dominant incumbent—whether private or public.

Garnham recognized the tendency toward oligopoly in broadcasting that follows from the superior economic efficiencies that may be realized by a single firm operating across several related markets. Recent history suggests that public firms are no less susceptible to such imperatives than are private firms, and the damage they do to diversity and pluralism is no less significant. The balance of probabilities suggests that both the economic objective of well-functioning competitive markets and democratic goals of diversity and pluralism are more likely to be achieved if the BBC is brought under a stronger regime of ex ante regulation than that currently proposed in the draft communications bill. A signal merit of both Brittan's and Garnham's discussions of broadcasting policy was their recognition of the intimate relationship in broadcasting between economic structure and political and democratic consequences. Though my discussion, like theirs, has focused on the economic, I hope that the potential consequences for democracy are clear. But in this, the third, cycle, the balance between embracing public service broadcasting as a counterweight to private oligarchy and avoiding the danger of public service broadcaster(s) becoming oligarchs that behave anticompetitively has tipped. In the two previous broadcasting policy cycles the balance of probabilities was that U.K. public service broadcasting was too weak. Now the principal U.K. public service broadcaster appears to be too strong. Regrettably, there is too little in the draft communications bill to address such concerns.

CONCLUSION

Unfortunately, it is difficult to avoid the conclusion that many provisions in the draft bill reflect a simple rolling forward of established arrangements for public service broadcasting rather than the result of a rigorous assessment of the contemporary performance, necessity, and value of public service broadcasting. Whether the scale and kind of intervention currently represented by U.K. public service broadcasters, and the level of intervention foreseen, is proportionate and appropriate is almost impossible to assess, for the U.K. has no clear definition of the deficiencies—actual, anticipated, or potential—of the broadcasting order that public service broadcasting is to redress. Undoubtedly there are deficiencies in the present, and any foreseeable future, U.K. broadcasting regime that justify a public service presence (e.g., to secure diversity in provision of news in some local U.K. broadcasting markets). If the broadcasting market is presumed not to be dynamic, public service broadcasting seems to make a positive contribution to diversity and pluralism; without it there would be fewer broadcasters. Radio and television provision would be less pluralistic and possibly less diverse. But if one assumes a dynamic market, this conclusion cannot so confidently be reached. Indeed, there is reason to believe that U.K. public service broadcasting, amply funded and enjoying a privileged regulatory regime, chills entry of new suppliers and services. The scale and character of BBC activities inhibit competition and militate against the achievement of core public service objectives such as diversity, pluralism, and quality. Whereas market opening initiatives, whether fostered by government (such as the independent producers' quota) or those initiated by commercial undertakings, such as Sky's entry to the U.K. television market, which ran against regulators' attempts to manage the market, suggest that diversity grows as competition intensifies.

Mark Thompson stated that the "future of public service broadcasting comes down to a question of belief, specifically, the belief that public service broadcasting can bring values and possibilities to bear on this grand digital future which the burgeoning, diversifying market won't" (Thompson 2000, 7). The ITC's audience research suggests this belief is widely shared in and outside Parliament, but the instruments, the *public service broadcasters* (and notably the BBC), charged with achieving the goals of *public service broadcasting* are likely to be tested severely. Competition-based regulation and the government's goal of fostering a dynamic, competitive, and innovative broadcasting market in the United Kingdom will, in the long run, create considerable pressure on the long established U.K. public service broadcasting ecology, however deeply and widely established public service broadcasters are currently valued by the U.K. public and however well the exceptional safeguards for the public service broadcasting status quo, currently embodied in the government's draft communications bill, survive. In the short term, the provisions of the draft bill justify John Hambley's melancholy judgment that the "pass has been sold." A better basis for the future would include clear and comprehensive Ofcom regulation of the BBC, a BBC that did less and focused more clearly on a distinctive, noncommercial, public broadcasting mission and mandate. This would necessitate clearer definition of public service broadcasting and a range of market opening initiatives (such as separation of BBC program supply from control of BBC channels) to foster entry, innovation, and initiatives from below.

It remains to be seen how much of the draft bill survives Parliament's consideration. At the time of writing, the balance of probabilities suggests that the provisions for the BBC will survive—not least because it is only the Conservative Party that has thus far explicitly voiced concern. But whether or not the bill, and U.K. public service broadcasting, survive in their present form, the structural contradictions between the dominance of public service broadcasting in the U.K. market and the doctrine of competition and markets makes the long-run future of U.K. public service broadcasting uncertain. The present structure of the U.K. broadcasting market thus lends support to Garnham's contention (1994) that there are strong tendencies toward oligopoly in broadcasting. Ironically, one of the strongest exemplars of Garnham's argument is the BBC.

NOTES

Thanks to Alan Bell, Tony Bennett, Martin Cave, John Hambley, Chris Hunt, Elizabeth Jacka, and Geoff Metzger for comments and information.

1. Official doctrine defines the five major terrestrial television channels (BBC1, BBC2, ITV, Channel 4, Channel 5), which together account for 80 percent of U.K. television viewing (ITC 2002), as public service broadcasting. Public service radio (some community services excepted) is provided solely by the BBC.

2. The BBC was awarded Multiplex B, and its partner, Crown Castle, was awarded multiplexes C and D. The BBC, Crown Castle, and BSkyB are partners in the ServicesCo company. ITC News Release 53, 2002.

3. In September 2002 the secretary of state approved the BBC's proposal for a further digital TV channel, BBC3.

4. Australia, Canada, Finland, France, Germany, Italy, Japan, Korea, New Zealand, Spain, Sweden, the United Kingdom, and the United States.

5. In 2001–2002 the BBC received £2.7 billion in public funding.

6. Channel 5 reaches only 80 percent of U.K. terrestrial TV homes.

7. Overall, 38 percent of U.K. TV homes have access to digital television as follows: satellite 24 percent, cable 8 percent, digital terrestrial television (DTT) 5 percent.

8. The independent producer quota was set at 25 percent, rather than the 40 percent proposed by Peacock. The BBC did not achieve the 25 percent quota in 2001–2002. PACT (see statement by PACT chairman Eileen Gallagher in *Media Guardian,* 29 July 2002, 4) has estimated that independent productions accounted for only 10 percent of the value of the BBC's television program budget.

9. In radio, the BBC accounted for 53 percent of radio consumption in the first quarter of 2002 (the BBC's radio share is overwhelmingly based on its dominance in the national, U.K.-wide radio market. BBC local and regional radio accounts for only 11.4 percent share of listening (some programs are simulcast on local and national services). National commercial radio accounts for 8 percent of listening. See www.rajar.co.uk/INDEX2.CFM?menuid=9.

10. Derived from the table of 2001 data at A23 in the draft regulatory impact assessment (DTI/DCMS 2002, 23).

11. Similar arguments were developed and mobilized by Andrew Graham, alone and also with Gavyn Davies; see, for example, Graham and Davies 1997. I have also added my piping to the basso notes of Graham and Garnham. See, for example, Collins 1990, 1997.

12. For discussion of public sector output maximization and anticompetitive behavior, see, for example, Lott 1999 and Sappington and Sidak's review (Sappington and Sidak 2000). Sappington and Sidak (2000, 290) state (in a review of Lott), "We find that public enterprises often have stronger incentives to pursue anticompetitive activities than do their private profit-maximising counterparts. Quite often, the less concerned the public enterprise is with profit, the stronger are its incentives to undertake activities that disadvantage competitors." If this analysis is applied to the

BBC, some murky waters and counterintuitive arguments emerge. For example, a BBC proponent might argue that the more commercial the BBC became the less prone it would be to act anticompetitively, whereas an opponent might argue that the more effective the BBC's "Chinese walls" between its public and commercial activities the more likely it would be to act anticompetitively.

13. Garnham, for example, argued that "linking the licence fee to RPI, let alone RPI minus x percent, places a sharp squeeze on the BBC" (Garnham 1994, 15). Graham concurred and advocated an "increase in the real revenue of the BBC" possibly from "increases in the license fee well above the RPI" (Graham 1999, 45). Garnham and Graham's arguments bore fruit and in 2000 the secretary of state authorised a license fee set at RPI + 1.5 percent until charter renewal in 2006–2007. The BBC's guaranteed growth in income contrasts with a decline in the advertising revenues that sustain its terrestrial competitors (these fell by 8 percent from 2000 to 2001 and are likely to have fallen further in 2001–2002) (DTI/DCMS 2002, table A 23, 23).

14. See also Elstein 2002.

15. The chairman of the Competition Commission made a similar point in his evidence to the Puttnam Committee on 27 May 2002.

16. The comparison with ITV is most relevant because of the higher degree of vertical integration in the BBC and ITV relative to Channel 4 and Channel 5.

17. Educational publishers have also expressed alarm at the prospect of the BBC entering, and perhaps foreclosing, the digital online educational market.

18. The Puttnam Committee referred to the "dominant market role" of the BBC (Puttnam 2002, para. 212).

19. The principal BBC subsidiaries are BBC Worldwide (exploiting BBC intellectual property in the United Kingdom and overseas), BBC Technology (links from studio to transmitter, etc.), BBC Broadcast (subtitling, etc.), and BBC Resources.

20. The Davies Report recommended sale of BBC Resources, stating, "We . . . consider that steps should be taken to realize the value of the business for investment in improving the quality of BBC services" (Davies 1999, 100). However, BBC Resources has not been sold. Indeed, a significant part of BBC Resources was reintegrated into the BBC Home Services in 2001. A BBC source argued that the facilities market is oversupplied and in consequence little would be realized from a sale. Balanced against the loss of quality control and of reserve capacity that would be entailed in a sale, the value likely to be realized would be insufficient to make a sale worthwhile. BBC Resources lost £13 million in 2000–2001 and £6 million in 2001–2002. It is open to question how a nonpublic firm would behave in like circumstances.

21. It is worth observing that concern about U.K. broadcasters' ability to exercise market power is not confined to concern about the BBC. I have referred earlier to Yeo's remark about the BBC and BSkyB, and Vickers also commented on BSkyB in this connection (discussion of BSkyB is beyond the scope of this chapter).

22. Implying a position where the undertaking in question can act to an appreciable extent independently of competitors and/or customers.

23. The Producers' Alliance for Cinema and Television, the trade association of independent producers.

24. PACT CEO John McVay, interview, 15 July 2002.

25. The BBC exculpates itself by claiming that the status of one of its suppliers changed during the relevant accounting period and could no longer qualify as an in-

dependent producer. However, this suggests that the BBC treats the independents' quota as a ceiling rather than a floor.

26. The BBC *Annual Report* for 2001–2002 includes other shifts of activities between commercial and public service sections, for example, part of BBC Resources from commercial to public service and BBC Technology from public service to commercial (BBC 2002, 81).

27. Interview, 12 September 2002. Artsworld is a U.K. subscription-financed digital television channel carried on Sky's satellite platform. Currently Artsworld has fewer than 50,000 subscribers. In mid-2002 there was serious concern about the prospect of the imminent closure of Artsworld's services.

28. He stated, "The BBC has so much commercial power it distorts the market for all of us—especially small channels like Artsworld." He instanced the lack of salience given to non-BBC services in the BBC magazine *Radio Times;* the BBC's ability to cross-promote its undertakings across a variety of platforms and media; and the use of the abundant resources of the parent BBC to fund promotional activity (e.g., a launch party for BBC 4), which Artsworld and other small competitive channels could not and cannot afford.

29. Hambley acknowledged that the separation of BBC Worldwide from the public service side of the BBC made it hard to formally sustain a case that the BBC was guilty of anticompetitive behavior of refusing to supply programs to a competitor. However, Hambley referred to negotiations with BBC Worldwide the previous year in which Artsworld expressed interest in acquiring rights to fifty BBC programs from a list of one hundred presented by BBC Worldwide, only to be told that forty-six of the fifty were no longer available. The BBC wished to reserve the programs in question for subsequent transmission itself. The author heard a similar tale from the chief executive of another U.K. television channel. The BBC declined to supply programs from its catalogue because it might, at an unspecified future date, wish to transmit them itself. Such decisions might be lawful commercial behavior but are not always easily reconciled with the general public interest in access to public service programming.

30. Interview, 2 October 2002.

31. See *Ariel*, 18 September 2002, 6.

32. That is, after the announcement of the BBC's U.K. History Channel.

33. An arts channel that went off the air in consequence of the BBC's impending launch of BBC4.

34. Interview, 30 September 2002.

35. *"Eastenders* five nights a week is no justification of the licence fee, a range of diverse, high quality programs is."

36. Hambley cited Sky's growing commitment to cricket and investment in "Music Choice Europe" as other cases in point.

37. The terms of the framework directive do not extend to content issues.

REFERENCES

Annan, Noel Lord. 1977. *Report of the Committee on the Future of Broadcasting.* Cmnd. 6753. London: HMSO.

Ariel. London: BBC.

BBC. 1992. *Extending Choice: The BBC's Role in the New Broadcasting Age*. London: BBC.

———. 1999. "Licence Payers Say 'Yes' to Proposals for New BBC Public Services." BBC News Release. www.bbc.co.uk/info/news/news202.htm.

———. 1999a. "Details of BMRB International Report on Attitudes to Licence Fee." BBC News Release. www.bbc.co.uk/info/news/news203.htm.

———. 2002. *Annual Report and Accounts 2001/2002*. www.bbc.co.uk/info/report2002.

Brittan, Samuel. 1987. "The Fight for Freedom in Broadcasting." *Political Quarterly* 58, no. 1: 3–23.

Collins, Richard. 1990. *Culture, Communication, and National Identity: The Case of Canadian Television*. Toronto: University of Toronto Press.

———. 1997. "Public Service and the Media Economy." *Gazette* 60, no. 5: 363–76.

———. 2002. "The Future of Public Service Broadcasting in the United Kingdom." In P. Donges and M. Puppis, eds., *Die Zukunft des Öffentlichen Rundfunks*, 111–30. Cologne: Herbert von Halem Verlag.

Davies, Gavyn. 1999. *Review of the Future Funding of the BBC: Report of the Independent Review Panel*. London: Department of Culture, Media, and Sport. www .culture.gov.uk/global/publications/archive_1999/funding_bbc.htm?properties= archive%5F1999%2C%2Fbroadcasting%2FQuickLinks%2Fpublications%2F default%2C&month.

DTI/DCMS [Department of Trade and Industry and Department of Culture, Media and Sport]. 2002. *A New Future for Communications. Communications Bill. Draft Regulatory Impact Statement*. Norwich: Stationery Office.

———. 2002a. *Draft Communications Bill*. Cm 5508-I. Norwich: Stationery Office.

———. 2002b. *The Draft Communications Bill. The Policy*. Cm 5508-III. Norwich: Stationery Office.

Elstein, David. 2002. "Paying for Auntie." *Financial Times*, 19 September 2002, 19.

European Parliament and the Council. 2002. *Directive 2002/21/EC of the European Parliament and of the Council on a Common Regulatory Framework for Electronic Communications Networks and Services (Framework Directive)*. 7 March 2002, OJ L 108/33.

Garnham, Nicholas. 1994. "The Broadcasting Market." *Political Quarterly* 65, no. 1: 11–19.

Graham, Andrew. 1999. "Broadcasting Policy in the Multimedia Age." In A. Graham et al., *Public Purposes in Broadcasting*, 17–46. Luton: University of Luton Press.

Graham, Andrew, and Gavyn Davies. 1997. *Broadcasting, Society, and Policy in the Multimedia Age*. Luton, U.K.: John Libbey.

ITC [Independent Television Commission]. 2000. ITC *Consultation on Public Service Broadcasting*. London: Independent Television Commission.

———. 2001. *Public Service Broadcasting What Viewers Want*. London: Independent Television Commission.

———. 2002. *Television Audience Share Figures*. 14 February 2002. www.itc.org.uk/uploads/TELEVISION_AUDIENCE_SHARE_FIGURES16.doc.

———. 2002a. *Comparative Review of Content Regulation*. A McKinsey Report for the Independent Television Commission. Mimeo. London: Independent Television Commission.

———. 2002b. *Memorandum to the Joint Scrutiny Committee on the Communications Bill.* 23 April 2002. www.itc.org.uk/uploads/MEMORANDUM_TO_ THE_JOINT_SCRUTINY_COMMITTEE.doc.

Jowell, Tessa. 2002. "Media Future Comes into View." *The House,* 27 May 2002, 12–14.

Kuhn, Raymond, and Mark Wheeler. 1994. "The Future of the BBC Revisited." *Political Quarterly* 65, no. 4: 432–40.

Liddiment, David. 2002. "Cut the BBC's Umbilical Cord." *Media Guardian,* 14 October 2002, 5.

Lott, John. 1999. *Are Predatory Commitments Credible? Who Should the Courts Believe?* Chicago: University of Chicago Press.

Merrill Lynch. 2002. *U.K. Free-to-air Television.* London: Merrill Lynch.

Peacock, Alan. 1986. *Report of the Committee on Financing the BBC.* Cmnd. 9824. London: HMSO. The Peacock Report.

Pilkington, Harry. 1962. *Report of the Committee on Broadcasting 1960.* Cmnd. 1753. London: HMSO.

Puttnam, David Lord. 2002. *Report of the Joint Committee on the Draft Communications Bill.* Vol. 1, Report HL Paper 169-I. HC 876-I. London: TSO.

Sappington, David, and J Gregory Sidak. 2000. "Are Public Enterprises the Only Credible Predators?" *University of Chicago Law Review* 67, no. 1: 271–92.

Thompson, Mark. 2000. "Zapped: Why Public Service TV Has to Change." Speech presented at the Banff Television Festival. www.bbc.co.uk/info/news/news245.htm.

Vickers, John. 2002. "Competition Policy and Broadcasting." Speech presented to the IEA conference on the Future of Broadcasting, 24 June 2002. www.oft.gov.uk/news/speeches/2002/competition+policy+and+broadcasting.htm.

Yeo, Tim. 2002. "Switching On to the Digital Changes." *The House,* 27 May 2002, 16.

10

Broadcasting and the Market
The Case of Public Television

Giuseppe Richeri

YET ANOTHER CRISIS FOR PUBLIC TELEVISION?

The problems and future prospects of European public television services have been widely studied and discussed from many points of view. Why, then, propose this theme as a subject for reflection? Have there been changes that open up new prospects in this field? I think so. I believe that in the past few years a number of different factors have been coming together in a way that creates a crisis in public television services and also marks the beginning of their final marginalization or their end.

Public television services have gone through a number of crises that have reduced their size and scale of operations. Of all the crises, the one with the biggest impact throughout Europe concerned ending the state monopoly on television service and inaugurating hitherto unprecedented competition between public and "commercial" broadcasters. In Italy, where this took place in the quickest and most chaotic way, the effect was probably greater than elsewhere, and the crisis manifested itself in various forms, many of which were also present in other European countries (Richeri 1986).

THE FUNDAMENTALS OF PUBLIC SERVICE BROADCASTING

In general, the drastic reduction of public service broadcasting services throughout Europe is the result of the progressive erosion of the principles that have traditionally justified a state monopoly in this field, and the subsequent ever growing criticism of the services provided by public service broadcasting, its forms of financing, its competitive advantages over private broadcasters, its relationship with government, and so on (Groombridge and Hay 1995).

By comparing radio and television legislation in the largest European countries, it is possible to identify at least four main ideas that, in part and in various combinations, have underpinned state interest in broadcasting services, the forms of public financing (license or public subsidy), and the identity and orientation of services in the "public interest" (Blumler 1994). The first and most neutral of these ideas has a technical basis. The shortage of broadcasting facilities for television signals (i.e., hertzian frequency) actually creates a "natural monopoly" that must be taken into account and managed in the interests of everyone. The principal aim has been to use this monopoly in order to provide television broadcasting throughout the country and to offer every citizen equal access to the programs. Public service broadcasting is therefore conceived of as a huge technical infrastructure that must guarantee universal access.

The second idea is of a cultural order in which public service broadcasting is given the task of satisfying the citizen's right to information, education, and entertainment as well as promoting national culture and shared values. Public service broadcasting therefore takes on the role of a great national education agency that supports, integrates, and develops the pedagogical functions of the school.

The third idea is of a political nature and is based on the desire to guarantee participation and pluralism. Broadcasting services, therefore, have a fundamental role in democracy: public services have a duty to broaden citizen participation, guarantee freedom of information, and embrace all forms of political, social, and cultural trends. Public radio and television constitute the great modern agora, where a plurality of voices is heard and where public opinion is formed. The fourth idea has a legal basis in which television and radio guarantee the right to freedom of expression and information as laid down by constitutions throughout Europe. Since public service broadcasting can be used to assert these rights, it should be promoted and made effective.

These key ideas on which public service broadcasting and the monopoly system are based have come under attack with various degrees of intensity, depending on the country, because of technical factors, political reasons, or a changing social and cultural climate. It is important to remember this fact and the trauma and difficulties it has caused many European public service broadcasters (Iseppi and Bossi 1998).

CHANGE IN THE 1980s

From the 1980s on, scientific and technological progress in the electronics, optical electronics, and aero-spatial fields created new opportunities. New prospects for growth in the transmission of radio-electrical signals were opened up. Improvements in transmission and reception quality and better management of hertz frequencies created greater channel availability. At the same time, more attention was focused on the fields of satellites and cable networks, leading to an increase of broadcasting channels and television signal delivery. The first idea to be rejected was the "natural monopoly." The change from a situation where frequencies were scarce to one where there was an abundance of available channels demolished one of the strongest arguments of even the most resolute defenders of public monopoly (Foster 1992).

During the course of the 1980s, the ideological and cultural climate changed considerably as a result of a combination of three factors: on an individual level a "return to the private," on the economic level the ideology of competition and the company, and on a social level the crisis of the welfare state. This helped weaken the idea of public broadcasting based on its role as a service and as a cultural and social promoter and based on public financing. At the same time, the public to which the radio and television services catered was no longer homogeneous and unified, but rather a number of publics with increasingly fragmented characteristics, interests, and tastes. Furthermore, the various audiences were increasingly more educated and had more diverse tastes in both origin and content.

The idea of a public service that satisfied the presumed cultural needs of an indistinct mass of viewers was at odds with the reality of a plethora of audiences that had moved on from needs to cultural demands, had distinct tastes, and was able to independently choose from the various products offered and broadcast by the diverse systems and channels. From many quarters it was claimed that public service broadcasting alone was not able to deal adequately with the new situation and that private television companies could guarantee the multiplicity of supply needed to satisfy the ever more diverse cultural demand (Missika 1997).

The cultural need for a public service broadcaster therefore became less evident and sustainable. From a monopoly position, public radio and television became one of the players in competition with other private players. In the same way, the political idea on which public television was based became undermined. Freedom of expression and pluralism were no longer regarded as rights under threat, which had therefore to be protected and guaranteed within the confines of public service broadcasting, but rather as freedoms. From a political point of view, the problem was not that of guaranteeing a space—public television—for exercising freedom of expression and pluralism but of allowing this freedom to express itself through a variety of means and mediums.

In many quarters, it was therefore claimed that competition and comparison could define space for freedom and pluralism better than a monopoly could. Finally, it was argued that the legal notion of the "public interest" attributed to public television could be applied to all public and private television companies, as long as appropriate regulations were in place ensuring that private enterprises kept their sphere of activities within public interest objectives (independence and pluralism of information and culture, national program broadcasting quotas, advertising limits, protection of minors, etc.).

The criticism and undermining of the key principles on which public service broadcasting and monopoly practice were based, even if they were questionable in part, have caused a loss of legitimacy and a search for a different role. Public television must find a new identity within the new configuration of public–private television that allows it to differentiate itself from private television and to take on the role created by the changed context of the 1990s (internationalization, technological development, multimediality, etc.).

Without competitors, public service broadcasting based its activities on the logic of supply: the great presumption of public television was to give the public what was "good" for it. According to this logic, production and programming were the paramount functions of television. Going over to a plurality of competing companies, television activity is now based on demand: audience background, behavior, and consistency are now at the center of attention and audience ratings become the measure of success since, in a competitive environment, public viewing figures are not a secondary consideration but something that needs to be tackled with success (Richeri 1992).

THE CRISIS ON VARIOUS FRONTS

In Europe, public service broadcasting had to quickly face up to a competitive situation without the necessary means, know-how, or policies. For a long time, its identity was tied to its functions as a public service, which were more and more conditioned by the need to face up to competition. This has meant focusing on the audience as the market on which advertising revenue depends and, within limits, to justify the fact that public financing is the exclusive province of public television. In Europe during the last few years, public service broadcasting has had to cope with three distinct crisis factors. Above all there has been *a legitimacy crisis*. Freedom of expression, public access, and political and cultural pluralism, which, at least theoretically, characterized and legitimized the work of public broadcasters, now seem better guaranteed by competition among a variety of broadcasters.

Second, there has been a *financial crisis:* The change from monopoly to marketplace has had a profound effect on public television costs and income. Competition has caused a steady increase in daily broadcasting hours,

Table 10.1.   Revenue Share per Television Company Type (percentage)

	1990	1995	2000	i.m.a.
Pay TV	6.1	13.9	22	22.9
Commercial TV	37	34	32	6.5
Public Service TV	56.9	52.1	46	5.8
Total	100	100	100	8.1

Source: Processed data from Observatoire Européen de l'Audiovisuel and Radiotelevisione Italiana.
Note: i.m.a. = average investment per year

in the costs for acquiring television rights (for sports and entertainment), and in the fees for the most popular and attractive TV professionals and personalities (presenters, *compères,* anchormen, etc.). But income has not grown at a parallel rate (Peacock 1986). Third, there has been an *identity crisis*: Public broadcasters have been obliged to change the very basis of their identity moving from the principle of supply to that of demand, focusing no longer on program quality but on audience quantity (Tracey 1998).

One way or another, public broadcasters have got over the crisis caused by the new competitive context without abandoning the objectives for which they were created. However, they have had to give up some of their distinguishing features as well as an increasing number of viewers (Giauque and Perellon 1997).

Today in Europe, public corporations continue to occupy a central position in the television market. At a European level they control 46 percent (see table 10.1) of all the resources destined for terrestrial television, and their share of the viewing public ranges from 30 percent to 50 percent in every European country.

Generally speaking, they still offer a better guarantee than commercial broadcasting of universal access to the television service, information pluralism and cultural diversity, support for production, and diffusion of national cultural production.

Throughout Europe today, public television is facing new problems that may relegate it to a marginal role and thus change the characteristics of present-day television systems.

INCREASES IN COSTS AND INVESTMENTS

The first problem concerns the growing inflation of costs for production or acquisition of the most attractive television production such as fiction and sport (Jezequel and Lange 2000). This prevents public television from maintaining high-quality schedules for fiction and entertainment, which in most cases do not differ from those of their commercial competitors. However, an even more difficult situation was created by the unprecedented explosion in spending for rights to sporting events (Oliver 2001). Soccer is a classic case.

In the last ten years the rights for broadcasting premier league matches have risen exponentially everywhere. With respect to 1990 they are forty-three times higher in the United Kingdom, eighteen times higher in France, and ten times higher in Italy. However, there have also been sharp cost increases in the rights to broadcast attractive sporting events like Formula 1 motor racing, tennis, and skiing, not to mention the Olympics or the world soccer championships.

Public television corporations have found it increasingly difficult to meet these costs, and the most attractive sporting events have in many cases disappeared from their schedules with a consequent significant loss in their popularity. During the first half of 2002, there were signs suggesting an inevitable reduction in payments for rights to televising sports events, in particular soccer. On the one hand the crashes of the Kirch group in Germany and ITV Digital in the United Kingdom were largely put down to the excessively high costs incurred for obtaining the rights to sporting events. On the other hand, the television rights to the world soccer championships in summer 2002 were offered at such high prices that in some countries there were no buyers, in others negotiations were difficult and forced significant price reductions, in others the match broadcasts did not generate sufficient advertising revenue to cover the rights costs.

Although an unbreakable ceiling seemed to have been reached, when the autumn round of negotiations for the rights to the sporting events for the following seasons started, prices, especially for the rights to soccer, continued to rise in most European countries. In France, in order to secure the television rights to the French First Division championship (Ligue 1), Canal Plus agreed to pay €480 million for the next three years as opposed to the €320 million paid for the previous three years.

The explosion in the cost of programs that traditionally symbolized public service broadcasting is accompanied by the need to maintain high investments that often do not generate sufficient returns to compensate (Arthur Andersen 1998) The second problem concerns the continuously growing investment necessary to keep a central role in the national broadcasting system. The high turnover rate of the technical means of production and broadcasting, brought about by increasing technological change, forces all broadcasters to update constantly. This becomes more demanding for public broadcasters because they have to guarantee everybody cutting-edge technical quality and must constantly update equipment, even if they have yet to pay for it.

The development of new telecommunications networks capable of supplying editorial content in more accessible, widespread, and customized forms opens up new areas for growth and competition where public broadcasters must be present and maintain high levels of quality. However, these activities are often very costly, with uncertain or much delayed returns. This situation forces more and more public broadcasters to develop business policies that try to increase their incomes. But these kinds of activities do not reflect the nature of public service. Such is the case with regards to cable or satellite theme channels, Internet services, and those related to interactive TV that are offered on digital television platforms.

Creating a website has cost some public broadcasters (e.g., the BBC) up to €150 million; high-range theme channels cost the public service broadcasters on average between €25 million and €50 million per year, and high levels of investment are needed to set up and manage interactive TV services. However, the forms and uses of public broadcaster financing impose restrictions that reduce or prevent the commercial exploitation of these activities.

RESOURCE RESTRICTIONS

An increase in resources proportional to the sharp increase in costs caused by content price inflation and by the need to increase investments in technological updating and diversification of services and assistance has not occurred.

Between 1996 and 2000 the average annual rate of growth of revenue of public television in the European Union collected through public financing (license fee, aids, grants, etc.) was 3.3 percent, which in most cases was just slightly higher that the average rate of inflation (table 10.2). It is interesting to note that in the same period

1. public television revenues derived from commercial activities (advertising, sponsoring, program sales, merchandising, etc.) increased at an annual rate of 8.5 percent;
2. the proportion of commercial revenues in public television financing has gone up from 29 percent to 32 percent;
3. in commercial television this has grown at an average rate of 17.7 percent;
4. the share of public assets in overall European broadcasting financing has fallen sharply from 38 percent to 27 percent.

The license fee paid by all television owners, which makes up about 90 percent of public financing, is a tax that depends on political decisions. Governments are reluctant to increase it because a tax rise is unpopular and the tax itself is coming under increasing criticism (Richeri 1992). The criti-

Table 10.2.   Revenues of Public Service Television in the European Union (1996–2000) (€billion)

	1996	2000	a.a.r.g.
Public income	14.1	17.2	3.3%
Commercial income	5.99	8.52	8.5%

Source: European Audiovisual Observatory, 2002.
Key: a.a.r.g. = average annual rate of growth

cism is of three kinds: the first refers to the fact that the audience share of public service channels is in slow but continual decline, while the fee is paid by all viewers irrespective of the use made of it. The second refers to the fact that the fee affects direct or indirect competition between private and public-service broadcasters (one competes for audience share to improve advertising revenue while the other does so in order justify its role, although both reasons apply in the case of some public-service broadcasters) because it gives a big advantage to the latter. The third refers to the fact that, in most cases, you cannot tell the difference between public TV and commercial TV programs, while the broadcasting of programs which are supposed to be financed by the fee is steadily going down. As a result large increases in the license fee will become more and more unlikely (Davies 1999).

Between 1996 and 2000 public television advertising revenue in the EU rose overall by 7.6 percent—less than the rate of inflation recorded in most European economies. At the same time, the advertising revenue of the private broadcasters rose in monetary terms by 12.5 percent (table 10.3). Public broadcasters who also obtain revenue through advertising (like France Television, Rai in Italy, and ZDF and ARD in Germany) cannot substantially increase this resource for mainly three reasons. In some countries, the advertising revenue of public service broadcasters cannot exceed the ceiling set by law to limit their influence. Moreover, public television channels schedule less time for advertising than is permitted to commercial broadcasters.

The third reason is to limit the negative effects excessive pursuit of audience share could have on public television program content. Quite apart from the influence of the general economic climate, it is unlikely that public television channels can record sharp increases in advertising revenue where it is allowed.

State funding of public television for the supply of special services (destined for school, for abroad, etc.) cannot provide solutions either. On the one hand the quantity of funding is based on the cost of the service requested, and so there is little margin for its use in covering other costs. On the other hand, any form of state financing of public television is carefully controlled by the European Union with the aim of avoiding public funds interference in the market.

Table 10.3. Television Advertising Revenue in the European Union (€million)

	1996	*2000*	*a.a.r.g.*
Public TV	4.1	5.48	7.6%
Private TV	10.2	17.04	12.5%

Source: European Audiovisual Observatory, 2002.
Key: a.a.r.g. = average annual rate of growth

Some European public broadcasters have ventured into financial activities (equity interests in commercial companies; for example, France Television has shares in Television par Satellite, a pay-TV digital platform; Rai in Tele+, an Italian pay-TV channel) and commercial ones too (the sale of products or television channels, activities particularly significant in the case of the BBC and Rai who set up theme channels and sell them to pay-TV platforms).

However, these activities have and will continue to have secondary roles since they have nothing to do with the institutional role of public television; their excessive growth would be in contradiction with the objectives of a public service.

EUROPEAN UNION RESTRICTIONS

In the second half of the 1990s, the European Union had to intervene to define the boundaries of public television more rigorously. There were two reasons for this move. On the one hand, some of the main private European broadcasters (TF1, Mediaset, Antena 3, Telecinco, etc.) criticized the various forms of financing public television received from the state in different countries (revenue derived from license fees plus various subsidies, increases in capital, loans on easy terms, contributions, etc.). The consequence of such financing for public television was its competitive advantage in the audience rating war and in acquiring advertising investment. On the other hand, a number of critics observed that public television program content resembled private television too much as a result of competing with it and experiencing a loss of identity and original role. Public television programming was (and still is) accused of abandoning variety of supply and quality, which public service broadcasting should guarantee, in favor of scheduling programs aimed solely at conquering high viewer ratings.

The intergovernmental European conference, held in Amsterdam in June 1997, confirmed the right of state members to finance their public radio-television services but imposed certain restrictions. In the Protocol of Amsterdam, the document that contains the conference resolutions, it is stated that public service broadcasting in the member States of the European Union is "directly linked to the democratic, social and cultural needs of each society as well as to the need to preserve pluralism in the media." But the right of state members to finance public service broadcasting is recognized "in so far as such funding is granted to broadcasting organisations for the fulfilment of the public service remit as conferred, defined and organised by each Member State and insofar as such funding does not affect trading conditions and competition in the Community."

In the protocol, public service is not restricted to a specific company like a public television company, but it is possible to award public financing (license fees, etc.) to private companies that agree to insert public service programs (informational, cultural, educational, for minorities and the socially discriminated, etc.). Furthermore, it is clearly stated that public financing is legitimate if it is designed to carry out a remit that is conferred, defined, and specifically organized to be in a position to identify programs that are within the remit with respect to other television programs.

Since then in Europe it has become necessary to identify and separate much more clearly than before public service state-funded activity from commercial activity that cannot be financed with public funds.

The application of the Protocol of Amsterdam has been very slow and in some cases is still ongoing. It is a difficult process that in some ways implies a fundamental overhaul of existing public television organizations. Its application basically requires three specific steps. First, as mentioned before, it is necessary to define exactly what public service broadcasting consists of so that its characteristic elements with respect to private television broadcasting can be determined. This is the job of the state (government, parliament, authority, etc.).

Analytic accounting must be applied in order to precisely identify program costs (and measure how much public financing has been invested). Apart from the direct external costs (of the suppliers), you need to identify the internal direct and indirect costs (as a proportion of general costs) that can be attributed to each program. On this basis you can carry out separate accounting between public service activities and commercial activities and find out how public financing is used to avoid its being employed in activities that can distort the market, such as competition between public and private television.

In countries where public television is subject to the pressure of audience ratings, this has created some problems that do not have easy solutions. Up to what point is it possible to distinguish in a discriminating way the contents of a television channel that is predefined as being within the remit of a public service from those that do not come within that remit? It appears difficult to distinguish a public service TV serial, show, light music concert, or talk show from its commercial counterpart just as it is difficult to characterize the connection between spectacular sporting events and public service. How far is it possible in the overall expenditure of a television schedule to credibly ascertain the costs of public service programs (financed by the license fee) with respect to those that are not categorized as such and can only be financed by advertising (sponsors, etc.)? In reality, the path to follow if European Union indications are to be respected cannot be that of distinguishing public service programs, financed by a tax, from others financed by advertising, but by separating according to channel.

The most probable result with this approach, which has been at the center of debate in many countries, especially Italy and France, is that the public service channel or channels will find themselves bereft of most attractive, popular so-called commercial programs, and will have significantly reduced audiences. Meanwhile, the channels with commercial-type activities, which have been wrongly managed until now by public broadcasters, will sooner or later be privatized.

On the privatization of public service broadcasting, a topic that is much discussed in many European countries, the proponents of this solution are growing in numbers. This prospect has reached its most advanced stage in Italy, where the government recently proposed a law on television reform that provides in the short term for the privatization of RAI (the Italian public service broadcasting company), using a mechanism that should guarantee broad-based shareholding (no party will be able to hold more than 1 percent of the capital).

THE EVOLUTION OF TELEVISION SYSTEMS

The general evolution of television systems does not favor the prospects of public service broadcasting. In all European countries and elsewhere, the television system is characterized by four notable trends. The continuing multiplication of television channels, which until now have used satellites and cable television networks, can also continue in the next few years through new technical platforms such as terrestrial digital television and broadband networks. It is now difficult to identify the resources necessary to sustain recent projects, those about to take off, or those in preparation. It is certain, however, that in the next few years in Europe, the number of multichannel households will grow as a result of the development of digital television platforms and the increasing supply of both free and pay-TV channels by both public and private broadcasters. The experience of countries where there are a large number of households who have access to a wide range of television services indicates an interesting development, which is the progressive splintering of the audience due to the growing number of channels.

What happened in the United Kingdom is a case in point. In 1988, before the advent of the multichannels of Sky Television and then BSkyB, the BBC picked up 50 percent of audience share: BBC1 had 38 percent and BBC2 had 11 percent. In 2002, in households equipped with cable (NTL and Telewest) or satellite channels (BSkyB), the BBC had 27 percent of audience share: BBC1 20 percent and BBC2 7 percent. The situation in the United Kingdom mirrors what happened to the three big networks in the United States over the last twenty years and indicates which way television is going in other European countries. The channels penalized by this development are not only the public TV channels, but all the traditional big free-access all-purpose channels. In other words, development in European television systems is leading toward a structural situation where public television (and not only) will probably experience a constant reduction in audience share. This trend will inevitably reach a point where public TV audience ratings will no longer be high enough to justify its public interest role, which is the basis for its public financing: if the average overall audience of the public broadcaster falls below a certain level (20 percent?) it would seem more difficult to oblige all TV households to pay a license fee.

Another difficult problem now arises. The average hourly broadcasting cost per viewer will increase, reducing the possibility of maintaining high production standards and acquiring attractive quality content. This situation already exists in some circumstances and will probably get worse over time. It is therefore probable that as the television audience continues to splinter due to the increasing number of channels, it will become necessary to reduce average hourly broadcasting expenditure, thereby causing further loss of audience share and creating a downward spiral that will be difficult to check. The alternative is to maintain program investment at current levels, with the risk that the cost per viewer of public service broadcasting reaches levels that no government or authority can possibly justify.

THE IMPACT OF DIGITAL TELEVISION

The prospect of abandoning analog and going to digital TV, instead of brightening the outlook for public service broadcasting, suggests it is at the end of the road. Let's see why.

All European governments have plans on their agenda to go totally digital, even though there are a lot of doubts as to when this might happen. The terrestrial television sector, by far the most important, will, in fact, develop digitally much more slowly than predicted, especially since households with a modest income need to be taken into account. In 2003, digital television is now a reality throughout Europe. The most common platform at the moment is that offered by satellite and, in some countries, cable networks are rapidly updating to digital. Meanwhile, the first experiments in terrestrial digital carried out in Spain and the United Kingdom have not been successful economically and have had to change ownership and business model. Nevertheless, the aim of a quick total substitution of analog terrestrial television with a digital version is still very much to the fore.

It is a very complex aim to accomplish because the complete abandonment of analog television can only come about when all households are equipped with televisions that are capable of receiving digital broadcasts. For a smooth transition to be achieved, the new terrestrial digital networks must cover the whole country, there must be accessible and attractive programs on offer and effective promotional and marketing campaigns for the new television channels, interactive services must be offered by digital TV, and a large proportion of these channels and services must be free, that is, paid for by a license fee or by advertising.

There are at least three reasons why governments are interested in speeding up the transition from analog to a totally digital TV. The first is a more efficient use of scarce natural resources. Digital broadcasting allows a reduction in the number of frequencies used for broadcasting thus making space for other new mobile communication services which need an increasing number of hertz. The second reason is basically social. Digital TV can be used to access the Internet. This scenario is the quickest route for governments to create Internet access for all. Once transition to digital TV is accomplished, all households will be able to access the so-called information society services—online interactive services (e-learning, e-government, e-commerce, etc.) from which many governments are expecting economic, social, and cultural advantages. Such an aim cannot be entrusted to the personal computer that a solid minority of households are not able to use or have no intention of buying or using.

The third reason is linked to economic factors. The transition from analog to digital TV entails the complete substitution of all the means of production, transition, and reception and the beginning of a new cycle of growth that could offer some electronic companies new opportunities for expansion.

The transition seems inevitable, but the time scale is not at all clear. Public broadcasters, due to their very nature, are being encouraged to take a leading role by setting up the simulcast stage (supplying the same broadcast using both analog and digital technology) and also new digital channels so as to stimulate the acquisition of digital TV access systems in households. In order to take part in the process and stay ahead of the rest of the field, in order to provide simultaneous analog and digital distribution, in order to take full advantage of digital television in terms of multichannels, interactive TV and interactive multimedia services, the public broadcaster must be in a position to invest heavily in technology, programs, and professional integration and development.

As we have seen, present sources of financing—the license fee and advertising—have many restrictions and are unlikely to generate sufficient financial resources to cover investments in digital technology. Public service broadcasters cannot afford to stay out of terrestrial digital TV for very long for various obvious reasons, but also because it would mean a loss of image and speedy relegation to a secondary role. However, becoming a major player right from the start means finding the necessary resources to cover spending and manage the new channels and services. One way of finding economic stability in this picture is to raise new revenue based on direct payment of new services by the consumer. This scenario, which is incompatible with the principles and the role of public service television, may not be the only and inevitable direction public service broadcasting in Europe will take.

Among the growing incertitude shown until now by all European public broadcasters in front of digital television transition, BBC looks like an exception. For Freeview, the digital terrestrial platform backed by BBC with Crown Castle and BSkyB, the corporation envisaged (Gibson 2002) spending £3.5 billion (5.8 billion) in the next ten years. But the government at the beginning of 2003 announced a wide-ranging review of the BBC as part of the preparations for the renewal of its royal charter in 2006 and, in particular, the license fee model.

There is strong pressure to change the traditional financing of the BBC. Two possible solutions would strongly reduce the central role held by BBC in the British television broadcasting system. One is to fund BBC by subscription. Barry Cox, deputy chairman of Channel 4 and influential adviser on media policy to the government, said in an article for *Media Guardian* (27 January 2003): "The BBC has great creative strength and understand the tastes of many different audiences. And that strength is precisely why it can and should afford, in the digital world, to rely on our willingness to pay for it voluntarily." The second solution, very dangerous for BBC and in line with the Amsterdam Protocol, would have the government set up a public service broadcasting fund to which all broadcasters, not just the BBC, would be able to bid for cash.

CONCLUSION

Public television services have succeeded so far in keeping a central position in all European countries. Everywhere they have received the confidence of the states that assign to them functions of relevant general interest. Public television services draw a big share of the audience. But on close analysis, even if they appear to be strong, the situation is tight, due to a series of difficulties that have been contributing to the progressive marginalization of public television services, or the end of them entirely. Several factors are working against public television, including difficulties in raising new revenue to keep up with the rising costs of production and the transition to digital services, the prospect of the increasing fragmentation of the audience, and growing political pressure and criticism directed toward public broadcasting.

Three recent cases offer reason for pessimism about the future of public television. In the Netherlands, the government decided to eliminate the license fee revenue of public television services and transferred the revenue to the general budget of the country. A debate has begun in Great Britain about the renewal of the Royal Charter on which the financial framework for public service broadcasting is based. One proposal under discussion is to change the public broadcasting financing system by moving to a spontaneous revenue system like the one of pay-TV or even to put up for auction parts of public television services that will be given to private or public winners with economic resources collected by license fees. In Italy, the government television bill presented to the Parliament at the end of 2002 proposed the privatization of RAI, the company that has managed the television public service since its beginning.

The increasing competition between public and private broadcasters and, in many cases, the importance of advertising revenues, are leading public broadcasters to schedule new, more commercially oriented program choices, reflecting less preoccupation with traditional public service values (quality, diversity, culture, etc.). That tendency is giving to social and political groups with a critical attitude toward public broadcasting more and more occasions to criticize financing by license fee.

During the last ten years we have seen the strong, constant growth in the cost of producing fiction and sports broadcasting. This phenomenon has led to continual increases in scheduling costs and it has forced public television stations to give up very successful programs, for examples, Premier League football (soccer) or other very popular sports events. These kinds of programs are now offered instead by private broadcasters or by pay-TV stations.

As costs rise, finances targeted for television public services slow or stagnate. During the 1990s, the medium rate of growth of advertising investments tageted to television has been everywhere lower than what was recorded in the 1980s. Adding to this tendency, advertising revenues destined for public broadcasting were restricted, on the one hand, to avoid an excessive influence on scheduling contents and strategy and, on the other hand, to avoid having those revenues siphoned by private broadcasters.

But even the revenues derived from the license fee, which represent the prevalent part of revenues of almost all public television services, have not increased according to need, since they are linked to political decisions that are controversial and often delayed or restricted because of concerns about tax increases. In addition, the revenue system based on license fees has come under criticism and it has been increasingly questioned in the current political climate, including by an increasing number of television viewers. With revenue not increasing at the same rate as costs, officials are forced to consider downsizing the services offered, in terms of both quantity and quality, thus reducing audience choices.

Public television services face a number of other difficulties throughout Europe in the future. The decision to gradually shift from analog to digital terrestrial television generates two main problems. The first concerns the cost of the transition for broadcasters. In the last few years in most European countries, public television broadcasters have not managed to gain sufficient license fee increases to enable them to finance the transition to digital service. The second problem concerns the fact that digital terrestrial television will require an increase in the number of available television channels and a consequent fragmentation of audience. Free-to-air national channels are likely to lose audience share, continuing the process that began when satellite and cable services were introduced. In light of these developments it is unlikely that public broadcasters will be able to maintain the same investment and quality standard of scheduling when audience size declines.

REFERENCES

Arthur Andersen. 1998. *The Impact of Digital Television on Supply of Programs: A Report for the European Broadcasting Union*. Geneva: EBI.

Blumler, Jay G. 1994. *Television and Public Interest: Vulnerable Values in Western European Broadcasting*. London: Sage.

Davis, Gavyn. *The Future Funding of the BBC: Report of the Independent Review Panel*. London: Department of Culture, Media, and Sport.

European Audiovisual Observatory. 2002. *Yearbook: Economy of the European Audiovisual Industry*. Strasbourg: Council of Europe.

Foster, Robin. 1992. *Public Broadcasters: Accountability and Efficiency*. Edinburgh: Edinburgh University Press.

Giauque, David, and Juan Perellon. 1997."La SSR aux defies de la concurrence du marché audiovisuel." In M. Finger, S. Pravato, and J. N. Ray, *Du monopole à la concurrence*. Lausanne: IDHEAP.

Gibson, Owen. 2002. "BBC's Digital Dream to Cost £3.5 bn." media.guardian.co.uk/broadcast/story/0,7493,749181,00.html.

Groombridge, Brian, and Jocelyn Hay, eds. 1995. *The Price of Choice: Public Service Broadcasting in a Competitive European Market Place*. London: John Libbey.

Humphreys, Peter. 1996. *Mass Media and Media Policy in Western Europe*. Manchester: Manchester University Press.

Iseppi, Franco, and Vittorio Bossi. 1998. *Il ruolo e la missione del servizio pubblico radiotelevisivo*. Roma: Edizioni Radiotelevisione Italiana.

Jezequel, Jean-Pierre, and André Lange. 2000. *Economy of European TV Fiction: Market Value and Producers-Broadcasting Relations*. Strasbourg: European Audiovisual Observatory.

Missika, Jean-Louis. 1997. *Les enterprises publiques de television et les missions de service publique: Rapport de mission au ministre de la culture et de la communication*. Paris: Ministere de la Culture et de la Communication.

Oliver, Mark. 2001. "The Rise of the Broadcaster-Owned Sport Agency." *European Sport Rights Market* in *Sis Briefing*, August–September 2001. Geneva: European Broadcasting Union.

Peacock, Alan. 1986. *Report of the Committee on Financing the BBC*. London: HMSO.

Richeri, Giuseppe. 1986. *Television from Service to Business*. In P. Drummond and R. Paterson, eds., *Television in Transition*. London: British Film Institute.

———. 1992. *La TV che conta: Televisione come impresa*. Bologna: Baskerville.

———. 1994. *La transicion de la television*. Barcelona: Bosch Casa Editorial.

Tracey, Michael. 1998. *The Decline and Fall of Public Service Broadcasting*. Oxford: Oxford University Press.

11

Living with Monsters
Can Broadcasting Regulation
Make a Difference?

Sylvia Harvey

This chapter explores both free market and Marxist critiques of broadcasting regulation with a view to assessing the continuing viability and purpose of regulation as an instrument of public policy making. It is based on three assumptions. First, it is in the public interest that broadcasting should reflect the experiences, dilemmas, and conflicts of particular societies, providing (among other things) a forum that is coextensive with electoral boundaries. Second, the content and quality of radio and television programs has social, cultural, and sometimes political significance; because of this, democratic governments have a duty to ensure universal access, monitor standards (through independent, intermediary bodies), and enable pluralism and diversity of expression. Third, where broadcasting markets have failed to reflect either the diversity of indigenous cultures and concerns or the relevance of international issues, governments have a duty to seek alternative means to compensate for such failure, enabling freedom of expression that is linked, where possible, to the nonviolent resolution of conflicts between groups or nations. This principle relates as much, in my view, to conflicts between men and women over child care, access to resources, and the inviolability of the person as it does to conflicts between ethnic groups and between nations. As the German filmmaker Alexander Kluge put it, "the public sphere is the site where struggles are decided by other means than war" (Hansen 1993).

In the first part of this chapter I address some general issues to do with the relevance of regulatory studies for a political economy of broadcasting and explore various critiques of regulation. I then consider selected examples of regulatory intervention drawn from different countries and periods and designed to illuminate different approaches to the concept of the public interest in broadcasting. In the second part I examine some positive examples of regulatory practice and assess the prospects for forms of regulation that are consistent with democratic objectives, while noting that regulation is largely the province of nation-states that are themselves torn by internal and transnational conflicts of interest.

THE CRITIQUE OF REGULATION

Enlarging "Political Economy"?

The various "political economies" of the media have systematically linked issues of power and control to the empirical facts of investment and profitability on the one hand and to the generation of publicly shared meanings and values on the other. These approaches have been ambitiously holistic in wishing to situate and understand the media within "society as a whole" and the "economy as a whole," seeking to establish a virtually unbreakable bond between politics and economics. Of course, this bond can only be established through a sideways move into the controversial field of studies in the social circulation of meaning, a field that has both theoretical and empirical coordinates. While approaches from political economy have asserted the more or less determining force of economic relations on media output, they have also been subject to the criticism that content has a relative autonomy of its own and that the making of meanings by cultural producers and consumers cannot be seen as a simple effect of ownership and economic power. In this regard the famous assertion by Marx and Engels (*The German Ideology*, 1846) that the "ideas of the ruling class are in every epoch the ruling ideas" (Marx and Engels 1974, 64) has been seen to operate at a level of generality that may not be entirely helpful in tracing the generation and circulation of meanings in the age of mass literacy and then of mass communication.

However, the proposition that the making of meaning is not absolutely determined by owners and investors in the cultural industries is widely matched by a recognition that class identity and loyalty, social prejudice, cultural capital, and economic power can combine to ensure the marginalization of certain views and the widespread erasure or absence of certain experiences and cultures in the universe of media representations. Thus the issue of power—of who determines who may say what, when, and where, how loudly, and to how many people—remains inevitably center stage for those concerned with the social impact and significance of cultural production and cultural expression.

What remains deeply problematic for a political economy of the media, most particularly one that holds strongly to the idea of class difference and class power, is the role of the state in regulating the media. While liberal theory sees the state as essentially impartial, "holding the ring" between competing social and economic forces and interests, some branches of Marxist theory have seen the state as the agent of those who are most economically powerful within society. This latter position offers us the class state, not the neutral state, the state whose raison d'être is to defend the interests of the class in power, the ruling class. At its most pessimistic this view holds that the courts, the schools and universities, the media, and even Parliament or Congress itself are the tools or agents of the economically powerful. When such a view is applied to the media, civil servants and regulators, television executives and filmmakers are seen to have no choice but to manage institutions, tell stories, and represent views that support those who hold economic power. There is, as it were, no representational space for resistance. From this point of view there appears to be no ground on which democracy might be built, short of some global and electronic world equivalent of the storming of the Winter Palace.

For this reason different currents within Marxism and, in a more mainstream way, within European socialism and social democracy have come up with a view of the role of the state that is more complex and nuanced. The state is then seen not as some vast and untouchable throne of power but as something more like an open and muddy soccer pitch, across which charge various forces and interests, sometimes winning, sometimes losing.

The soccer pitch metaphor allows us to consider one of the many activities of the state—the regulation of broadcasting—as an arena of conflict and contestation whose institutions and officers may act sometimes in the interests of national and multinational capital but also, and sometimes, with a sense that the public interest may at times be distinct from corporate interests. The middle section of this chapter traces some of those instances of regulatory intervention (whether by regulatory bodies, legislators, or the courts) and presents them here as instances of a kind of international "case history" of public interest regulation. Moreover, it is proposed here that just as the "sidestep" into the analysis of meaning making has enlarged the field of political economy, making its application in the realm of media studies more robust, so too a different kind of "sidestep" into the realm of regulatory studies may enlarge and strengthen the domain of political economy. This is so because the regulation of broadcasting is one of the factors (varying considerably between countries and cultures) that make up the "conditions of existence" for cultural production and the circulation of cultural commodities.

What's Wrong with Regulation?

The Marxist Critique

It may be useful at this point to examine both Marxist and liberal critiques of regulation. If we take Marxism to be a political philosophy that is characterized by its advocacy and defense of working-class interests, linked to the proposition that the state in capitalist societies inevitably represents the interests of the economically dominant class, then it will come as no surprise to discover its argument that regulation by such a state is incapable of advancing working-class interests. Thus, the argument runs, the bourgeois state is bound to reproduce itself, working at times with the instruments of physical repression and at times through a more subtle and complex process that naturalizes and legitimates its power and the interests of the dominant class—the "state as the organ of class rule," as Lenin put it (Lenin 1969, 28).

Where the state is seen to be already partisan in this way, it cannot serve the interests of different social classes and, by extension, cannot be an instrument of democratization. According to this view, both the politicians who make up the legislature and the individuals who together form the regulatory body (for example) would be incapable of defending any interests other than those of big business. Any talk of citizenship, public interest, or communicative rights would be just that—talk—and incapable of winning any real gains for the makers and users of broadcasting programs. From this perspective the concepts of "diversity and pluralism" are viewed as a cynical cover for a deeply unrepresentative media system, and it is believed to be impossible that broadcasters might be as attentive to the cultural interests of the exploited, the marginalized, and the oppressed as to those of the wealthy. In addition, the principle of "freedom of expression" (at least in public) is believed to be operationalized in such a limited way that any serious challenge to existing hierarchies and forms of social order is ruled out in advance. In summary and schematic form, these grand and "broad brush" propositions can be seen to deny that the state in capitalist societies can act in the general interest, to deny that there is any meaningful diversity or pluralism in the media, and to argue that freedom of expression is only available to the rich and powerful.

As already noted, many of the newer or "post-Leninist" currents in Marxism—developed in the 1960s and 1970s but with their roots in the work of earlier theorists such as Antonio Gramsci—rejected this totalizing view of the state. By the late twentieth century the idea that the state was a locus of struggle and contestation was no longer clearly distinct from the social democratic tradition, which had believed all along that the state, governments, and the "parliamentary way" could be mobilized as agents of progressive social change. In the social democratic camp the word "progressive" never took on the connotations of class war with its belief in the fundamental incompatibility of working class and capitalist class interests. In the field of European broadcasting regulation it should come as no surprise, therefore, to discover that the principles of broadcasting regulation are most certainly not rooted in the theory of class antagonism.

By the end of the twentieth century, the differences between Marxists and social democrats on the issue of class antagonism and the role of the state had paled into relative insignificance compared with the militant and expansionist views of the neoliberals, for whom the market and not the state was the only game in town. Moreover, the process of global liberalization has itself introduced a new complexity in the political realm. Thus some of the currents of European social democracy have swirled away from their historical sources and joined the liberal, free market stream, creating a curious political hybrid whose prospects are not yet clear.

It will be useful now to match this rather schematic account of a Marxist critique of the role of the state (and, by extension, of regulatory bodies) with a brief examination of some of the liberal or free market criticisms of regulation.

The Liberal Critique

There are, broadly speaking, three arguments against government regulation from a liberal perspective, although this section of the chapter also considers the other side of these arguments, namely, the defense of regulatory intervention.

First, there is an argument about properly functioning markets; second, there is a debate about the appropriate exercise of political power; and third, there is an argument about censorship and freedom of speech.

The market distortion argument. It has been argued that government intervention distorts the market, and that the long postwar history of Keynesian economic policy is a prime example of this. In the field of broadcasting it has been suggested that detailed and intrusive content regulation by politicians or public officials, along with monopoly public ownership, has created a broadcasting system that is not "market worthy." This kind of broadcasting is believed to reflect the tastes and choices of regulators instead of recognizing and responding to the preferences of audiences.

There are at least two problems with this argument in its pure form. The first is that it is agreed by advocates of a free market that the natural tendency toward monopoly paradoxically requires the state to step in to ensure that adequate competition is maintained and that dominant players neither stifle innovation nor inflate prices. The then chairman of the U.S. Federal Communications Commission (FCC), Reed Hundt, noted this point in a 1996 speech: "it is . . . the 'paradox' of competition that although firms compete to win, the ultimate victory is monopoly. So the ever-present job of government is to write the rules that invent, revive and sustain competition, while inviting instead of deterring or inhibiting innovation, entrepreneurship and investment" (Hundt 1999, 285).

Thus some measure of state intervention in defense of competition is required. In the field of telecommunications in the United Kingdom this intervention has delivered benefits to consumers in the form of new services and lower prices. Competition in broadcasting, however, has had less predictable outcomes and here it is important to remember the goals of competition. It is not an end in itself but is designed to ensure innovation and efficiency in production so that the rational and knowledgeable consumer can select the product of highest affordable quality at the lowest price. Already we can see that it is difficult to apply the propositions of classical economics to the exercise of consumer choice in broadcasting. This is partly because programs may have been paid for by advertisers and not audiences, partly because there is no universal pricing mechanism, and partly because of the extraordinary range of tastes, interests, and priorities in this field.

This observation may lead us to the second of the problems with the radical "anti-intervention" argument. When we observe the actual consequences of increased competition in the field of broadcasting, we can find instances of lowered standards in public affairs journalism (Barnett and Seymour 1999), decreased audience choice, and a reduced range of programming genres (Stone 2000; Nason and Redding 2002). Or we may find increased costs, for example in access to sporting events or popular foreign TV series. There is little point in facilitating the entry of newcomers into the field if the service they offer is of inferior quality or higher cost. There is, as already suggested, some evidence from qualitative as opposed to quantitative research that *decreased* choice may be the result of competition where there has been a rush to the middle ground in the commissioning of programs, and where ratings anxiety and risk aversion become the sad progenitors of unadventurous programming.[1] Where audiences have shown a willingness to pay more for enhanced or specialist "niche" services it is, in my view, right to facilitate the provision of new services, but not in a way that places existing, high-quality, and universally accessible public services at risk or destroys them in the interests of commercial competitors.

The political control argument. The First Amendment to the U.S. Constitution, "Congress shall make no law . . . abridging the freedom of speech, or of the press" (Wilson 1993, 48), famously seeks to prevent government from interfering with free speech rights. In the United States this important statement of principle has, with some exceptions, underwritten a minimalist approach to broadcasting regulation, where the state and not big business has been seen to pose the greater threat to freedom of expression. Various attempts by the FCC to produce regulations enabling pluralism on the airwaves have run into problems as a consequence of this. In Europe a history of dictatorial control of broadcasting (in Nazi Germany, in Franco's Spain) has also generated considerable concern about the need to ensure political pluralism. But this has connected to a wider debate about the social and civic purposes of the medium and to the role that broadcasting might play in the development of democratic politics. Janet Morgan, a former adviser to the BBC, sketched out some of the broader issues at stake: "The issue is not one of technology or economics but of politics, of how as a society we wish to use our joint resources and collectively manage our affairs" (MacCabe and Stewart 1986, 31).

Recognition of the public interest in the field of broadcasting seems to require that the broader communicative needs of a society are facilitated. This is the "public sphere" argument in defense of regulated broadcasting (Habermas 1989). However, the argument loses its force in a culture where broadcasting is seen as predominantly a branch of the leisure industry.

The censorship argument. Third, it has been argued that government intervention in the regulation of broadcasting content constitutes a form of unacceptable censorship and a contravention of free speech rights. In a sense this grows out of the arguments about political control. But there appear to be some important differences of opinion between the United States and various European countries regarding individual and corporate free speech rights in the field of broadcasting. The constitutional courts in both France and Germany have emphasized the civic duties of broadcasters. In 1994 the French court, for example, found that the principle of freedom enshrined in the Declaration of Human Rights

> would be meaningless if the public, for whom broadcasting in all its forms is intended, had no access, either in the commercial or the public service sector, to programs which guarantee freedom of expression for different groups, out of respect for the absolute need to provide truthful information. (Robillard 1995, 61)

Over the years there have been numerous instances of unacceptable government interference in the content of broadcasting but this of itself does not seem to rule out a role for the state in *enabling* the public exchange of ideas through this medium.

REGULATION IN HISTORICAL CONTEXT

Broadcasting as Information or Entertainment

In the 1920s political systems emerged that were based on universal adult suffrage. They absorbed the political shock waves that had emanated from the creation of a "workers state" in Russia in the previous decade. At this juncture two alternative paths for the ordering of broadcasting were adopted. One approach gave primacy to the role of the state (even where program makers enjoyed some relative independence from government pressure). The other approach gave primacy to the creation of a broadcasting market developed by business entrepreneurs capable of uncovering the potential economic value embedded in applications of the new technology.

The first approach has tended to see broadcasting primarily in terms of the contribution that the provision of information makes to the conduct of the political process. The second has tended to emphasize the entertainment role of the medium and its potential for profitability. The foregrounding of the entertainment value of broadcasting has—arguably—followed that other great model for the creation of a successful cultural business, namely, the Hollywood film industry. Coincidentally, the American film industry was establishing the basis for its global success during the 1920s, the first decade of broadcasting, and this was to provide useful models for global media corporations at the end of the twentieth century. These two approaches of "information-opinion-politics" on the one hand and of "entertainment" on the other, provide—broadly speaking—the basis for the very different broadcasting systems that developed in Western Europe and the United States.

The State and Broadcasting

The sharpest contrast in methods (the extreme ends of the spectrum, as it were) can be observed by comparing the approaches developed in the 1920s in the fledgling Soviet state and in the United States, then emerging as the dominant economic and political world power. In Soviet Russia broadcasting was seen, above all else, as a medium of political communication or propaganda to be controlled by the one Communist party and designed to educate and mold the thoughts and beliefs of millions. In the United States hundreds of individuals and companies seized the initiative and began broadcasting radio signals of all kinds before there was a fully fleshed-out legal framework for the allocation of frequencies (Douglas 1987). In America the educational and informational potential of radio was noted and advocated by many voluntary bodies—churches, universities, trade unions (McChesney 1993). Its role as an entertainment and money-making invention was also recognized: radio might "lighten" and well as enlighten the lives of millions. We also now know that during the American New Deal period of the 1930s the great "interventionist" Franklin Roosevelt, although he secretly explored the potential for nationalizing radio, drew back from the brink not wishing to jeopardize his relations with the industry (McChesney 1993, 185). Europe, by contrast, was the home of nationalized or firmly state-regulated broadcasting; it was "another country" and they did things differently there.

However, as we examine the history of broadcasting regulation, the simple dichotomy between state primacy and market primacy turns out to be too simple. In both Europe and the United States, far though they might both seem to be from the advocacy of direct state ownership and party-political control, the new medium of communication was seen to have potentially major consequences for social and political order. A clear legal framework and close government involvement was therefore seen to be required. In the course of the twentieth century the sense of order inscribed in broadcasting has changed considerably from imperialist supremacism, racism, and male chauvinism to more inclusive but also more populist modes. And while the John Reithian elitism of the BBC has provided both a strength and a weakness for British broadcasting, an apolitical populism has perhaps been a more consistent feature of the American system.

A few examples drawn from the history of broadcasting regulation in the United States, Britain, France, and Germany demonstrate both the variety of approaches and the ways in which they reflect the contours of each country's underlying political and constitutional features. These examples remind us that broadcasting is not a phenomenon of the natural world, despite its reliance on the physical facts of engineering science; rather, it is shaped by the exercise of human choices, desires, and priorities.

On the spectrum of state intervention, developments in the United States can be seen to embody the least interventionist approach together with a commitment to maximum openness and opportunity for individual entrepreneurs. Here too broadcasting was to some extent seen as a kind of public trust, and licenses were allocated by the Federal Communications Commission (FCC) and its predecessor, the Federal Radio Commission, to serve the "public convenience, interest, or necessity" (Radio Act of 1927; in Barnouw 1966, 301). The secretary of commerce, Herbert Hoover, established a series of radio conferences in preparation for the 1927 legislation and supported the principles of private ownership and a large measure of industrial self-regulation. But Hoover also recognized the cultural status and significance of the new medium. "It is inconceivable," he declared, "that we should allow so great a possibility for service to be drowned in advertising chatter" (McChesney 1993, 13; Barnouw 1966, 96). His curt dismissal was short-lived, and most subsequent commentators have testified to the central role played by advertising in the American broadcasting industry (Sterling and Kittross 2002; *CNET Investor* 2002).

In the period after World War II the FCC established a range of regulations designed to serve the public interest, including the 1949 *Report on Editorializing by Broadcast Licensees,* more commonly known as the Fairness Doctrine. This regulation required broadcasters to give adequate information about public issues and, in particular, to offer fair coverage that accurately reflected opposing points of view (Kahn 1984, 279–80). Moreover, where sponsorship was not available to underwrite the costs of presenting alternative views, the broadcaster was obliged to present such material at its own expense. This interventionist approach was endorsed by the U.S. Supreme Court in its famous Red Lion judgment of 1969: "It is the right of the viewers and listeners, not the right of the broadcasters, which is paramount. . . . It is the right of the public to receive suitable access to social, political, esthetic, moral and other ideas" (Kahn 1984, 287). Such distinguished support for public interest intervention became politically unacceptable in the deregulatory Reagan era, and in 1987 the FCC suspended the Fairness Doctrine. This suspension was in response to two main arguments: (1) that enforced "fairness" was having the "chilling effect" of causing journalists to avoid controversial issues, and (2) station owners argued that the rule contravened their own free speech rights to use the airwaves as they saw fit (Harvey 1998).

In most European countries, since the early days of broadcasting, advocacy of the public or the national interest was taken to justify much higher levels of state intervention than were common in the United States. The meaning of both "public" and "national" interest has been hotly contested as, for example, the coverage of the General Strike in Britain or of the Vietnam War in the United States testifies. One key example of alternatives to market provision can be traced to the United Kingdom in the 1920s, when a group of commercial radio manufacturers were persuaded by the government's post office to come together in a kind of business cooperative to provide a monopoly service to the whole country. This novel and uncompetitive business was then transformed into a not-for-profit organization, the British Broadcasting Corporation (BBC), in 1927. Since then and to the present day, the BBC has continued to operate under the terms of its renewable Royal Charter, supported by a compulsory license fee payable by all households with broadcast receiving equipment.

In the year 2000–2001 the BBC's license fee was worth just over £2.3 billion ($3.3 billion) and compares favorably with other revenue sources available to U.K. competitors: total net television advertising was then worth around £3.3 billion and subscription revenue £1.9 billion (BBC 2001, 66; ITC 2001a, 36). Interestingly the U.K. license fee is worth around twice as much as the total revenue of American public television, estimated to be worth $1.6 billion in 2000 (Public Broadcasting Service 2002).

Unlike the Public Broadcasting Service (PBS) stations in the United States, which have around a 3.5 percent share of the total television audience (Gunzerath 2000; Public Broadcasting Service 2002),[2] the BBC in 2000 took a 38 percent share of the U.K. television audience (including all terrestrial, cable, and satellite channels but excluding video viewing) and a 52 percent share of the national radio audience (BBC 2001, 10–14). Within the British regulatory framework, the BBC is exclusively funded by the national license fee and receives no U.K. advertising revenue.

The closely regulated and relatively well-resourced duopoly of BBC and Independent Television (ITV) only faced multichannel competition from the late 1980s.[3] However, by 2001—just over ten years into the multichannel era—the old duopoly seemed to be doing relatively well in the new market conditions. With the addition of the new advertising-funded terrestrial Channels 4 and 5, the free-to-air terrestrial system of five channels retained an 80 percent share of the total U.K. television audience.[4] The large number of new competitor cable and satellite services shared just under 20 percent of the audience between them, with the News International stable of twenty Sky channels taking a 6 percent share (ITC 2002). Since 1989 these new services have ushered in the world of pay-TV in the United Kingdom and have begun to change the basic features of the broadcasting economy, accelerating the processes of commodification and commercialization. As one senior U.K. television executive observed in 1995, television viewing accounted for some 70 percent of all leisure time but attracted only 10 percent of leisure spending (Elstein 1995). This is now changing as more people spend more money buying access to television programs. Although not-for-profit broadcasting in the United Kingdom (and the citizenship requirements that it underwrites) appears to be holding its ground, there is fierce competition for audiences with some reduction in viewer welfare; the future is difficult to predict.

The development of market competition has had a determining effect on broadcasting systems, but political intervention has also played a part, even where some multiparty states have sought to check the power of the party in government. In the United States, for example, the Communications Act of 1934 ensured that of the seven commissioners who constituted the FCC only four might be members of the same political party. Appointments were (and are) made by the president with the advice and consent of the Senate. In the United Kingdom the principle of bipartisanship was less explicit and more powers were reserved for the government of the day, taking decisions essentially behind closed doors. Thus the first five governors of the BBC were selected and appointed by the relevant minister, then the postmaster general, although officially these appointments are made by the king or queen. Although the chosen mode of operation, through a Royal Charter, was believed to give the then monopoly broadcaster greater flexibility than either dependence on parliamentary statute or company law would have done, the government held the BBC on quite a short leash. This is so despite the formal statements in the charter and in parliamentary speeches concerning the importance of the BBC operating independently of government. In 1926, for example, the deputy postmaster general had this to say: "I want to make this Service not a Department of the State, and still less a creature of the Executive, but as far as is consistent with Ministerial responsibility, I wish to create an independent body of trustees operating the Service in the interest of the public as a whole" (Briggs 1961, 329).

Fine words are not always reflected in practice, and the lack of bipartisan specifications in the regulations dealing with the appointment of BBC governors has resulted in some instances of directly partisan appointments. This was thought to have occurred in the 1980s during the latter part of Margaret Thatcher's premiership (Goodwin 1998).

In France and Germany, there has been similarly strong involvement from the government of the day in making key appointments in the field of broadcasting. This has had variable effects on programming output from the conservative statism of the French ORTF in the 1970s to the social critique and stylistic experimentalism of ZDF in Germany (Humphreys 1996, 146; Sergeant 1999, 47; Hartnoll and Porter 1982). In France television broadcasting remained a state monopoly until the 1980s; the state controlled the broadcasting budget and made all key appointments.

In Germany the relationship between state and broadcasters and the highly distinctive methods of regulation adopted embody a reaction against the methods of National Socialist control of broadcasting during the 1930s. There are perhaps three key features of the system. First, the Federal Constitutional

Court, the highest legal authority in the country, has played a key role in the development of broadcasting in the period after World War II, grounding its judgments in the right of freedom of communication enshrined in Germany's Basic Law and requiring broadcasters to enable the "free, individual and public formation of opinion" (Hoffman-Riem 1996, 119). According to the court neither government nor powerful forces in the private sector should be able to determine individual opinion. A 1986 ruling established the constitutionality of private broadcasting (introduced for the first time during the 1980s), although this is seen as complementary to public broadcasting. And a 1994 ruling confirmed the importance of television license fee funding for the public sector as a guarantor of political and economic independence (Robillard 1995, 79).

Second, the postwar German state was reconstituted according to federalist and decentralizing principles. In this it resembles the United States but not France or the United Kingdom. In a departure from the characteristic methods of probably most other states, the German regional governments, or *Länder*, were given responsibility for all cultural and broadcasting matters. There can thus be no equivalent of a Federal Communications Commission, and both public and private broadcasters are regulated by a complex array of bodies created by the *Länder*.

Third, the contemporary German state is characterized by a deep-rooted commitment to pluralism and proportionality. It thus escapes the majoritarian "winner-take-all" impulses of France and the United Kingdom. Although many broadcasting appointments are deeply politicized, the regulatory bodies are composed of nominations received from a mixture of political parties (in accordance with their proportional presence in each regional parliament), churches, worker and employer organizations, and other designated social interest groups. These broadcasting councils are designed, as Hoffman-Riem notes, to "reduce the risk of one-sided use of broadcasting" (Hoffman-Riem 1996, 124). Both public and private broadcasters are required to ensure pluralism and diversity of viewpoint in their program content.

Broadly speaking, commercial interests in the United States have prevented the FCC from acting to promote the public interest in the area of program content, and consumer choice in the market has been regarded as a sufficient mechanism for ensuring diversity and pluralism. This ethos has made quality, pluralism, and even fairness no-go areas for the American regulator. In most European countries, by contrast, there is a long history of attachment to non–market-based public service broadcasting, and to some form of regulation for quality and diversity. This continues to make it difficult for multinational corporations to dominate, although their share of the market has been growing.

BROADCASTING REGULATION AND THE DEMOCRATIC PROJECT

There can be little agreement on what constitutes the successes and failures of regulatory intervention if there is disagreement about its goals. In some areas it may be fairly easy to measure success: available electricity supply, safe drinking water, smooth road surfaces, trains that run on time, lower infant mortality rates. Some things are fairly easy to quantify. The problems arise particularly in respect of qualitative judgments and most especially in the cultural arena (Corner and Harvey 1996, 234–35; Harvey 1999). Moreover, as I indicated earlier, there are disagreements about the purposes of broadcasting. If the broadcasting of accurate, impartial, and complex information, the airing of controversies, the formation of informed citizens, the production of acute and original drama are regarded as important objectives, then broadcasting develops in one direction; where market choices are regarded as sufficient guides and the manufacture of entertainment is divorced from its social impact then broadcasting adopts a different social role.

On the assumption that quality, fairness, diversity, and pluralism (in both fictional and factual programming) are important issues for the shaping of broadcasting policy, the final section of the paper explores some positive examples of regulatory intervention.

These examples are drawn from the United Kingdom, Canada, France, and Germany and are designed to cast some light on the following issues: the rationale for "fairness" or "impartiality" rules, the cultural purpose of national and regional origination quotas, and the consequences for audiences of the creation of new broadcasting institutions.

The quality of programs can be affected by a variety of factors; one particularly sensitive area concerns the reporting of major controversies, including political disagreements. We know that during periods of dictatorship audiences have not been able to rely on broadcasting to give them an accurate or considered view of the world, though this is also true of some forms of unregulated commercial broadcasting. The requirement for broadcasting impartiality established in U.K. law (and similar in intention to the discarded U.S. fairness provisions) includes a provision for opinionated, "personal view" programs and offers, perhaps, an example of good practice. While most television viewers are probably unaware of the existence of the impartiality code, it appears to be valued in its effects in that audiences record higher levels of trust in television as a source of news than in newspapers (Towler 2001, 26; Hargreaves and Thomas 2002, 49). The impartiality rule is, in a sense, an imposition (prohibiting broadcasting institutions from "taking sides" on major controversies) and this might be seen, from an American perspective, to interfere with the free speech rights of broadcasting corporations—placing the needs of viewers and listeners above the rights of broadcasters. However, it does provide the necessary if not sufficient condition for accurate and fair-minded news and public affairs broadcasting (Harvey 1998). In countries where a high value is placed on the principle of informed citizenship, "impartiality" may provide a useful statutory check on both the political aspirations of media owners and the self-regulation of journalists.

A further dimension of content regulation concerns support measures for the production of indigenous and local or regional programming. These provide opportunities for program makers and meet fairly widely evidenced audience preferences in this area (ITC 2001b). In Canada there has been a long tradition of encouraging the availability of Canadian programming (Holznagel 1996, 205–15; CRTC 2001). And in the European Union there is a requirement (rather unevenly applied) for the screening of a majority proportion of programs of European origin (Goldberg, Prosser, and Verhulst 1998, 61). Regulations in France, Germany, and the United Kingdom have encouraged the development of regional broadcasting. Individual U.K. broadcasters (the BBC, ITV, and Channel 4) have adopted policies designed to ensure significant investment in programs made throughout the country and not only in the capital city; in the case of Channel 4 this has become a license requirement (ITC 2001a, 80). Such investment has created and sustained, to some extent, a new pluralism of nonmetropolitan voices (Harvey and Robins 1993).

Finally, we may note two examples of the creation of broadcasting institutions that have fostered innovative and critical forms of cultural production and extended the range of choices available to viewers. First, Channel 4 (U.K.) was established in 1982 on a not-for-profit basis, although funded by advertising. It operated under a statutory remit to foster experimentation and innovation in the form and content of programs, to serve minority audiences, and to cater to interests not met by other broadcasters. Channel 4 was a risky initiative receiving some public "pump priming" in its early stages. But it established its financial viability within five years and attracted a wide range of audiences, with a 10 percent audience share in 2001 (Harvey 2000; Channel 4 2002, 72). Second, Canal Plus was established in 1984 as the first of the privately owned French services. Although it broke with the principle of public monopoly broadcasting, it was itself the product of public debate and government support for the French film industry. It was given a special obligation to finance and showcase French feature films and proved highly successful in this role, with an audience share of 4.5 percent in 1996 (Chaniac 1999, 60).

From these examples we can see some of the ways in which viewers, considered as citizens, can benefit from statutory intervention. It is clear, however, that in the new multichannel, mobile telephone, and Internet-imbued culture the old role of public service broadcasters is under notice of change if not eviction. A number of analysts have commented recently upon the risks to democracy that accompany the new fragmentation of audiences as the million "one-to-ones" of mobile telephony and the other new media usher in, perhaps, a new and electronic version of the "lonely crowd." Nicholas Garnham has noted the danger of societies fragmenting into a series of mutually uncomprehending quasi-public spheres and argues for the importance of a "common arena for critical public debate and decision-making" (Garnham 2000, 187). Edwin Baker has noted the threat of the disappearance of a "common public realm of discourse" (Baker 2002, 290).

Company mergers, cost cutting, and vigorous international marketing are all signs of the new corporate priorities for continuing capital accumulation in broadcasting as elsewhere. Of course, corporations can be large without being "monstrous," and there are many senior executives who would prefer to balance social and ethical considerations against purely business objectives. Nonetheless the relentless pursuit of shareholder value in conditions of intensified competition may place corporate decision makers on a collision course with the communicative requirements of a democratic state.

The reach of public broadcasting is weak in North America but still relatively strong in western Europe, and it remains to be seen in what ways electorates and governments will respond to these weaknesses and opportunities. Increased competition in the multichannel environment has made it more difficult for private broadcasting companies to retain their historic levels of profitability, and this creates real difficulties not only for the businesses themselves but also for governments. It is not, therefore, easy or straightforward to make recommendations about forms of regulatory intervention that will improve the services available to users, though the problems, at least, are becoming clearer. In the context of still rapid technological change, governments that prefer to see only a cornucopia of choice and not the erosion of choice, that act primarily to facilitate business in crisis and not to improve standards of public communication and debate, cannot be seen as acting in the interests of democracy.

NOTES

I wish to thank the Center d'Études sur les Médias in Quebec, Canada, for giving me the opportunity to research aspects of the history of broadcasting regulation for a seminar held in Montreal on 15–16 May 2002.

1. The economists Gordon Hughes and David Vines give an interesting example of the loss of consumer welfare that can be one of the unexpected results of competition. They describe two ice cream sellers on a beach who chose to stand next to each other in the center of a beach to achieve maximum market share; had they spaced themselves out across the beach, bathers would have enjoyed better service (Hughes and Vines 1989, 55).

2. I base this estimate of audience share on Gunzerath's figure for average household use of television in the United States as seven hours and twenty-four minutes per day in 1998–1999 and the PBS estimate that the average household tuned in to public television for approximately eight hours per month in October 2001 (Gunzerath 2000; PBS 2002).

3. ITV was established by the Conservative government in 1955 as a privately owned and advertising-funded network of stations based in the regions and nations of the United Kingdom.

4. Channel 4 was established in 1982 as a nonprofit subsidiary of the regulatory body and subsequently as an independent trust. Channel 5 began broadcasting in 1997 and is owned by private investors.

REFERENCES

Baker, Edwin. 2002. *Media, Markets, and Democracy*. Cambridge, Mass.: Cambridge University Press.

Barnett, S., and E. Seymour. 1999. *"A Shrinking Iceberg Travelling South": Changing Trends in British Television: A Case Study of Drama and Current Affairs*. London: Campaign for Quality Television.

Barnouw, E. 1966. *A Tower in Babel: A History of Broadcasting in the United States*. Vol. 1. New York: Oxford University Press.

BBC. 2001. *Annual Report and Accounts 2000–2001*. London: BBC.

Briggs, A. 1995 [1961]. *The History of Broadcasting in the United Kingdom*. Vol. 1, *The Birth of Broadcasting, 1896–1927*. Oxford: Oxford University Press.

Chaniac, R. 1999. "Two Programming Models." In M. Scriven and M. Lecomte, eds., *Television Broadcasting in Contemporary France and Britain*, 58–70. New York: Berghahn.

Channel 4. 2002. *Report and Financial Statements 2001*. London: Channel 4.

CNET Investor. 2002. "Veronis Suhler Stevenson Issues Annual Communications Industry Report." 2002. http://investor.cnet.com. Accessed 28 October 2002.

Corner, J., and S. Harvey, eds. 1996. *Television Times: A Reader*. London: Arnold.

CRTC. 2001. *Broadcasting Policy Monitoring Report 2001*. Ottawa: CRTC. www.crtc.gc.ca/ENG/publications/reports/PolicyMonitoring/2001/bpmr.htm.

Douglas, S. J. 1987. *Inventing American Broadcasting, 1899–1922*. Baltimore: Johns Hopkins University Press.

Elstein, D. 1995. Forman Lecture. Granada Centre for Visual Anthropology, University of Manchester. Unpublished speech delivered on 7 December.

Garnham, N. 2000. *Emancipation, the Media, and Modernity: Arguments about the Media and Social Theory*. Oxford: Oxford University Press.

Goldberg, D., T. Prosser, and S. Verhulst. 1998. *EC Media Law and Policy*. Harlow, U.K.: Addison Wesley Longman.

Goodwin, P. 1998. *Television under the Tories: Broadcasting Policy, 1979–1997*. London: British Film Institute.

Gunzerath, D. 2000. "Audience Research Trends." www.nab.org/research/reports/audienceresearchtrends.

Habermas, J. 1989. *The Structural Transformation of the Public Sphere: An Inquiry into a Category of Bourgeois Society*. Translated by Thomas Burger with the assistance of Frederick Lawrence. Cambridge: Polity. First published in German in 1962.

Hansen, M. 1993. "Unstable Mixtures, Dilated Spheres: Negt and Kluge's *The Public Sphere and Experience*, Twenty Years Later." *Public Culture* 5: 179–212.

Hargreaves, I., and J. Thomas. 2002. *New News, Old News: An ITC and BSC Research Publication*. London: Independent Television Commission.

Hartnoll, G., and V. Porter. 1982. *Alternative Film-making in Television: ZDF—A Helping Hand*. BFI Dossier, no. 14. London: British Film Institute.

Harvey, S. 1998. "Doing It My Way—Broadcasting Regulation in Capitalist Cultures: the Case of 'Fairness' and 'Impartiality.'" *Media, Culture, and Society* 20: 535–56.

———. 1999. "Broadcasting Regulation: Satanic Censor or Angel of Enlightenment." *Screening the Past*, November 1999. www.latrobe.edu.au/www.screeningthepast.

———. 2000. "Channel 4 Television: From Annan to Grade." In E. Buscombe, ed., *British Television: A Reader,* 92–117. Oxford: Clarendon.

Harvey, S., and K. Robins, eds. 1993. *The Regions, the Nations, and the BBC.* London: British Film Institute.

Hoffman-Riem, W. 1996. *Regulating Media: The Licensing and Supervision of Broadcasting in Six Countries.* New York: Guilford.

Holznagel, B. 1996. "Canada." In W. Hoffmann-Riem, ed., *Regulating Media: The Licensing and Supervision of Broadcasting in Six Countries,* 191–221. New York: Guilford.

Hughes, G., and D. Vines, eds. 1989. *Deregulation and the Future of Commercial Television.* Aberdeen: Aberdeen University Press/David Hume Institute.

Humphreys, P. J. 1996. *Mass Media and Media Policy in Western Europe.* Manchester, U.K.: Manchester University Press.

Hundt, R. E. 1999. "The Hard Road Ahead: An Agenda for the FCC in 1997." In P. Aufderheide, ed., *Communications Policy and the Public Interest: The Telecommunications Act of 1996,* 283–93. New York: Guilford. Extracts from a speech delivered on 26 December 1996.

ITC. 2001a. *ITC Annual Report and Accounts 2000: Licensing and Regulating Commercial Television.* London: ITC.

———. 2001b. *Public Service Broadcasting: What Viewers Want.* London: ITC.

———. 2002. *Television Audience Share Figures: Twenty-First Quarterly Report.* London: ITC. www.itc.org.uk/news/news_releases/htm.

Kahn, F. J., ed. 1984. *Documents of American Broadcasting.* Englewood Cliffs, N.J.: Prentice-Hall.

Lenin, V. I. 1969 [1917]. *The State and Revolution.* Moscow: Progress.

MacCabe, C., and O. Stewart, eds. 1986. *The BBC and Public Service Broadcasting.* Manchester, U.K.: Manchester University Press.

Marx, K., and F. Engels. 1974 [1846]. *The German Ideology.* London: Lawrence & Wishart.

McChesney, R. W. 1993. *Telecommunications, Mass Media, and Democracy: The Battle for the Control of U.S. Broadcasting, 1928–1935.* New York: Oxford University Press.

Nason, S., and D. Redding. 2002. *Losing Reality.* London: Third World and Environment Broadcasting Project.

Public Broadcasting Service. 2002. "The Public Television Audience." http://pbs.org/insidepbs/facts.

Robillard, S. 1995. *Television in Europe: Regulatory Bodies. Status, Functions, and Powers in 35 European Countries.* London: John Libbey.

Sergeant, J.-C. 1999. "The Future of Public Broadcasting." In M. Scriven and M. Lecomte, eds., *Television Broadcasting in Contemporary France and Britain,* 107–19. New York: Berghahn.

Sterling, C. H., and J. M. Kittross. 2002. *Stay Tuned: A History of American Broadcasting.* Mahwah, N.J.: Lawrence Erlbaum.

Stone, J. 2000. *Losing Perspective: Global Affairs on British Terrestrial Television, 1989–1999.* London: Third World and Environment Broadcasting Project.

Towler, R. 2001. *The Public's View 2001.* London: ITC. http://itc.org.uk.

Wilson, V., ed. 1993. *The Book of Great American Documents.* Brookeville, Md.: American History Research Associates.

12

Capitalism's Chernobyl?
From Ground Zero to Cyberspace and Back Again

Vincent Mosco

PRE-9/11

New York's World Trade Center was arguably the first material manifestation of the postindustrial society idea, which was hatched intellectually a short subway ride away at *Fortune* magazine when Daniel Bell was labor editor. It took root later on, further up the subway line at Columbia University, where Bell was professor of sociology. Scholarly attention to the concept of a postindustrial society has understandably focused on the idea and its history. But, particularly in light of the September 11 attacks, it is important to reflect on its physical birth in the Twin Towers.

The Trade Center project grew out of a fierce debate in the 1950s and 1960s, when a dispute about urban redevelopment—what to do with Lower Manhattan—effectively became the first surrogate for an argument about the meaning and significance of a postindustrial society. In brief, on one side were proponents of strengthening the existing mixed economy of blue- and white-collar labor and affordable housing. On the other were supporters of a postindustrial monoculture of office towers and luxury housing. The latter, led by David and Nelson Rockefeller, won out over a movement that included the noted urban specialist Jane Jacobs (1961) and other critics of the view that New York City would inevitably lead the way to a postindustrial service economy (New York City Planning Commission 1969; Regional Planning Association 1968).

New York City once provided one of the best examples of a diverse, post-Fordist socioeconomic order, led by small and medium-sized enterprises. It had a strong public infrastructure, long before Piore and Sabel (1984) made the so-called second industrial divide popular and before scholars and planners flocked to Bologna to document the success of the "Third Italy" (Best 1990). All of this ended between 1959 and 1975, when New York eliminated 440,000 of 990,000 manufacturing jobs. By the early 1990s the total of industrial jobs eliminated rose to 750,000. In 1967 alone, as Danny Lyon powerfully documents in his now deeply haunting photographic essay, over sixty acres of buildings in Lower Manhattan were destroyed, an area four times larger than the site of the WTC attack (Lyon 1969, 3). As a result, Lower Manhattan, including the Trade Center and the luxury housing complex Battery Park City, which literally rose out of the Hudson River from material dug out of the ground to create the towers, became the icon for a postindustrial society (Darton 1999; Doig 2002; Fitch 1993).

MYTHS OF CYBERSPACE

The postindustrial society idea grew into a myth, understood not as a falsehood but in the anthropological sense as a transcendent story providing a social identity. In the 1980s and 1990s, with the arrival of global computer communication, it broadened into a set of myths connecting cyberspace to the end of history, the end of geography, and the end of politics. Computer communication, now the Internet, provides the most recent version of what James Carey (1992) calls the "electrical sublime," at once the banal infrastructure for globalization and the spectacle of universal intelligence celebrated and venerated in the breezy triumphalism of *Wired* magazine and the unsettling visions of people like theologian Teilhard de Chardin (1959). Writing before the Internet era, Teilhard is praised today for his image of the noosphere, a literal atmosphere of thought mounting in pressure on a world whose linked intelligence prepares the way for an evolutionary leap. Cyberspace provides a transcendent spectacle, what Leo Marx dubbed the "rhetoric of the technological sublime," which sends up hymns to progress that rise "like froth on a tide of exuberant self-regard sweeping over all misgivings, problems, and contradictions" (1964, 207). Cyberspace renews what was once promised by telegraph, telephone, film, radio, and television by offering the literal connections, the missing links that will bring about the end of history, the end of geography, and the end of politics.

Cyberspace has anointed our time with an apocalyptic quality—the end of history. It becomes, in the work of Frances Fukuyama (1992), Nicholas Negroponte (1995), and Ray Kurzweil (1999), to name just some of the leading gurus, a radical disjunction in time, opening the way to a new era no longer confined by economic, technological, or even biological limitations that heretofore marked every historical period. For Fukuyama cyberspace enables liberal democracy to mark the end point in an evolutionary process that has taken people through stages of development (e.g., hunting and gathering, agriculture), modes of thinking (mythic, religious, philosophic), and forms of governance (tribal, feudal, communist, fascist). For the former director of MIT's noted Media Lab, Nicholas Negroponte, the end of history comes with the end of an analog world and the arrival of a digital one to which we must accommodate our lives. In straightforward prose, he offers a prophet's call to say good-bye to a world of atoms, with its coarse and confining materiality. Instead, he welcomes the digital world, with its infinitely malleable electrons that transcend temporal constraints. The world of atoms is ending, he says, and we must learn to be digital.

Ray Kurzweil brings the ballast of strong technological credentials (including widely used aids to the blind) to a best-selling book that casts the end of history in biological terms. The radical disjunction means the end of death as we know it, because we are rapidly developing the ability to preserve our intelligence in computer software so that "life expectancy is no longer a viable term in relation to intelligent beings" (1999, 280). For Kurzweil, one of history's fundamental problems is that we have been dependent on the "longevity of our *hardware*," that physical self which he condemns through Yeats as "but a paltry thing, a tattered coat upon a stick." History ends as we "cross the divide" and "instantiate ourselves into our computational technology" (Kurzweil 1999, 128–29).

Cyberspace helps us cross the spatial divide, putting an end to geography as we know it. For Frances Cairncross (1997), this means the "death of distance," as cyberspace permits us to experience what it means to be anywhere at any time of our choosing. Accepting this view, Kenichi Ohmae (1990, 1995) celebrates a "borderless world" where any attempt to create boundaries is doomed to failure or what William Mitchell (1999) calls an "e-topia" of near boundless choices for where and how we live and work. For him, the web does not just extend geometry: "It negates geometry" (Mitchell 1995, 8). Even someone like Margaret Wertheim (1999), who takes a less triumphalist view, nevertheless sees cyberspace as spatially disjunctive, exploding the singularity of the Enlightenment's vision of one empirical space and introducing an experience reminiscent of the medieval era where existential space was inherently dual. The medieval mind, she contends, saw space as secular and spiritual; today the divide is between material space and cyberspace.

Finally, cyberspace promises to close politics as we know it by undermining organizational constraints on building networked democracies and by sweeping away age-old strategic military thinking (Mosco and Foster 2001). In the work of the Tofflers (1995), George Gilder (2000), George Keyworth and other members of the Progress and Freedom Foundation, the end of politics means more than just deploying computer communication to create democracy.

Cyberspace redefines what we traditionally called politics by grounding power in networks rather than in institutions. New economic power rests in malleable structures, systems with nodal points whose power comes not from geographical supremacy but from networked interdependence and flexibility. Real-time and twenty-four hour networks of information flows topple the physical city and the nation-state too, creating new laws to which politics must comply or face extinction. Proponents of this vision go as far as to envision a quantum politics whose indeterminacy mirrors that of the subatomic world.

The end of politics also means the end of fear, particularly the traditional fear of military attack because computer communications enables a defense against it. Specifically, the need for offensive weapons and strategies of mutually assured destruction fade away as ballistic missile defense systems lift a protective umbrella to shield the world. Ronald Reagan first called for such a system, with his Strategic Defense and Strategic Computing Initiatives, telling Gorbachev that he could see the "hand of providence" in it. George W. Bush has brought it back to life with plans for a complete defense against nuclear attack. Once again, we hear the words of a new dawn in global security, of world peace, driven by a kind of "machina ex deo" that transforms politics as we have known it throughout history (Mosco and Foster 2001).

MYTHS MATTER

There are several ways to respond to these myths of cyberspace, including simply debunking them. Indeed, the history of communication technology, including the telegraph (Standage 1998), telephone (Martin 1991), radio (Douglas 1987), and television (Fisher and Fisher 1996) reveals a pattern. Each of these arrived with the triumphalist expression that they mark a break with history, the death of distance, and an end to the politics of division, if not the arrival of world peace. Admittedly, each typically contains a subtext that worries about harmful social impacts on the family, privacy, and authentic communication. But each wave of communication technology, including associated systems like electricity, had its time to bask in the glow of the technological sublime before the inevitable routinization set in, and the return of a view that Raymond Williams gave some conceptual heft: technology is little more than a congealed social relationship. It is capable of good as well as evil and, as it literally withdraws into the woodwork of homes and offices, considerable banality.

James Carey (1992, 200) said that "nostalgia for the future" has turned out to be one of our most potent pastorals. Even after what is arguably the greatest collapse in modern business history, after millions of people lost billions of dollars in the telecommunications and dot-com industries alone, people still believe. Forget the crash, forget banality; the December 2002 issue of *Wired* magazine offers a cover and several feature articles on computers, science, transcendence, and religion. The highlight is a feature by its irrepressible editor-at-large Kevin Kelly, who announces in the title that "God Is the Machine." If you happen to wonder which machine, he concludes that the "universe is not merely like a computer it *is* a computer" (Kelly 2002, 183).

It is therefore useful to address myths by taking them seriously. In this view, their value is determined less by whether or not they are empirically true or false, but rather by whether they are living or dead. What keeps myths alive? One answer is that myths are sustained by social practices that involve the leadership of storytellers whose accomplishments in one arena give them a platform to promote myths. Bill Gates's ability to sustain a business monopoly gives him the space to mythologize about revolution and transcendence in his books *The Road Ahead* (1995) and *Business at the Speed of Thought* (1999). The storytelling no longer takes place around a campfire, but through a dense and recombinant field of media that amplify, simplify, and modify the tales of Gates, Negroponte, Gilder, the Tofflers, and others, for the world's audiences. These deceptively simple stories of a new age, new economy, next new thing, also contain the sophisticated practices perfected by magicians and conjurers over the centuries. These protective covers, including what Barthes (1972) called the process of inoculation, even find a role for the ancient and wily trickster, now taking on the shape of the computer hacker.

DIGITIZATION AND COMMODIFICATION

Myths can be understood for what they reveal, the desire for genuine community, but also for what they conceal. The myth of cyberspace is a primary example of what Barthes meant when he defined myth as depoliticized speech. Myths conceal a great deal about the politics of cyberspace and here it is useful to focus on the relationship between the processes of digitization and commodification. Digitization refers to the transformation of communication, including words, images, motion pictures, and sounds, into a common language. It provides enormous gains in speed and flexibility over earlier forms of electronic communication, which were largely based on analog techniques (Longstaff 2002). Mythmakers jump from here to the view that the world of atoms is developing into a virtual utopia. This is mistaken because it neglects to recognize that digitization takes place along with the process of commodification or the transformation of use to exchange value.

The expansion of the commodity form provides the context for precisely how digitization develops. It is used first and foremost to expand the commodification of information and entertainment content, deepen the commodification of labor involved in the production, distribution and exchange of communication, and expand markets in the audiences that take in and make use of digitized communication (Mosco 1996). Digitization takes place in the context of powerful commercial forces and also serves to advance the overall process of commodification worldwide. Cyberspace can be seen to result from the mutual constitution of digitization and commodification.

Digitization expands the commodification of content by extending the opportunities to measure and monitor, package and repackage entertainment and information. Packaging material in the paper-and-ink form of a newspaper or book has provided a flexible, if limited, means to commodify communication by offering an adequate form in which to measure the commodity and monitor purchases. Challenges arose when what Bernard Miège calls "flow" type communication systems arose, most significantly television (Miège 1989). It forced the question, How does one package a television program for sale to a viewer? Initially, commodification was based on a relatively inflexible system of delivering a batch of channels into the home and having viewers pay for the receiver and for a markup on products advertised over the air. This system did not account for different use of the medium, nor did it make any clear connection between viewing and purchasing. It amounted to a Fordist system of delivering general programming to a mass audience that was marketed to advertisers for a price per thousand viewers. Each step along the way to the digitization of television has refined the commodification of content, allowing for the flow to be "captured" or, more precisely, for the commodity to be measured, monitored, and packaged in increasingly more specific and customized ways. Early cable television improved on commodification by charging per month for a set of channels. As this medium has become digitized, companies now offer many more channels and package them in multiple ways, including selling content on a pay-per-view basis. Material delivered over television, the Internet, or some combination of these and other new wired and wireless systems can now be packaged and repackaged for sale in some related form with the transaction itself measured and monitored by the same digital system.

The recursive nature of digital systems expands the commodification of the entire communication process. Digital systems that precisely measure and monitor each information transaction can be used to refine the process of delivering audiences of viewers, listeners, readers, movie fans, telephone and computer users to advertisers. Companies can package and repackage customers in forms that specifically reflect both their actual purchases and their demographic characteristics. These packages, for example, of eighteen- to twenty-five-year-old women who order pop music concerts on pay-per-view television can be sold to companies that spend more for this information because they want to market their products to this specific sector with little advertising wasted on groups who would not be interested or able to buy. This refines the commodification of viewers over the Fordist system of delivering mass audiences to advertisers, and it is being applied to almost every communication medium today.

The labor of communication is also being commodified. The replacement of mechanical with electronic systems cut thousands of jobs in the printing

industry as electronic typesetting did away with the jobs of linotype operators. Today's digital systems allow companies to expand this process. Print
reporters increasingly serve in the combined roles of editor and page
producer. They not only report on a story but also put it into a form for transmission to the printed and increasingly electronic page. Companies generally retain the rights to the multiplicity of repackaged forms and thereby
profit from each use. Broadcast journalists carry cameras and edit tape for
delivery over television or computer networks. The film industry is starting
to deliver digital copies of movies to theaters in multiple locations over communication satellite, thereby eliminating distribution of celluloid copies for
exhibition by projectionists. Companies sell software before it has been de-
bugged on the understanding that customers will report errors, download
and install updates, and figure out how to work around problems. This ability to eliminate labor, combine it to perform multiple tasks, and shift labor to
unpaid consumers further expands the revenue potential (Hardt and Brennen 1995; McKercher 2002; Sussman and Lent 1998).

CORPORATE INTEGRATION AND CONCENTRATION

The mutual constitution of digitization and commodification contributes to
the integration of the communication sector and the concentration of corporate power within it. The adoption of a common digital language across the
communication industry is breaking down barriers that once separated print,
broadcasting, telecommunications, and the information technology or computer data sectors. These divisions have been historically important because
they contained the legal and institutional marks of the particular period in
which they rose to prominence. The print publishing industry is marked by
a legal regime of free expression, limited government involvement, and local ownership. Broadcasting and telecommunications rose to prominence
alongside the rise of powerful nation-state authority and national production, distribution, and exhibition systems. Western legal systems placed a
greater regulatory burden on radio, television, and telephone systems, going
as far as to create publicly controlled institutions in these sectors in order to
accomplish national objectives that included reflecting a national identity
and building a national market. National firms were more likely than was the
case in print publishing to control commercial broadcasting and telecommunications systems.

The information technology or computer data industry took off in the
post–World War II era and embodies the trend away from nation-state regulation, except to advance the expansion of businesses and control by multinational firms. There are numerous legal and institutional struggles in this
sector, but unlike the broadcasting and telecommunications sectors, the
computer industry faced no public interest or public service responsibilities,

no subsidized pricing, no commitment to universal access, and no expectation that national firms would be more than one step on the way to multinational control (Schiller 1999; McChesney 1999). This has become the model for the convergent communication industry.

The growing integration of communication sectors into a consolidated electronic information and entertainment arena helps explain the unprecedented acceleration in mergers and acquisitions. Communication systems in the United States are now largely shaped by a handful of companies, including U.S.-based Microsoft, AT&T, General Electric, Viacom, Disney Corporation, AOL–Time Warner, and the Liberty Media Corporation. There are others, including non–U.S. based firms like News Corporation, Bertelsmann, Vivendi Universal, and Sony. Each of these firms has a significant transnational presence through outright ownership, strategic partnerships, and investment ("The Big Ten" 2002).

Concentration is far from an exclusively American phenomenon. The Canadian communication arena is arguably more highly concentrated, with four firms in the most dominant positions: BCE, Rogers Communication, CanWest, and Quebecor. (Some might add a fifth firm, Shaw Communication.) BCE alone has spread over a wider terrain than even its admittedly larger American and European counterparts. The company's former chair and CEO boasts about what would be the American equivalent of BCE: "Start by combining the telephone businesses of Verizon Communications and SBC Communications. Then add Verizon's wireless operations, and America Online's Internet customers. Fold in ABC's television network, the ESPN cable sports network and the Direct-TV satellite service. Finally, tack on The New York Times" (Simon 2001). Marveling at Bell's ability to dominate the Canadian industry, a correspondent concludes that American antitrust officials and regulators would not permit such a conglomerate to be assembled in the United States (Simon 2001). Whether this is true is debatable, but the combination of growing concentration and diminishing regulation certainly leads some to fear that cyberspace will be little more than a commercial space with less than adequate room for diversity and the clash of ideas so vital to democracy (Sunstein 2001).

The transformation, however, is far from complete. Canadian communication firms, like their counterparts in the United States, Europe, and elsewhere face enormous pressures toward regional and global integration (Mosco and Schiller 2001). In order to expand transnational corporate communications, nationally controlled institutions would have to be eliminated, or at least marginalized, and public service principles would have to be sharply reduced or eliminated entirely. American corporate and political leaders lobbied furiously beginning in the 1980s to advance these changes in an even more expansive campaign to liberalize trade and investment rules. Playing important roles in this process were government initiatives, private economic diplomacy, bilateral negotiations between states, and multilateral organizations such as the World Bank, the International Monetary Fund (IMF), and the World Trade Organization (WTO). The Free Trade Agreement (FTA), which brought together Canada and the United States, and the North American Free Trade Agreement (NAFTA), which added Mexico, made up significant initiatives within this larger movement. Each was perceived as the beginning of a broader push for the liberalization of global trade and investment within the organizational context of the frameworks established by the General Agreement on Tariffs and Trade (GATT) and now the World Trade Organization.

TENSIONS AND CONTRADICTIONS

Media concentration is a powerful force, but it often does not produce the synergies that companies anticipate and sometimes results in content that does not succeed in attracting audiences. Digitization is not a flawless process and technical problems have slowed its development. Furthermore, we can observe significant political contradictions. The dominant political tendency today is neoliberalism, which was founded on the retreat of the state from vital areas of social life, including regulating and setting policy for the communications industry, where the state was once directly involved in the construction of infrastructure, the establishment of technical standards, the regulation of market access, and even the direct provision of services. According to neoliberalism, such functions are best provided by the private sector with minimal state involvement. Neoliberalism aims to customize state functions, tailor them to suit business needs, and thereby avoid the problems that the vision of the state as a universal or public space, open to a wide range of contestation, used to provide.

The communication arena demonstrates that it is not so easy to accomplish this feat. Consider first the development of technical standards. Digitization requires common technical standards to harmonize the processing, distribution, and reception of digital signals. It is one thing to turn audio, video, and data streams into digital packets; quite another to ensure their flawless flow through global grids. To accomplish this, it is essential to set a wide range of standards for the equipment necessary to encode and decode signals and for managing data flows through networks. Achieving such agreement is normally quite difficult. Competing firms are reluctant to cooperate because they resist sharing sensitive and valuable information. Societies have traditionally dealt with this problem by establishing government agencies or private–public partnerships to serve as independent standards arbiters. Almost a century and a half ago, competing telegraph interests established the International Telecommunication Union (ITU), a global body composed of mainly government organizations and managed on a one-nation, one-vote basis to set global standards for the new technology. Over the years, the ITU expanded its role as each new communication technology came along. For example, it set standards for the telephone, allocated broadcasting frequencies, and eventually the orbital locations of communication satellites.

However, conflict grew at the ITU as the number of nations increased, including former colonial societies eager to create standards to expand widespread access to communication technology and not just the profits of communication companies. As a result, core capitalist powers, led by the United States, began to consider alternatives. These included political bodies like Intelsat, a global communication satellite organization whose rules permitted Western control, and more recently private corporations, primarily ICANN, the Internet Corporation for Assigned Names and Numbers, which essentially establishes standards for the Internet. The goal of these organizations has generally been to set business-friendly standards without sacrificing global credibility.

However, it is increasingly difficult to accomplish this because digitization is now global and the competition to dominate markets for the short term by controlling one phase of a rapidly changing system or for the long term by setting an important standard (such as for a computer operating system) is intensifying. Furthermore, the number of global interests is expanding so that even something as seemingly innocuous as setting a national suffix for a web address becomes a political question when, to cite one particularly fractious case, it is Palestine petitioning for .ps. Should the common ".com" suffix expand to include "union" as one public interest group proposed? Private businesses expect to depoliticize these issues by setting up Western controlled private or only quasi-public standards organizations. But they are actually only displacing tensions and contradictions.

In 2002 ICANN ultimately succeeded in eliminating democratically elected members, but this does not likely guarantee smooth functioning (Jesdanum 2002). This got rid of elected board members like Ken Auerbach who tried to democratize ICANN but consistently ran up against age-old bureaucratic and political problems. Auerbach met ICANN executives' refusal to provide him with the organization's records by turning to a judge who supported the dissident director's request. ICANN responded by eliminating Auerbach and other elected board members (Geist 2002a). One telecommunications analyst calls for the elimination of ICANN, charging that the agency descended to a new low by meeting in locations that are distant from most of the activists who have been pressing for change in order to keep them from showing up at meetings. The decision to eliminate elected board members was made at an ICANN meeting in Shanghai, China (Weinstein 2002). Consider the irony of an international organization set up to address needs of the new online global community, doing what it can to keep its representatives as far away as possible. Is this the real meaning of the end of geography?

In light of these developments, one should therefore not be surprised that ICANN's legitimacy should suffer. Moreover, it should come as no surprise that a 2001 report found more than five hundred top-level domains being operated around the world by some two hundred administrators, all outside the official domain name system (Weiss 2001). How many more rogue networks will be added to that total as ICANN withdraws legitimacy from its system? What about the protests that accompanied its decision to remove elected members of its board? One consequence has been a stepped-up effort to shift international decision-making power over domain names to the ITU, which in October 2002 approved a resolution on managing multilingual domain names. One analyst has gone as far as to suggest that the ITU will likely emerge as the "governance leader" (Geist 2002b). Nevertheless, this alternative, setting up genuinely public, national, or international regulatory authorities, a central feature in the expansion of communication during the Fordist period, invites turning this arena into a highly contested terrain.

This contradiction has also marked debates about how to expand access to technology in order to build markets and how to ensure some measure of privacy to create consumer confidence in the technology. For example, in the early days of radio, business felt it did not need government to regulate frequencies. The result was near chaos, as broadcasters poached each other's frequencies and the air was filled with worthless static. Business brought in the state to bring order to the chaos and it succeeded. But in doing so, it opened this private arena to the wider public, which used the opportunity to fight for public broadcasting and the regulation of private station content. The technology has indeed changed but the political economic dynamic has not; and so the same tensions and contradictions mark the world of digitization (Lessig 2001).

Consider the burst of the telecommunications bubble. Once industry giants like Nortel, Cisco, Lucent, and now WorldCom (this icon of the telecom boom was bounced from the NASDAQ and S&P 500 in 2002 and had its credit rating reduced to junk status) have shrunk into economic obscurity. Between 2000 and 2002, Nortel and Lucent lost 98 percent of their stock value and, between the two alone, shed 148,000 jobs out of a total of more than 500,000 lost in the telecommunications industry. WorldCom's demise is extraordinary even in the context of the most substantial crash in the history of the telecommunications industry. Once America's second largest telecommunications carrier, WorldCom filed for bankruptcy in July 2002. With $107 billion in assets, it was the largest such action in U.S. history. As of October 2002 the company was charged with $7.4 billion worth of accounting irregularities. Building its capitalization on a variety of shady practices, including its incorrect claim that Internet traffic was doubling every hundred days, a claim dignified in government reports that repeated it, WorldCom appeared to be the new model for the Internet-savvy telecommunications industry. Aided by the Telecommunications Act of 1996, which diminished scrutiny over the company, WorldCom enjoyed a blank check from regulatory authorities. As a former deputy general counsel at the FCC put it, "the agency was oblivious to the enormous accounting fraud at WorldCom." He now calls for stripping the company of the licenses and certifications it needs to do business (Sidak 2002, A31). But WorldCom, though arguably the worst case, was hardly alone. At the end of 2001, the eight largest telecommunications companies collectively owed $191 billion and with demand flat, there was little prospect of debt repayment (Goodman 2002). This was partly because even companies like AT&T and Sprint, which have not been accused of WorldCom's offenses, faced enormous pressure to meet the results that WorldCom appeared to be generating. Unable to do so legitimately, their stock value was pummeled, and the companies were forced to restructure operations and replace senior management (Schiesel 2002).

Global Crossing is a small company that was touted by Internet guru George Gilder as a solid contender for domination of the telecommunications industry in the new century. This firm, led by a protégé of junk bond felon Michael Milken, managed to raise $750 million almost overnight, went public, reached a value of $30 billion, built a transatlantic fiber network valued at much less, and with a glut in capacity (95 percent of fiber network capacity goes unused) collapsed in January 2002. The company's share value declined by 99 percent to 13.5 cents a share and it filed for bankruptcy, the largest one by a telecommunications company, joining other high fliers like 360networks, which Gilder forecast would battle Global Crossing for telecommunications supremacy in the twenty-first century, in bankruptcy in 2001 (Romero 2002). Fearing a case of "Enronitis," the FBI and the Securities and Exchange Commission launched investigations into Global Crossing in February 2002. As it turns out, the company was literally connected to the icon of corporate malfeasance, Enron, in a complex deal brokered by a third party that enabled both Enron and Global Crossing to circumvent accounting rules and book revenue, and allowed Global Crossing to hide a loan (Barboza and Romero 2002, C5). This appears to be part of a wider practice whereby Enron and other energy companies sought to demonstrate that they were comers in the broadband communication business by trading broadband capacity with one another, thereby pumping up the appearance of their activity in the broadband market (Barboza 2002, C1).

Comparing the telecom situation to Enron, a business correspondent concluded in March 2002 that a "tragedy of identical plot, but with far more damaging implications" is playing out in telecommunications. Unlike the saga of Enron, however, this is not about a single company with mischievous executives; "this tale is about an entire industry that rose to a value of $2 trillion based on dubious promises by Wall Street and company executives for an explosive growth in demand." Cozy relations among formally competing firms led to what seems to be agreements to pad demand forecasts, overvalue assets. and otherwise cook the books (Morgenson 2002, sec. 3, p. 1). Insiders were able to dump their stock at inflated prices before the collapse set in (Berman 2002). According to one article, as "the fiber optic fantasy slips away," the promise of universal access to broadband communication remains just a promise (Romero and Schiesel 2002). Meanwhile, in another spin of the wheel, even well-known bankers like Felix Rohatyn, who once engineered a bailout when New York City declared bankruptcy, calls for a return to rigorous regulation to combat what he calls the "betrayal of capitalism" (Rohatyn 2002a, 6). According to this pillar of the establishment, "I believe that market capitalism is the best economic system ever invented for the creation of wealth; but it must be fair, it must be regulated, and it must be ethical. The excesses of the last few years show how the system has failed in all three respects . . . the system cannot stand much more abuse of the type we have witnessed" (Rohatyn 2002b, 6).

Finally, a similar conundrum shapes the issue of privacy. The drive to use communication and especially the new media of cyberspace to expand the commodification process now includes personal identity. The threat to privacy is not just an offshoot of technology or a correctable oversight but is intrinsic to the commodification process. Consequently, the struggle for personal privacy is part of a wider struggle against the expanding commodity. Among many examples, consider a January 2001 Nortel Networks announcement of a new line of "personal content" network software that the company proposed to sell to Internet service providers. The software would package online services to suit individual preferences. It would do so by tracking every choice a user makes on the Internet and configuring the network to deliver efficiently the kinds of material typically selected. In effect, Nortel would add to the value of the Internet by making it more responsive to customer profiles. But in doing so, the company would make it possible to gather, package, and share information on customer choices. The response of one privacy activist focuses on the company's responsibility charging that it is "unacceptable" to enable Internet service providers to watch where customers are going. However, Nortel's behavior is less a matter of corporate irresponsibility and more that of a company which needs to expand the commodification of its major resource, the Internet. Nortel's product reflects a fundamental contradiction besetting the business of cyberspace—the conflict between the goals of building consumer confidence to turn the Internet into a universal market and commodifying without government intervention whatever moves over the Internet, including personal identity (Associated Press 2001).

THE "ANTIGLOBALIZATION" MOVEMENT

Corporate power in cyberspace is also threatened by social movements that make extensive use of computer communication. Indeed, cyberspace advances a form of political convergence that makes increasingly transparent the divisions between consumption and labor. It fosters an antiglobalization movement that merges the politics of labor from an earlier era (Denning

1996) with the politics of representation that that marked a more recent time (Klein 2000). Mass demonstrations in Seattle, Prague, Quebec, Genoa, and Washington, D.C., as well as the global movements organized around culture jamming, are grounded in a powerful, broad-based understanding of the convergence of labor and consumption in the world today. These movements understand the links between Nike ads and sweatshops making running shoes, as well as between familiar brands like Wal-Mart, Esprit, Kmart, and JCPenney and slave labor. For example, the connections between business and exploitation were documented in a chilling 2002 account of slavery in the mahogany-rich forests and fast food–producing cattle ranches of Brazil (Rohter 2002). Global social movements are today based on the ability to strip the cover from the gloss of a brand to reveal not only the exploitation of labor but also the commercialization of life worldwide and destruction of the earth's environment.

The convergence between labor and consumption demonstrates that convergence does not just mean plugging a cable modem into a PC. For some, these global social movements hold out hope for a renewed public sphere, cosmopolitan citizenship, and a genuinely democratic cyberspace. The convergence of labor and consumption and the politics of citizenship, which seem to mark so much of what is all too glibly called the antiglobalization movement, may be the most significant form of convergence to understand today.

POST-9/11

There was more such hope before the events of September 11. The sociologist Ulrich Beck called 9/11 "capitalism's Chernobyl" because it undermined faith in neoliberalism (Beck 2001). Beck suggests that we need to think much more seriously about the vulnerabilities that follow directly from a global political economy rooted in networks of communication and transportation.

Multiplying global communication and transportation links also multiplies the number of nodes from which to attack and the number of nodes that are open to attack. (Mohammed Atta, who helped fly an aircraft into one tower, made his booking on the American Airlines website; others used Travelocity.com.) Clashing with this process is the tendency of neoliberalism to promote a retreat from the state, which means a retreat from the collective management of expanding networks at the national and international levels. Beck perceptively concludes:

> Today, the capitalist fundamentalists' unswerving faith in the redeeming power of the market has proved to be a dangerous illusion. In times of crises, neoliberalism has no solutions to offer. Fundamental truths that were pushed aside return to the fore. Without taxation, there can be no state. Without a public sphere, democracy and civil society, there can be no legitimacy. And without legitimacy, no security. From this, it follows that without legitimate forums for set-

tling national and global conflicts, there will be no world economy in any form whatsoever. (Beck 2001)

Even at the highest levels of neoliberal orthodoxy are heard what were once considered heretical calls for a return to a more active state in regulation, policy, and security.

The tale of the Twin Towers also reminds us that massive government economic and political support was essential to remake Lower Manhattan and sustain the entire district. The World Trade Center, this icon of postindustrialism, was built because the state condemned the existing properties, appropriated the land, paid for construction, provided tax subsidies higher than anywhere else in the city, and filled the often vacant towers with state government workers (taking up fully fifty stories of one of the towers) (Darton 1999; New York City 2001; Goldberger 2002, 91). It also built a tax-subsidized luxury housing district adjacent to the towers (Battery Park City) and subsidized a high-tech district now in decline (Silicon Alley). Government moved one of the city's elite public schools to the area and added a state-of-the-art park at a time when city schools and parks were suffering from years of neglect. Strengthening the state apparatus can produce mixed results indeed (Mosco 1999).

Returning to Ground Zero suggests that we have come a long way from the breezy triumphalism of the dot-com boom, and we do not know where it will lead. Sober second thoughts might increase support for a cosmopolitan politics, if not a new internationalism. But perhaps that will not be the case and we will find ourselves facing, at first regionally and then perhaps even globally, what Robert Kaplan has called *The Coming Anarchy* (1997).

REFERENCES

Associated Press. 2001. "Nortel Unveils New Technology Tool." January 30.

Barboza, D. 2002. "Signs of Manipulation in Broadband Trading." *New York Times*, May 17, C1, C7.

Barboza, D., and S. Romero. 2002. "Enron Is Seen Having Link with Global." *New York Times*, May 20, C1, C5.

Barthes, R. 1972. *Mythologies*. Translated by A. Lavers. New York: Noonday.

Beck, U. 2001. "Globalisation's Chernobyl." *Financial Times*, November 6. news.ft.com/ft/gx.cgi/ftc?pagename=View&c=Article&cid=FT3U5G8OOTC&live=true. Accessed November 20, 2002.

Berman, D. 2002. "Before Telecom Bubble Burst, Some Insiders Sold Out Stakes." *Wall Street Journal*, August 12.

Best, M. 1990. *The New Competition: Institutions of Industrial Restructuring*. Cambridge: Harvard University Press.

"The Big Ten." 2002. *The Nation*. www.thenation.com/bigten. Accessed January 28, 2002.

Cairncross, F. 1997. *The Death of Distance*. Boston: Harvard Business School Press.

Carey, J. W. 1992. *Communication as Culture*. New York: Routledge.

Darton, E. 1999. *Divided We Stand: A Biography of New York's World Trade Center.* New York: Basic.

Denning, M. 1996. *The Cultural Front.* London: Verso.

Doig, J. W. 2002. *Empire on the Hudson: Entrepreneurial Vision and Political Power at the Port of New York Authority.* New York: Columbia University Press.

Douglas, S. 1987. *Inventing American Broadcasting, 1899–1922.* Baltimore: Johns Hopkins University Press.

Fisher, D. E., and M. J. Fisher. 1996. *Tube: The Invention of Television.* New York: Harcourt Brace.

Fitch, R. 1993. *The Assassination of New York.* New York: Verso.

Fukuyama, F. 1992. *The End of History and the Last Man.* New York: Avon.

Gates, B. 1995. *The Road Ahead.* New York: Viking.

———. 1999. *Business at the Speed of Thought.* New York: Warner.

Geist, M. 2002a. Internet Overseer Takes Wrong Path on Accountability. *Globe and Mail*, August 8, B12.

———. 2002b. "Internet Turf War Playing Out." *Globe and Mail*, November 7, B15.

Gilder, G. 2000. *Telecosm: How Infinite Bandwidth Will Revolutionize Our World.* New York: Free Press.

Goldberger, P. 2002. "Groundwork." *New Yorker*, May 20, 86–96.

Goodman, P. S. 2002. "Telecom Sector May Find Past Is Its Future." *Washington Post.* www.washingtonpost.com/wp-dyn/articles/A36589-2002Jul7.html. Accessed November 20, 2002.

Hardt, H., and B. Brennen, eds. 1995. *Newsworkers: Toward a History of the Rank and File.* Minneapolis: University of Minnesota Press.

Jacobs, J. 1961. *The Death and Life of the Great American Cities.* New York: Random House.

Jesdanum, A. 2002. "ICANN's Contrarian Gets the Boot." *SiliconValley.com*, October 29. www.siliconvalley.com/mid/siliconvalley/news/editorial/4384835.htm. Accessed November 1, 2002.

Kaplan, R. 1997. *The Coming Anarchy.* New York: Knopf.

Kelly, K. 2002. "God Is the Machine." *Wired*, December, 180–85.

Klein, N. 2000. *No Logo.* Toronto: Knopf Canada.

Kurzweil, R. 1999. *The Age of Spiritual Machines.* New York: Viking.

Lessig, L. 2001. *The Future of Language.* New York: Random House.

Longstaff, P. F. 2002. *The Communications Toolkit.* Cambridge: MIT Press.

Lyon, D. 1969. *The Destruction of Lower Manhattan.* New York: Macmillan.

Martin, M. 1991. *"Hello, Central": Gender, Technology, and Culture in the Formation of Telephone Systems.* Montreal: McGill-Queen's University Press.

Marx, L. 1964. *The Machine in the Garden· Technology and the Pastoral Ideal in America.* New York: Oxford University Press.

McChesney, R. 1999. *Rich Media, Poor Democracy.* Urbana: University of Illinois Press.

McKercher, C. 2002. *Newsworkers Unite: Labor, Convergence, and North American Newspapers.* Lanham, Md.: Rowman & Littlefield.

Miège, B. 1989. *The Capitalization of Cultural Production.* New York: International General.

Mitchell, W. J. 1995. *City of Bits.* Cambridge: MIT Press.

———. 1999. *E-topia.* Cambridge: MIT Press.

Morgenson, G. 2002. "Telecom: Tangled in Its Own Web." *New York Times*, March 24, sec. 3, pp. 1, 7.

Mosco, V. 1996. *The Political Economy of Communication.* London: Sage.

———. 1999. "New York.com: A Political Economy of the 'Informational' City." *Journal of Media Economics* 12, no. 2: 103–16.

Mosco, V., and D. Foster. 2001. "Cyberspace and the End of Politics." *Journal of Communication Inquiry* 25, no. 3: 218–36.

Mosco, V., and D. Schiller, eds. 2001. *Continental Order? Integrating North America for Cybercapitalism.* Lanham, Md.: Rowman & Littlefield.

Negroponte, N. 1995. *Being Digital.* New York: Knopf.

New York City. Office of Management and Budget. 2001. Statement by the Mayor. New York, April 25.

New York City Planning Commission. 1969. *Plan for New York City.* New York: New York City Planning Commission

Ohmae, K. 1990. *The Borderless World.* New York: HarperCollins.

———. 1995. *The End of the Nation-State.* New York: Free Press.

Piore, M. J., and C. F. Sabel. 1984. *The Second Industrial Divide.* New York: Basic.

Regional Planning Association. 1968. *The Second Regional Plan.* New York: Regional Planning Association.

Rohatyn, F. 2002a. "The Betrayal of Capitalism." *New York Review of Books,* February 28, 6.

———. 2002b. "From New York to Baghdad." *New York Review of Books,* November 21, 4, 6.

Rohter, L. 2002. "Brazil's Prized Exports Rely on Slaves and Scorched Land." *New York Times,* March 25, A1.

Romero, S. 2002. "In Another Big Bankruptcy, a Fiber Optic Venture Fails." *New York Times,* January 29, A1, C10.

Romero, S., and S. Schiesel. 2002. "The Fiber Optic Fantasy Slips Away." *New York Times,* February 17. www.nytimes.com/2002/02/17/business/yourmoney/17BAND.html. Last accessed November 20, 2002.

Schiesel, S. 2002. "Trying to Catch Worldcom's Mirage." *New York Times,* June 30, sec. 3, pp. 1, 14.

Schiller, D. 1999. *Digital Capitalism.* Cambridge: MIT Press.

Sidak, J. G. 2002. "The F.C.C.'s Duty." *New York Times,* October 8, A31.

Simon, B. 2001. "A Telecom Umbrella Extends Its Shadow." *New York Times,* December 24, C3.

Standage, T. 1998. *The Victorian Internet.* New York: Walker.

Sunstein, C. 2001. *Republic.com.* Princeton: Princeton University Press.

Sussman, G., and J. Lent, eds. 1998. *Global Productions.* London: Sage.

Teilhard de Chardin. 1959. *The Phenomenon of Man.* New York: Harper.

Toffler, A., and H. Toffler. 1995. *Creating a New Civilization: The Politics of the Third Wave.* Atlanta: Turner Publishing.

Weinstein, L., 2002. "ICANN Needs Another Long Trip." *Wired,* November 18. www.wired.com/news/politics/0,1283,56398,00.html. Accessed November 19, 2002.

Weiss, T. R. 2001. "ICANN, under Fire, Targets Alternate Top-Level Domain Name System." *Computerworld,* May 31. www.computerworld.com/governmenttopics/government/legalissues/story/0,10801,60980,00.html. Accessed November 20, 2002.

Wertheim, M. 1999. *The Pearly Gates of Cyberspace.* New York: Norton.

13

New Media and
the Forces of Capitalism

Robin Mansell and Michèle Javary

If the analysis of economic power is made central to a discussion of the likely future development of the new media—the technologies and services based on digital networks and platforms—the important role of financial capital in the new media markets cannot be ignored. This chapter considers the role of financial capital in forging the emerging structure of the new media markets in the United Kingdom. It highlights the need to give greater consideration to the legislative framework for regulation in order to protect certain aspects of the public interest in a high-quality and relatively low-cost new media infrastructure. Measures additional to those proposed in the draft communications bill of May 2002 in the United Kingdom are needed.

Those who adopt a social constructivist position with respect to the new technologies, such as MacKenzie (1996, 6), generally ask about who the new technologies are likely to be good for. As MacKenzie puts it, "different people may see a technology in different ways, attach different meanings to it, want different things from it, assess it differently. . . . Technologies . . . may be best because they have triumphed, rather than triumphing because they are best." This observation is undoubtedly accurate, but this type of approach to the analysis of the implications of the new media technologies and their consequences does not enable us to consider the principal economic forces that are shaping the new media environment.

Another viewpoint has been expressed by Castells (2000, 1), who adapts Freeman's (1982) earlier discussion of techno-economic paradigms to argue that the new media represent a "cluster of inter-related technical, organizational, and managerial innovations, whose advantages are to be found in their superior productivity and efficiency in accomplishing an assigned goal." He goes on to suggest that "they process the goals they are programmed to perform. . . . To assign different goals to the programme of the network . . . actors will have to challenge the network from the outside . . . around alternative values." The implication is that some components of the new media might be produced and consumed outside the constraint of capitalist forces of production. This controversial point is not the one that is of particular interest in this chapter. Instead, we want to focus on the implications of Castells's observation with respect to the "goals" that the new media technologies and services are being "programmed to perform."

In this chapter, we first consider the way the predominant logic of new media development is being understood by many policy makers and the particular way in which these observers regard the market as the key "driver" for the development of the new media landscape. Second, by examining the roles of financial capital and governance processes in the Internet service provider (ISP) market in the United Kingdom, we highlight trends that appear to run counter to the conclusion that the predominant market logic is consistent with the public interest in new media services. Our analysis indicates a need for regulation of certain aspects of the new media markets that extend into the Internet realm. This view is a departure from the predominant one that advocates Internet self-regulation as the best means of protecting the public interest in the United Kingdom.

The position developed in this chapter is consistent with Trebing's (1995, 1998) argument with respect to market developments in the U.S. telecommunication and ISP industries. He claims that these developments are inconsistent with an adequate standard of protection of the public interest. Similarly, Bar and colleagues (1999) indicate that sustained regulatory intervention is needed to encourage the evolution of an open Internet environment in the United States. Their views contrast with those of Oxman (1999), who argues that given the immaturity of the ISP market in the United States, there is no basis for regulatory intervention.

THE LOGIC OF NEW MEDIA MARKETS

The predominant logic of the new media marketplace has been articulated in various international policy forums in recent years. There is a widely promoted vision of an emergent global knowledge society. As the deputy secretary general of the Organization for Economic Cooperation and Development

(OECD) put it during a conference in 2001, "the world has become a real global place; not just a global market place. . . . The global distribution of skills and knowledge is the precondition for the distribution of wealth in the world economy."[1] The secretary-general of the OECD also observed that "education and e-competence are essential . . . governments must adopt 'best practices.'" As the chairperson of the Group of Eight's Digital Opportunities Task Force put it, "The ICT revolution could be a powerful driver for empowering the world's poor; strong partnerships and reciprocal listening are essential. . . . The divide is about information, knowledge and global identity."

This vision of a global knowledge society is accompanied by a very specific view of the economic logic of the new media marketplace. It is at the heart of the predominant thinking that informs much of the "knowledge society" debate. This view is one in which the whole of society is expected to benefit when markets are fully open to the flow and circulation of capital which, in turn, is expected to stimulate investment in ever greater bandwidth and subsequently new digital content.

The building of inclusive local and global virtual communities is expected to be achieved by the establishment of trusted social networks. These, however, are to be underpinned by competitive markets in all aspects of information and communication service supply. In addition, as digital services spread as a primary economic activity, countries should comply with existing taxation regimes. No new taxes should be imposed on online service revenues regardless of shifts in the tax base with the growth in the importance of electronic services or in the face of social need.

The constitution of the institutional rules of the game—the policies and regulations that apply globally, regionally, and nationally with respect to trade, intellectual property rights, telecommunication and broadcast services, and Internet-related activities—should be accomplished according to a one-size-fits-all model. Market forces should be unleashed and "light touch" regulation should prevail. The underlying rationale for this economic logic is, as argued by an economist who advises policy makers on trade issues, that "investing in innovation (in digital technologies), human resources and knowledge provides an endless mechanism for growth." He argued during the same conference that there is no foreseeable "ceiling on rates of growth because of the processes of learning, competence building, and capability accumulation that are enabled by investment in new technologies."

This is the prevailing logic of the new media paradigm. It goes hand in hand with the view that the knowledge (or information) society, resting on new media technologies, is beneficial for economic growth and well-being. It is closely linked to the argument that regulation of the new media is not a major concern given the innovative capacity and competitiveness of the new media firms.

However, some Internet industry analysts reach a different conclusion. For example, Huston observes that, in spite of the flurry of entry into and exit from an important segment of the new media marketplace, the ISP markets in the industrialized countries,

> underneath the veneer of a highly competitive Internet service market is a somewhat different environment, in which every ISP network must interoperate with neighbouring Internet networks in order to produce a delivered service outcome of comprehensive connectivity and end-to-end services, and therefore, every ISP must not only coexist with other ISPs but also must operate in cooperation with other ISPs. (Huston 1999, 1)

This is the cooperative ethos that is widely believed to be embedded in the Internet's architecture and is also believed to be associated with the socially enabling features of the new media environment (Castells 2001).

Huston goes on to argue that Internet carriage service (i.e., Internet traffic distribution) has become a commodity service that provides little opportunity for product differentiation. In the traffic wholesale business, a relatively low rate of financial return is the norm. Most ISPs are seeking to participate in service retail markets where there is a potential for differentiating products and increasing profit margins. Huston suggests that the "Internet market is not a sustainable open competitive market. Under such circumstances there is no natural market outcome other than aggregation of providers, leading to the establishment of monopoly positions in the Internet provider space" (Huston 1999, 23). This opens the possibility that the competitive process in the ISP market may lead to variety reduction through increasing concentration in the industry. Such a reduction would be inconsistent with the public interest in new media services, as we indicate in the following sections of this chapter.

ISPs are retailing a host of information products and services under a variety of business models and they are becoming significant intermediaries between citizens or customers and information creators (Eliasson 1999). Their potential for growth depends upon whether they can "lock in" customers in a way that establishes a foundation for their growth. As Eliasson suggests, the ISPs are linking communication transport infrastructures with the "syndication of electronic content" (6). Consolidating this linkage requires new combinations of capabilities for knowledge generation in order to create new value-added products and services. To achieve this linkage between the carriage of "bits" and the supply of information services, new financial flows must be organized and controlled, and conditions must be put in place to secure economic returns.

The ISP market in the United Kingdom comprises not only many entrepreneurial ventures but also incumbents that emerged from the privatization of public utilities, including the electricity and telecommunication firms as well as the broadcasting authorities. Since the mid-1990s, the incumbents have been seeking to strengthen their positions in market segments related to services for consumers and small businesses as well as those aimed at the large corporate users. By the end of the 1990s, the incumbents acquired many of the successful early entrants. They also forged global partnerships and/or merged their operations with American-owned companies. In the next section we examine several aspects of the dynamics of the relatively new ISP industry.

FINANCIAL FLOWS AND NETWORKS OF INVESTORS

The ISP market in the United Kingdom has been characterized by the convergence of the ISPs with the telecommunication network operators. Various developments in the ISP and the telecommunication market have provided the foundation for a process of convergence in the knowledge base that supports the emerging new media industry. On the one hand, there is an ongoing process of consolidation of the economic and corporate governance of the ISP industry; on the other, there are successive waves of intense entrepreneurial activity and new entry in the ISP market.

The first wave of activity in the dial-up ISP market from about 1995 to 1999 included major efforts to coordinate and control financial flows. In many cases there was evidence of the frequent presence of a common investor among those investing in the United Kingdom ISP market.[2] For example, the American-based FMR Corporation (also known as the Fidelity Group) has significant holdings in America Online (AOL), Verio, and WorldCom, all of which were active in the ISP market in the United Kingdom. Verio is a large web-hosting company and business-oriented ISP. FMR is related to two other players in the telecommunication and ISP market in the United Kingdom. One is Colt Telecom, an indirect wholly-owned subsidiary of FMR Corporation. Colt Telecom is a partner of NTL Group Ltd., alongside Energis. Another significant investor is Brooks Fiber Property, a wholly-owned subsidiary of WorldCom. More than a quarter of Verio stock is held by two of the prominent firms in the ISP market in the United Kingdom.

There are strong efforts to achieve the coordination and control of knowledge flows within these networks of organizations. This is illustrated by the shared directorships between AOL and WorldCom and between WorldCom and Verio, as well as within a partnership between AOL and Verio. For example, AOL's chairman and chief executive is a member of the board of WorldCom. He is also a member of the board of directors of the New York Stock Exchange. WorldCom's director is a member of the board of Verio. WorldCom gained a presence in the ISP market in the United Kingdom through a merger with UUNET in 1998. AOL's partnership with Verio was forged in the United States and was an element in the development of AOL/CompuServe's leadership in the United Kingdom after the company's launch in January 1996. AOL has an exclusive agreement with Verio.

The technological, financial, and knowledge networks that support the growth of these ISPs in the United Kingdom are shaping this segment of the industry and enabling new forms of service differentiation through various forms of market control. The need to achieve economic power in the market requires control over components of the knowledge base for new media service supply. Building a new industry in an uncertain technological and commercial environment requires massive investment. The process of building the ISP market is giving rise to corporate relationships that in turn are influencing market dynamics.

The implications of the linkages between sources of finance and control over the strategic behavior of enterprises are central themes in the literature on the determinants of corporate organization and industrial structure. In the 1980s research by Scott (1985, 1986) and Mintz and Schwartz (1985) revisited debates about the role of finance and corporate control in the economy (Berle and Means 1932). Drawing on Mintz and Schwartz's work, Scott (1993) argues that, while decision making may be insulated from direct intervention by shareholders, shareholder control derives from property relationships and the legal rights conferred by share ownership. Share owners have rights over the disposition of income and they have voting powers with respect to corporate affairs.

In questioning the polarized views of the liberal management and the Marxist theorists, Scott (1993, 295) argues that control should not be considered in terms of a simple relationship between ownership and managerial powers of decision making. Instead, control should be considered in the context of the institutional constraints that are exercised by shareholders over decision making. These constraints are embedded in any given share ownership structure. He argues that "it is now the strategic actions of the financial intermediaries in Britain and in the United States which are most influential in determining the constraints under which enterprises act" (Scott 1993, 295). For Scott, issues of ownership and control must be considered in the light of relations of power operating through networks of intercorporate relationships.

The ISP market in the United Kingdom displays networks of intercorporate relations established through shareholder arrangements that bind (multinational) financial organizations and firms. Sometimes these relationships are reinforced by interlocking directorships. The significant presence of a small number of large financial institutions as shareholders is one of the phenomena at the heart of the emerging ISP networks in the United Kingdom. These institutions include the Prudential Corporation, HSBC Holdings, Mercury Assets Management, and Merrill Lynch and Company in the United Kingdom, and the FMR Corporation in the United States. Some of the developments in the ISP market in the United Kingdom appear to corroborate Scott's assessment of the significance of institutional shareholders within networks of corporations. However, another set of dynamics is at work that we consider in the next section.

ENTREPRENEURIAL DYNAMICS:
MARKET EXPANSION AND CONTRACTION

The ISP dial-up market in the United Kingdom is highly dynamic with waves of new entrants and disputes between the larger, as well as the larger and smaller, players. Mergers, acquisitions, and bankruptcies are frequent. Despite rapid change, there is a tension between the forces of an expansionist market and the forces of contraction, control, and consolidation.[3]

In the early phase of ISP development, from about 1995 to the end of 1999, the design and delivery of dial-up Internet access was closely linked to the technological and financial governance structures of the existing voice telecommunication network in terms of cost accounting and revenue sharing. The incumbent, British Telecom, dominated call origination and network control. It achieved this largely through its control of the local loop infrastructure. In this phase, the entrepreneurial firms were limited in their efforts to provide services by a call revenue sharing model enabling pay-as-you-go ISP services. The new market entrant ISPs innovated by taking advantage of a technological opportunity. They often started up as self-financed ventures that subsequently attracted venture capital. The new entrants were swiftly acquired by the largest players. However, another round of entrepreneurial dynamics in 1998 gave rise to a new set of players providing "free" Internet access to build a mass dial-up Internet market.

The lowering of barriers to entry stimulated the ISP market as service providers took advantage of the benefits of lower costs and growing revenues from call termination. The confidence and market leverage of regional, as well as other larger, licensed telecommunications operators and service providers, increased as they captured a larger share of the call termination market. By 1999, British Telecom faced growing competitive pressures in the call termination market and traffic bottlenecks on its voice telephony network.

From the spring of 1999 to the end of January 2001, competitive pressures between British Telecom and other telecommunication service providers and collaborative ventures began to drive innovation in technology and service platforms for pioneering unmetered Internet access. This triggered regulatory intervention in the wholesale call origination market where British Telecom continued its dominance. During this phase, a "freefone 0800" model was used to launch unmetered Internet access. This was underpinned by an interim flat rate Internet access call origination (FRIACO Hybrid) wholesale product offered by British Telecom and approved by the regulator, the Office of Telecommunications. British Telecom launched its own unmetered retail Internet access product—SurfTime—in April 2000.

During this period there was a frenzy of competition. Many of the new entrants lacked both the technological capability and the managerial competency to sustain their growth. Their primary aim was to achieve a market position that might yield high financial rewards in the stock market and/or rewards through acquisition. Most of these new ventures failed in the face of the strategies of larger incumbents. Nevertheless, the competitive pressures led to strong ISP market growth and to greater pressures on the telecommunication infrastructure.

The incumbent British Telecom at this stage sought to recover a larger share of call termination costs through its interconnection agreements with its competitors, a controversial move that had to be resolved by the Office of Telecommunications. During this period, however, these arguments over the new terms and conditions for Internet call revenue sharing between British Telecom and its competitors resulted in a slowdown in the design and rollout of a technology platform capable of supporting the creation of unmetered Internet access products and services at the retail end of the market.

The ISPs' failure or incapacity to estimate and control demand for their services and the variable underlying costs of their capacity requirements led to growing service disruptions, failures, and bankruptcy. British Telecom's introduction of SurfTime just before the launch of the FRIACO Hybrid gave the company an opportunity to build market share in the unmetered segment of the retail ISP industry. By early 2000 a new phase of market contraction had begun.

From the spring of 2000 to the spring of 2002, British Telecom began to reassert its dominance in call origination and termination in the dial-up ISP sector by gaining regulatory support for its wholesale pricing of dial-up products. It also strongly influenced the design of its unmetered Internet access platform. During this period yet another round of entrepreneurial entry coincided with the emergence of a few hub or intermediary ISPs.

During these periods there was a constant process of strategic repositioning. This underpinned the expansion and contraction of the dial-up ISP market. This market was being shaped by the interests of ISPs, the incumbent and new entrant telecommunication infrastructure providers, and by the progressive implementation of regulatory interventions. In February 2002, British Telecom announced a major decrease in broadband wholesale prices, giving rise to a new round of market expansion for the ISPs as they raced to offer broadband services for the mass retail market. The "always on" services are likely to overtake the dial-up market.

Throughout these phases of ISP market evolution, there have been continuities, discontinuities, cumulativeness, and feedback processes in the market. The interaction of technological innovation, changing governance structures and regulation, financial flows, and the aspirations of entrepreneurial new entrants and incumbents are interwoven and display signs of "cumulative causation" (Myrdal 1944). This is creating a trajectory for the transformation of the industry's private and public governance and market structure.

The ISP market reflects the transition from the "old telecommunication" to the "new telecommunication" institutions and regulatory practices. During most of the period considered here, the incumbent British Telecom has been a reluctant follower of developments in the ISP market. It has influenced the pace of change as well as the strategic options available to new entrants in the wholesale and retail segments of the market. In some respects these developments are reminiscent of earlier incumbent telecommunication operator strategies to maintain market control in the face of new entry (Mansell 1993).

Financial risk has been distributed toward the new entrants who, in many cases, lack the financial, technological, and organizational (networking) capabilities of the incumbent. Nevertheless, the pioneering efforts of entrepreneurial companies have been the catalysts for learning and experimenting with novel formulas to combine, produce, and manage Internet access products and services. Both competitive and collaborative forces are altering the market and institutional governance structures that enable the delivery of new Internet products and services.

In the most recent phase of development—the push toward broadband using asynchronous digital subscriber lines—the Office of Telecommunication's regulatory interventions may not have been sufficient to halt another round of ISP market contraction. British Telecom is restructuring and strategically repositioning in the broadband market. This suggests that even if the phases of contraction and expansion of the ISP market prove to experience Schumpeterian (1942) cycles, there is a need for regulation to ensure that a high quality of service to end users is maintained, even in the face of oligopolistic market competition.

THE NEW MEDIA PARADIGM UNDER CAPITALISM

In the ISP market in the United Kingdom the expectation is for an increasingly rapid turnover time of capital and a rapid growth in profits. Speculation on the growth potential of the ISP market is dependent on the exploitation of new media technologies. There is a transition from the older to the newer technologies that requires both sustained large-scale capital investment and substantial learning time, especially in the case of the Internet. High-bandwidth infrastructures are expected to create the conditions for the delivery of a large throughput of new media services. However, the capital invested in the infrastructure has an engineering life cycle spanning several decades. This is creating intense pressure for the realization of short-term expectations for a return on capital for smaller and larger service providers.

In the ISP market, the risk for investors is substantial. As a result, there is tension between the financial expectations of investors and the constraints of the new media system. This tension is being eased through strategies that promote a rapid scaling up of the use of available infrastructure capacity— the rush to broadband (Mansell and Nikolychuk 2002). In the ISP market, the main strategy is to exploit scale economies in infrastructure provision through consolidation between ISPs and facility providers. Service providers are also seeking to achieve economies of time through the intensive marketing of higher value added services.

The ISP strategies for achieving rapid returns on the financial backers' investments differ somewhat from those that characterized the separate telecommunication carriage and content industries. It is not surprising that the major firms in the ISP market are devising strategies aimed at achieving quasi-monopolistic positions in differentiated segments of the market. However, the implication of convergence is that they must also redefine the scope of the ISP market in a bid to increase their capacity to integrate and systematize learning to support new media market growth. If they succeed, this will continue to create conditions for optimizing their use of network capacity and securing a return on capital at a pace that could meet the expectations of the financial institutions.

On the one hand, the nascent characteristics of this market and the appearance of multiple new entrants suggest that diversity is the trend for the future. On the other, the role of financial capital in this market suggests that the dynamics of the ISP market are inconsistent with the public interest in a new media marketplace that takes account of the interests of citizens, consumers, and small firms. The evidence for this is that the ISP market does not appear to be delivering a very high quality of service for many individuals and smaller firm users. For instance, the rate of dial-up failure is high, and companies are offering technical support to their customers at premium telephone tariffs ranging from fifty pence to one pound per minute. The broadband Internet access market is growing rapidly, but it is unclear how this will impact the quality of service available to Internet users.

Stock market investors began to curtail the ISP boom as the speculative future failed to materialize in line with early expectations. In order to sustain a high level of capitalization, the major suppliers in the ISP market need to learn how to transform prophecy into reality. As they do so, the risk to the public interest in diverse content and new services is likely to grow.

The risk associated with the new media or networking paradigm is that it may be very unstable. It may exacerbate various kinds of insecurities and it may lead to inclusion in the "knowledge society" on very unequal terms, as well as to outright exclusion (Mansell and Steinmueller 2000). Those who adhere to the vision of the positive features of the new media paradigm described above point to the diversity and declining costs of new media services. Most people in the United Kingdom can now be connected to new media networks and services, either in their own private spaces or at publicly accessible sites. Adherents to this view suggest that, in the United Kingdom, the development of the new media under the forces of capitalism is unfolding in a way that is consistent with inclusive social goals and continuing economic growth.

The changes in the legislative environment for regulation in the United Kingdom reflect this view.

In the light of technological convergence, the issues of whether and in what form regulation should be applied to the rapidly changing new media markets are more complicated than they were in the monopoly era of telecommunication and free-to-air broadcasting. They are also infinitely more complicated than the regulation required to encourage a competitive market for the supply of voice telephony services. The Communications Bill of 2002 (Department of Trade and Industry and Department of Culture, Communication, Media, and Sport 2002) in the United Kingdom is intended to promote a strategic view across the whole of the communication sector. It is a response to the explosion in the volume of data communication and to the convergence of services using digital technologies.

The government of the United Kingdom is emphasizing the need for a coherent, integrated, and balanced approach that minimizes regulatory burdens. The new integrated regulatory agency is expected to "secure public policy objectives with regard to the protection of consumers and citizens, but with the minimum of regulation that is necessary to achieve the required result" (DTI/DCCMS 2002, 27); that is, it should take a "light touch" approach. The legislation is expressly drafted to ensure that the new Office of Communication (Ofcom) will not regulate the content on the Internet, but it is silent with respect to other aspects of the presently unregulated ISP industry.

In its decision not to regulate the Internet, the government is defining regulated services as those being "available for reception by members of the general public" (DTI/DCCMS 2002, 48), thus excluding video on demand but acknowledging that the secretary of state could amend the definition to take account of matters such as the expectations of the public about content, child protection issues, and technological change. The new regulatory institution is expected to address issues of media literacy, but to do so by developing a better understanding of the different types of media services, both licensable and nonlicensable and, in particular, the Internet. No mention is made of the changing networks of financial control in the new media industry represented by the ISPs nor of the public interest considerations that these developments may give rise to. With respect to the broadcasting industry, it is asserted that "in the future new technologics may increase choice and competition in communications markets to the point where there is no longer any need for ownership rules to guarantee plurality of media voices" (DTI/DCCMS 2002, 56). Further,"any consequent consolidation in the TV industry will benefit consumers and companies alike" (DTI/DCCMS 2002, 58). Yet the ISPs are offering platforms for the delivery of the broadcasting industry's content and the present phase of consolidation is tending to suppress diversity and high-quality services.

The development of the ISP market in the United Kingdom provokes questions about the need for new forms of regulation to ensure that the forces of capital in the market for Internet access and related services produce outcomes that are more in line with public interest considerations such as the availability of diverse, low-cost, good-quality services. Is there a case for regulatory intervention to protect the public interest in the deployment of services that use the Internet as a platform?

Adopting Corsi's viewpoint, we should not regard firms as "powerless economic agents adjusting passively to parametrically given techniques, prices and quantities but [rather] as agents actively seeking the reorganization of production and market activities in the context of rival's possible reactions" (Corsi 1991, 124). If we understand the current competitive process in the new media markets in this way, there are many reasons for concern about the motives and practices of the firms that are operating in these marketplaces.

One reason is suggested by the dynamics of the ISP industry and the implications of the interplay between technological change and the control and coordination of the knowledge base and capital flows within the industry. Arguably, the processes of "creative destruction" (Schumpeter 1942) associated with technological change in this industry are not leading to the erosion of market power but to its reconstitution. Insofar as this is so, it is inconsistent with the public interest in an open network "commons."

Clark (1939, 1961) argued that a good system of public control must be democratic, powerful, and adaptable. Based on these criteria, he sought to introduce incentives into the process of public control or regulation to divert management away from subverting regulation and toward the goal of improving efficiency. The ISPs seem mainly concerned with maximizing shareholder value, a concern that appears to overshadow a concern with "efficiency" in the sense that might be expected in an intensely competitive marketplace. This observation seems particularly apt in the light of the largely favorable reception of the new communications legislation by both the regulated and unregulated components of the new media industry.

However, it is not simply efficiency considerations that must be of concern to policy makers when they consider whether certain components of the new media industry (i.e., some Internet-based firms) could require government regulatory oversight. The continuing waves of expansion and consolidation of the ISP market have implications for the diversity and costs of the content of the new media. This raises many social and cultural issues that have been addressed in the framework of conventional regulation of the older broadcast media. They are no less relevant to the new media.

CONCLUSION

Developments in the ISP market in the United Kingdom suggest a trend toward an oligopolistic industrial structure, together with a continuous process of expansion and contraction. The present dynamics of "cumulative causation" are inconsistent with the idea of a network "commons" that is responsive to a wide range of social values. The trend appears to favor the consolidation of the ISP market in the hands of financial investors whose primary interest is in the rapid turnover time of capital rather than in the long-term development of diverse, low-cost services targeted at citizens, consumers, and smaller firms. They favor an effort among the large suppliers to consolidate the knowledge base (competencies and capabilities) to succeed in the new markets. They also are giving rise to barriers to entry for small suppliers that confront constraints on their capacity to expand and to offer financially viable services. Alongside these developments, Internet platforms are being designed and deployed using architectures and pricing regimes that do not always favor the incumbents in the market. When new entry opportunities do emerge, there are strong indications that entrepreneurial activity drives the expansion of the market—for a period of time at least.

The overall trajectory of movement toward an oligopolistic market structure, however, is creating pressures for reduced service variety. This outcome runs counter to the view that the new media and the Internet's open architecture are optimized to encourage diversity in the supply of content and information services. The investigation of economic power in the ISP market is crucial in order to expose the interdependencies of technological change, innovation, and the role of finance. The trend in ISP market development is consistent with the interests of large corporations and the expectations of investors for strong revenue growth and rapid capitalization. It is also consistent with the Schumpeterian "creative gales of destruction" that so often accompany innovations in technology, business organization, and governance. As the new media paradigm takes hold, the outcomes of these developments for citizens, consumers, and smaller firms must be considered as matters for policy and for regulatory intervention, even within the framework of new "flexible" legislative and regulatory initiatives in the United Kingdom.

The combined forces of the financial flows and networks of the large players with interests in the ISP market and the speculative behavior of the small entrepreneurs are giving rise to a process of "cumulative causation" and to feedback loops that tend to reinforce the positions of the dominant and traditional telecommunication infrastructure provider, British Telecom. At the same time, they are giving rise to reductions in the quality of service available to some end users of ISP services.

Garnham (1990) argues in support of a political economy of communication that is concerned with how power is structured and differentiated. He favors an examination of the processes involved in the development of the media and communication industries in the context of the specific and changing dynamics of capitalism. In this chapter, we have addressed one small aspect of the way in which the system of social relations, governance processes, and market power in the present historical period is being reproduced through the predominant vision for global knowledge society.

The study of the new media under the forces of capitalism must focus on the continuing "industrialization of culture" (Garnham 1986, 31)—on the way symbolic forms are produced and circulated as commodities. New combinations of technological, financial, and knowledge networks are enabling the lock-in of customers and citizens to an increasingly oligopolistic industry. The vision of a global knowledge society that has captured the imagination of policy makers and many others is predicated on intense competition in the industry that provides access to the Internet and is increasingly involved in the provision of the content of the Internet. The evidence, at least in the United Kingdom, shows that this vision is only partially accurate. There is intense competition, but it is complemented by strong cooperation and by the consolidation of market power in the ISP industry. There is a case for national governments to create legislative frameworks that will enable intervention in an attempt to ensure that the new media market evolves in a way that is more consistent with the public interest.

NOTES

1. This articulation of the vision was presented at the OECD Emerging Market Economy Forum on Electronic Commerce, Dubai, UAE, 16–17 January 2001. Mansell served as rapporteur. Otherwise unattributed quotations in this paper are drawn from her working notes on the meeting.

2. An extended version of this discussion appears in Javary and Mansell 2002.

3. This section is based on research conducted by Javary under a grant from the Economic and Social Research Council Award No. R000223599 in the United Kingdom (Javary 2002).

REFERENCES

Bar, F., S. Cohen, P. Cowhey, B. DeLong, M. Kleeman, and J. Zysman, 1999. *Defending the Internet Revolution in the Broadband Era: When Doing Nothing Is Doing Harm*. Berkeley Roundtable on the International Economy, University of California at Berkeley, E-economy Working Paper no. 12, August.

Berle, A. A., and Means, G. C. 1968 [1932]. *The Modern Corporation and Private Property*. Rev. ed. New York: Harcourt Brace.

Castells, M. 2000. "Materials for an Exploratory Theory of the Network Society." *British Journal of Sociology* 51, no. 1: 5–24.

———. 2001. *The Internet Galaxy: Reflections on the Internet, Business, and Society*. Oxford: Oxford University Press.

Clark, J. M. 1939. *Social Control of Business*. New York: McGraw Hill.

———. 1961. *Competition as a Dynamic Process*. Washington, D.C.: Brookings Institution.

Corsi, M. 1991. *Division of Labour, Technical Change, and Economic Growth.* Aldershot, U.K.: Avebury.

Department of Trade and Industry and Department of Culture, Communication, Media, and Sport. 2002. *Draft Communications Bill: A New Future for Communications.* London, May. www.communicationsbill.gov.uk/policy_narrative/550800 .html. Accessed 29 November 2002 (see also Communications Bill, www .parliament.the-stationery-office.co.uk/pa/cm200203/cmbills/006/2003006.htm. Accessed 29 November 2002.

Eliasson, G. 1999. "The Internet, Electronic Business, and the EURO—On Information Products, Market Transparency and Internet Economics." Mimeo. Royal Institute of Technology, Stockholm, 2 February.

Freeman, C. 1982. *The Economics of Industrial Innovation.* 2d ed. London: Frances Pinter.

Garnham, N. 1986. "Contribution to a Political Economy of Mass-Communication." In R. Collins, J. Curran, N. Garnham, P. Scannell, P. Schlesinger, and C. Sparks, eds., *Media, Culture, and Society: A Critical Reader,* 9–32. London: Sage.

———. 1990. "Media Theory and the Political Future of Mass Communication." In F. Inglis, ed., *Capitalism and Communication: Global Culture and the Economics of Information,* 1–19. London: Sage.

Huston, G. 1999. "Interconnection, Peering, and Settlements." Presentation made to INET '99, San Jose. www.potaroo.net/papers/inet99/peering.htm. Accessed 29 November 2002.

Javary, M. 2002. "Governing the 'New Economy': Internet Provider Market in the United Kingdom." *ESRC End of Award Report,* R000223599, Lewes, U.K., October.

Javary, M., and R. Mansell. 2002. "Emerging Internet Oligopolies: A Political Economy Analysis." In E. S. Miller and W. J. Samuels, eds., *The Institutionalist Approach to Public Utilities Regulation,* 162–201. East Lansing: Michigan State University Press.

MacKenzie, D. 1996. *Knowing Machines: Essays on Technical Change.* Cambridge: MIT Press.

Mansell, R. 1993. *The New Telecommunications: A Political Economy of Network Evolution.* London: Sage.

Mansell, R., and L. Nikolychuk. 2002. *The Economic Importance of Electronic Networks: Assessing the Micro-level Evidence Base.* Final Report prepared for the Prime Minister's Strategy Unit, Cabinet Office, London, 26 August. www.cabinet-office.gov.uk/ innovation/2002/electronic/attachments/LSE.pdf. Accessed 29 November 2002.

Mansell, R., and W. E. Steinmueller. 2000. *Mobilizing the Information Society: Strategies for Growth and Opportunity.* Oxford: Oxford University Press.

Mintz, B., and M. Schwartz. 1985. *The Power Structure of American Business.* Chicago: University of Chicago Press.

Myrdal, G. 1944. "Appendix 3: A Methodological Note on the Principle of Cumulation." In *An American Dilemma: The Negro Problem and Modern Democracy,* 2: 1065–70. New York: Harper.

Oxman, J. 1999. *The FCC and the Unregulation of the Internet.* Working Paper no. 31. Washington, D.C.: Federal Communications Commission, Office of Plans and Policy.

Schumpeter, J. A. 1962 [1942]. *Capitalism, Socialism, and Democracy.* New York: University Library, Harper & Row.

Scott, J. 1985. *Corporations, Classes, and Capitalism.* 2d rev. ed. London: Hutchinson.

——. 1986. *Capitalist Property and Financial Power: A Comparative Study of Britain, the United States, and Japan.* Brighton, U.K.: Wheatsheaf.

——. 1993. "Corporate Groups and Network Structure." In J. McCahery, S. Picciotto, and C. Scott, eds., *Corporate Control and Accountability: Changing Structures and the Dynamics of Regulation,* 291–304. Oxford: Clarendon.

Trebing, H. M. 1995. "Structural Change and the Future of Regulation." *Land Economics* 71, no. 3: 401–14.

——. 1998. "Market Concentration and the Sustainability of Market Power in Public Utility Industries." *National Regulatory Institute Quarterly Bulletin* 19, no. 1: 61–67.

14

Dismantling the Digital Divide

Rethinking the Dynamics of Participation and Exclusion

Graham Murdock and Peter Golding

CLOUDY SKIES

On the cover of his manifesto for the network revolution, *The Road Ahead* (1995), Bill Gates of Microsoft is photographed bathed in light, standing on a long, straight, empty road stretching to the far horizon. For those not trained in reading visual connotations, the copy on the flyleaf helpfully explains that the book offers a look ahead at "how the emerging technologies of the digital age will transform all our lives" by allowing everyone to travel the "information highway" whenever they wish (Gates 1995). Behind him, the thin band of early morning cloud looks set to disperse at any moment. Other commentators of the time, however, saw more substantial breaks in the blue skies of upbeat speculation. Far from being a universal movement changing everyone's life for the better, the "digital revolution," mounting evidence suggested, was adding to the advantages of the privileged while systematically excluding the poor and marginalized.

Although the shift from analog to digital technologies was in the early stages of altering the possibilities offered by telephones and television sets, the most widely used domestic communications equipment, debate about its social impact quickly fixed on the emerging Internet. The reasons were not hard to find. First, the Net is a uniquely versatile system. It is simultaneously a distribution channel for information and entertainment services, a conduit for commercial transactions, a means of interpersonal communication, a forum for social exchange, an electronic library, museum, and college, a space of individual expression and creativity, and an arena of social and political organization. Second, by removing the technical barriers to access, the launch of the World Wide Web in 1990 and the development of the first easy-to-use web browsers (Netscape Navigator in 1994 and Internet Explorer in 1995) held out the promise of universal participation.

This prospect was particularly attractive to both the new-style Democrats led by Clinton and Gore in the United States and the New Labour "modernizers" led by Tony Blair in the United Kingdom. As a solution to the problems generated by the accelerating dynamics of marketization and the decline of public welfare systems, it offered several advantages. It was relatively inexpensive in terms of the public investment required, it offered scope for partnerships with private companies, and it could be presented as a creative and forward-looking response to the inevitability of technologically driven change. Its political advocates saw the Net playing a central role in reorganizing education, retraining redundant workers for jobs in the information economy, repairing relations between citizens and government, and revivifying declining communities.

Promoting universal access also addressed anxieties about the future of citizenship in the digital age. If we define citizenship as the "right to participate fully in social life . . . and to help formulate the forms it might take in the future" (Murdock 1999, 8) then clearly, "as more forms of communication, social networking, community organisation, and political debate and decision making gravitate to online media, those without access to the technology will be shut out of opportunities to practice their full citizenship" (Warschauer 2003, 28). To be disconnected is to be disenfranchised.

The argument that there were substantial gaps in Internet access rapidly gained currency in public discussion, and was given authoritative backing by the National Telecommunications and Information Administration, the arm of the U.S. Department of Commerce charged with advising the government on telecommunications and information technology issues. It had begun mapping the contours of digital exclusion in the early 1990s with a research program named Falling Through The Net. The first report, published in 1995, bore the somewhat old-fashioned sounding title, *A Survey of the "Have-Nots" in Rural and Urban America*. Three years later, however, when the second installment came out, the rhetoric had shifted decisively and the report's title, *New Data on the Digital Divide,* confirmed this couplet as the dominant characterization of the problem.

This easily remembered phrase proved irresistible to journalists, policy makers, and academics looking for a handy encapsulation of a complex problem. Unfortunately, the one-dimensional thinking hinted at by the fact that it is singular rather than plural has been carried over into many of the descriptions and explanations of the problem it has generated, leading in turn to inappropriate and ineffectual policy interventions. To move forward we need to dismantle the "digital divide," as both a conceptual framework and a guide to action.

ONE-DIMENSIONAL DEFINITIONS

Much writing on the "digital divide" focuses on whether or not people have basic access to an Internet-enabled computer. This is often measured by a version of the catchall question Senator Joe McCarthy put to suspected "subversives" in 1950s America: "Are you now or have you ever been . . . ?" Successive surveys conducted by the Pew Research Center in the United States, for example, ask, "Do you ever go online to access the Internet or World Wide Web? The equivalent question on the Eurbarometer surveys, which provide the most widely used figures for European countries, is, "Do you have access to, or do you use, the Internet or World Wide Web." For governments and free market enthusiasts wishing to show that access is steadily rising as the price of a basic PC falls, these elastic definitions have clear advantages. As a basis for systematic analysis of digital participation and exclusion, however, they are useless. By lumping together experienced home users and people who have tried a terminal in a public location once or twice, they systematically conflate very different levels of access and use. People "living in poorer neighbourhoods may be able to surf the Web from public libraries, schools, and community centres, or even cyber cafes, but this is not the same thing as having automatic access via high-speed connections at home and the office. Nor is it the same as having all Internet, all the time" instantly downloadable via portable devices (Norris 2001, 92).

Because the Internet supports both vertical, top-down dissemination systems and horizontal, peer-to-peer networks, it has generated a wide range of applications that compete for users' time and commitment. Corporations and governments are primarily interested in establishing vertical connections. They envisage an e-society built around responses to centrally produced materials. To this end they are busily constructing virtual shopping malls and entertainment districts, distance learning networks, and e-government systems that allow users to download official information, complete required forms, and send e-mails to politicians and ministers. Alongside these heavily managed interactions the Net also allows individuals to keep in touch with family and friends, post their own opinions and creative work, and participate in virtual communities based around shared interests, beliefs, or experiences. As a consequence, full digital citizenship is not simply a matter of guaranteeing basic access. It requires command over the resources that underwrite people's capacity to use the Net creatively as a space of self-expression and social participation. Analyzing the allocation of these resources requires us to jettison the idea that the "digital divide" is a single, simple dichotomy between those on- and offline, and to focus instead on people's opportunities to use the Net to "achieve cooperative and participatory status in the social and economic life of the larger community" (Wilhelm 2000, 73). To do this we need to examine hierarchies of access and differences in use among those who are connected (Selwyn 2002, 10). Like entry to a first job, initial access to the Internet is more usefully seen as the first stage in a career that may be marked by stasis, frustration, and dropping out as well as progression, not the moment that solves the problem by removing someone from the figures for unemployment.

MISSING CLASS

Enthusiasts of leaving access to the unfettered play of market forces were adamant that uneven take-up was a temporary condition. They envisaged Internet access following the dissemination curve established for television sets, with relatively affluent early adopters taking the initial risks on an emerging technology and blazing a trail for the rest to follow as machines became more reliable and easier to use, and as prices steadily dropped. Adam Clayton Powell III, vice president of technology and programs at the conservative think tank Freedom Forum, was in no doubt that this "trickle-down process" had run its course by the end of the 1990s, and that "now that some personal computers cost less than TVs . . . every American who wants one is getting [one]" (Powell 2001, 313). There was therefore no need for intervention in the marketplace or public spending on improving access for the poor. He saw ill-informed journalists being duped by special interests. "Misled by stereotypes, misinformed about survey techniques, and misdirected by interest groups, the media have treated the digital divide as a crisis requiring government intervention. As a result, billions of dollars might be spent to address needs that no longer exist" (Powell 2001, 309).

That a firm believer in free markets as the least worst allocation mechanism should see the "trickle-down" effect solving the problem of unequal access is entirely predictable. That it should be partially endorsed by Manuel Castells is rather more surprising. He too is convinced that "as computer prices fall, and more applications can be found on-line, minorities and low-income groups are likely to find . . . fewer obstacles to owning a home computer" (Castells 2001, 253) and that "for most people, including most individuals from minority groups, access to the Internet is likely to become pervasive" (Castells 2001, 254). He concedes that this process of steadily widening inclusion will stop short of "the poorest, most discriminated segment of population—this furthering their marginality" (Castells 2001, 254), but envisages this lumpen group as relatively small. This is an odd conclusion for someone who, elsewhere in his work, is well aware that the rollout of personal computers has coincided with a "structural trend toward increasing inequality" (Castells 2000, 80) in a number of advanced capitalist countries, including the United States. As we argued over a decade ago, this trend, combined with the pattern of constant innovation and upgrading in the home computer market, means that far from closing the gap "poorer groups are chasing a moving and fast-receding target" (Murdock and Golding 1989, 192). Evidence collected since then has confirmed this conclusion.

As clusters of technologies, home computers differ from television sets (the main reference point for "trickle-down" models) in four important respects. First, access to the full range of creative and communicative possibilities offered by PCs requires users to invest in additional software and hardware. Anyone wanting to create and exchange photographs, for example, will need a scanner or digital camera. These "extras" are not usually included in basic starter packages. Second, now that home computer ownership has leveled out (at around 45 percent of households in the United Kingdom), it is more profitable for manufacturers to add value to exiting products and target the "high-margin but narrow upper end of the market" (Warschauer 2003, 64) than to persuade "nonadopters" to buy an entry-level machine. Third, the invitation to existing users to continually upgrade is supported by a vigorous policy of planned obsolescence whereby new software will not run on older, less powerful machines with limited memory. Fourth, using a computer for communications requires users to be linked to the Internet via a telephone or cable network. The nature of this connection has a major impact on both the quality of people's experience of being online and the range of activities they can engage with.

Most domestic users have a standard dial-up connection over a conventional telephone line. This is slow, vulnerable to interruption, and limited in capacity. In contrast, broadband links, over a dedicated cable network or adapted (ADSL) telephone connection are much more versatile. They are always on, they download web pages almost instantaneously, and they can comfortably handle video and other "bulky" materials. Because these features offer immediate gains in areas like video conferencing and electronic trading, the rollout of broadband in the United Kingdom has been business driven. As a consequence installation has been concentrated in regions that are major locales for high-tech industries. Whereas London is more or less 100 percent covered, this figure drops to 55 percent in the mainly rural areas of Wales and the South West (Cabinet Office 2001). However, even where households are passed by a broadband connection, the relative expense compared to dial-up charges remains a major deterrent. As a consequence, even the most optimistic industry estimates see domestic take-up reaching no more than 30–40 percent by 2005. Households that are able to upgrade their connection will enjoy cumulative advantages. Additional gains will accrue to those owning a laptop computer and thus able to use the increasing number of Internet "hot spots" now being established in airports and city centers using wireless connections. However, because laptops remain significantly more expensive than basic desktop machines, this increased flexibility of use will remain confined to more affluent users. As Castells notes, because of these innovations in network infrastructures, "it could well happen that while the huddled masses finally have access to the phone-line Internet, the global elites will already have escaped into a higher circle of cyberspace" (Castells 2001, 256). Far from catching up, those with basic computers will have all the running and connecting they can do to keep in the same place, while nonowners fall further and further behind, a dynamic that Anthony Wilhelm has dubbed the "Red Queen effect" after the tetchy monarch in Lewis Carroll's *Through the Looking Glass*. She summarily dismissed Alice's claim that "if you ran fast for a very long time, you'd generally get to somewhere else" (Wilhelm 2000, 123).

Despite the evidence, market advocates stubbornly refuse to acknowledge the structural basis of unequal access and display a manifest impatience with population groups who are unwilling or unable to take advantage of the plenitude being offered to them. As the advocates of "e-Europe" in the European Union recently noted, Europeans "ought to realize the efficiencies and opportunities intrinsic in the adoption of these technologies" (European Commission 2002b, 17). If they persist in refusing, it is the task of policy to remove the scales from their eyes. Benjamin Compaine sees such interventions as so much wasted effort. He presents the 40 percent of Hispanic households in a U.S. survey who said that they don't own a computer because they "don't need" one as prima facie evidence of what he calls "voluntary" nonparticipation (Compaigne 2001b, 328), rather than a signal that they have been written out of technological change, both materially and symbolically. By arguing that the laggards are too timid, inadequate, or uninterested to see the manifest benefits of joining the "digital revolution," this blame-the-victim ideology neatly transfers the explanation for differential participation from structural dynamics to personal failings. Whether presented in the laissez-faire version favored by Compaine or the dirigiste variant championed in Brussels, it ignores the fact that the development of the Internet has coincided in time with a strengthening of income differentials (Golding 2000).

The growing evidence of a persistent "one-third/two-thirds" divide across many contemporary capitalist countries is seen at its most intense in U.K. experience. The official Households Below Average Income (HBAI) statistics show that in 1999–2000 around 14 million people (25 percent of the population) were living below half average incomes after housing costs. This is almost three times higher than in 1979, when 5 million people (9 percent of the population) were poor (Howard et al. 2001, 30). A subsequent report published in December 2002 shows that 12.9 million people were living in households with less than 60 percent of median income. While government action had begun to reduce the volume of households, and children, in poverty as the twenty-first century began, the figures remain double what they were twenty years ago (Palmer et al. 2002). Moreover, in buoyant economies such as the United Kingdom's, the differentials in rewards in the labor market are also widening as those in secure and flourishing sectors accelerate away from a growing segment of the working population in insecure and low-paid employment. While top earners in the United Kingdom saw a 7.3 percent rise in average weekly earnings between 2000 and 2001, for the lowest paid 10 percent the increase was only 4.5 percent. In April 2001 the bottom 10 percent of employees were earning below £207 per week, less than half the average wage of £444 per week. In contrast, the top 10 percent earned, on average, more than £722 per week (Jenkins 2002, 130–32).

These widening divisions are strongly reflected in patterns of computer ownership and Internet access. Although U.K. government research suggests that the overall percentage of households with PCs and home access to the Internet rose from 18 percent in mid-1999 to 44 percent in September 2002 (ONS 2003), this total figure conceals very substantial differences among social classes. While 82 percent of households in the richest 10 percent by gross income had home access, this figure drops to 10 percent for the lowest decile, and is well below half in all five of the lowest decile groups (ONS 2003, 4). These figures confirm the pattern revealed by previous studies (e.g., Russell and Drew 2001), leading a government report to conclude that "there is little evidence that the market will close this gap" and that the differential "if anything is widening" (Office of the e-Envoy 2001, chap. 3). Surveying the evidence, another government-sponsored research team concluded that even if penetration naturally passed 60 percent there would still be "an unconnected or excluded group of over 20 million citizens" (Booz, Allen, and Hamilton 2000, 13).

FORGOTTEN CAPITALS

This basic pattern is both familiar and widely documented, with a recent sixteen-nation study confirming "multiple links" between Internet access on the one hand and income levels and patterns of income distribution on the other (Bauer, Berne, and Maitland 2002, 122). But as research on the early adoption of home computers demonstrated, differential command over material resources is not the only explanation of social variation in access and use (Murdock, Hartmann, and Gray 1992). There are "noneconomic determinants of exclusion" (Wilhelm 2000, 49). A number of writers have recently developed multidimensional resource models in an effort to take account of these additional factors (e.g., Wilhelm 2000, chap. 3; Warschauer 2003, chap. 2), but in our view the framework developed by Pierre Bourdieu, suitably reworked, remains the most useful place to start.

Bourdieu argues that all social practices are decisively shaped by stratified access to three basic clusters of resources (or "capitals" as he prefers to call them): economic, social, and cultural. The term "economic" is problematic here, since it tends to focus attention exclusively on the distribution of income to the neglect of two other measurable resources that play a major role in shaping user careers: "free" time and the availability of safe, private space. Consequently we prefer the term "material resources."

Understanding the differential allocation of these resources within as well as between households is crucial to explaining unequal access and use. Despite the proliferation of access points at work and in public places, for most people, the Internet remains primarily a domestic technology. When asked in a recent U.K. survey, for example, 79 percent of respondents said they used the Internet in their own homes, as against 35 percent saying they used it at work and only 8 percent saying that they used it in a public library (ONS 2002, 4). This does not mean that all household members necessarily have equal access, however. On the contrary, the allocation of usable space and "free" time will vary considerably depending on the overall size of the dwelling and the use of rooms and on the internal distribution of control. Knowing that a household has an Internet-enabled PC tells us nothing about where it is located, who has access to it when, or how use may be constrained by lack of privacy or interruptions and competition from other household members. Consequently, to understand fully how differential command over material resources shapes patterns of participation and exclusion, it is essential to explore gender and generational dynamics *within* households, looking particularly at divisions of labor and patterns of power and authority (see, e.g., Murdock, Hartmann, and Gray 1992; van Zoonen 2002).

Bourdieu defines his second form of capital, social capital, as the "sum of the resources that accrue to an individual or group by virtue of possessing a durable network of . . . relationships of mutual acquaintance and recognition" (Bourdieu and Wacquant 1992, 119). In recent years its role in underwriting social participation has attracted renewed attention from social scientists concerned about the erosion of community in an increasingly individualistic era, most notably Robert Putnam, who defines it simply as "about networks" (Putnam 2001, 171). Circles of friends and acquaintances can play a major role in encouraging people to try the Internet for the first time and in sustaining their commitment and developing their capacity to become creative and contributory users. The help offered might range from "observing computer use at a friend's house" or "hearing how a neighbour uses the internet" (Warschauer 2003, 156) to borrowing and exchanging software and troubleshooting problems. In addition to these specific forms of support, there also is a generalized benefit in belonging to a social network whose members are all online. Conversely, disconnection makes initiating, sustaining, and developing use much more difficult.

A national survey conducted in the United States at the end of 1999 asked those without a computer at home what the main reason was. Almost half

(47 percent) said they didn't "need one" (National Public Radio et al. 2001, 275). As noted earlier, conservative commentators like Benjamin Compaine interpret these and similar findings as evidence of "voluntary nonparticipation" rooted in a "refusal to see the personal value" of being connected (Compaine 2001b, 328). Work on social capital, however, suggests that people were simply being realistic. If the survey's compilers had thought to ask, they might have found that their respondents saw no need for a PC because no one else they knew had one. There is little point in being able to send an e-mail if no one you want to contact can reply. In the United Kingdom in 2002, for example, almost twice as many people living in neighborhoods classified as "prosperous professional" claimed to have used the Internet as those living on council housing estates "in greatest hardship" or with high unemployment (86 percent compared to 44 percent). Moreover, this gap had widened since 2000 (Russell and Stafford 2002, 2). Instead of blaming the victims for their lack of interest, analysis needs to explore how the unequal distribution of computer experience across both work situations and neighborhoods helps create networks that cumulatively reinforce participation on the one hand and exclusion on the other.

This stratified distribution of social capital intersects in turn with the unequal allocation of cultural capital, which we can define here as the complex of symbolic resources required to exercise full command over the meaning- and knowledge-producing potentials offered by the Internet. These resources comprise competencies, literacies, and identities. Clearly users need to be familiar, competent, and comfortable with the full range of available software packages. However, to use the Net as a means of individual expression and social communication, rather than just a device for downloading and interacting with preprepared materials, they also need to possess the range of literacies required to operate effectively and creatively as both producers and consumers, speakers and listeners, in the social contexts they choose to enter. Finally they must be able to recognize themselves as "at home" online.

Here again, the easy assumption that people voluntarily choose not to participate conceals the major role played by the promotional culture surrounding the Internet. For the marketing reasons mentioned earlier, advertisements for Net-enabled home computers tend to feature mobile executives, affluent families, eager children, or absorbed adolescents, rather than the poor and elderly, which may go some way to explaining why age gaps on the Net have proved so resilient. For example, recent U.K. government figures, based on a conveniently elastic definition of "access" that embraces once in a lifetime experimenters alongside obsessive hobbyists, found that by September 2002 only 17 percent of those over sixty-five had accessed the Internet, compared to 94 percent of adults between sixteen and twenty-four (ONS 2003). The process of cultural marginalization initiated by imagery in the publicity surrounding the Net is further compounded by the language and mode of address employed on many websites. Those that mimic the visual field of youth-oriented cable channels like MTV tend to alienate older users, while the formal language employed on sites developed by government agencies deters low-income users all too familiar with being talked down to by bureaucracies.

In their eagerness to go beyond the "economic inequality" explanation for differential patterns of Internet access and use, and to demonstrate the central role of noneconomic resources and dynamics, some revisionist commentators have been tempted to present them as freestanding forces. The consistently strong correlation between home computer access and educational attainment, for example, has been used to argue that education is more important than income in "facilitating or inhibiting Internet access" (Nie and Erbring 2000, 269). This neatly sidesteps decades of research demonstrating an enduring connection between parental class position (as indexed by occupation and income) and children's chances of succeeding in the education system (measured by the length of full-time education received and the number and level of formal qualifications obtained). Despite repeated reforms, for example, the British education system continues to favor children from professional, managerial, and white-collar homes. As Pierre Bourdieu famously argued, this is in large part because it demands that everyone possess what "it does not give" in the form of the linguistic competences and prior familiarity with officially approved forms of culture and knowledge required for academic success (Bourdieu 1973, 80). Children from families that have already ensured that they posses these resources enjoy a head start in the race for educational attainment. Conversely, children from families with linguistic and cultural resources that are not recognized or required within the curriculum find it hard to catch up and are more likely to "fail" and leave the system at the minimum age.

The fit between parental class, educational success, and subsequent earnings is tight, but, as Bourdieu points out, not perfect, for two reasons. First, there is certain amount of upward and downward mobility between generations. Second, because of the overall structure of the occupational reward system stocks of cultural capital do not always translate into equivalent holdings of economic capital. Teachers may have substantial cultural resources (as measured by educational qualifications) but earn relatively little while a self-made businessman who enjoys a high income may have left school with little or no formal certification.

A similar complexity also characterizes the relations between occupation and Internet use. To understand how work experience impacts on home Internet use, we need to know whether or not people have access at work as well as how they use their connectivity. A range of jobs involve workers in using computers in some capacity, but most only require competence in operating standard software packages for word processing, spread sheets, and information searching. Comparatively few encourage creative use, and in most work settings the surveillance systems installed to monitor employee Internet use actively discourage peer-to-peer exchange other than job-related e-mails. Consequently, as Pippa Norris points out, whereas managerial and executive staff are likely to enjoy flexibility of use, with subsidized laptops and home access "to facilitate connectivity with the office," manual workers are far less likely "to acquire the skills and experience in the workplace that breed comfort and familiarity with the Web at home" (Norris 2001, 80). Teachers, on the other hand, may build up creative Internet skills through their involvement in online learning and exchange initiatives but are unlikely to enjoy the subsidies to home use offered in the corporate sector.

Following Bourdieu, we can characterize social locations as points within a three-dimensional space fixed by intersecting inequalities of command over economic, social, and cultural resources. This is not to say that these dimensions are of equal weight in determining domestic Internet access and use, however. Economic position continues to determine "in the first instance," in two ways. First, parental position plays a central role in structuring past access to the core cultural resources conferred by family upbringing and education. Second, as we have noted, present position regulates access to high-end PCs and broadband connections at home, the conditions under which they are used, and the availability of the network resources provided by white-collar employment and neighborhoods with high densities of connectivity.

MACHINE ROOMS

Policies designed to widen and deepen Internet participation need to take these multiple aspects of economic location fully into account. To date however, the U.K. government's aim of creating an "internet for all the people" (Blair 2000) has consistently worked with one-dimensional models and instrumental assumptions.

Most initiatives have been underpinned by variants of technological determinism and have assumed that simply making machines and connection available in schools, libraries, community centers, and private homes will "bridge the digital divide and ensure that everyone has the opportunity to benefit from new technologies" (Wills 2001, 198). They have taken little or no account of the part played by social and cultural dynamics in sustaining user careers and fostering creative and participatory uses. This is not surprising, since the primary rationales for getting everyone online are instrumental. Some initiatives have set out to address the perceived failings in core public sector services: education, welfare, health, tax, and public bureaucracies. Others have attempted to reduce unemployment by retraining workers for routine participation in an increasingly computerized economy, a strategy typified by the "UK Online Computer Training" initiative, launched in the spring of 2000 to provide "basic ICT skills to 50,000 unemployed and economically inactive people" (BMRB Research 2002, 1). Employment-related schemes have been viewed as a cost-effective way to compensate for the education system's failure to address business needs with sufficient vigor. As the government's *UK Online* report notes, there is particular concern that the "digital content industry" responsible for designing commercial websites is "not getting the right people with the right mix of knowledge and skills coming from education into the labour market" (Cabinet Office 2001, 31). It goes on to note that the sector is "particularly concerned to secure a better dialogue with the higher education sector over skill needs" (Cabinet Office 2001, 31). In this context university commitments to mobilizing Internet use in the service of independent thought, self-expression, social responsibility, and civic participation are surplus requirements.

The pursuit of these instrumental, business-oriented rationales at the national level has received strong backing from the European Union. A recent European Commission report, for example, makes no attempt to disguise its disappointment with members who have failed to follow Britain's proactive lead. As it wearily points out, most EU action to date "has not involved legislation. Instead it has relied on peer pressure . . . to make sure the individual EU countries actually do what they have promised each other to promote e-Government, e-Health, e-Content and similar initiatives" (European Commission, 2002a, 11). On closer inspection, however, the priorities are rather less comprehensive than this promotional rhetoric would suggest, with the present targets set for "e-Europe" placing particular emphasis on enhancing the digital literacy of the workforce and introducing the European computer driving license.

In the U.K. context, sensitivity to business interests has extended to the operation of publicly funded schemes to increase Internet access and competence, many of which have been run as public–private partnerships. As we shall see, public purposes have not always been best served by businesses aiming to make a profit from their participation.

To meet the ambitious timescale set for universal Net access as cost effectively as possible, the majority of U.K. government schemes have concentrated on providing public terminals with the overall aim of ensuring that 98.6 percent of the population would be no more than five miles from an access point by the end of 2002. Initiatives have included National Lottery money to enable all public libraries to go online, increased funds to help all schools get connected, and a phased launch of one thousand ICT learning centers across the country. However, a policy action team convened by government to evaluate the impact of these various interventions "found a range of barriers which prohibit the establishment of successful ICT points and constrain the involvement of the target audience" (Policy Action Team 15 2000, 5). Not surprisingly, given the scatter-gun nature of intervention, they identified a range of organizational failures, most notably lack of coordination among the various government departments involved and the general lack of "a joined up approach" capable of integrating national and local strategies and sharing good practice. When users were questioned, the "real and perceived" cash costs of access once again emerged as a major deterrent to participation, but their answers also highlighted the key role played by failures to provide appropriate social and cultural resources together with convenient and safe space and free time. They found many of the venues chosen difficult to get to, open at unattractive times, and insufficiently secure. They complained about the lack of the child care support needed to free up uninterrupted time to spend in front of the screen. They found that much of the content they encountered was unattractive, was unsuitable for their needs, did not talk to them in ways they felt comfortable with, and was overly dependent on levels of literacy they did not feel they possessed. Finally, they regretted the lack of accessible social support, a finding that led the action team to recommend that future projects should mobilize "local ICT champions and mentors who are drawn from the same background as the community they serve" (Policy Action Team 15 2000, 6). Nor do these problems disappear when computers are placed in the homes rather than in public locations, as the career of the Computers With Reach project, Britain's most ambitious venture in this area to date, clearly demonstrates.

This was an initiative spearheaded by Chancellor Gordon Brown. Taking note of the growing income differential in Internet access in the United Kingdom, he saw the country moving rapidly toward a society divided between "a wired superclass and an information underclass" (Brown 2000, 8). His solution was to put the "equipment, as well as the opportunity, directly into people's hands" (Brown 2000, 8). To this end, in his budget of March 1999, he set aside £15 million to provide personal computers to 100,000 low-income households. Once potential recipients had been identified by local charities and voluntary groups, IT companies were brought in to buy up old PCs from companies and public sector organizations, refurbish them, and deliver a package containing an Internet-ready machine, software, and printer to participating households. They would be paid £210 for each package with the recipient contributing £60. The scheme worked most effectively when it was administered by a public sector body and fully funded out of public money, as in Liverpool where it operated under the I Take My Place initiative with regeneration money covering the £60 cost of the package, and the locally based project team taking responsibility for distributing the machines and providing continuing support. Where the scheme was run on a commercial basis, however, experiences were often less positive. In some pilot areas people paid their £60 fee in advance but waited up to six months before their machine was delivered. Nor were suppliers under any obligation to install it or provide starter tutorials for first-time users. Some participants returned home to find their machine left on the doorstep. Help with ongoing problems and queries was also often difficult and expensive to access. Because the initial contracts had failed to specify the terms and conditions under which help lines should be operated, some suppliers took the opportunity to charge premium rates of £1 per minute for calls from users, many of whom found it difficult to follow instructions that made few concessions to beginners. Despite working well in areas where it was linked to existing public initiatives, in February 2002 the initiative was quietly shelved. As a "source close to the scheme" told journalists, the relevant minister had come to believe that "it doesn't have enough positives" (quoted in Humphries 2002).

ECONOMIC MIGRATIONS

Faced with the manifest failure of attempts to create a universally wired society using public and domestic PCs, policy makers in Britain have begun to transfer their attention to Internet-enabled digital television services. Noting the low figures for personal computer ownership on deprived council estates, for example, the policy action team argues that because "television is ubiquitous, digital television may offer a more likely future route to home access in these neighbourhoods" (Policy Action Team 15 2000, 4). The problem is that the two modes of Internet access are not equivalent. Digital television offers less comprehensive and far more carefully directed online possibilities.

The commercial option is typified by Sky TV's satellite delivered service, which is centered around shopping opportunities rather than spaces for political debate, social participation, and personal creativity. Audiences don't even need to interrupt their regular viewing. Purchasing opportunities can be accessed directly from the main program menu as an integral part of a carefully constructed flow of materials. As the division's managing director of Sky Interactive told an industry gathering, "We are not competing with the PC. We are competing for a slice of the four hours a day that people sit down in front of the box to be entertained. Interactivity has to be an integral part of the viewing experience" (Florsheim 2001, 2). In his conjectures on the future of the Internet Robert Putnam asks if it will "become predominantly a means of active, social communication or a means of passive, private entertainment" (Putnam 2001, 179). Sky and other commercial television entrepreneurs are in no doubt. Their preferred future will be built around a shopping mall with integrated entertainment facilities, not a library, university, town meeting, or café conversation.

The vision being promoted by the BBC and other public service television channels is rather less restrictive, with organizations using their websites to continue and amplify the momentum established by broadcast programs through e-mail feedback, online discussion, and additional web-based resources and links. However, the network employed remains overwhelmingly vertical rather than horizontal. It privileges two-way links between dispersed, individual, and a central originating node rather than peer-to-peer connections. Its primary tasks are to promote the organization's programs and associated merchandise, polish its brand image, and cement audience loyalty.

At the same time, public broadcasting, for all its failings, offers perhaps the best chance of building a digital commons, open to all, hospitable to personal creativity and participation, and capable of supporting the collective debate required to underwrite full citizenship in the digital age (see Murdock 2001). As a place to start, it has three advantages. It is an already familiar, valued, and trusted presence in people's lives. It is free at the point of use. And it addresses audiences as members of moral and social communities rather than consumers with current credit cards. Constructing this new communal space, however, requires three minimum conditions to be met. First, it must operate horizontally as well as vertically. Second, it must find productive ways of harnessing both the expertise and resources offered by public broadcasters and other public institutions—libraries, museums, galleries, and universities—with the vitality and grassroots participation fostered by social movements and community groups on line. Third, it must guarantee universality of access by making the necessary equipment available to anyone who wants it. Finding creative and practical solutions to these challenges is arguably the most important task now facing anyone committed to providing the minimal conditions for digital citizenship.

REFERENCES

Bauer, J. M., M. Berne, and C. F. Maitland. 2002. "Internet Access in the European Union and in the United States." *Telematics and Informatics* 19, no. 2: 117–37.

Blair, A. 2000. Speech presented to the Knowledge 2000 Conference, 7 March. www.number-10.gov.uk/output/Page1521.asp.

BMRB Research. 2002. *An Evaluation of UK Online Computer Training.* Research Brief no. 329. London: Department for Education and Skills.

Booz, Allen, and Hamilton [consultancy]. 2000. *Achieving Universal Access.* London: Booz, Allen, and Hamilton.

Bourdieu, Pierre. 1973. "Cultural Reproduction and Social Reproduction." In Richard Brown, ed., *Knowledge, Education, and Cultural Change,* 71–112. London: Tavistock.

Bourdieu, P., and J. D. Wacquant. 1992. *An Invitation to Reflexive Sociology.* Oxford. Polity.

Brown, Gordon. 2000. *Britain and the Knowledge Economy.* Speech presented to the Smith Institute, 16 February. www.hm-treasury.gov.uk/press/2000.

Cabinet Office. 2001. *UK Online: The Broadband Future: An Action Plan to Facilitate Roll-Out of Higher Bandwidth and Broadband Services.* London: Cabinet Office, Office of the e-Envoy.

Castells, Manuel. 2000. *End of Millennium.* 2d ed. Oxford: Blackwell.

————. 2001. *The Internet Galaxy: Reflections on the Internet, Business, and Society.* Oxford. Oxford University Press.

Compaine, Benjamin M., ed. 2001a. *The Digital Divide: Facing a Crisis or Creating a Myth?* Cambridge: MIT Press.

————. 2001b. "Declare the War Won." In *The Digital Divide: Facing a Crisis or Creating a Myth?* 315–35. Cambridge: MIT Press.

European Commission. 2002a. *Towards a Knowledge Based Europe: The European Union and the Information Society.* Brussels: Directorate General for Press and Communication.

————. 2002b. *Communication from the Commission to the Council, the European Parliament, the Economic and Social Committee and the Committee of the Regions.* COM. 2002. 263. Brussels. European Commission.

Florsheim, Jon. 2001. "Sky Gets More Active." Speech presented to the IEA Conference, London, 12 November.

Gates, Bill. 1995. *The Road Ahead.* New York: Viking Penguin.

Golding, P. 2000. "Forthcoming Features: Information and Communications Technologies and the Sociology of the Future." *Sociology* 34: 165–84.

Howard, M., A. Garnham, G. Fimister, and J. Veit-Wilson. 2001. *Poverty: The Facts.* 4th ed. London: Child Poverty Action Group.

Humphries, Paul. 2002. "Recycled PCs for the Poor Scheme Crashes." *Guardian Unlimited,* February 8. http://society.guardian.co.uk/regeneration/news/0,8367,646636,00.html.

Jenkins, J. 2002. "Patterns of Pay: Results of the 2001 New Earnings Survey." *Labour Market Trends,* March, 129–39.

Murdock, Graham. 1999. "Rights and Representations: Public Discourse and Cultural Citizenship." In Jostein Gripsrud, ed., *Television and Common Knowledge,* 7–17. London: Routledge.

————. 2001. "Against Enclosure: Rethinking the Cultural Commons." In David Morley and Kevin Robins, eds., *British Cultural Studies,* 443–60. Oxford. Oxford University Press.

Murdock, Graham, and Peter Golding. 1989. "Information Poverty and Political Inequality: Citizenship in the Age of Privatised Communications." *Journal of Communication,* Summer, 180–95.

Murdock, Graham, Paul Hartmann, and Peggy Gray. 1992. "Contextualising Home Computing: Resources and Practices." In Roger Silverstone and Eric Hirsch, eds., *Consuming Technologies: Media and Information in Domestic Spaces,* 146–60. London: Routledge.

National Public Radio et al. 2001. "Survey of Americans on Technology." In *The Digital Divide: Facing a Crisis or Creating a Myth?* 274–77. Cambridge: MIT Press.

Nie, N. H., and L. Erbring. 2000. *Internet and Society: A Preliminary Report.* Stanford: Stanford Institute for the Quantitative Study of Society.

Norris, Pippa. 2001. *Digital Divide: Civic Engagement, Information Poverty, and the Internet Worldwide.* Cambridge: Cambridge University Press.

Office of the e-Envoy. 2001. *UK Online: Annual Report.* www.e-envoy.gov.uk/oee/oee.nsf/sections/index/$file/index.htm.

ONS [Office of National Statistics]. 2002. *Internet Access: Households and Individuals.* London. ONS.

————. 2003. *Internet Access: Households and Individuals.* London. ONS.

Palmer, G., M. Rahman, and P. Kenway. 2002. *Monitoring Poverty and Social Exclusion*. York: Joseph Rowntree Foundation.

Policy Action Team 15. 2000. *Closing the Digital Divide: Information and Communication Technologies in Deprived Areas: An Executive Summary*. London: Department of Trade and Industry.

Powell, Adam Clayton, III. 2001. "Falling for the Gap: Whatever Happened to the Digital Divide? In Benjamin M Compaine, *The Digital Divide: Facing a Crisis or Creating a Myth?* 309–14. Cambridge: MIT Press.

Putnam, Robert D. 2001. *Bowling Alone: The Collapse and Revival of American Community*. New York. Touchstone.

Russell, Neil, and Nick Drew. 2001. *ICT Access and Use: Report on the Benchmark Survey*. Research Brief no 252. London: Department for Education and Employment.

Russell, Neil, and Neil Stafford. 2002. *Trends in ICT Access and Use*. Research Brief no. 358. London. Department for Education and Skills.

Selwyn, N. 2002. "Establishing an Inclusive Society? Technology, Social Exclusion, and UK Government Policy Making." *Journal of Social Policy* 31, no. 1: 1–20.

Van Zoonen, L. 2002. "Gendering the Internet: Claims, Controversies, and Cultures." *European Journal of Communication* 17, no. 1: 5–23.

Warschauer, Mark. 2003. *Technology and Social Inclusion: Rethinking the Digital Divide*. Cambridge: MIT Press.

Wilhelm, Anthony G. 2000. *Democracy in the Digital Age: Challenges to Political Life in Cyberspace*. New York: Routledge.

Wills, M. 2001. "Forward: PAT 15: Information Technology." In *National Strategy for Neighbourhood Renewal: Policy Action Team Audit,* 197–98. Report by the Social Exclusion Unit. London: Cabinet Office.

15

Building the Information Society in EU Candidate Countries

A Long Way to Go

Jean-Claude Burgelman, Elissaveta Gourova, and Marc Bogdanowicz

Recently the governments of the candidate countries—Central and Eastern European countries that will join the European Union over the years to come (CEEC10) and the Mediterranean countries (Malta, Cyprus, Turkey)—have put high priority on the utilization of information and communication technologies (ICTs) as an important tool for acceleration of reforms, modernization of the economy, and overall integration into the European Union (EU).[1] Their commitment to join the efforts to build a larger European information society (IS) is reflected in the eEurope Plus Action Plan, which mirrors the objectives and deadlines of the eEurope Action plan of the EU member states.

As well as carrying out comprehensive political, economic, and social reforms, candidate countries face the challenge of calibrating IS policy within their overall development.

This chapter aims at providing insight into the major challenges confronting the candidate countries in the development of an information society for all. It focuses on the status and trends in the candidate countries in the three enabling areas for building an IS: networks (infrastructure), applications (info-structure), and skills (capabilities). On this basis, it attempts to highlight a number of future opportunities and possible barriers for IS development in candidate countries.

INFRASTRUCTURES

Availability and Use of Technologies

The rate at which an information society can be constructed is strongly dependent on the availability and affordability of ICTs to individuals, organizations, and the society as a whole.

Despite large differences in their initial status and ongoing reforms, all candidate countries have established conditions that facilitate the rapid diffusion of ICTs and a wide diversity of networks and services. At present a number of public or closed user-group networks, with national or regional coverage, provide access to voice, data, and images via satellite, cable, or wireless facilities. Consumers have various means and opportunities for communication, work, or entertainment, using fixed, mobile, or cable television (CATV) networks, as well as specialized networks for financial services, administrative, or research communications.

The high rate of adoption of technology and the introduction of changes in the telecommunications market raise expectations that candidate countries will be able to catch up in technological terms in a short period of time. However, the introduction of modern technologies is not supported by an even development at local, national, and regional levels. As progress in ICTs is correlated to a large extent with the level of economic development and the purchasing power of the population, countries with low per capita gross domestic product (GDP) are not capable of sustaining a high rate of ICT growth or high teledensity. On average, the candidate countries continue to lag behind EU member states in all measures of ICT access and usage. Advanced technologies for the provision of Internet access to end users, such as DSL, WAP, and CATV, are still in the early phases of deployment. Some candidate countries, however, are performing well. Estonia, Malta, Cyprus, and Slovakia, for example, have a higher Internet penetration than some EU member states. Furthermore, Estonia and Slovenia have reached the EU average level in terms of mobile usage and personal computer penetration. It should also be noted that CATV is quite well developed in most candidate countries. More than 50 percent of all households with television in Slovakia, Romania, and Malta, for example, have CATV connections. CATV may thus be considered an essential future opportunity for the provision of low-cost information and communication services to end users.

The overall economic situation in candidate countries—and the resulting uneven revenue distribution—is widening the gap between the people who can access the market of advanced technologies and services and those for whom they are a luxury. Additionally, the digital divide that is emerging in candidate countries is complex. At the moment there are large differences in technology diffusion based on geographic location, economic and social status, or age. In Turkey nearly 77 percent of all computers are owned by 40 percent of all households (Turkish National Information Infrastructure Master Plan, TUENA). These belong to the highest socioeconomic status groups, while the low economic status group, with around 40 percent of the households, owns only 10 percent of all computers. In Hungary Internet usage is dominated by educational institutions (44 percent), followed by corporate and government users (29 percent), and finally users at home and in small offices (27 percent) (ITU 2001). In Latvia and Bulgaria, fewer than 15 percent of households have computers (Eurostat 2001). In Estonia 58 percent of Internet users are between nineteen and twenty-nine years old, while only 7 percent of the users are between fifty and seventy-four (Baltic Media Facts 2001). The high price of equipment and services is a serious barrier for the wide use of new communication technologies. Hungary and Poland, for example, have the highest Internet access charges during off-peak time among OECD countries.[2] The low teledensity and long waiting lists in some of the candidate countries (e.g., more than 3 percent of the population in Poland, Romania, Bulgaria, and Turkey) also hamper Internet penetration and impose serious threats of growing regional disparities in the provision of access to new communication networks and services.

The deployment of online payment systems and security enhancing technologies is another critical issue for the take-up of e-commerce. In the candidate countries e-payment solutions are still in their infancy and awareness of Internet security threats is not widespread, except in banking, telecommunications, government and IT sectors, and the oil and gas industry. The high level of fraud and the lack of risk management skills in the CEEC10 are considered to be major reasons for the underdevelopment of new payment solutions. All existing Internet security technologies (e.g. authentication, firewalls, encryption, antivirus screening, etc.) are known and used in candidate countries, but their penetration has still not reached a critical mass. Besides, small and medium-sized enterprises (SMEs) try to solve security issues in-house without using professional security services (CEEBIC 2001). In comparison to the other OECD countries, Turkey, Poland, and Hungary are lagging behind with very few secure servers per million inhabitants (OECD 2001a). It is promising, however, that the candidate countries are trying to follow the new technological solutions for reliable and secure systems. As a Netcraft survey pointed out, the number of secure servers in the Czech Republic almost doubled from March to December 1999, and in Poland, Slovenia, Hungary, Estonia, etc., it increased by more than 50 percent (UN Economic Commission for Europe 2000). See table 15.1.

Industrial Position

The economic transformations in the last decade, the inflow of foreign direct investment (FDI), and the ability of companies in the candidate countries to absorb new technologies and integrate large production chains have contributed to the emergence of new patterns of local industry specialization.

Table 15.1. Selected Telecommunications Indicators

	Total Lines per 100 inh.		Mobile Lines per 100 inh.([1])		PCs per 100 inh.([1])		TV Sets per 100 inh.		CATV Users per 100 inh.
	1999	2000	1999	2000	1999	2000	1999	2000	1999
Bulgaria	38.9	44.3	4.3	8.2	2.7	4.4	37.2	37	6.9
Cyprus	62.99	64.72	22.5	26.2	16.7	28	27.5	28	6.1
Czech Republic	57.1	77.6	19.0	29.2	10.7	13.1	36.6	44	8
Finland	130	n.a.	66.8	72.8	36	n.a.	40.7	n.a.	17.8
Greece	92	n.a.	31.4	55.7	6	n.a.	31.3	n.a.	3
Estonia	64.1	n.a.	26.8	32.0	13.5	n.a.	37.3	36	8
Hungary	51.7	60.8	16.2	29.7	7.4	n.a.	50.3	n.a.	14
Latvia	42.6	46.9	11.2	15.6	8.2	n.a.	39.4	39	5
Lithuania	39.4	43.0	9.0	11.4	5.9	n.a.	55.4	73	7
Malta	52.04	52.76	9.7	21.1	18.1	21.0	66	n.a.	13.7
Poland	36.9	44.5	10.2	15.0	6.2	15.5	23.9	24	8
Romania	23.5	32.3	6.2	12.6	2.7	3.2	19.1	20	16
Slovakia	47.9	52.9	17.0	21.5	7.4	n.a.		23	
Slovenia	76.1	104.7	31.5	57.4	25.3	27.3	38.0	41	13
Turkey	30.74	31.37	12.5	19.3	3.2	4.6	33.02	33	1.17

Source: Eurostat 2001.

Recent analysis by the Vienna Institute for International Economic Studies (WIIW) indicates that in many CEEC10, manufacturing industries belonging to the ICT sector are increasing exports to the EU15, see table 15.2 (Havlik et al. 2001). Hungary is in a very strong position, as it has significant specialization in office machinery, computers, and electronic components, while in Poland the TV, radio, and recording equipment industry has been a top exporter since 1995. Estonia has been selected as a manufacturing and assembly center by high-tech Scandinavian and western companies. Malta has a comparative advantage in electronic products, which accounted for about half of its exports in 1999 (Eurostat 2000), while the Turkish electronics industry, in its exports of consumer electronics and telecommunications equipment, achieved an output of US$1.6 billion in 1996 (Acar et al. 2001).

The information technology (IT) hardware market in the CEEC10 has grown remarkably over the past few years, mainly due to government procurement projects and foreign investments. It should be noted that as a percentage of GDP, ICT expenditure in Hungary (6.42 percent), Slovakia (5.98 percent), and the Czech Republic (8.49 percent) is higher than in Germany (5.27 percent) and Finland (5.88 percent), while in Romania (1.78 percent), Bulgaria (1.76 percent), and Turkey (2.47 percent) it is still very low (World Bank 2001). However, according to Eurostat data (Eurostat 2000), the size of the IT hardware market in 2000 in all candidate countries was about €5 billion (Poland and Turkey taking more than 60 percent of the whole market), compared to €235 billion for the EU15.

Domestic IT companies in most of the candidate countries, without financial resources to modernize their production, were not able to compete with multinationals and have shrunk into small producers in limited niche markets. Many hardware companies have been integrated into the product life cycle of western companies through subcontracting or outsourcing, assembly, distribution, reverse engineering, and so on. In order to benefit from local expertise, many foreign companies have invested in software houses (e.g., in Estonia, Bulgaria, and Hungary) or have outsourced their work, taking advantage of the high quality and low prices in computer software markets in the CEEC10. Estonian IT companies, for example, are becoming more and more integrated into the supply chains of their Nordic counterparts, thus getting leading edge know-how and project management expertise. With its well-educated population and government emphasis on ICT development, Estonia is considered an excellent test market for new technologies (CEEBIC 2000). In Latvia, despite the availability of good specialists, insufficient government support and access to venture capital are limiting the competitiveness of IT companies. Other drawbacks are the lack of marketing skills in many companies and the mismatch between university training and practice (Ernst and Young 1999).

Software services represent one of the fastest growing sectors of the IT market in the candidate countries. Particularly strong growth is seen in the market for packaged software, such as PC applications software, enterprise resource planning applications, and application tools for database development and management. Most growth in the software and services sector is derived from large-scale projects in banking, financial services, government administration, telecommunications, and industry. Many domestic software companies have exploited local knowledge of customers and the local language as competitive assets. Local firms play an essential role as system integrators, value-added service providers, software developers, and training centers, and thus dominate the segment for computer-connected services such as installation, implementation, and customer training (Weber et al. 1999). They are often ahead of foreign companies in the local market in areas like company management, financial accounting software, banking software, and software for SMEs.

The telecommunication market is characterized by diverse trends. On the one hand, new operators and service providers are entering the market. On the other, companies are building new alliances and consolidating in order to deal more effectively with increased competition and rapid technological change. For example, the structural changes in CATV markets (e.g., Bulgaria, the Czech Republic, Latvia, and Estonia) are related to the growing need for investment in interactive services for end users. Only Malta and Turkey still have monopolies in CATV. Furthermore, increasing competition from mobile, satellite, and CATV operators confronts incumbent operators with the challenge of solving problems resulting from rigid organizational structures, lack of skilled manpower and market experience, as well as the relative inability to address user expectations for new services and quality offerings.

Infrastructure Challenges

These trends in the ICT sector show the ability of local industry to use its knowledge of local customers, culture and language, and geographical location as competitive tools in finding market niches and even going beyond national borders. Although the candidate countries are not able to compete with major foreign manufacturers and leading multinational ICT companies, they show signs of engaging foreign companies in investment in domestic manufacturing and technology transfer. Subsequently, public procurement policy and the investment climate might be important tools for further development of local branches of the ICT industry, especially where domestic traditions in this area and relevant experience are available.

In the rapidly changing technological and market environment, companies in the candidate countries face growing challenges for preserving and further expanding their market presence. Interconnection, Internet peering and settlement, technological conversion, and globalization are likely to further increase the complicated task of telecommunication managers and the newly established regulators. The demands on regulatory and competition

Table 15.2. Gaining and Losing Industries in Exports to the EU15, 1995–1999

		BG	CZ	HU	PL	RO	SK	SL	EE	LV	LT
TV, radio, and recording equipment NACE 3230	Exports 1999, Euro mn	13.3	135.6	1548.3	556.9	-	47.7	-	91.5	-	15.5
	Average annual change (percent)	84.8	31.4	52.9	59.2	-	39.9	-	56.5	-	72.8
	Competitive gain 95-2000	11.8	74.5	1167.9	440.5	-	31.0	-	71.1	-	13.1
	Market share in EU15, 1999 (percent)	0.08	0.81	9.26	3.33	-	0.29	-	0.55	-	0.09
TV and radio transmitters, line telephony equipment NACE 3220	Exports 1999, Euro mn	3.2	62.7	62.4	-	32.0	-	-	221.2	-	-
	Average annual change (percent)	62.9	63.1	49.0	-	179.3	-	-	316.1	-	-
	Competitive gain 95-2000, Euro mn	2.5	48.6	42.2	-	31.2	-	-	220.0	-	-
	Market share in EU15, 1999 (percent)	0.02	0.43	0.42	-	0.22	-	-	1.50	-	-
Electronic components NACE 3210	Exports 1999, Euro mn	7.4	326.9	332.8	196.9	-	40.8	43.9	-	-	32.4
	Average annual change (percent)	20.0	29.8	68.1	12.9	-	35.0	12.0	-	-	4.0
	Competitive gain 95-2000, Euro mn	2.8	177.3	278.6	39.4	-	24.8	7.6	-	-	-3.7
	Market share in EU15, 1999 (percent)	0.03	1.24	1.26	0.75	-	0.15	0.17	-	-	0.12

(continued)

Table 15.2. Gaining and Losing Industries in Exports to the EU15, 1995–1999 (continued)

		BG	CZ	HU	PL	RO	SK	SL	EE	LV	LT
Office machinery and computers	Exports 1999, Euro mn	-	188.8	1879.4	-	57.2	128.9	12.5	29.9	1.8	-
	Average annual change (percent)	-	20.0	109.8	-	167.0	149.8	16.1	-16.4	85.5	-
NACE 3001 and 3002	Competitive gain 95-2000, Euro mn	-	58.4	1740.3	-	55.6	124.2	2.6	-57.7	1.6	-
	Market share in EU15, 1999 (percent)	-	0.31	3.13	-	0.10	0.21	0.02	0.05	0.0	-

Source: WIIW (2001).
Note: The NACE numbers are taken from the European international standard industry classification.

authorities to safeguard competition and market rules, as well as to mobilize technical, organizational, and other means to ensure the protection of consumers, and trust and confidence in electronic communications are also increasing in this dynamic environment.

Despite their growing use of ICTs, candidate countries are exposed to serious risks that advanced technologies will widen the existing gap between rich and poor, young and old, and thus may endanger social cohesion and generate political backlash. Low investment opportunities of domestic companies and purchasing power of the population limit the growth of the sector and the achievement of a critical mass of users. Therefore, an important objective of ICT policy is to ensure that all citizens and businesses gain equal opportunities to access and use at a reasonable price modern, efficient, and high-quality technologies and services. Respect for consumer rights and the participation of all in the IS also raises issues for user support, ease of use of equipment, interfaces, and services, as well as the application of the principles for interoperability.

While universal access is highly dependent on the availability of networks, the development of alternative access technologies (e.g., wireless, satellite, and cable) might facilitate leapfrogging over fixed telephone infrastructure deficiencies. Their spread, along with increasing competition in the market, provides opportunities for communication and faster Internet connection at lower prices. The development of specialized networks (e.g., administrative and research) and setting up public access centers might have an impact in the long run on the provision of access to disadvantaged regional communities. The preferential treatment of similar centers and the development of SME-oriented centers, especially in less developed regions, might also contribute to overcoming their isolation and low technological status, creating new opportunities for people and enterprises, and fostering innovation.

INFO-STRUCTURES AND CONTENT

The Strong Development of Content and Applications

During the last decade populations in candidate countries have been offered generalized access to international information sources. There has also been a blossoming of national online content initiatives. The rapid growth of domestic websites and web portals in local languages and the provision of governmental interactive services and online content have been stimulated to a large extent by the strong demand from businesses and civil society. A survey in Turkey, for example, outlines the population's very favorable attitude to the use of national information infrastructure for communication with other people or enterprises and for access to public services, information, and culture (TUENA 1998).

Many domestic websites provide opportunities for communication and exchange of ideas (through discussion forums), for online travel bookings, and for tourist information, library searches, and so on. Most public authorities in the candidate countries focus on the establishment of new information systems and public registers and on the modernization of existing ones, as a basis for development of e-government and provision of one-stop shopping. Some initiatives for tax payment over the Internet and the announcement of governmental decisions and public tenders are seen as the first steps toward government-to-business and government-to-citizens e-commerce.

The development of IS applications in health care, transport, culture, and tourism, for example, is also gaining importance in the candidate countries. In all these countries, higher education seems to be the leading application sector, whereas electronic applications are not so widespread at other educational levels or in local administration (see table 15.3). A number of projects have focused on the preservation of traditions, folklore, and national heritage for future generations, making them available to other people all over the world. In Latvia and Lithuania, for example, access via the Internet has been provided to museums and art galleries, while in Slovakia most of the large public libraries are online. The progressive deployment of global positioning systems, geographic information systems, sophisticated traffic monitoring systems, and travel information services also allow vehicles to avoid delays in delivery of goods and to optimize their routes, and in general aim at improving transport logistics, efficiency, and safety.

In the area of health care, ICTs have been used in many cases for improving the quality of medical services and making specialized knowledge available to hospitals and primary health care organizations. Regional health care networks are supporting remote diagnosis and consultation. For example, the Baltic International Telemedicine Network is providing a joint forum for the development of occupational health and safety.[3]

E-business Trends

Despite the fact that business players have undertaken different initiatives for providing end consumers with online services, creating virtual shops or taking first steps toward setting up systems for e-banking and e-business, the business-to-consumer market is still very limited. The few customers who use the Internet do so predominantly to receive information and to order products or services, paying on delivery. Business-to-business commerce is also in its infancy—companies use electronic networks mainly to access market news/analysis and new business offers, and to communicate with suppliers—while contracts and business deals are carried out by direct contacts and by traditional means.

Table 15.3. Public Supply: Percentage of Websites per Sector

	Primary, Secondary Schools	High Schools, Universities	Ministries	Local Authorities	Hospitals	Museums	Libraries
Cyprus	6	38	100	n.d.	8	11	1
Czech Rep.	27	86.9	100	12.9	62.2	52.1	7
Estonia	37.8	75.8	100	66.8	28.2	26.8	4.3
Hungary	28	30	100	21.42	52.87	19.91	9.5
Latvia	14.1	84.8	100	14.3	8	77.4	2.4
Lithuania	11.6	100	100	16.5	22.1	93.75	17.2
Malta	6	4	35	21	20	21	2
Poland	14.5	90.6	100	51	19	17.7	6.3
Romania	0.5	17.8	62.5	9.2	1.9	1.8	0.1
Slovakia	1.67	100	100	9	11	33.7	75
Slovenia	84	89	100	70	54	45.9	96.9
Turkey	1	100	100	4	6	30	8

Source: Eurostat 2001.

Table 15.4. Competitiveness Indicators in Internet

	Note	BG	CZ	DE	GR	HU	PL	RU	SK	TU
E-mail Does your company use e-mail?	Rank 1 = strongly disagree 7 = strongly agree	55 5.48	16 6.9	21 6.8	51 6.3	40 6.5	54 5.5	56 4.9	53 5.8	22 6.8
Internet for information Share of companies that use Internet for general information	rank percent	56 83.9	9 100	16 100	32 98.2	42 97	29 98.5	57 83.9	54 87.1	20 100
Internet for supplier relations Share of companies that use Internet for supplier relations	rank percent	56 47.1	29 68.4	12 75.9	50 54.9	54 49.4	30 67.3	44 59.6	13 75	40 61.8
Internet for customer service Share of companies that use Internet for customer service	rank percent	57 37.1	20 81	10 84.1	48 63	55 45.7	40 70.7	59 33.3	21 80	44 67.6
E-commerce Share of companies that use Internet for e-commerce	rank percent	58 12.8	31 45	5 67.5	54 24.4	53 24.7	15 55.3	55 22.5	9 62.3	42 39.4

Source: Centre for Economic Development 2000; quoted at the World Economic Forum.

According to a regional survey of SMEs in Poland (Chmielarz n.d.), 75 percent of those interviewed consider the Internet to be an excellent promotional medium for products and services and 48 percent would use it to create their corporate image. Only 31 percent of companies declare that they use the Internet, or are going to use it, to sell their products or services. There is not much difference in attitudes between Hungary, Turkey, Bulgaria, the Czech Republic, and Slovakia, where more than 83 percent of companies use the Internet for information (see table 15.4). In this field, only a few champions exist in the candidate countries. Estonia clearly is one, as Estonian banks have more than 330,000 Internet bank customers, putting it on a level with the highly developed Nordic countries (Siil 2001).

As in most EU countries, the spread of ICTs among companies in the candidate countries is a market-driven phenomenon. Most companies see no real strategic reason to go online (Eade 2000). It is regarded as little more than an extra or a question of image, and ICTs are not perceived as contributing to competitive advantage, not even as an integrated tool for viable business. There are expectations, however, that with increased competition, companies will reconsider e-business alternatives for higher efficiency and competitiveness. Multinationals that establish branches in the candidate countries increasingly require e-business capability on the part of their suppliers and the banking sector. They bring in e-business models, forcing both their partners and competitors to respond; it is the fear of falling into obsolescence that apparently drives most e-business in the candidate countries.

As already stated, investment capacity, especially domestic investment, is still relatively weak, and in such circumstances risky options are usually left aside. Internal organizational factors may well be the biggest obstacle to making the right decisions and overcoming organizational inertia: cultures of entrepreneurship, e-business education, e-readiness, and leadership are aspects that remain to be dealt with. Additionally, the conservative attitude of most customers, and some businesses, the lack of trust in security of technologies, and the fear of misuse of personal and business information further influence companies' investment and adoption of ICT-based strategic options. Insufficiently developed logistics systems and lack of professional home delivery services are further obstacles in this respect, as well as the predominance of English-language materials on the web. Recent overviews also found that all candidate countries face common technical obstacles to the take-off of e-commerce, related to the limited diffusion of ICTs, banking products, and security-enhancing technologies (PricewaterhouseCoopers 2000).

Many companies in the candidate countries will soon be in a position to adopt and apply e-commerce technologies in order to leapfrog economic development and hence join the EU on a more competitive basis. Only countries such as Estonia and possibly Slovenia may be in a position to successfully meet this ambitious challenge.

The Government's Role in Raising Participation

Government initiatives in the candidate countries are proactively focused on the establishment of a favorable environment for development of e-commerce and a knowledge-based economy. Influenced by the EU accession negotiations, governments in CEEC10 have undertaken many actions in order to facilitate the transition toward an information society, for example, development of IS strategies and action plans, setting up of coordination mechanisms, introduction of appropriate regulatory environment, awareness raising on ICT use, and so on (EU/CEEC Joint High Level Committee 2000).

The process can be seen as one of "capacity building." In the case of the candidate countries it involves establishing and developing new institutions, providing a regulatory tool kit, developing skills in its use, and, most importantly, establishing the credibility of the regulator. Front-end expenditure on these activities is expected to produce significant long-term benefits.

The establishment of public gateways to electronic information and services is another important tool for providing all citizens with equal access at affordable prices and raising participation. Access to online services in a social location different from work or home has been provided in the candidate countries in various forms, for example, information kiosks, stand-alone terminals, telecenters, community centers, and clubs (Milne and Creighton 2000). Centers in rural areas also fulfill some intermediate functions related to technological assistance to users and consultations, and have particular importance for bridging the regional digital divide.

Despite these many efforts, candidate countries are still not well prepared to take advantage of e-commerce. An assessment of global e-readiness carried out by McConnell International in August 2000 considered Central and Southern Europe "a most e-ready region."[4] In particular, the report stated that the highly skilled population and a reasonable level of information security in these countries considerably reduce e-business risks. Nonetheless, in many countries there is substantial room for improvement in the e-business climate, especially the regulatory environment (see table 15.5).

Info-structure Challenges

Linguistic diversity, cultural heritage, media pluralism, technical and media competencies, and the supply capacity and knowledge base that already exists provide the candidate countries with an opportunity to make the most of production and provision of content. However, the promotion of cultural diversity on the Internet and access to world cultural heritage via the new

Table 15.5.   Assessment of E-readiness in Central and Southern Europe

Country	Connectivity	E-leadership	Information Security	Human Capital	E-business Climate
Bulgaria	1+	2	1	2	1+
Czech Rep.	2+	2	2	2	1+
Estonia	2+	3	2	3	3
Greece	2	1+	2	2	1
Hungary	2+	2−	2	3	2
Italy	2+	2	3	2+	2
Latvia	1+	1+	2	2+	2+
Lithuania	2	2	2	2	2
Poland	1+	2	2	2+	2
Portugal	2+	3	2+	2	2+
Romania	1	2	1	2	1+
Russia	1	1	1	2−	1
Slovakia	2	1+	2+	2	1+
Slovenia	2+	2+	2	2	1+
Spain	2+	2+	2+	2+	2+
Turkey	2	2	1+	2+	2

Source: McConnell International 2000.
Key:
+/−   Indicates improvements/weakening relative to prior time periods
1   Substantial improvement to the conditions necessary to support e-business and e-government
2   Improvement to the conditions necessary to support e-business and e-government
3   Majority of conditions suitable to the conduct of e-business and e-government

electronic media is likely to require the joint efforts of the international community. It must develop the necessary technological tools to offer linguistic diversity (also in other alphabets) and avoid the often cited trap of worldwide Americanization of cultures.

The advent of Internet and digital broadcasting platforms will raise several new issues for the candidate countries related to the protection of consumer and citizen rights, such as the availability of quality content in an overall context of below-average per capita revenues and the protection of intellectual property. In fact, the challenge of how to prevent the infringement of ethnic, religious, and minority rights, as well as human dignity, is a global prerequisite. However, in the newly established democracies of the candidate countries it is more challenging to find the right balance of regulatory and self-regulatory rules, and to ensure both freedom of information and expression and protection of citizens and users from illegal or harmful content and disclosure or misuse of private information.

In order to maximize the potential for the content industry in candidate countries, it is of vital importance to build up a critical mass in investment and usage, and to create awareness of the profitability and potential benefits of public and private partnerships. In this area valuable lessons can be learned from EU experience. This does not mean mimicking western European development procedures but adapting the lessons learned to the local situation.

Public availability of electronic sources of information, knowledge, and culture, and access to online applications for health, education, and transport could give wide opportunities for innovative socioeconomic development, could enable governments to meet democratic objectives, and could enhance communication among citizens and businesses. Simultaneously, governments would fulfill their role as a driving force toward an "information society for all." A major challenge therefore will be to establish methods of governance that offer new tools for managing the public sphere democratically.

The private sector will play a vital role in this endeavor. While incumbent media companies further develop the repurposing and cross-promoting of content across multiple distribution channels, net-native companies could offer targeted content or delivery options in niche markets. The key here, fundamental to a competitive industry, is for the candidate countries to become producer rather than consumer countries. A challenge for candidate countries is to achieve balanced deregulation. They need to create an economy that is sufficiently stable and regulated to attract investment and promote entrepreneurship, but at the same time liberal and open enough for companies to explore their objectives with the freedom to create profitable businesses.

Candidate countries still have a long way to go to meet the objectives of e-business. The future competitiveness of their enterprises will also depend on fast access to up-to-date information, electronic communication with partners and customers, innovative marketing strategies, and the use of web page and database references in highly rated sites. In particular, ICTs open up possibilities for their many small firms to become aware of the needs of global conglomerates. However, this has to be managed, structured, and supported on the solid foundation of an efficient logistics system. The lack of appropriate technologies, skills, technical and management personnel, as well as limited awareness of the potential advantages of ICTs, may hamper this development.

CAPABILITIES AND SKILLS

ICT-Based Trends in Education

The CEEC10 face greater challenges than the EU15 countries in the provision of the kind of education needed for the digital age, as massive economic and social changes are going on. Due to the large economic decline in these countries, state support for education has been seriously reduced in real terms. This is exacerbated by a transition to a more decentralized educational system and the consequent emergence of regional disparities in the provision of education and training. Generally speaking, disparities in educational opportunities between students with different backgrounds are increasing (Gourova et al. 2001). The introduction of private education and the nationalization of resources in secondary education have further widened the educational divide. On the other hand, the availability of elite schools has made it possible to maintain a good level of student knowledge in mathematics and science in some countries (OECD 2000).

Despite these growing disparities in education and the problems encountered at regional levels, the introduction of ICTs has now become an important educational topic and is firmly on the national policy agenda of candidate countries. The main activities focus on developing new methodologies, programs, and educational content, and supplying the necessary equipment and connectivity in schools.

Though candidate countries acknowledge the role of ICTs as enabling technologies and as a necessity for all, they differ in their education policy goals. Most of them focus primarily on ICT education as a separate subject. The objectives pursued by candidate countries cover a wide range of fields: programming, use of software, information searches, and communication via a network (Bulgaria, Romania, Slovenia) or aim at familiarizing pupils with ICT (Hungary) and enabling them to acquire basic knowledge (Poland, Estonia) (EURYDICE 2000).

The availability of computers and their connection to the Internet are essential for ICT-based learning processes and have dominated the first phase of introduction of ICT education. In Hungary all secondary schools are connected to the Internet and, as a result of the School-Net project launched in 1996, many schools have been equipped with computer laboratories, with six to eighteen multimedia computers each (UNESCO 2000). In Latvia the ratio of students per computer has halved in the period 1997–2000, reaching 32.3 students per computer in 2000. In this country 20 percent of secondary schools in rural areas and 49 percent of those in cities have permanent connections to the Internet (Bicevskis et al. 2001). With 66.4 students per computer, Bulgaria is lagging far behind.

Even where technologies and skills are available, the integration of ICTs in the learning process is hampered by the lack of appropriate electronic books or multimedia tools in the local language. The dominance of English as lingua franca of the information age is often considered a barrier for enhanced ICT usage. However, the emphasis of candidate-country governments and the collaboration of all actors—teaching staff, software developers, content producers, learning content distributors, and so on—might facilitate the development of educational materials meeting e-learning requirements.

The availability of technologies and tools is a necessary condition, but the key factor for success in the e-learning field is the human factor. While at the policy level it is clear that schools should be connected to the Internet, the ability of teachers to adapt effectively to new technologies in the learning environment is problematic despite many training programs to retrain teachers and prepare them for the changing learning environment. There are concerns about how to motivate young people to choose the teaching profession as a career and how to encourage teachers to use ICTs efficiently and move toward a more open learning process and self-development on the job.

It is not only a problem in the candidate countries that non-ICT teachers often oppose the mediator role of machines in human communications and refuse to implement ICTs. Best-practice cases indicate that good management and internal organization in schools, as well as the human approach to the problems of teachers, are important factors contributing to successful ICT integration in education, high teacher motivation, and innovation. The success of e-learning reforms will also probably depend on the availability to teachers of a robust and user-friendly e-learning environment—availability of relevant software, suitably designed educational portals, and the opportunity to access educational forums.

Training the Workforce

Competitiveness appears increasingly dependent on the ability of a company to develop, recruit, and retain a technologically literate workforce. Moreover, the transitional period and in particular the restructuring of the economy have seriously affected both vocational education and traditions of on-the-job-training, breaking off existing links with enterprises, and cutting down the support system for learning. Also, insufficient financial resources limit the ability of enterprises to provide on-the-job training and qualification courses to their employees.

Many initiatives aimed at responding to the increased training needs of the labor force, and focusing on building an open, flexible and transparent lifelong learning system, are under way in all candidate countries (European Training Foundation 2000). Schemes aimed at encouraging company training activities have been launched in Cyprus, Malta, and Hungary. In Slovenia existing company-based training facilities have been transformed into intercompany or regional practical training centers. The focus in most cases is on areas where the demand and potential for economic gain are greatest (business, law, ICTs, foreign languages, etc.). Along with forms of traditional training, candidate countries are also seizing the opportunities that distance education offers them. "Virtual universities" and distance-training courses have developed, mainly through the financial support of international institutions (e.g., EU, UNDP, World Bank, etc.).

The training of managers and leaders is another essential issue. While the Mediterranean countries have longer experience with market economies, the transition decade has faced the CEEC10 with the challenge to prepare managers able to raise the competitiveness of their companies and adapt them to the rapidly changing technological and market conditions. Although there are some indications that individual entrepreneurship is driving the uptake of economic activity in candidate countries, in particular in the services sector, the lack of entrepreneurship and aversion to risk are claimed to be weaknesses of businesses in the CEEC10 (EBRD 2000). As the European Bank for Reconstruction and Development (EBRD) pointed out in the 2000 transition report, foreign investors have experienced more difficulties in finding good managers than IT or financial staff.

A cross-country survey of the European Training Foundation in Slovenia, Romania, and Poland observed that a great majority of managers still see themselves primarily as functional specialists and professionals (Gudic 2000). Strategic thinking seems to be underdeveloped and strategy is misinterpreted or even confused with tactics, tools, and instruments. Considerable managerial and leadership potential has been recognized in the nonmanagerial groups of young talent and professionals, though this is still underutilized.

The application of innovative management techniques constitutes a serious need in candidate countries. These could be introduced, for example, as company praxis value analysis, business process reengineering, project development and management, benchmarking of competitive capacity of companies, technology watch, or quality management methodologies. Such techniques would help companies develop more forward-looking attitudes and focus on human resources, technology, and markets (European Commission, DG Enterprise 2001). In particular, SMEs lack the resources or know-how to think in strategic terms, and their use of advanced technologies is relatively low.

Within the EU negotiation process, special attention is devoted to supporting the development of SMEs and providing the necessary training for managers, decision makers, and public sector employees. In particular, the introduction of ICT in the public sector, the focus on e-learning, and e-government raises the issue of strengthening general and special ICT competencies in all public institutions. At the same time, it calls for increasing decision makers' awareness of the opportunities provided by new communication tools for companies, individuals, and society as a whole, in order to be able to take appropriate decisions to facilitate ICT development. Courses on management of change, quality management, business administration, and so on, are organized to complement the traditional degree programs or build part of special programs developed jointly by universities and companies according to management needs. International collaboration and networking are other important action lines providing local companies the opportunities to benefit from external experience and to develop the necessary managerial capabilities.

ICT Professionals

Despite the recent slowdown of the new economy and the cutting of many IT jobs in developed countries, the ICT sector in candidate countries is still trying to bridge technology gaps. ICT growth and good working conditions have attracted many young people. Some CEEC10 (e.g., Latvia, Bulgaria), while worrying about future shortages, consider the availability of highly qualified IT specialists as an important strength for sector growth. In particular, the expansion of software applications in many CEEC10 has been facilitated by the existing human capital accumulated previously in the sector (Kubielas and Yegorov 2000).

In general, it is difficult to assess the real situation in the ICT-sector labor market for all candidate countries, due first to a lack of employment data by branch of activity and second to contradictory views on the future availability of ICT professionals. Employee groups state that there are enough highly skilled professionals while IT associations often claim job shortages (e.g., in Turkey, Cyprus, Bulgaria). It has also been estimated that in Estonia in 2000–2002 there would be shortages of about 1,200 people for the IT industry and 12,000 IT specialists for other sectors. In Hungary shortages have been predicted to reach 9,500 by 2002 (European Commission 2001).

The OECD provides some insight into employment in the ICT sector as a share of the business sector in some candidate countries. Hungary takes third place among OECD countries, while Turkey and the Czech Republic are below the OECD average (OECD 1998). The telecommunication industry makes up over 70 percent of the ICT sector employment in Turkey, while in the Czech Republic and Hungary, ICT manufacturing and services dominate.

Immigration policies of developed countries aimed at attracting workers from other countries with IT skills are exacerbating the situation. A World Economic Forum survey (quoted in a 2001 working document on Bulgarian technology development from the Center for Economic Development) states that talented people would rather remain in Poland and the Czech Republic, whereas the probability of a brain drain is much higher in Bulgaria and Slovakia. In Latvia, some hopes are expressed that talented people at present working abroad will return, but the best IT specialists are unlikely to emigrate due to the high living standards they enjoy there (Tukisa 1999). According to OECD estimates, around 50 percent of all Turkish postgraduate students in the United States are potential emigrants (OECD 2001b).

There are also more general threats based on trends in higher education and research. Many students who study communications or computers are no longer interested in postgraduate education or research careers after obtaining their master's degrees in most CEEC10. In Latvia, professors are worried that the present achievements in higher education in ICT are based on the scientific potential of the past. Young people are not choosing university careers now, thus putting into question the longer-term prospects for the training of ICT professionals (Tukisa 1999). Furthermore, foreign-owned companies and banks provide better employment conditions and have attracted the best trained specialists, often leading to a lack of skilled personnel in local companies and research units. In Estonia, for example, the Tallinn Technical University has lost dozens of highly educated employees to the banks (Kalja 1999).

The problems that the educational systems in candidate countries at present face—the skills mismatch of the workers and the very fast outdating of competencies—often motivate larger companies to establish their own programs in order to retrain employees. In Bulgaria, Cisco has its own academy; in the Baltic states Microsoft runs authorized training programs; and IBM computer classes are part of the University of Latvia. This tendency to private certification is particularly important for the enterprises involved in ICT development and maintenance, as well as the major users and providers of knowledge-intensive services. Specialized training and retraining courses are offered for bank and telecommunications employees and computer specialists.

Capabilities and Skills Challenges

Responding to the needs of rapidly changing technological development and the shift toward a knowledge-based economy requires the right skills and capabilities as much as it requires the best possible info-structure or infrastructure. Addressing the problem of missing skills and capabilities, however, is primarily a question of setting the right institutional and cultural priorities and involves a cross-sectoral and long-term policy approach.

A clear challenge for all the candidate countries is to create an adequate e-learning environment, not just equipping schools with computers but also focusing on the effective use of ICTs in education. A key issue is to strengthen teachers' competencies and their ability to absorb innovative approaches in the learning process. This requires that the candidate countries also consider how to motivate teachers to make the necessary professional and personal effort and to assist them in their new role of facilitators.

Building partnerships and strengthening collaboration of educational institutions with companies, labor authorities, or NGOs might be a useful step toward meeting the objectives of e-learning, and even wider targets such as overcoming the skills shortages, increasing employability, and meeting present and future market demands for highly skilled employees. Time pressure and increased competition is driving companies to focus on the skills and knowledge base of their future employees and customers, thus investing in education and collaborating with general vocational schools or universities. Faced with a shortage of money for education, public authorities need to encourage these trends and make full use of them.

In addition to the requirements for specialized knowledge and skills among employees, managers, and ICT professionals, candidate countries need educated citizens who are able to use the computer networks and are interested in the new services and tools. It is vital for future development that everyone is provided with the opportunity to obtain the knowledge and skills needed to use basic IS services—regardless of age, disability, income, or gender. Subsequently, public policy needs to redirect its focus toward a more balanced development in education so that neither young nor old are left behind.

There are further issues that the candidate countries need to solve—how to guide the mobility of IT specialists and researchers and make use of it, how to explore the opportunities provided by ICTs for work, education, and regional development—to mention only some.

CONCLUSION

These trends illustrate candidate countries' capacity to catch up in techno-logical terms and integrate existing global companies, as well as their po-tential for finding competitive niches for local industry, mainly in software and services, using local knowledge and geographic situation as competitive assets. Some of them may even go beyond their immediate domestic mar-kets. In particular, info-structures and content present great opportunities for candidate countries to utilize media production capacities (TV, editing, cin-ema, press, etc.), cultural heritage, and traditions for today's business pur-poses.

However, the low investment capabilities of the industry and the low pur-chasing power of the population hinder balanced development and the building of a critical mass of usage. Therefore, it is necessary to mobilize public–private partnerships to raise awareness and participation, and to meet the demands for services and content by business players and society in general.

The key issue here is the formation of human capital. Candidate countries are focusing on meeting human resource needs in the ICT sector and gener-ally building excellence in some areas of science and technology, while do-ing little about their largely ICT illiterate population. If candidate countries really wish to achieve a knowledge-based society, the strong correlation be-tween income level, education, and ICT know-how points to the need for a holistic policy approach addressing all levels of society and all categories of the population.

These difficulties and opportunities have to be seen against the back-ground of the overall challenges candidate countries face in the transition to market economies and democratic societies. Their policy makers will be un-der huge pressure to respond to the legitimate short-term needs and current problems rather than the rather long-term issues of development of an in-formation society. Striking a balance between these two sets of policy objectives (acute societal day-to-day needs and IS needs) is probably the most difficult policy challenge.

Clearly choices made today will drive their economies and societies to alternative scenarios:

1. If present development imbalances are not addressed, the candidate countries will build a society that will succeed in making ICT islands but will maintain large disparities between countries, regions, and groups of people in this domain as in others.
2. If the candidate countries wish to establish a more inclusive and democratic information society, a policy push is needed, as well as sufficient financial support, to achieve balanced ICT development. In times of restricted public resources, striking the balance between competitive objectives, targeting the major relevant factors of long-term development, and acting cooperatively with the private sector could become the guidelines of a sort of "Marshall Plan" for the information society.

NOTES

1. The views expressed in this chapter are not necessarily those of the European Commission. This chapter is based on the work undertaken for the IPTS Enlargement Futures Project: www.jrc.es/projects/enlargement.

2. www.oecd.org/dsti/sti/it/cm.

3. www.bitnet.promotor.telia.se; www.balticseaosh.net.

4. The e-readiness ratings combine a dynamic evaluation of the relevance and accuracy of available quantitative data with an understanding of cultural, institutional, and historical factors relevant to the actual situation in each country. The ratings measure status and progress on five interrelated attributes: connectivity, e-leadership, information security, human capital, e-business climate. See "Risk E-business: Seizing the Opportunity for Global E-readiness," www.mcconnellinternational.com/strategies2.html#readiness2.

REFERENCES

Acar, A., et al. 2001. *A Brief Review of the Current Status of E-Turkey*. Ankara: METU Software Research and Development Center.

Baltic Media Facts, Ltd. 2001. Surveys. www.bmf.ee.>www.bmf.ee.

Bicevskis, J., et al. 2001. "The LIIS and E-Latvia." *Baltic IT&T Review* 20: 49; also www.liis.lv/english/main.htm.

CEEBIC. 2000. "Telecommunications Services." www.mac.doc.gov/eebic/countryr/estonia/market/EstTeleServices.htm.

———. 2001. "Hungary—Market Research." www.mac.doc.gov/eebic/countryr/hungary/market1.htm.

Center for Economic Development. 2001. *Analysis of the Bulgarian Technology De-velopment.* Working paper, p. 110. www.ced.bg/projects11/documents1/an_t_dev .PDF.

Chmielarz. n.d. *E-commerce from the Point of View of Medium-sized Businesses in Poland.* Warsaw, Poland: Warsaw University, Management Department.

Eade, Ph., et al. 2000. *A Survey of E-business, Business Central Europe.* Delia Meth-Cohn.

EBRD. 2000. *Transition Report.* London: European Bank for Reconstruction and De-velopment.

Ernst and Young. 1999. "Opportunities for Investment and Co-Operation in the IT Sector in Latvia: A Study of the IT Services Sector." *Baltic IT Review* 15.

EU/CEEC Joint High Level Committee. 2000. *Progress Report.* europa.eu.int/ information_society/international/candidate_countries/doc/summary_report.pdf.

European Commission, DG Enterprise. 2001. *Innovation Policy in Six Applicant Countries: The Challenges.* Brussels: European Commission.

European Training Foundation. 2000. *Review of Progress in Vocational Education and Training Reform of the Candidate Countries for Accession to the EU in the Light of Developments in European Policy on Vocational Training.* www.etf.eu.int.

Eurostat. 2000. *European Union FDI with Candidate Countries: An Overview.* Statis-tics in Focus 26. Luxembourg: European Commission.

———. Eurostat. 2001. *IS Statistics,* 27. Statistics in Focus. Luxembourg: European Com-mission.

EURYDICE 2000. *ICT in the Education Systems in Europe.* www.eurydice.org.

Gourova, E., et al. 2001. *Technology, Knowledge, and Learning.* Enlargement Futures Report Series 3. November, 63.

Gudic, M. 2000. *Assessing Management Training Needs in Central and Eastern Eu-rope: Cross-country Survey.* European Training Foundation. www.etf.eu.int/P.

Havlik, P., M. Landesmann, and R. Stehrer. 2001. *Competitiveness of Industry in CEE Candidate Countries.* Vienna: Vienna Institute for International Economics.

ITU. 2001. *Internet in a Transition Economy: Hungary Case Study.* www.itu.int/ti/ casestudies.

Kalja. 1999. "Early Activities in the Field of Software Process Improvement in Esto-nia." *Baltic IT Review* 15: 59.

Kubielas, S., and I. Yegorov. 2000. "Strategic Alliances and Technology Transfer in Central and Eastern Europe." *Science and Public Policy,* August 2000.

Milne, C., and S. Creighton, eds. 2000. *Universal Community Service: Access for All to Internet Services at Community Level.* Strasbourg: Council of Europe DH-MM.

OECD. 1998. *Measuring the ICT Sector.* Paris: OECD.

———. 2000. *Measuring Student Knowledge and Skills: The PISA 2000 Assessment of Reading, Mathematical, and Scientific Literacy.* Paris: OECD.

———. 2001a. *Science, Technology, and Industry Scoreboard.* Paris: OECD.

———. 2001b. *International Mobility of the Highly Skilled.* Paris: OECD.

PricewaterhouseCoopers. 2000. *EU Enlargement Challenges.* Focus on E-business. London: PricewaterhouseCoopers.

Siil, I. 2001. *Estonia: Preparing for the Information Age.* International Council for IT in Government Administration (ICA), ICA Information no. 74. www.ica-it.org.

TUENA.1998. *Turkish National Information Infrastructure Masterplan*. TUENA Final Report. www.tuena.tubitak.gov.tr.

Tukisa. 1999. "An Important Anniversary for the University of Latvia's Mathematics and Informatics Institute." *Baltic IT Review* 15: 11.

UN Economic Commission for Europe. 2000. *Internet Infrastructure Development in Transition Economies*, 76–78. www.unece.org.

UNESCO. 2000. *World Communication and Information Report 1999-2000*. Paris: Unesco.

Weber, M., et al. 1999. *The Wider Picture: Enlargement and Cohesion in Europe*. Futures project Series no. 15. Seville, Spain: JRC-IPTS.

World Bank. 2001. *World Development Indicators 2001*. www.worldbank.org/data/wdi2001/index.htm.

16

Romanticism in Business Culture
The Internet, the 1990s, and the Origins of Irrational Exuberance

Thomas Streeter

Most would agree that, in the contemporary world, business shapes culture, and many would add that business also *has* a culture (or cultures) of its own. But cultural processes also play a role in *constituting* business. Whether or not Weber was right about the role of the Protestant ethic in creating modern industrial capitalism, there are key moments when markets, property relations, and enterprises are constituted, come into being, in conditions deeply shaped by cultural constructs. The cultural visions that drove the "irrationally exuberant" Internet economy of the 1990s, this chapter suggests, provide a case study of such a moment.

It is important that, in retrospect, so much of what happened in the 1990s looks frivolous, that it was embedded in hype and cultural trends. But we would do well to look beyond the assumption that 1990s Internet enthusiasm was merely a momentary group psychosis that can be cured if we all return to business fundamentals. James Carey and John Quirk note that, ever since the development of the telegraph, new technologies have been greeted by what they call the "rhetoric of the electrical sublime," an expression of a quasi-religious faith in the power of new technologies to overcome social and material constraints (Carey and Quirk 1970). Clearly the enthusiasm for the Internet in the 1990s is a dramatic example of what Carey and Quirk are talking about. But Carey and Quirk's insight, coupled to the extraordinary events of the late 1990s, raises further questions: Why does this pattern persist? What are its effects? How does it connect to everyday life? to social structure? This chapter explores some possible answers to those questions; it suggests how some specific cultural patterns interacted with political economic shifts.

The chapter begins by describing characteristic online experiences of the early 1990s and then proceeds to locate those experiences in the U.S. political context of the time, particularly struggles over the relations between government and business in technological and economic development. It shows how certain subjective experiences associated with the burgeoning online world interacted with specific political economic events—particularly the failure of corporate and government elites to anticipate the Internet. This interaction lent itself to an iconoclastic, counterculture-influenced ethos that in turn laid the foundations for the Internet stock bubble.

MODEMS AND MIDDLE MANAGEMENT IN THE EARLY 1990s

The Internet did not appear from nowhere in the early 1990s, even though it seemed to. By 1990, regular users of the Internet in private and public research labs around the world had been noticing the dramatic growth in the Internet's richness as more and more people became connected. The more people who were using the Internet and the more services that were available, the more useful and interesting it became. Some readers may remember using Gopher information services back in 1992, for example.

Recall what it was like back then. By 1992 or 1993, computers had become a commonplace of office life; word processing was routine, and a new computer had become a standard part of an academic job offer. Microcomputers had lost the sheen of newness that they had a decade before, along with their associations with entrepreneurial innovation.

E-mail was still somewhat exotic, and web browsing was unknown. Many had experimented with e-mail a bit, but typically within specific, confined worlds like CompuServe, Prodigy, local bulletin boards, or one of several restricted academic networks. "Going online" at the time was thus technically possible with the computers that were on the desks of journalists, academics, and other professionals, but it was a little out of the ordinary. If you weren't a computer professional, it was something you did out of curiosity; it took a substantial amount of time and was unlikely to yield much in the way of immediate practical value. For the vast majority, things that mattered still happened exclusively on paper or on the phone. In most offices, people who checked their e-mail on a regular basis were still a small minority, and if you went online you knew that most people around you did not.

Going online typically required purchasing and plugging in a roughly paperback book–sized modem (computers did not routinely come equipped with them). The modem had a bank of mysterious flashing red lights, and using it involved installing, configuring, and then running a "terminal" program, typing commands, listening to the squealing modem, and typing in another cryptic series of commands and passwords. There was no pointing and clicking yet in the online world. Just getting it going required at least forty-five minutes, and then figuring out what to do once you were signed on was a further challenge. Gateways between computer networks were still being constructed. As a result, to send, say, an e-mail from the BITNET network—then common at less technical universities—across the still limited Internet, for example, the e-mail addresses had to be sandwiched between quote marks and prefaced by "IN%"T_STREETER@uvmvax.uvm.edu"—and this technical detail was not easy to find out. Once you mastered such arcana, you could enter a secret world, in which some interesting things were going on and you could feel yourself part of a privileged few.

As the number of people with some variety of online access increased from month to month, more and more people had an experience of stumbling on something striking: it could be a surprising exchange on an e-mail discussion list, involving a tidbit of insider information from afar. Or it could be a titillating personal revelation; this was the moment when stories of e-mail romances began to circulate in popular folklore. It could be a new form of access to something or someone, like the personal MTV "gopher" created as a hobby by MTV vee-jay Adam Curry. Accessing his gopher gave one a kind of "personal" access to a media figure, to someone ordinarily shielded behind the glossy professionalism of the television screen. And then, with a 1960s flourish of rebellion, Curry announced his resignation from MTV on air. He said he was resigning in order to pursue his digital activities full-time, on the theory that the digital world was the wave of the future, and television was obsolete. If you were one of the still small number of people poking around on the Internet at the time, things like this generated a sense of being a privileged witness to something big going on.

The word "cyberspace" may have entered popular circulation as a word for the Internet in an e-mail message that circulated on a number of discussion lists in February 1993. It was the text of a speech that John Perry Barlow gave to a conference on national security held in Washington, D.C. As the message made clear, many members of the U.S. intelligence community (i.e., CIA, NSA, FBI) were present. Barlow's agenda was to educate this community about the value of protecting free speech and privacy in the digital realm.

Barlow began his talk this way:

I can't tell you the sense of strangeness that comes over someone who earns his living writing Grateful Dead songs, addressing people who earn their livings as many of you do, especially after hearing the last speaker. If you don't appreciate the irony of our appearing in succession, you have no sense of irony at all. . . .

The reason I am here has absolutely nothing to do with the Grateful Dead. I'm here because I met a fellow named Mitch Kapor in 1989. . . . we shared a sense of computers being more than just better adding machines or better type-writers. We saw that computers, connected together, had the capacity to create an environment which human beings could and did inhabit. . . . The people who share this awareness are natives of the future. People who have a hard time with it may always be immigrants.

When Mitch and I saw that computers had created a place, we started asking some questions about what kind of place it was. . . . We decided to name it Cy-berspace, after Bill Gibson's description of a futuristic place rather like it which we found in his novel Neuromancer.

At the time, reading a missive like this on one's monochrome screen, per-haps during a slow day at the office or perhaps late at night at home, had an arresting effect. The incongruous juxtaposition of a Grateful Dead lyricist with CIA officials was funny, of course, but also enticing. How many people get invitations to talk to CIA officials, much less go on to tweak the officials' noses and get away with it? Here was someone whose tax bracket and espi-onage experience were comparable to yours—modest—yet he was boldly preaching to an established, powerful, and sometimes violent institution. The situation suggested a new opening, a new avenue to power. As a reader of this text in early 1993, you felt uniquely privy to this intriguing opening because you were among the elite few who had mastered the arcane art of online access. The relative obscurity of the procedures needed to get the message only added to the aura of being part of a special group. And cru-cially, instead of downplaying his differences from his audience, Barlow of-fered them a choice between being one who "gets it" or one who doesn't. Accept his rhetorical universe, and you are a "native of the future." Reject it, however, and you are threatened with always being an immigrant there. You, who both got the joke and technically could get access to it, were in-vited to be one of the vanguard, one of Barlow's "natives of the future."

The effect was indeed delicious.

It is important to consider exactly what kinds of people were getting online access in the early 1990s. Typical discussions of social class and computer use focus on a "haves" versus "have-nots" continuum, where the concern is ex-tending the benefits of computer use lower down on the class ladder. But it is also illuminating to look upward on the ladder. Both Bill Gates and the jan-itor who empties your office trash bin can get along fine without desktop computers in their day-to-day work lives. Computers have become a central feature of the work lives specifically of the "knowledge" or professional classes, a group that includes middle managers, engineers, midlevel govern-ment bureaucrats, academics, and journalists—white collar workers.

Crucial to the character of the early 1990s, then, was the fact that online access came first among those *who did their own word processing* and thus had the necessary equipment and experience readily at hand. Graduate students and assistant professors were online before university presidents and provosts. Middle managers, technicians, and engineers were online before CEOs. Midlevel journalists were online before editors and managers. This is a relatively unusual pattern of technological diffusion. Networking entered social life through the same portal as the photocopy machine, rather than through the top-down diffusion patterns of the telephone or the consumer-distribution patterns of television. This pattern meant that the sense of something important happening in networking would hit the middle ranks of the knowledge class before it hit their superiors.

In the years leading up to 1995, the stage was thus set for the middle ranks to be treated to a drama of obliviousness from above, an object lesson in high-level bewilderment. It was the people who typed their own memos, reports, term papers, and journal articles who sensed the importance of the Internet first, and then watched the higher-ups struggle to catch up with them. "Cyberspace," with its hint of rebellion and lawlessness, better captured the sense of pleasure they felt in watching their secret world trump the staid world of their superiors.

As Barlow's message was circulating in e-mail discussion lists and newsgroups, the first issue of *Wired* had just hit the newsstands; within a year it would have a circulation of over 100,000 and a curious readership many times that (Koenenn 1994).

BACKGROUND: THE INFORMATION SUPERHIGHWAY, AL GORE JR., AND THE NSFNET

The practice of using government funds and institutions to encourage and guide technological innovation has been a constant in the background of U.S. policy for most of the twentieth century. In the 1980s, however, during the promarket, antigovernment years of the Reagan administration, enthusiasm for it reached a low ebb. One significant contributor to this was the rise of the microcomputer. In the 1980s, small computers surprised the corporate world and went from being a hobbyist's toy to a ubiquitous feature of the modern office, providing the occasion for the rise of new industrial empires like Apple, Compaq, and Microsoft. And this turn of events had more than a little impact on the political-economic imagination: the microcomputer had provided a sophisticated, high-tech glitter to the Reagan-era enthusiasm for markets, deregulation, and free enterprise. The microcomputer became an icon that stood for what's good about the market, inspiring leaders the world over to pursue neoliberal policies; Mikhail Gorbachev said it was the West's astonishing success in high technology, more than anything else, that inspired Soviet leadership to look for radically new economic models in the late 1980s.

Yet by the early 1990s in the U.S. context, all this was losing steam. Not only had the desktop computer become a commonplace of office life, but the companies that made microcomputers no longer seemed like the boisterous garage start-ups of popular capitalist mythology. By 1990 the least glamorous of the 1980s microcomputer companies, Microsoft, had achieved that much-prized and much-hated state common to technology industries: a practical monopoly. The gray, arrogant, predictable monopoly of IBM had been overthrown and replaced—by another gray, arrogant, predictable monopoly.

In a parallel development, neoliberal economic policy seemed to be on the wane, domestically at least. After the Reagan years, deregulation had lost much of its appeal even to the business community. The stock market crashed in 1987—the first such crash in the United States since 1929—and Silicon Valley was threatened by the Japanese, particularly in the area of memory chip manufacture. The wide-open, unfettered free market was looking a little less inviting and a little more threatening to significant groups of business leadership. As a result, for executives, the business press, politicians, and others who began their day with the *Wall Street Journal*, a principled hostility to government seemed a little less appealing. Corporate consortia and private–public partnerships were coming back in fashion.

Corporations, in sum, were quietly moving away from the rhetoric of competition and back toward asking for government help to organize and stabilize industries in classic corporate liberal fashion; calls from business for government to provide things like "level playing fields" and "regulatory backstops" were becoming increasingly common. And in some circles, the invitation to reregulate was not euphemistic. For example, some representatives of high-tech industries began calling for government coordinated "technology policy," which was a vague term for the use of government to provide things like tax incentives, research money, and antitrust waivers. Technological progress, many were beginning to believe, could not be left up to the market alone. *Fortune* magazine intoned, "What America wants, believe it or not, is proof that somebody's thinking about tomorrow. . . . A recent poll . . . asked respondents to pick America's most important goal for the next five years. By a large margin they selected 'strengthening technological and industrial leadership in the world'" (Kirkland 1991).

In the worlds of computing and high technology in the early 1990s, then, many of the individuals who were scanning for the next wave, the next best thing after the microcomputer, were looking toward networking, but most were imagining things happening in a more collective, centralized way. If there was going to be a digitalized, networked future it was going to be a joint project. It was not going to come out of garage start-ups but would involve some form of consortia, private–public coordination, and partnerships.

Indicative of the trend was the formation of General Magic by a consortium of computer companies in 1987.

In the late 1980s, the big corporate bets were being put on two models: one was television-based video-on-demand systems where the focus was creating something like an online digital video store. The other was a more magazine-like model, focused on subscription services like CompuServe and Prodigy. But as purely private ventures began to look less attractive, another, vaguely defined model started to gain momentum, this time with help from the government sector: the "information superhighway."

Many readers will remember all the talk about the "information super-highway" in the early 1990s. Because of the rich mix of political and economic energy to which the phrase became attached, it developed a lot of momentum. Politicians sought to ride on its coattails, and industry factions began to try to capture it; phone companies claimed they could provide the information superhighway, provided the government stayed out of it, thank you, and the cable industry countered by politically correcting the name of their newest technology from "500 channel TV" into "cable's information superhighway" (Stix 1993). "Information superhighway" became so common it sprouted its own metaphorical universe involving phrases like "road kill on the information superhighway." It's easy to forget, however, that for the first few years of this buzzword's flourishing, the "information superhighway" was not the Internet.

The phrase "information superhighway" has been around since at least the early 1980s, and the metaphor of an "information highway" for at least a decade before that.[1] But around 1990, "information superhighway" began to take on a very specific life inside the political circles of Washington, D.C. At the time, the U.S. economy was floundering, and the administration of George H. W. Bush was looking increasingly helpless on the economic front. *Fortune* magazine sniped that "the President has been disengaged, reactive, and inarticulate" on the economy (Kirkland 1991, 59). The Democrats in Washington sensed an opportunity—the slogan "it's the economy, stupid" proved devastating to Bush in the next election. But the problem for the mainstream Democrats was finding a way to differentiate themselves from the Republicans without opening themselves up to the label of "tax and spend liberals" that had been used so successfully against them in the previous decade by Ronald Reagan.

In the 1950s, Senator Albert Gore Sr. made a name for himself by shepherding the interstate highway system, which gave a huge boost to the auto industry and the economy in general, while profoundly shaping American life and culture around the automobile. It was one of the most successful and beloved massive government building projects of all time. To this day it stands largely above criticism. No doubt this rousing success was somewhere in the back of Senator Albert Gore Jr.'s mind when in 1989 he decided to get involved in a government-sponsored effort to further the science of computer networking. Gore's inspiration was to link up with various proponents of advanced computer networking in the engineering community, sponsor legislation that funded the development of a state-of-the-art computer network of networks, and call the project the "information superhighway."

The idea pressed several buttons at once. The high-tech industries, battered by Japanese competition and nervously groping for the next wave, looked favorably on this modest kind of government investment, which after all could save them the cost of a lot of high-risk R&D. Democratic politicians, like Gore Jr. himself, could use this safely as a model of "good" government intervention, undermining Republican efforts to maintain power by associating Democrats with government bureaucracy and excess. The project was wrapped in the glamorous aura of high technology and a positive vision of the future. And it appealed to a kind of economic nationalism. By 1991, a U.S. congressman argued for government involvement in the creation of a U.S. broadband network: "The Japanese will have an information superhighway by the year 2005 and the USA won't" (Stewart 1991). Small wonder, then, that Gore Jr.'s bill moved calmly through both houses of Congress and was signed by President Bush in 1991, providing $2.9 billion over five years for building something called the "NSFnet" (Quittner 1991).

Looking back on his leadership in developing legislative support for the National Science Foundation Network (NSFnet), Gore said during the 2000 campaign for U.S. president, "I took the initiative on the Internet." This statement was attacked in print by *Wired* magazine reporter and libertarian Declan McCullagh, and eventually twisted by various Republicans into a sound bite that Gore said he invented the Internet. From there it went on to become a favorite joke of late night comedians and a punch line in a TV pizza ad. It was a false slur, and it was irresponsible of reporters and politicians to repeat that sound bite up to the end of the campaign; it seems plausible that the "Gore said he invented the Internet" quip did at least as much damage to Gore's final vote count as Ralph Nader.

What's important about this episode is that, while the sound bite was factually untrue, it was funny. And it was funny because it appeals to a common skepticism about the orderly technocratic optimism of the managerial mode of thought associated with technology policy like Gore's. As far as Washington was concerned, the NSFnet was consistent with traditional corporate liberal policy: it was to be a technology test bed, something that would provide innovations that would eventually be implemented and broadly deployed by the private sector. And it would develop on a national basis, neatly coordinated by orderly consortia of established corporations like IBM and AT&T, perhaps eventually linking up with equally orderly systems developing in other nations around the world. It was all very high-minded. The "information superhighway" predicted by Gore's NSFnet initiative would be used by scientists for sophisticated research, and perhaps as a kind of electronic library where thoughtful patrons would quietly and studiously gather useful information. Gore did in fact take the initiative on the Internet, but what he had in mind was hardly the chaotic, explosive phenomenon that conveyed a cornucopia of pornography, pop culture, conspiracy theories, and irrational exuberance throughout the globe. He did not have in mind Grateful Dead lyricists tweaking the nose of the CIA.

Consider the difference between Gore's phrase, "information superhighway," all the rage in 1992, with Barlow's preferred term, "cyberspace." "Information superhighway" sounds clean, obedient, and orderly; it sounds a bit like a vision of the future from 1950s futurology, those pamphlets that many of us remember from our childhoods, with pictures of smiling, clean, deliriously happy families out for Sunday drives in their flying cars. The connotations of "cyberspace," in contrast, are darker, less regimented, more scary, more thrilling, particularly if one knows a little about the term's origin in the ur-cyberpunk novel, *Neuromancer*. Late at night, alone in one's cubicle, "cyberspace" had a much more alluring ring.

TROPES FROM THE COUNTERCULTURE: "THEY DON'T GET IT"

Louis Rosetto, creator of *Wired*—which he says he modeled on *Rolling Stone*—once dismissed *Newsweek*'s (and by implication all mainstream media's) technology coverage with the phrase: "they just don't get it" (Keegan 1997). The phrase is part of the rhetorical foundation of outlets like *Wired*; in their constant, cavalier dismissal of vaguely defined "old" institutions and points of view (e.g., Microsoft, television networks, government bureaucracies, Keynesianism), these media flatter readers by implicitly including them in the knowledgeable avant-garde. As in Barlow's speech to the CIA, the message seems to be, "You can be one of us, the mammals, whereas those powerful people are the dinosaurs."

When a marginal social movement accurately anticipates in the public eye a significant historical failure of judgment on the part of leadership, the effect can be powerful. Being right about something when the powers that be were wrong, for example, was a central collective experience of the 1960s counterculture. By 1969, the world had watched the television networks, the *New York Times*, and many members of the political establishment change their position on the Vietnam War. In the mid-1990s, it would be the failure to anticipate the importance of the Internet, or in the late 1990s the value of open software. And part of the power of such moments is that they open the door to iconoclasm and to new currents of thought: if the authorities are wrong about that one thing, what else might they have missed?

At the same time, this kind of collective experience establishes the conditions for a less clearly beneficial drawing of boundaries between those who know and those who don't. What this phrase does is tell the listener that he or she and the speaker are part of the elite group who "get it." The ones who don't could be the Pentagon, the media, or your parents; in any case, there's a thrill in the implication that you and I stand apart from despised others in the world.

If being right about a central event like Vietnam or the Internet gives the rhetoric of "getting it" force, accuracy in general is not necessary or even a precondition for the rhetoric to work. The Internet was not mentioned once in the first issue of *Wired*; Rosetto had to catch up to the Internet like everyone else in the media. And, more importantly, once the rhetorical ground is established by whatever means, a powerful trope for shutting down inquiry is made available. In the interview mentioned above, when Rosetto was asked if he's religious, he replied "no." When asked if he's an atheist, he also replied "no" and then continued: "It's not worth thinking about. . . . I mean, I've gone beyond it" (Keegan 1997). The rhetoric of "they don't get it" can create conditions that make this kind of shutting down of inquiry sound wise. The reader or hearer is made automatically wary of voicing any criticism, questioning, or complexity, even to themselves. Express doubts, and you risk being worse than wrong, you risk revealing yourself to be a dinosaur and thus no longer part of the privileged club: you just don't get it.

In one sense, the 1960s counterculture never went away. It just became available through popular memory as a set of cultural devices, a cultural tool kit for use by media executives, anti-abortion activists, rock bands, and left activists alike. It is a well-known fact (though not a well-theorized one) that the historical experience of the anti–Vietnam War movement and the counterculture left its mark on various segments of the computer engineering community, the "invisible colleges" within which the technology was developing. In the 1970s, the engineers at Xerox PARC made bean bag chairs into office furniture, and they were celebrated for their hacker rebelliousness by Stuart Brand in the *Village Voice* in 1972. Theodor Nelson's *Computer Lib* began circulating among computing professionals and amateurs in 1974, and he became a familiar side show at professional conferences during the decade. Steven Jobs and Steven Wozniak founded Apple computer in 1976, after making friends while phone phreaking in college and then attending meetings of the Homebrew Computer Club, which had been founded by activists with considerable countercultural and antiwar experience (Levy 1984). In general, the Cold War consensus that had formed the cultural glue of the military–industrial complex had become ragged and worn out; the formation of Computer Professionals for Social Responsibility around antinuclear issues took place in 1981. During the 1970s, in sum, a small community of computer engineers and tinkerers was envisioning computers through lenses that had at least echoes of the counterculture; this then provided a set of ideas and tropes that were available to be picked up by the larger culture and made into a vehicle for promoting new meanings, new habits of talk and action. By 1990, outlets like *Wired* and pundits like John Perry Barlow took that computer counterculture and, with far-reaching effects, used it to reframe the meaning of digital communications.

THE MOMENT OF MOSAIC: THE PLEASURE OF ANTICIPATION

By mid-1993, then, a growing crowd of midrank white-collar computer users was quietly gaining access to networked computing. Growing numbers of these were learning about and using the nonprofit, nonproprietary Internet, and these experiences were becoming increasingly inflected with countercultural habits and iconoclasm. The higher ranks of leadership, the CEOs and politicians, were largely oblivious to it all. This context proved fertile ground for a new, freely distributed computer program called Mosaic, the first successful graphical web browser. Mosaic 1.0 for the Macintosh and PC was released as a free download in August 1993 and spread like wildfire through the fall of that year. The program created an almost instant "wow" effect, motivating ordinarily bored or preoccupied cubicle dwellers to call a colleague and tell them, "you gotta try this thing." This was where it all started, the moment of takeoff for the Internet frenzy of the 1990s.

Mosaic was not the first web browser, nor even the first graphical web browser. The most advanced web browser in 1992, for example, was the X-Windows-based "Viola" (see fig. 16.1). Just like Mosaic, Netscape, and Internet Explorer, Viola had scroll bars, "Back" and "Forward" buttons in the upper-left corner, a globe icon in the upper right, a URL display, variegated fonts, and of course the ability to move to underlined links through the click of a mouse. Users of Viola knew that it was merely a stage in the evolution of the World Wide Web and in networking generally. A popular guide to the Internet of the time by computer administrator Ed Krol describes Viola in detail, but also discusses the features that would be included in future, more sophisticated browsers (Krol 1992). The book spends much more time on the web protocol itself, which in turn is listed alongside technologies like telnet, ftp, gophers, and other information-retrieval programs and protocols that were then spreading through the Internet.

More than a few computer professionals like Krol were thus very aware that there was something called the World Wide Web and that it was evolving; they were themselves already pointing and clicking their way around it on a regular basis. These people undoubtedly included others who, like Krol, worked for the National Center for Supercomputing Applications (NCSA) at the University of Illinois. Two NCSA employees, Eric Beena and undergraduate Marc Andreessen, decided to program a better browser near the end of 1992. They had undoubtedly seen Viola and heard arguments and visions like those presented by Krol, perhaps even from Krol himself. They were simply making their own contribution to an ongoing networking software evolution based on ideas that were already very much in the air around

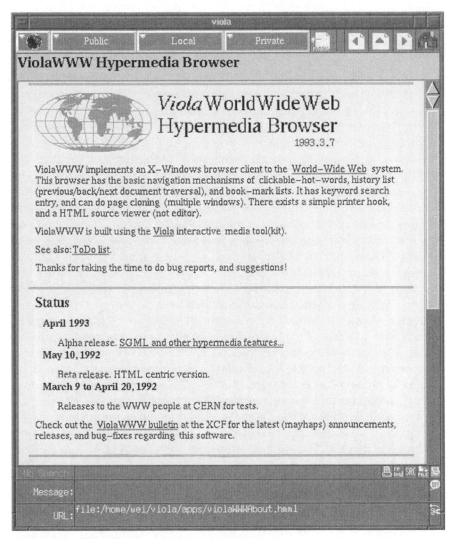

Figure 16.1. A screenshot of the Viola web browser

them. The main technical contribution of the first version of Mosaic for Unix they produced in the next few months was the ability to display images and a slicker, more inviting interface. Another important contribution was the production of PC and Macintosh versions of the browser, released in August 1993. These versions, programmed largely by undergraduates (partly in response to the enthusiasm generated by the first version within the existing Internet community), made the browsing experience more widely available. Technically speaking, Mosaic was a useful but modest contribution, arguably not as important as, say, SMTP, the WWW protocol itself, or the SLIP and PPP protocols that enabled connection to the Internet via modem. Mosaic was clearly not as important a technical contribution as the underlying TCP/IP packet switching protocol and all the software that had been written to implement it on a wide variety of computers. Mosaic did not make it possible to connect to the Internet. Other programs and protocols did that. And Mosaic did not make the Internet friendly; it simply made it somewhat friendlier. And it was not a question of efficiency. Mosaic was a slow, cumbersome way to get information, particularly on the graphics-impaired computers of the first years. Mosaic was a fine program, but it was not a revolutionary work of genius, by any definition.

So how did Mosaic become the "killer app" of the Internet, generating a flurry of interest in the Internet that took it out of the realm of technical experts into broad popular consciousness? Why was it that its successor, Netscape, launched the "Internet economy" of the 1990s? Part of it was simply the cumulative critical mass of people and technologies: enough computers were becoming graphics-capable, enough of those computers were becoming connected to local area networks (LANs), and enough of those LANs were being connected to the Internet that being on the Internet was becoming more and more valuable. Mosaic may have just come along at exactly the right time in that cumulative process.

Crucially, however, Mosaic wasn't so much efficient as it was pleasurable. Using Mosaic was one of the first really compelling, fun experiences available on the Internet. Some computer professionals tried to downplay it for that very reason: "Mostly, people use Mosaic to show off the money they spent on their PCs," observed one software executive. "You can call somebody over and say, 'Look at this.' It has got that kind of whiz-bang appeal. . . . It's like the first time you go through the library: It's fun to wander through the stacks, pulling down books. But that does wear off" (Hyatt 1994). But we now know in retrospect that the "fun" of web browsing was not about to wear off any time soon.

What kind of pleasure did Mosaic offer? Sociologist Colin Campbell has described what he calls "modern autonomous imaginative hedonism," a form of pleasure in which the anticipation of pleasure becomes part of the pleasure itself. It is characteristic of the consumer culture and romanticism generally (Campbell 1987). What one wants in this peculiarly modern form of pleasure, Campbell argues, is not desire satisfied but desire itself; it is the desire to desire. The pleasure of Mosaic was precisely this kind of pleasure. Mosaic did not so much show users something they wanted or needed to see as stimulate them to imagine what they *might* see. One of the early classic ways to demonstrate the web was to click onto the website for the Louvre, to watch grainy images of paintings slowly appear on the screen. This was not pleasurable so much in what it actually delivered—better versions of the same images generally could be found in any number of art books—but in how the experience inspired the viewer to imagine *what else might be* delivered. Mosaic enacted a kind of hope; it did not deliver new things so much as a sense of the *possibility* of new things. Surfing the web using Mosaic in the early days shared certain features with the early stages of a romantic affair, or the first phases of a revolutionary movement: the dreamlike experience of pointing, clicking, and watching images slowly appear generated a sense of anticipation, of possibility. Mosaic was not a case of desire satisfied, but of desire provoked.

In an important way, people need to imagine a technology, to envision it, before they can put it to use collectively. Any communication technology needs to be understood through a shared framework of meaning before it can become widely adopted and used. Furthermore, given the subsequent chain of events—the extraordinary explosion in the Internet, the stock market bubble—it is hard not to believe that something more than the accidents of gradual technological evolution contributed to the intense focus on Mosaic. Mosaic thus became invested with cultural significance far beyond its strictly technical value.

THE CREATION OF IRRATIONAL EXUBERANCE: NETSCAPE AND *WIRED*

In May 1993, as white-collar workers scattered through cubicles and offices across the land were quietly discovering the thrills of going online, as Andreessen and others worked on perfecting Mosaic, as the likes of John Perry Barlow and the editorial staff of *Wired* were spreading the tropes of the computer counterculture to the middle ranks, *U.S. News & World Report* published a "technology report" about the coming future of networked computing (Impoco 1993). The article, clearly a response to the enthusiasm surrounding Vice President Al Gore's "information superhighway" initiatives, began:

> The melding of the telephone, television and personal computer today has unleashed a dynamic digital revolution that promises to radically alter the way people live, work and play around the world. What new products and services can we expect from this technological upheaval? How big a market, exactly, are we talking about? And what, if anything, should the Clinton administration do to help foster these emerging technologies in America?

After framing its questions in terms of markets and products, the article went on to seek answers from "seven titans of technology": Bill Gates, shopping channel pioneer Barry Diller, AT&T chair Robert Allen, cable TV tycoon John Malone, IBM board vice chair Jack Kuehler, cell phone magnate Craig McCaw, and Motorola chair George Fisher. The article was thus organized around the assumption that, whatever happened, it would be shaped primarily by corporate leadership and corporate concerns, perhaps in interactions with government regulators spurred on by initiatives coming from the White House. Bill Gates predicted a wallet-size personal PC interconnected with home appliances. Others forecast a lucrative cornucopia of online shopping, ubiquitous multimedia communication for business executives, movies on demand, distance education via cable TV, and growing wireless data services. All expressed an ambivalence about government's role, expressing appreciation for the excitement generated by Gore and the Clinton White House but cautioning government regulators to stay out of the way of corporate initiatives. This was a view from the top, and no one mentioned the Internet.

Three months later, as Andreessen and company were releasing the first version of Mosaic for the Macintosh and the PC, the August issue of *Scientific American* appeared with a similar overview article (Stix 1993). In keeping with its more sophisticated readership, the article contained much more technical detail, comparing the bandwidth and cost of various transmission technologies like fiber optic cable and ISDN, for example, and its interviewees were less from the boardroom and closer to the research lab. But the basic organizing assumptions of the article were the same as the recent *U.S. News* piece: the bulk of the article focused on various corporations and their technologically linked interests, comparing and contrasting the schemes of various cable, phone, and media companies, interspersed with various inside-the-beltway regulatory concerns, such as common carrier principles.

The article, however, *does* mention the Internet. It opens with an anecdote about Internet Society President Vinton Cerf preparing for a congressional hearing by contacting thousands of enthusiasts over the Internet, pointing to the rapidly growing activity on the Internet as a potential "seed" of Gore's "National Information Infrastructure" (Stix 1993, 101). The article is titled "Domesticating Cyberspace," and it closes with a congressional representative echoing Barlow's metaphorical construction of the online world as a frontier: "Anything is a danger in cyberspace. . . . There are no rules. It's the Wild West" (Stix 1993, 110). The Barlow-inspired metaphorical constructs of its title and opening and closing paragraphs—a vision of a wild, expansive, exciting space on the Internet—would prove to resonate more profoundly than the content about corporate struggles, educational applications, and competing delivery technologies. Perhaps the *Scientific American* readership is specialized, but it includes politicians, executives, and—probably most importantly at this time in history—reporters.

This, then, was the moment when the Internet hit the media radar. As summer turned to fall in 1993, the Internet suddenly became an object of media fascination. A survey showed that during the fall of 1993, 170 articles appeared in major U.S. publications mentioning the Internet, as compared to 22 articles in the same period a year before (Bradner 1993). Scott Bradner, a senior Harvard computer network expert, Internet Society member, and columnist for the trade magazine *Network World*, observed with some astonishment,

> The Internet is suddenly popular. . . . For reasons best known to the media gods, articles about the Internet seem to be the thing to do these days. . . . All this

attention is flattering to those of us who have been proselytizing this technology for years. The problem is that I don't see any logical reason for the current attention. The Internet has been around and growing for more than a decade. Sure, its big (almost 2 million interconnected computers world wide) and growing fast (more than 7% a month), but it's been big and growing fast for quite a while now. It was certainly growing at least at this rate when *Time & Newsweek* were forecasting national video parlors for the kiddies instead of international on-line, real time, interactive current affairs in the schools. . . . The Internet has even shown up on the newspaper comic pages (Dilbert) and the *New Yorker*. Newspapers from the *Boston Globe* to *El Mercurio* in Santiago, Chile publish Internet e-mail addresses for those readers who would like to send electronic letters to the editor. Last month, I even found an article on the Internet in an airline flight magazine. (Bradner 1993)

As the excitement around the Internet gathered in the media, as *Wired* and John Perry Barlow framed computer networking in breathless, countercultural terms, as Mosaic circulated onto the increasing number of Internet-connected LANs, members of the business world slowly began to take note. In part, with their attention already directed toward networking by the "information superhighway" rhetoric, it might be unsurprising that those looking for business opportunities might follow the media toward the Internet. But another key factor was the Microsoft monopoly, which played a dual role: Microsoft's dominance in operating systems on the one hand represented the uninspiring end of the garage start-up days in microcomputing, thus motivating romantic entrepreneurs to look for something new. At the same time, it was well-known that Bill Gates had just become one of the richest men in the world, and that those who had heavily invested in Microsoft in the late 1980s were beginning to reap fabulous rewards. Microsoft was thus both a reviled corporate monolith and an object lesson: might something overthrow Microsoft just as Microsoft had overthrown IBM? Might that something have to do with the Internet? And might there be similar rewards to be reaped by those who accurately guessed what the next best thing would be?

Enter Netscape. The founding of Netscape is one of those oft-told business legends that get heavily mythologized, in a class with Edison's creation of the electric light, Marconi's transatlantic radio transmission, the creation of Apple computer in a garage, or Bill Gates's original deal to provide the operating system for IBM's first personal computer. The basics are that Jim Clark, founder of graphics workstation company Silicon Graphics (SGI), resigned from SGI in February 1994. Clark, as an executive, was not in the category of those who needed to do their own word processing. He stumbled on Mosaic as he was searching for a new direction in technology. He was introduced to the web browser by an underling at SGI sometime in the late fall of 1993, when the Internet craze and Mosaic were entering mainstream attention. Clark flew to the NCSA in Champaign-Urbana, Illinois, found Marc Andreessen, and founded a company to commercialize the program in the spring of 1994. With unprecedented haste, he launched the Netscape initial public offering (IPO) just over a year later. The most successful IPO in history, Netscape became the model for many subsequent IPOs, setting off the Internet stock craze.

It needs to be remembered that the excitement and behavior associated with the Netscape IPO was not just another case of routine, or even extreme, business hype. The Netscape IPO was unique because it marked such a sharp departure from any connection to business fundamentals, however defined. At the time of the IPO, the company had no profit and almost no revenues. It was giving its principal product away for free, and it had no crucial patents or other dramatic advantage in the browser market. Netscape was just one of about ten companies trying to commercialize Mosaic.[2] As the IPO approached in late summer of 1995, there were plenty of published warnings about the peculiarity of the event; as one reporter put it in the *Boston Globe*, "They are calling it the next Microsoft. And by the looks of its pitch to investors, it had better be. . . . Netscape . . . has no record of profits and has only generated $16.6 million in revenue in its first six months of sales. Microsoft Corp., by contrast, posted net profit of $39 million on sales of $198 million in 1986, when its market capitalization was a comparable $525 million" (Crosariol 1995). The facts were there, the cautions were there. And yet the IPO on August 9, 1995, exceeded even the already wild expectations. In early October 1995, one of the firms that so successfully managed the IPO, Hambrecht and Quist, hosted a packed conference on Internet investing, and later that month the American Stock Exchange tried to drum up support for its newly listed "Internet Index" options by hosting a party for brokers and traders at a "hip New York Internet coffee shop" (Lux 1995). The largest party ever thrown by capitalism had begun.

Why did Netscape get all this swooning attention? In part, Netscape grabbed the headlines because it was in Silicon Valley, in part because of Jim Clark's previous track record with SGI, and in part because Netscape hired Andreessen and many of the other original programmers of Mosaic. Netscape's first browser was a good one, particularly as it channeled its start-up funds heavily into rapidly improving the program, releasing frequent updates over the Internet, and quickly becoming the most popular browser.

To a very significant degree, Netscape followed a deliberate strategy of creating a media spectacle heavily centered on a romanticized, heroic construction of the computer counterculture. Very early on, Clark hired a publicist, Rosanne Siino from SGI, and told her to present Andreessen as the "rock star" of the company (Clark 1999, 99). Siino developed a strategy that carefully cultivated media attention framed in terms of "geek chic," deliberately taking reporters into the backrooms to show the chaos of the programmers' cubicles, programmers sleeping under their desks, and so forth (Clark 1999, 100). She successfully turned Andreessen into a celebrity: in 1995, Andreessen appeared on the cover of *Forbes ASAP* as "This Kid Can Topple Bill

Gates" (Clark 1999, 106). Andreessen was soon featured in *People* magazine and appeared on the cover of *Time* in his bare feet (Clark 1999, 194).

Wired magazine, or more precisely the cultural frame for interpreting computer communications that *Wired* so successfully propagated into American middlebrow culture, played an essential role in the phenomenon. *Wired* was barely more than a year old when Clark hired Andreessen and was full of adolescent hyperbole ("the digital revolution is the greatest development since fire"), and inaccurate predictions (issue 1 did not mention the Internet, and issue 2 implied that Richard Stallman's Free Software project was doomed [Garfinkel 1993]). Its eye-catching Day-Glo graphics and layout were sometimes unreadable. Furthermore, *Wired* did not invent the idea that Mosaic was the "killer app" of the Internet.[3]

But its impact on the cultural frames for understanding computer networking between 1993 and 1996 was profound and pivotal. As the Clinton White House and Congress took the "information superhighway" rhetoric off into dry committees spouting inside-the-beltway acronyms, businessmen could increasingly be seen thumbing through copies of *Wired* on airplanes, and terms like "cyberspace" began cropping up in newspaper articles and politicians' sound bites. Without *Wired*, it's not obvious that this countercultural framing of computer networking would have taken hold in the mainstream.

An illustrative and probably central moment occurred in October 1994, when *Wired* published an interview with Marc Andreessen, not long after he joined Netscape (Wolf 1994). The interview revealed that Andreessen had just abandoned the public sector for the private one in pursuit of wealth and glory; after playing a key role in creating Mosaic as a graduate student at the University of Illinois, Andreessen was lured to Silicon Valley. The article, grandiosely titled "The (Second Phase of the) Revolution Has Begun," was enamored with this twenty-something young man full of adolescent bravado and driven by a blurry but intoxicating vision of simultaneously getting rich and heroically setting the people free by slaying the dragon of the Microsoft monopoly and ushering in a social utopia.

It was all deeply contradictory. Andreessen repeatedly denounced Bill Gates, but Netscape's strategies were not so different from those of his Microsoft adversary. His approach was commercial and proprietary, after all, and he was more interested in creating than conforming to standards; his goal was to dominate rather than share in the web browser market. But those contradictions were typical of *Wired*: computer technology coupled to libertarian values would allow anyone who was hip enough to see it coming to successfully meld dreams of wealth with dreams of freedom, utopia, and individual heroism. But this dream was as powerful as it was wrongheaded.

What this article, and the mode of thought associated with it, did was take the dry industrial policy of the information superhighway and turn it into an unpredictable and thus tantalizing cyberspace; it was a rich if contradictory fusion of romantic individualism with economic libertarianism.

The article repeated the claim that Mosaic was the "killer app" of the Internet, predicted another revolution in the computer industry on parallel with the microcomputer revolution, and identified Andreessen's new company as the enterprise likely to dominate the new revolution. (This article may well have had the effect of a self-fulfilling prophecy as the other companies soon disappeared.) And it suggested that this represented the only possible threat to Microsoft's monopoly. This *Wired* article—and the vision of which it was emblematic—thus arguably played a key role in the ensuing explosion of both the Internet and the stock market by providing a particular vision that fused a 1960s-style romantic hope for radical change with pecuniary desire: those who regretted not investing in Microsoft in the 1980s might have a second chance. The article helped make markets hip and made hipness a way to make new markets.

Importantly, the article didn't just target a good investment or an exciting new technology or business as a normal trade magazine piece might have; it didn't put Andreessen next to the senior partner of the company, Jim Clark, who was an experienced Silicon Valley executive. Instead it separately interviewed the junior partner, Andreessen, and portrayed him as a subtle and potent mix of countercultural romantic hero and entrepreneur. This little bit of storytelling in turn provided a compelling model of personhood, a way of thinking about the relation of self and society in capitalism, that could be picked up by computer programmers, executives, and stock market investors alike. He wasn't the first businessperson portrayed this way: Steve Jobs and Wozniak had also been painted in a similar light in many a business profile. But it came at a crucial moment and it was colored this time around by the figure of archvillain Bill Gates. It was a way to culturally rescue business activity from the dreary image associated with large corporations, an exciting alternative to the man in the gray flannel suit and the tired technology policy of Gore's information superhighway.

CONCLUSION

The differences between cultural studies and political economy deserve less argument and more inquiry. What exactly are the relations between the cultural and the economic? The development and character of capitalism tends to be imagined in terms of things in the "guns, germs, and steel" category, things like technologies, resources, and geography. Economic development, most tend to assume, is about the efficiency with which the prosaic fundamentals of human life are produced and distributed, about things that change how much we have to eat or how long we live. Yet this way of thinking, for all its insight, can make us forget just how frivolous the development of capitalism has been at times. Think of the role of gold, spices, tea, tobacco, and beaver pelts in the development of mercantile systems and the early phases of the European colonization of the Americas. These were all trivial commodities of no major practical value, whose popularity largely reflected the fashion whims of the European upper class. Yet the basic systems of accounting and trade that laid the foundations for early modern capitalism, some would say for capitalism and the world system itself, were created around them.

Perhaps the Internet is playing a role like the one spices and beaver pelts played in their day. The Internet so far may have become important, not because of any huge material significance in its own right but because of the social visions and hopes invested in it, and the social arrangements to which those visions are giving birth. More specifically, the Internet in the first half of the 1990s enabled a certain kind of subjective experience for certain members of the "knowledge classes," an anticipatory subjective experience precisely about things to come, about imagined futures, which in turn interacted with ongoing events like Gore's "industrial policy" and a series of misguided efforts on the part of a corporate elite. Followers of Stuart Hall might call this a case of the "articulation" of a cultural formation with a political-economic structure; Weberians might call it a case of "elective affinity." In either case, the effects of that interaction were lively, even explosive. And we are still living with the results.

NOTES

1. For example, see Marbach 1983, 36: "This year alone, AT&T will install 15,000 miles of glass fibers in commercial systems across the country. Two 'information superhighways' being built of fiber-optic cable will link Boston, New York, Philadelphia and Washington, D.C."

2. In July 1994, at least ten companies had licensed Mosaic from the University of Illinois for commercial development, including the well-connected Spyglass and Spry (Corcoran 1994).

3. That distinction may belong to Robert Metcalfe, 3Com founder. In June 1994 he published a column in *Infoworld* that began, "Mosaic is doing for the Internet right now what VisiCalc, the proverbial killer application, did for the personal computer around 1980."

REFERENCES

Bradner, Scott. 1993. "Why Now?" *Network World.*

Campbell, Colin. 1987. *The Romantic Ethic and the Spirit of Modern Consumerism,* 77–95. Oxford: Basil Blackwell.

Carey, James W., and James J. Quirk. 1970. "The Mythos of the Electronic Revolution." *American Scholar* 39, no. 1: 219–41; 39, no. 2: 395–424.

Clark, Jim, with Owen Edwards. 1999. *Netscape Time: The Making of the Billion-Dollar Start-up That Took on Microsoft.* New York: St. Martin's.

Corcoran, Elizabeth. 1994. "Mosaic Gives Guided Tour of Internet: Companies Rush to Refine an On-Line Resource." *Washington Post*, July 11, F19.

Crosariol, Beppi. 1995. "Netscape's IPO Expected to Rocket." *Boston Globe*, July 25, F33.

Garfinkel, Simson L. 1993. "Is Stallman Stalled? One of the Greatest Programmers Alive Saw a Future Where All Software Was Free. Then Reality Set In." *Wired*, March-April.

Hyatt, Josh. 1994. "Hyperspace Map: Mosaic Helps Lead Users through Maze of Internet." *Boston Globe*, March 29, 1.

Impoco, Jim. 1993. "Technology Titans Sound Off on the Digital Future." *U.S. News & World Report*, May 3, 62.

Keegan, Paul. 1997. "Reality Distortion Field." *Upside.com*, February 1.

Kirkland, Richard I., Jr. 1991. "What The Economy Needs Now." *Fortune*, December 16, 59.

Koenenn, Connie. 1994. "E-Mail's Mouthpiece; In Just a Year, *Wired* Magazine Has Become the Guide down the Information Superhighway." *Los Angeles Times*, March 30, E1.

Krol, Ed. 1992. *The Whole Internet: User's Guide and Catalog.* Sebastopol, Calif.: O'Reilly & Associates, Inc.

Levy, Steven. 2001 [1984]. *Hackers: Heroes of the Computer Revolution.* New York: Penguin.

Lux, Hal. 1995. "Morgan Stanley to Launch Internet Derivative Products: As Amex Parties at an Interactive Coffee Shop." *Investment Dealers' Digest*, October 23, FE15.

Marbach, William D., with Phoebe Hoban, Richard Sandza, Ron Labrecque, Kim Willenson, Kim Foltz, and William J. Cook. 1983. "The Dazzle of Lasers." *Newsweek*, January 3, 36.

Metcalfe, Robert. 1994. "Mosaic Is Doing for the Internet Right Now What VisiCalc, the Proverbial Killer Application, Did for the Personal Computer around 1980." *InfoWorld*, June 6, 50.

Quittner, Joshua. 1991. "Senate OKs $2B for Work on National Computer Net." *New York Newsday*, September 12, 35.

Stewart, Alan. 1991. "NCF Flexes Its Muscles." *Communications International*, November, 12.

Stix, Gary. 1993. "Trends in Communications: Domesticating Cyberspace." *Scientific American*, August, 100–110.

Wolf, Gary. 1994. "The (Second Phase of the) Revolution Has Begun: Don't Look Now, but Prodigy, AOL, and CompuServe Are All Suddenly Obsolete and Mosaic Is Well on Its Way to Becoming the World's Standard Interface." *Wired*, October, 116–21, 150–54.

17

The Impact of the Internet on the Existing Media

Colin Sparks

This chapter discusses the Internet's likely impact on the existing mass media.[1] It begins with a brief examination of existing relationships between the mass media and the Internet, and considers what can be learned from them. Second, a range of different possible impacts is examined. Third, technical and commercial constraints on the process are considered and a model proposed for the likely impact. Almost all media today are conducted as commercial enterprises, and even those that rely on some form of subsidy, like the BBC in the United Kingdom, are increasingly obliged to behave like commercial enterprises. The primary condition for any other function of a commercial medium, whether it is cultural, political, or social, is that it can be shown to be an economically viable venture. Unless that condition is met, it has no long-term future. The main concern of this chapter is therefore with the business models available to the media in the online world. They will form the basis of any other impact that might be postulated.

Any work in this area is highly tentative for at least two reasons. In the first place, as a glance at any daily newspaper will make immediately apparent, this whole field is undergoing rapid technological and economic changes. There are frequent innovations in both the available technologies and in the degree to which they have been implemented. Sometimes very promising technologies emerge, are rapturously received, and then fade from the stage with extreme rapidity. In a similar fashion, new players emerge, new business initiatives are taken, and new mergers, acquisitions, and alliances are formed. Again, some are greeted with great enthusiasm and then fade rapidly into oblivion.

These inevitable accompaniments to the development of a new technology and a new industrial sector have been exacerbated by the extreme speculation that characterized the recent history of the Internet. Until April 2000, it was widely believed that this technology had transformed the nature of capitalism, that it had inaugurated a rapid and indefinite economic boom, and that those companies at the leading edge of the industry posed an irresistible threat to more traditional companies. This belief resulted in all sorts of wild speculative behavior. The stocks of "net native" companies were given very high valuations on markets around the world. Many non-Internet companies felt obliged to pay astronomical prices for small, untried Internet players in order to gain a toehold in the new business. This speculative boom crashed very rapidly in 2000 and was replaced by a pessimistic outlook in which even the real advantages of business use of the Internet have been disparaged. Dot-coms have collapsed in droves. The share prices of survivors, and of telecommunication companies that built their businesses on projections of indefinitely expanding demand, have fallen dramatically. Some have failed spectacularly. Boom has been followed by bust in the new economy, just as in the old one.

These extremes of sentiment have meant that it is extremely difficult even for the careful and experienced observer to determine which has a real potential and a real future and which is likely to prove worthless, for both the technologies and the business. Unfortunately, neither technical excellence nor entrepreneurial zeal represents an adequate criterion for making an informed choice, and unrelieved pessimism is equally ungrounded. This chapter attempts to avoid those pitfalls by abstracting from the press of daily events and considering trends. It is therefore neither technical nor economic but conceptual.

The second problem follows more or less directly from this state of uncertainty. Because the technical and business environment changes so rapidly, and because there are so many competing models, it is very difficult to draw firm conclusions based on convincing and substantial evidence. The historical experience is very short indeed (even in Internet time, which allegedly moves four times as quickly as offline time). The new technology has not yet reached maturity in technical, social, or economic form. The number of variables is high and the number of imponderables higher. In short, it is difficult to avoid what amounts to speculation. There is no obvious solution to this problem except to acknowledge the danger, try to ensure that whatever reliable evidence is available is used judiciously, accept that many of the conclusions reached here will be mistaken, and try to avoid the sort of ungrounded utopian imagining that is so prominent a part of writing about this field. There is a difference between informed speculation based on a survey of the existing incomplete evidence and the cyberbabble that pervades this field.

THE CURRENT SITUATION

In February 2002 there were, according to one of the best-known estimates, 13,536 mass media organizations with Internet presences (Editor and Publisher Online 2002).[2] Among these were some 4,065 magazines, 5,000 newspapers, 2,233 radio stations, and 1,429 television sites. Three things are worth noticing about these figures. In the first place, they are the evidence of a relatively recent phenomenon. As recently as 1993, there were only around 20 freestanding electronic versions of newspapers, and at that time it was by no means apparent to anyone that, in the very near future, the Internet, and more specifically the World Wide Web, was to become overwhelmingly the main technology of electronic distribution. The real growth in the number of newspapers, and then of other media organizations, took place in late 1994 and early 1995, and the rise since then has been very rapid and, up to the present, uninterrupted (Sparks 2000a).

The number of online newspapers has continued to increase despite the collapse of the dot-com boom and the more general slowdown in the world economy. The number of papers around the world seems to be reaching a maximum, although there was a moment in 1998–1999 when this also appeared to be the case, so it is impossible to draw a firm conclusion at this stage. It may simply be that the impact of the recession has meant a temporary halt to the expansion. On the other hand, there is little evidence of newspapers and other media withdrawing completely from the Internet. What is common is an effort to cut the costs of the online operation. In the United Kingdom, the Express Newspapers Group sold off some of its more successful Internet properties and reduced its presence in 2001. Its remaining web presence is a purely token one.[3] This is an extreme form of a process that one discovers almost everywhere: online media outlets have reduced staff, cut costs, reduced investment in technical development, and attempted to squeeze their expenses so as to balance their revenues, which are much less than was predicted by some of the prophets of the new age.

These pressures are even more intense for "net native" titles, which lack even the financial safety net of an established offline business. The webzine Salon.com is a good example. This project attracted a great deal of attention and funding at its launch in 1995, but it has experienced continued losses, up to a total of $79,740,000 by September 2002. Despite critical acclaim for its content, by June 2002 it announced that it would close unless it could find new funding (Byrne 2002a). It managed to stave of that immediate crisis by persuading existing investors to put up another three-quarters of a million dollars and agreeing to a deal with HBO to generate and pursue story ideas. But the company continued to operate at a loss. These financial difficulties were reflected in the price of its shares. In the years of the Internet boom, Salon Com, as it then was, traded on the NAS-DAQ national market, but on 25 September 2001 the renamed Salon Media Group failed to meet the listing standards and was moved to the SmallCap market, which has different and lower requirements. On 11 November 2002, it was taken off the SmallCap market because it was unable to meet the listing standards of this market, and forced to trade on the Over the Counter Bulletin Board Exchange, which is a home for "penny stock." The company has managed to continue by means of desperate financing initiatives and ruthless cost cutting. As they put it in the September 2002 *Quarterly Report:*

> Salon's independent accountants have included a paragraph in their report for the fiscal years ending March 31, 2002 and 2001 indicating that substantial doubt exists as to Salon's ability to continue as a going concern because it has recurring operating losses and negative cash flows, and an accumulated deficit. Salon has eliminated various positions, not filled positions opened by attrition, implemented a wage reduction of 15% effective April 1, 2001, and has cut discretionary spending to minimal amounts, and predicts it may reach cash-flow break even for its quarter ending September 30, 2003. Salon needs to raise additional funds and is currently in the process of exploring financing options. (Salon Media Group 2002, 14)

Even very large companies with definite revenue streams in both the offline and online world find the current situation difficult, as the case of AOL-Time Warner demonstrates. Overall, while the traditional media have not retreated from the Internet, they all now appear to be readier to apply the logic of business rather than the logic of experimentation to their online operations.

Second, offline media across the spectrum from print to broadcasting have strong online presences. The full range of different kinds of outlet is present, and their patterns of development are similar to those of newspapers. The consequence of this is that spaces that are different and distinct in the offline world are copresent online. The boundaries between different media, if indeed they continue to exist, are drawn in different ways in the online world. Some of the content thought to be characteristic of one medium in the offline world (e.g., moving pictures on television) might be differently and more widely present online (e.g., as an element in a newspaper website). In a similar fashion, the boundary between the media—as businesses and as social practices—are refashioned in the electronic world. It is no longer quite so clear what constitutes a part of the "mass media" and what constitutes some other sort of social or economic activity. Some of the content of the mass media might now be found in online situations that are remote from the traditional media organizations.

Third, the online media are present around the world, but the economic logic that shapes the distribution of the offline media operates even more strongly online (Sparks 2000b). The main online media are concentrated in the advanced countries, and within that in North America, notably the United States. To a much lesser extent, they are present in Europe. Asia, which has more than half of the world's population and, in Japan, contains the world's second largest economy, does not have proportional representation in the online world. Africa, which is the poorest continent in material terms, is also the poorest continent in online provision.[4]

What we can conclude, in this case with some certainty, is that the offline media today take the online world very seriously indeed. Of course, the total number of media sites is insignificant compared to the millions of total sites. It is also true that a minority of titles and stations in the offline world have established online presence. However, enough of the media have ventured into cyberspace to make the lessons they have learned there worth thinking about and using as a starting point for further analysis.

THE IMPACT OF THE INTERNET

One of the reasons for this stampede online is that it is clear that the Internet alters the existing processes of production and distribution, and thus impacts on the business models of the established media, in at least the following ways:

1. Delivery through the Internet entails a common technology. Existing media have sharply differentiated delivery technologies. The printed press uses ink on paper. Its symbolic content is embodied in a physical commodity that must be delivered by physical transportation, either to a retail outlet or direct to the customer. Broadcasting uses the electromagnetic spectrum. Its programs are delivered through a transmitter network, either wirelessly or through cable. To receive it, however, a special technology is required—the radio or television receiver and sometimes the satellite dish. All content on the Internet is in digital form and it is, to date, mostly transmitted by wired means, although it will increasingly use wireless technologies for at least some functions. Reception today is usually through the personal computer, although the television set, the mobile telephone, and the game console are increasingly used for some functions. The previous distinctions of content and delivery technology that formed central constraints on the consumption patterns and the business logic of different media are replaced by a single kind of content—digitized information—transmitted along common channels and available through common reception technologies.

2. Production and distribution on the Internet lowers entry barriers for some media. The nature of printing technology means that a substantial

investment is essential in order to enter most press markets. This problem is particularly acute for daily newspapers, which must invest in large printing presses, purchase large quantities of newsprint and ink, contract with an extensive distribution network, and hire many printers and distributors, and so on, before they can begin publishing. Similar, if smaller, costs are present for all printed media products. Broadcast media require, apart from the costs of production, a license from the appropriate authority and access to a transmitter and relay network, either terrestrial or satellite, that can carry their signal to the target audience. On the Internet, while the costs of producing the symbolic content remain, and perhaps even increase, the distribution costs are much smaller and there are no licensing or transmission charges. While it is necessary to have space on a server for the content, the customers generally pay for the connection charges and purchase the reception equipment themselves. It becomes feasible for new entrants (e.g., companies operating only on the Internet with relatively low capital investment) to enter the online market place and compete with giant media corporations.

3. Delivery through the Internet erodes established patterns of media consumption. Existing media are consumed according to patterns of social behavior that are embedded in daily routines. Newspapers and magazines are delivered to the home or are purchased from retail outlets as discrete commodities. They are published at definite and fixed intervals in the day, week, or month. They are consumed in locations and at a pace determined by their readers. Radio broadcasting is normally a background medium consumed while engaged in some other primary function, which may be mobile, for example, driving, doing housework, or working at a computer. Television is normally consumed as a primary activity, or alongside other primary activities. It is predominantly fixed in location, in the home, and used during leisure hours, with the timing of programs being mostly outside of the control of the consumer. Once a sociable activity, it is increasingly a solitary pursuit in the richer countries, as the number of television sets per household multiplies, although restrictions on digital television have in some countries partly reversed that trend. The main form of consumption of the Internet, at least at present, is integrated into patterns of computer usage, at home, at work, or at both. These are primary activities, and usually solitary. Consumption is not bound by time: so long as there is a functioning telecommunications link and the ISP server is not down, it is possible to go online. It is a much less patterned activity and can thus encroach on the time budgets devoted to other media. The online news site, for example, is always available and can provide a source of information during times that previously were devoted to reading offline newspapers or watching television news.

4. The Internet erodes advantages based on physical space. Most existing media circulate in strictly defined areas. In the case of the printed press, there are physical limits to how far a daily newspaper can be transported before it is outdated. Other printed publications, with a longer periodicity, do not suffer from this problem so acutely. But since they normally depend on advertising revenue, they tend to circulate within regions (mostly defined by national boundaries) in which advertising campaigns are reasonably homogeneous. Most terrestrial broadcasters, particularly those using line-of-sight technologies, are strictly limited by the nature of their transmitter networks, which tend to be designed to reach territories defined either politically, as in a state or region, or commercially, as in a viable advertising market. Satellite broadcasting and shortwave radio can overcome these geographical limitations and played important commercial and political roles in the past. But they remain systems grounded in defined physical spaces. The Internet, by contrast, is a global medium. It is designed to permit complete interconnectivity between individual computers whatever their geographical location. Its structure was not designed to divide the world into geopolitical or geocommercial regions. Publishing on the Internet is thus not constrained to a particular physical place: output is available anywhere in the world there is a telephone line and a suitable computer. In the offline world, local daily newspapers could build their position insulated by geography from their competitors. Online, they all inhabit the same space and all face direct competition from the *New York Times*, *Le Monde*, or *Asahi Shimbun*.

5. The Internet erodes advantages based on time of production and distribution. The offline media are all geared to particular windows of distribution. Thus the morning paper has a different agenda to one produced in the evening. The prime-time television program is expected to display characteristics different from that of the daytime program. For Internet-based productions, there is no "time of publication" that must be the same for all parts of the product. News services on the Internet, for example, update their offerings in ways that were previously available to broadcasters but not to newspapers. The extent to which "rolling" or "breaking" news actually changes over any twenty-four-hour period is debatable, but clearly the organizational culture of journalists, their professional ideology, and important elements of production of news events are structured by times of publication and thus of deadlines. The destruction of these fixed points implies a transformation in the processes of newsgathering.

6. The Internet is a competitor for revenue streams. The traditional mass media have three main sources of income. The first is subsidies, usually in the form of license fees for broadcasters but also in some countries in the form of payments or allowances to the press, or specially selected

sections of it. The second is subscription, whether in the form of payment for a newspaper or a restricted television outlet. The third is advertising, which to date is the dominant form of revenue for both broadcasters and the press. At least in this stage in its development, the Internet is not a serious competitor for subscription-based services, outside of very specialized areas like financial news and pornography. Almost all newspapers, for example, have found it more or less impossible to charge for access to their basic online news services, although there are recent signs that more of them are attempting to develop new models of content management that will allow them to charge for at least some services. While the Internet has in the past commanded substantial subsidies, directly from government and indirectly from Universities, and there are likely to be continuing efforts to ensure that access is available to poorer sections of society, there is little evidence that such support extends beyond the provision of infrastructure. Content is, of course, internally subsidized as part of the business plans of companies wishing to develop a net presence, but this is more a form of marketing than media activity proper, and thus does not impinge directly on the existing media. The main area where the Internet competes directly with the established media is as an outlet for advertising revenues. Not only do online media products compete with offline media for advertising, but also there are Internet-specific operations that are designed as vehicles for various kinds of advertising. While the total amount of online advertising expenditure is small at present, the special features of the Internet, and in particular its searchable nature, make it a particularly attractive location for the classified advertising that provides the majority of revenue for most newspapers in developed market economies. Looking for a car, a job, or a house is much easier online than offline, and the web is natural home for those kinds of classified advertising, which everywhere make up a huge proportion of newspaper revenue. There is a fourth form of revenue, the use of data about the audience for commercial purposes like direct marketing, that is a minor part of the revenues of most offline media. Like classified advertisements, they promise to be much more easy to exploit online.

7. The Internet allows the disaggregating of editorial and advertising material. The overwhelming majority of the existing mass media package advertising and editorial material together. While the editorial material provides the main point of attraction for the audiences, advertising provides the main revenue stream. Media that contain only one or another of these two streams certainly exist, but they flourish in the margins of the business. The Internet, with its searchable nature, allows the separation of these two different aspects of media content. It is no longer necessary for the reader to be exposed to the advertising message in order to gain access to editorial mate-

rial, nor is it necessary to be exposed to editorial material in order to gain access to advertising.

8. The Internet provides channels whereby both news sources and advertisers can develop direct relations with readers and customers. In the offline world, there is no alternative to relying on the media to aggregate both audiences and the different kinds of material they consume. Online, the news source (e.g., a governmental body) can make its informational material available directly to the potential audience. The advertiser too can make the promotional message directly available to interested consumers. Groups of regular advertisers in a particular sector, such as people who advertise certain kinds of jobs, can establish their own web presence to act as an outlet for their material independent of the media that they are forced to rely upon online. The pressing needs that brought together a mass public and the mass media in the offline world, and thus provided the basic economic model of most commercial media, no longer apply online.

9. The Internet erodes the boundaries between editorial, advertising, and transactional activities. In the offline media, conventions have developed that distinguish editorial content from advertising material. Distinguishing between material, whether designed as news or entertainment, that commands its place in the media as a result of the editorial decisions of the professional staff and that which is present because the owners have been paid to include it has often been eroded in practice. Product placement, "advertorial" copy, advertising supplements, and so on, have a prominent place in many offline media. Nevertheless, they are generally perceived, both inside and outside the industry, as infractions of the proper norms of the media business. These conventions do not yet exist in the online world, and there are strong grounds for believing that the direction of development for online media suggests that they may never evolve. Not only will the distinction between editorial and advertising material probably be less visible than in the offline world, but also there will be a tendency to link both of these with directly transactional material encouraging, for example, the purchase of goods.

10. The Internet provides opportunities for selective consumption. The audience for the media is no longer obliged to purchase the whole package in order to enjoy the attractive parts. People can now select what is to their taste from a number of different sources. Traditionally the newspaper and the general broadcast channel aggregate a variety of different kinds of content aimed at different tastes. Perhaps no single individual consumes the whole package but is unable to bypass the package as a whole: if you like the sport from one newspaper and the political commentary from another, you must buy both titles to enjoy the small bits you enjoy. Online, consumers can go more or

less directly to those parts that are to their taste, irrespective of what else the title offers, and they can configure their consumption to include only what they individually want. This phenomenon, usually known as the "daily me," has been the subject of much discussion. Here we need only note that it poses considerable problems in terms of how the producers find an economic reward for their efforts in such a fragmented market.

11. The Internet is dialogic in its technical structure. The traditional mass media are essentially monologic communication technologies. One paper or station has many readers, listeners, or viewers. The Internet, by contrast, was originally designed as a point-to-point medium. It therefore permits the possibility of interactivity to a much greater extent than do the existing media. In principle, at least, this opens the possibility of much greater audience participation in the production of media artifacts. This dimension of the Internet has also been the subject of a great deal of discussion, for example, in terms of its implications for the nature of journalism. Again, we are not going to explore the wider aspects of this debate but simply note that as the production of new, interactive, material becomes generalized, the costs to the media companies will be greater, since they will need to generate this in addition to their existing offline material.

The above list of eleven points is far from exhaustive and tells us little about what the relative weight of each will be in the longer-term future of online media. The different factors influence different parts of the overall production and consumption of the media and thus evolve according to different social dynamics. Taken together, however, these factors suggest that the nature of competition in the media sector is likely to become much more intense. The relatively settled models, which evolved over time, provided for each class of media a niche in which it was possible to combine different elements of production, consumption, and revenue generation into a profitable concern. While the success or failure of individual titles was much more uncertain, the niches themselves had a familiarity and stability. It is unlikely that they will be reproduced even approximately in the online environment. The impact is likely to be differential, depending on the nature of the media sector under consideration. The potential will be realized through the interaction of at least two other sets of factors, one technological and the other economic.

TECHNOLOGICAL CONSTRAINTS

One major factor determining the speed with which media can be ported onto the web is the amount of information stored in each artifact. Some kinds of artifacts (e.g., theatrical release motion pictures) constitute extremely large files when rendered in digital form. Others (e.g., text-only newspaper articles) are relatively compact in digital form. For an artifact to be transported to the web, it is necessary that a medium of sufficient capacity be available to keep it in a form suitable for transmission, that sufficient bandwidth exists actually to transmit it to the receiver in an acceptable time period, and that a reception device appropriate to the medium be available to the receiver at the time of consumption. To turn the receiver into a customer requires in addition a reliable means of payment acceptable to both parties in the transaction. The ease with which a particular medium can take advantage of the Internet thus rests on three technical issues: the availability of suitable storage, distribution, and display.

I wish to advance as a working hypothesis that the greater the informational content of a class of media artifacts, the more difficult and protracted is the task of transforming it into an Internet-based medium. At one extreme it is very unlikely that the technologies will be available, in the near future of even the most advanced countries, to make the widespread home viewing of movies in quasi-theatrical form a realistic proposition. On the other hand, adequate technologies already exist and are widely deployed in advanced countries for the production, marketing, distribution, and consumption of online newspapers and magazines.

Innovation in mass storage and display remain relatively unexplored areas compared to the issues around distribution. Here there are two dynamics operating. The first is the installation of higher capacity systems (e.g., fiber optics cabling) giving greater physical bandwidth in transmission. The second is the development of compression systems able to utilize existing bandwidth more efficiently, of which the currently dominant form is DSL. Since the latter enables telecommunications operators to utilize existing networks for the provision of higher bandwidth services to domestic customers, and is thus much less demanding of capital investment than the construction of a wholly new broadband network, this is a very attractive option, at least in markets with a well-established and comprehensive local loop based on copper wires. The implication of these technological factors is that, except for the most bandwidth-intensive applications, the timescale in which it will be feasible to provide a wide range of online media to the home or office is relatively short in countries with well-developed telecommunications markets.

Such markets, however, are very far from universal internationally, and even a brief discussion of technical issues leads us inevitably to confront the fact that the opportunities to participate in these developments, as a vendor or as a consumer, will not be equally distributed. We can reasonably say that, in the highly wired nations of the developed world, the technical possibility of delivering and displaying full-motion video is already present on a large scale and will soon be widely (although not universally) available. On the other hand, accessing even the least bandwidth-hungry media in online form will remain an extremely rare, if not unthinkable, experience for much of the world's population. The obstacle to wider access is not only that most people in the world do not have access to a computer, they also do not have access to the necessary telecommunication link, and often even not the electrical supply, that is necessary for Internet use.

As we saw above, the evidence for the existing distribution of online media shows that it closely reflects well-established patterns of social differentiation. The "global north" is richly provided with online newspapers, magazines, radio and television stations. The "global south" is poorly provided with these facilities, with evidence from Africa suggesting that those that do exist are oriented toward elite groups. The patterns of consumption will reproduce these familiar inequalities in even more acute form. It therefore seems likely that in the foreseeable future the online media will be even less well placed to overcome patterns of social advantage and disadvantage that are strongly reflected in the availability of offline media. With the exception of television, the latter required only limited expenditure on the part of the consumer and could therefore be relatively widely available even to poorer and more remote communities. The delivery of media through the Internet, on the other hand, supposes a substantial investment in reception equipment and telecommunications that will act as substantial barriers to the world's poor for a long time to come.

ECONOMIC CONSTRAINTS

To say that something is technically possible, however, is not to say that it will occur, even in countries with relatively low barriers to access. In a commercial media environment, the decisive question is economic profitability, not technological feasibility. Even where the technology is already in place for the distribution and reception of a particular artifact via the Internet, there remains the question of whether it is profitable to do so.

Until very recently, one of the main reasons for an offline media company to have an online presence was not directly commercial. In the first place, having a website has been seen as an important marker of being abreast of developments and thus has the same sort of function as other kinds of corporate image advertising. Second, even the most experimental sites provided valuable intelligence for the operating company and its employees, in an environment in which experienced staff are at a premium. For many media companies, the slogan There to Learn and Not to Earn accurately described much of their activity in the years up to 2001. Third, as the movie *Blair Witch Project* is usually taken to show, an online presence can have an important place in the existing offline functions of a company (in that case, marketing). Such positional functions are undoubtedly important and will continue to provide some rationale for an online presence. But if current levels of investment are to be sustained, there must be some prospect of determining a viable business model. As we saw above, the collapse in advertising revenue that has accompanied the recent recession increased the pressure on all media, whether offline or online, and this has meant increased stress on finding ways of generating revenue from all possible sources, including web activities.

The construction of an online presence that represents a positive addition to the company's balance sheet involves three sets of considerations.

1. There are incremental costs involved in a web presence. In addition to the irreducible essential costs of physical presence like space on a server and reliable telecommunications links, it is not self-evidently the case that the same content can be presented online without modification. At the very least, content generated for the offline world needs to be revised and repurposed to suit the needs of the online environment. In newspapers, for example, it seems to be the case that rather different kinds of material are required, presented in very different ways, for an online venture as opposed to an offline one. Whether such a difference is apparent in a medium like the video release of a theatrical feature film is another matter: the sale of a downloadable version might require rather different packaging than in the case of a physical commodity, but it is not clear that the basic content will need to be altered significantly.
2. The discovery of a satisfactory revenue source for the online world is not immediately obvious for every business. In some media, notably the newspaper press, it has proved very hard to charge for access to basic services in the same manner as is done offline. In other cases, notably the music business, there is a well-developed online market in illegal copies, as well as a number of businesses providing copies of contested legality. Ensuring that online distribution is secure remains a continuing problem, since the main revenue stream for this industry has traditionally been the sale of individual copies of the product. Advertising, on the other hand, while well-adapted to the online world, has the problem that we identified above of potentially becoming detached from an editorial vehicle and placed with a more efficient web-only advertising oriented host. In only one of the potential revenue generating areas is the online environment naturally better than the offline: the gathering of detailed customer information and its potential use in various forms of direct marketing.
3. The impact of a successful online venture on its offline parent is likely to be considerable. The circumstances in which it will be possible to port a media business wholesale to the web and completely close down its offline operation are likely to be rare. In the newspaper business,

there has been at least one case involving a recent start-up that failed to establish a viable offline circulation and retreated to the less costly world of online distribution, but such events are not commonplace. In most cases, there will certainly be a period, probably a very protracted period, during which it will be essential to maintain both offline and online operations. While the market might expand as a result of the new distribution medium, it is by no means certain that individual companies will benefit, since as we have seen, the online market encourages new forms of competition. It is therefore likely that most companies will find themselves with higher costs arising from serving a market of the same size through two channels rather than one.

Taken together, these three problems mean that very few, if any, of the thousands of online media actually make any money at present. Many of those that claim to do so are almost certainly enjoying various forms of indirect subsidy, like free access to news feeds, from their offline parents. It is likely that, despite the common delivery channel and very limited range of reception devices, there is not one single business model. Rather, there will be a range of successful models depending on the exact nature of the medium involved and the kind of market into which it is seeking to sell. There will also be, of course, a big range of unsuccessful models.

TOWARD A TYPOLOGY OF ONLINE OPPORTUNITIES

Putting these factors together, we can derive a typology of the impact of the Internet in terms of the shift in revenue sources and the likely timescales within which the different media will need to respond. As we have seen, this timescale will be quite different in richer than in poorer countries; here we concentrate on the impact in the richer ones since we have more evidence and information in those cases.

The primary determinant for timescale is taken to be the technical demands of the medium, here simplified to the need for the widespread deployment of an adequate delivery mechanism. On this axis, the point of direct engagement with the web is either near or present for all of the media companies reviewed, although the technologies at stake are far from being universally diffused even in the most wired of nations. It is, however, sufficiently diffused that, for some forms like music, online distribution is a clear threat to their main revenue source. For others, like the merchandising associated with a particular film, the engagement with the web is as yet as a supplementary means of retailing that adds to the workings of a basically offline operation. Table 17.1 is an attempt to summarize the likely effects of the web on existing media businesses.

If we turn our attention to the available revenue sources, the nature of the Internet means that technology clearly presents new opportunities that are

Table 17.1. The Impact of the Internet on Existing Businesses

Medium		Offline Revenue Source	Bandwidth/ Compression Demand	Online Revenue Source	Point of Threat	Commercial Threat
Film	Theatrical	Ticket	Very high		Distant	
	Video rental	Hire fee	High		Near	
	Video sale	Retail sale	High	Retail sale	Near	Low
	Broadcast	Wholesale	High		Distant	
	Merchandise	Retail sale	Low		Present	
TV	Free to air	Advertising	High	Advertising +Transaction	Present	
	Subscription	Regular fee	High	+Occasional fee	Present	Medium
	PPV	Occasional fee	High		Present	
Radio		Advertising	Low	Advertising +Transaction	Present	Medium
Newspapers		Advertising +Subscription	Low	Advertising +Transaction	Present	High
Magazines		Advertising +Subscription	Low	Advertising +Transaction	Present	High
Music		Retail sale	Low	Retail sale	Present	Very high

Key: Point of threat = the time at which the impact of the Internet becomes substantial
Commercial threat = degree to which online developments threaten the revenue streams of offline media

present only partially, if at all, in the offline world. The first is gaining revenues from transactions facilitated by contact mediated through the agency of proprietary content. The interactive nature of the Internet means that purchase can be directly linked to exposure in a much more efficient manner than was previously possible. The second possible new revenue source lies in the gathering of customer data, since it can subsequently be traded or otherwise commercially employed. On the other hand, there looks to be a reduction in the variety of different revenue sources that have sustained some industries, since some do not port very easily onto the web.

One interesting consequence of this tabulation is its suggestion that the revenue streams of the different media will tend to converge in the online world. This form of "convergence" so far has been little explored, since most inquiries have focused on either technical factors or corporate mergers. The offline world is characterized by a diversity of revenue streams, but only some of these are likely to be able to transfer to the online world. The fact that some will make the transition and others will not is important to the overall shape of the media business.

Some revenue streams, particularly those concerned with discrete units of symbolic material (e.g., copies of films or recordings) can in principle be transferred to an online environment, although this model does not appear to work for regular publications like newspapers and magazines. Such a transfer will not be without effects, particularly on the existing distribution infrastructure. The networks of video rental shops and music retailers, for example, are likely to come under considerable pressure as the hit-driven core of their businesses migrates online. Securing those copies legitimately purchased through online means from subsequent unauthorized reproduction is likely to be extremely difficult, not only for the music business but also for the media that rely on such a revenue stream. One probable consequence will be a shift away from impossible-to-enforce rental to direct sale, and a consequent repricing of products to reflect the continuing likelihood of unauthorized reproduction.

The fact that the subscription revenue stream dries up for many media means that advertising and transactions are the central financial resources of a range of activities, supplemented perhaps by sales of customer data. These markets are likely to be more hotly contested than was the offline advertising market, partly because of their increased importance to survival and the fact that previously distinct media like television and newspapers will now be operating in the same commercial space, but partly also because of a change in the nature of their operation. In the offline world, distinct media had different functions for advertisers, and media were purchased in a "mix" designed to give certain kinds of exposure to well-defined audiences. Online advertising has some important limitations (e.g., for luxury goods) resulting from the inferior reproductive capabilities of the CRT compared with color printing on high-quality paper; it also has important advantages. The first of these is the ease of linking advertising with transactions, as noted above. The second main advantage is the facilities that the medium provides for marketing and advertising to be much more closely tied to the interests of the particular consumer. The gathering of customer data means that the kinds of advertising offered to particular individuals can be customized to take advantage of interest profiles that can be derived from studying the patterns of their web usage. What they see can be linked to what they are interested in, and these interests can be tied directly to a particular e-mail address, providing the opportunity for highly targeted direct (electronic) mail advertising campaigns much more sensitive than the pile of (unwanted) printed material that drops through the offline letterbox each morning.

This latter potential suggests that the most likely medium to attract large quantities of advertising will be the one that can, first, persuade individuals to register and repeat their visits frequently and, second, prove sufficiently "sticky" to allow the construction of a detailed profile of the interests of the individual to be constructed from the trajectory displayed in a site. That suggests that the most economically viable media will be those that can provide the widest range of editorial content. These successful sites, of course, are likely to be owned by the largest and richest of offline media, or large and rich pure Internet operations that have acquired access to premium media content. These are the companies that have the deepest pockets and the widest range of staff needed to produce the rich content that will attract large numbers of visitors, persuade them to spend some time on the site, and to return to it frequently. To the extent that media properties are able to establish themselves as the sites of substantial transactional activity, there will also be an advantage to brands that command a high degree of trust or are associated with luxury goods. On all of these counts, the media most likely to be successful online are the ones that have substantial financial backing, strong brand identity, and an elite customer group in the offline world.

One major consequence of these purely business factors is that the technical promise of increased plurality online will be difficult to realize in practice. The technical properties of the medium may, as already noted, permit easier access to new competitors. But the logic of doing business online suggests that thousands of new entrants will extend, rather than erode, the dominance of the large media corporation or the large online competitor. The problem of the diversity of voices will not be solved by technological change alone.

CONCLUSION

The Internet has already had a major impact on all the offline media. Literally thousands of newspapers, magazines, radio and TV stations have established online presences, and they have been joined by some purely online ventures. The online world alters the ways in which all the media are produced and distributed, the ways in which they can be consumed by their audiences, and the technical, temporal, and geographical boundaries that have until now helped structure the industry.

The fact that these online media depend on relatively high levels of distribution and reception technology suggests that their short-term impact is likely to be most marked in the world's richer societies, and even there it is far from certain that they will be universally diffused. The evidence suggests that access to cultural goods in the online world will demonstrate similar forms of stratification to those known to exist offline. Digital divides will continue for a long time, both between the poor and the rich within societies and between poor and rich societies.

Although the technology of online production and distribution offers considerable cost advantages, particularly to media that, like newspapers and magazines, depend on the physical distribution of bulky products, it is likely that the considerable costs of producing a high-quality online edition will have to be borne in addition to the costs of the offline edition, at least for most media for the foreseeable future. To the extent that audiences and advertising are attracted to the new online editions, they eat into the revenue streams of existing offline media. It is questionable whether, up to the present, many, or even any, online media are really profitable operations. The current advertising slump has led a few media companies to withdraw from the online environment, but for the majority there is increased pressure to locate funding to support what has become an expensive habit.

In order to become profitable operations, they need to develop robust online revenue streams. Subscription and rental do not appear easy to transport onto the web. Direct sale is easily transportable for primarily symbolic commodities, but this raises serious copyright problems that are not easily resolved. Advertising, and the greatly enhanced opportunities for linking it directly with transactions, appear to provide an attractive source of online revenue. The two problems here are, first, that classified advertising is easily disaggregated from editorial copy and, second, that the disappearance of distinctions between media will greatly increase competition for advertising. One possible response to that threat would be to use the editorial copy to construct profiles of the individual consumer that could be used as the basis for personalized advertising and direct (e-)mail campaigns. In order to do this successfully, it is necessary to attract the same customers frequently and for extensive visits. The ability to construct sites that can do this is likely to reside with large corporations with deep pockets. It is therefore likely that the most commercially successful media will be those that already dominate the offline world.

Even if it does prove possible for some online media ventures to establish stable revenue streams from their online operations, the size of such streams, and whether they will be adequate to cover costs, remains uncertain. The current pessimism among all media arising from the serious slump in overall advertising will certainly evaporate in an economic upswing, but it has illuminated the issues very clearly indeed. Probably some online media operations will be able to generate sufficient revenues at least to cover their "above-the-line" operating costs: they will continue to exist. Others will be maintained even though they are loss makers because they are part of an overall corporate marketing strategy, and their value is measured more in terms of visibility and image than in terms of revenue. A few, notably those of the public service broadcasters, may be sustained for entirely noncommercial reasons, it being considered that they constitute such an important part of the remit of their parents that they deserve continuing support. For many other sites, however, there will be no prospect of raising sufficient revenue to break even, at least in the near term. Such sites will be under continual pressure from managements concerned with profitability and shareholder value, and some, perhaps many, of them will forced into closure.

Clearly the outcomes of the Internet's impact on the traditional mass media will be extensive, but it is likely to reproduce the disparities in media availability that exist both between countries and within countries. The struggle to find a workable business model that will permit profitable online operation is likely to result in the continued, or even increased, domination of the supply of media artifacts by the same large corporations that dominate offline media.

NOTES

1. Because this chapter focuses on the Internet's impact on existing media, I have relatively neglected the question of companies operating only in the online environment ("pure-play dot-coms"). Obviously they have an impact on the existing media, which I treat primarily as a function of reduced barriers to entry. This also includes direct takeovers, of which there are some famous examples. While recent developments have reduced the visibility of this class of company, it remains interesting from a theoretical point of view. The maturing of the medium might again render pure-play dot-coms serious players, albeit in a less exaggerated form than was the case a couple of years ago.

2. More up-to-date figures are not available. The U.S. trade magazine compiled the database used here for a number of years, but apparently ceased production in the course of 2002. This is a good demonstration of the points that I am making about the increasing centrality of purely business decisions in online operations.

3. Northern and Shell, the company that owns the Express Newspaper Group, is a subject in itself, which I do not pursue here. Parsimony online is also present offline, in terms of the staffing, wages, and conditions of journalists on the newspaper titles. See Byrne 2002b.

4. A comparison of the relative preponderance of offline with online newspapers shows that the distribution of online resources is much more unequal. The Internet has reinforced rather than abolished the stark inequalities that are the central reality of the contemporary world.

REFERENCES

Byrne, Ciar. 2002a. "Cash Crisis Threatens Salon.com." *Media Guardian,* 27 June 2002. media.guardian.co.uk/newmedia/story/0,7496,745081,00.html. Accessed 27 June 2002.
———. 2002b. "Media: Is This the Future for Subs?" *Guardian,* 4 November 2002.
Editor and Publisher Online. 2002. www.mediainfo.com.
Salon Media Group. 2002. *Report for Quarter Ending 30 September 2002 (Form 10-Q).* Available at www.sec.gov. Accessed 11 February 2003. Filed with SEC 30 September 2002.
Sparks, C. 2000a. "From Dead Trees to Live Wires: The Internet's Challenge to the Traditional Newspaper." In J. Curran and M. Gurevitch, eds., *Mass Media and Society,* 268–92. 3d ed. London: Arnold.
———. 2000b. "The Distribution of Online Resources and the Democratic Potential of the Internet." In J. van Cuilenberg and J. van der Wurff, eds., *Media and Open Societies.* Amsterdam: Het Spinhuis.

18

Audiences on Demand

Oscar H. Gandy Jr.

THE AUDIENCE COMMODITY

The tensions between political economists and scholars identified with cultural studies have been most sharply drawn around the study of the audience.

Discussions, arguments, and occasionally harsh words have been exchanged over the tendency among political economists to focus on production, whereas those concerned with cultural studies have emphasized the role of consumption, or reception as some seem to prefer (Garnham 1995; Grossberg 1995). Although recent efforts to combine perspectives have met with limited success (Hagen and Wasko 2000), this fundamental difference in orientation remains.

Livingstone (1998) suggested that audience research was at a crossroads and it was time for some careful reflection about a variety of implied audiences. However, her list of core constructions of the audience failed to include the *commodity audience*. Political economists recognize the commodity audience as a special product of the media industry that is served up in response to the demands of advertisers and political strategists (Croteau and Hoynes 2001).

The commodity audience is the focus of this chapter. After discussing some of the critical differences between conceptions of the audience as commodity and the audience as public, market, and victim, I will examine some of the issues and concerns that arise when the private and social value of the commodity audience is shaped by considerations of race, class, and ethnicity.

Political economists credit Dallas Smythe (1977) with introducing us to the commodity audience. As Meehan (1993) reminds us, Smythe's engagement with this idealized audience met resistance because to many it seemed to be a "return to vulgar Marxism" (Meehan 1993, 379). Unfortunately, many of the scholars identified with critical theory sought to distance themselves from an analytical stance that foregrounds the manipulation of "subjects," at a time when individual agency and "resistance" were being celebrated in the offices down the hall. At the same time, scholars more closely identified with the mainstream media industry had already begun to make this relationship far more explicit than at any time in the past (Ettema and Whitney 1994; Webster and Phalen 1997).

Even though Ang (1991) characterized the study of the commodity audience largely as a project doomed to failure, the attempt to classify and characterize audiences in an effort to rationalize their control has become normalized as a way of life for those for whom the production of audiences is a routine activity.

Although the production of audiences is obviously far less precise than the production of manufactured goods such as automobiles and shoes, the underlying logic is essentially the same. Indeed, the relationships between productive resources and outputs can be estimated in similar fashion, and the search for greater efficiency and competitive advantage is a common goal in this industrial sector (Gandy and Signorielli 1981).

Smythe's pursuit of the commodity audience may have been sidetracked by an emphasis on determining more precisely the nature of the "work" that the audience was performing for capitalism, yet I would suggest that there is a great deal more to be explored in this regard (Jhally and Livant 1986).

CONSUMERS OR COMMODITIES?

The primary distinction between audiences as consumers and audiences as commodities emerges in the realm of advertiser-supported media. It is here that particular attributes of the audience become especially relevant. It is here that the traditional anonymity of the market relationship becomes a limitation for the sellers of audience. It is here that concerns about privacy and discrimination become salient (Cohen 1996; Gandy 1995). It is also here that the interests of advertisers displace the desires of audiences. It is vitally important to understand how this displacement works.

In part, it is the nature of the medium and the structure of transactions that determine how strongly the distorting influence of advertiser involvement will be felt. Mainstream economists have tended to discuss this problem in terms of the distinctions between public and private goods.

Public goods are characterized by two attributes that introduce problems for the establishment of a commercial market for particular commodities. Public goods are characterized by "nonrivalrous consumption," meaning that consumption by one person does not limit the ability of another to consume it. The second attribute is termed inappropriability, which means that excluding nonpayers from gaining access to and consuming the goods is difficult. In sum, the commodification of information is severely challenged by the status of information as public goods.

Media systems vary in the degree to which they are able to overcome the limitations imposed by the public goods character of information. Broadcast media provide information primarily in the form of public goods in that there is virtually no limitation on the ability of additional listeners or viewers to consume the content, as long as they have a receiver capable of translating the broadcast signal into an intelligible display. Thus it is only by limiting access to receivers, or to the code for translation, that nonpayers can be excluded from gaining access to and consuming this content.

Technical, economic, and legal developments have been pursued with great vigor in the attempt to transform public goods into private goods or commodities. Technological systems create the equivalent of turnstiles, where each customer pays a fee to gain access. Legal regimes such as copyright establish ground rules for access and use and recommend penalties for noncompliance.

In the developing Internet environment, problems of arbitrage and noncommercial redistribution of content have yet to be solved. Neither copyright management technology that involves sophisticated encryption nor the threat of criminal sanctions seems to have deterred consumers from "sharing" music and video in digital form (Lessig 1999). I wish to suggest that it is the far earlier introduction of advertising as the favored solution to the public goods problem that has introduced the most troublesome disturbance into the media environment.

THE PROBLEM WITH ADVERTISERS

Advertisers are consumers of audience attention, not content. Advertisers think of audiences as markets, but they purchase access to them as commodities. Some producers of media content may be unconcerned about or indifferent toward the attributes of those who consume its products. For the publisher of books, for example, all that matters is that consumers are willing and able to pay. Advertisers, on the other hand, have an apparently insatiable interest in knowing as much as they can about a potential consumer. Ideally advertisers would like to know each consumer as a unique individual, even down to the details of cyclical variations in mood.

In the idealized market, producers of media goods delivered in tangible form maximize profits by maximizing sales while minimizing costs. Even in the market for tangible media goods, there are important differences in production and distribution costs that have implications for the rate of exploitation, but the underlying logic is the same: the more the merrier. This begins to change in the context of advertising as a form of finance.

As the number of goods and providers in the market increases, it becomes more difficult for producer and consumer to find each other. In the ideal, we might think of advertising as serving an important function in markets by providing consumers with price, quality, and availability information that would enable product markets to clear. Unfortunately, the reality is far from the ideal.

The supply of market information is not without cost, and advertisers seek to avoid "wasting" their promotions on reaching segments of the population that have limited potential as consumers. This means, of course, that advertisers are always seeking to purchase access to precisely the "right" audience.

Unlike individual consumers, who are relatively powerless in the market for content and have to choose from whatever the market has to offer, advertisers have considerable market power. As a result, they are able to influence what the market supplies. Major advertisers are said to be on the "short side" of the market (Bowles and Gintis 1992) and consequently are able to consume access to audiences that have been literally produced on demand.

RACE AND AUDIENCE PRODUCTION

An important tension is created when some media, such as newspapers, find themselves torn between the demands of two sets of consumers—readers and advertisers (Baker 1994, 2002). There are critical insights yet to be developed about the ways in which the demands of audiences as consumers are balanced off against the demands of advertisers, who are more concerned about the "quality" of the audience than they are with the quality of the materials that are used in producing them.

Among the most important insights to be pursued are those related to the externalities, or the uncompensated social effects that flow from the use of particular sorts of content to attract the most desirable audience (Baker 2002). Those external effects tend to be related in important ways to the distinctions between desirable and undesirable audiences that are correlated with ethnicity, race, and class.

Until quite recently, very little attention had been paid to the social consequences that flow from the differential production of audiences defined by race (Gandy 1998; Turow 1997). Scholars concerned with consumption, reception, and resistance within the scope of cultural studies have tended to discuss these audiences as "spectators," but scant few have explored their status as commodities produced for the global market (Negus and Román-Velázquez 2000).

As Garnham has reminded us, it is necessary to understand the relations between production and consumption, as well as supply and demand, at several different levels and moments in time (1990, 12–13). This understanding must of necessity include the complex forces that shape the demands of consumers and the equally complex set of forces that determine what sorts of commodities would be offered to satisfy those demands.

Although political economists have paid attention to the development of "just-in-time" manufacturing techniques that enable the production of "job lots" of tennis shorts in precisely the colors that are popular in one region of a specific urban market, they focus primarily on the impact of this technology on the labor force (Mosco 1996). Color is largely irrelevant to their analysis.

When we shift our attention to the newsroom, however, we have reason to be concerned when we learn that producers are selecting stories in order to supply audiences in the colors that their advertisers demand (Heider 2000). According to one inside observer, "At the network level, producers are 'carefully taught'. . . that white viewers (whom advertisers regard as having greater purchasing power) will tune out if blacks or Latinos are the principal characters in segments on their shows." We are told that comments by producers such as "'they are bad demos' or 'it's not good television' are euphemisms for 'avoid stories about African Americans'" (Westin 2001). When pressed, producers will say about this racial seminar, "It's a subtle thing. A story involving blacks takes longer to get approved. And if it is approved, chances are that it will sit on the shelf a long time before it gets on the air. No one ever says anything. The message gets through." Like the just-in-time manufacturing of tennis shorts, the technology of audience production has incorporated Nielsen ratings that enable minute-by-minute assessment of the quality and character of the audience being produced. As a result, the schedule of later stories in the program may actually be adjusted in response to early assessments of audience quality. We need to know a great deal more about these aspects of audience production.

The Value of the African American Audience

The segmentation of audiences reflects the differential value placed on each segment by those who are in the market for access to audience attention. Only naive models of the market for audience attention assume that each member of the audience is valued precisely the same (Wildman and Karamanis 1998).

The valuation of audiences extends beyond simple measures of income to include specific social categories. On the average, advertisers pay higher rates per thousand for young, affluent magazine readers than they do for older adults. Indeed, younger readers between twenty-nine and thirty-nine years of age are valued at 7.5 times the rate paid for consumers a bit long in the tooth. Those who are both young and affluent are valued at 48 times the rates paid for access to seniors who have to struggle to get by on limited fixed incomes (Koschat and Putsis 2000).

Segmentation by race and ethnicity reflects a similar process of valuation. Media targeted to African American and Hispanic audiences offer commodities that the market values considerably less than those produced by general, or white-targeted, media (Ofori 1999). The lower value placed on minority radio audiences is reflected in two practices that have become commonplace among advertisers: a "dictate," or admonition to media buyers to avoid placement of ads on stations that target black or Hispanic audiences, and the demand for a "minority discount" for accepting "lower-quality" audiences that just happen to get mixed in.

Economic analysis of radio advertising provides evidence of this sort of discrimination. This analysis makes use of a power ratio that compares the station's share of audience with its share of advertising revenue. Stations with power ratios above 1.0 are assumed to have an audience that is valued above its unit value; those with ratios below 1.0 have undervalued audiences. In 1996 the average power ratio for minority-targeted stations was 0.91, while that for general market radio was 1:16.

In 1999 the disparity actually increased. The average power ratio for minority-targeted stations was 0.72, in comparison to an average of 1.15 for general market stations (Ofori 2001, 4).

The racism at the base of these data reflects a desire by some advertisers to avoid being associated with minority consumers. This is a view that accepts the expectation that white consumers will not buy products identified with black and Hispanic consumers. The association of low-status consumers with a given product is believed to reduce the status benefits that would be derived by those who tend to seek status enhancement through conspicuous consumption (Veblen 1953). Another racist concern, often expressed as an inside joke, is that advertisers are interested in "prospects rather than suspects" (Ofori 1999, 27) or "people who actually shop, not shoplift" (Flint 2002).

Clearly the African American audience is undervalued as a market segment, which is not to say that African Americans have no value on the open market for audiences. During the good times in the U.S. economy in the early to mid-1990s, when spending for advertising was increasing across the board, less than 1 percent of the $160 billion spent on marketing to consumers was targeted to African Americans. A comparative lack of interest in gaining access to African American consumers is also reflected in data from the most precisely targeted media—direct mail. Here as well, African Americans tend to be ignored.

While 79 percent of marketers who reportedly targeted black consumers used direct mail, an African American household receives about 20 percent of the volume of marketing mail that the average household receives (Reese 1997).

The Internet

We are just beginning to take note of the Internet, and there are not many studies available for review. A small number of the published studies of user and nonuser populations have attempted to develop compelling explanations for the observed disparities in access and use between groups defined by race, ethnicity, and class.

An important contribution to that discussion was made by a public service organization rather than a mainstream media scholar. The Children's Partnership commissioned a study of urban residents, and its report emphasized the concerns of non-English speakers. It concluded that despite the popular image of the Internet as reducing the friction of space and place, Internet users were online most often in search of information about local events, problems, and resources. A large segment of the population of nonusers was reportedly unable to find the sorts of local information that it needed most (Children's Partnership 2000). The information superhighway was not designed to take them where they apparently needed to go.

Those who provide Internet-based services to communities defined by race and ethnicity follow the well-worn paths established by traditional media (Hirsch 1968). These providers emphasize the economic value of the consumers that can be reached through the portals they maintain. *Black Enterprise* magazine reported online subscriber demographics from 1998 indicating that it could provide access to a very narrow segment of the black population with an average household income of $73,000 and an average net worth of $273,000 (*Black Enterprise* 2002). A black-targeted web portal, blackvoices.com, reported that its registered members had a mean household income of $70,000 (blackvoices.com 2002).

Clearly these providers are trying to sell access to a very select population of African Americans, given the fact that the median household income for African Americans was estimated at less than $28,000 in 1999 (*Money Income* 2002). It would be hard to argue that this privileged segment of the black population has the greatest need for information. Instead, we see that as in other commercial media environments, advertising provides an economic subsidy to those in the audience who need it least (Baker 2002).

CONSIDERING A RACIAL CLASS

Political economists who criticized cultural studies work that focused on audiences as consumers (Garnham 1995) often focused on the apolitical nature of the sorts of identities that emerge through consumption. Outside the bounds of this continuing debate, some discuss the possibility of a racial class that would be more political than cultural. These scholars tend to emphasize the role that identity plays in the development of social movements (Gunier and Torres 2002).

New social movements are considered to be important from a perspective on agency that emphasizes the ability of groups to engage in collective mobilization around common interests. The process of mobilization both reflects and shapes an activist culture. It is unclear whether protests over concerns as mundane as the withdrawal of a favored product or a popular television program can ever equal the sort of protest cultures that developed in response to the labor or civil rights movement (Hart, Esrock, D'Silva, and Werking 2001). Similar questions can be raised about the viability of social movements based on racial group membership that are shaped in large part through the consumption of targeted media content.

This is a problem of class consciousness, and it should apply to our definition of a racial class as one with explicit political goals. It seems clear that the development of class consciousness requires the existence of substantial class conflict and an awareness of the social processes that assign people to antagonistic classes. Although there is reason to doubt that the relationships which have helped mobilize activists worldwide around environmental issues are the equivalent of the relationships that mobilized industrial labor, it is fairly easy to understand the ways in which charges of environmental racism help mobilize a racial class (Blais 1996).

Less well understood are the ways in which a larger "cluster of social movements" (Preston 2001, 266–70) can be mobilized in the face of the pressures toward polarization that media technology enables (Sunstein 2001) and advertisers seem to promote (Turow 1997).

Racial Class Formation

Ideally, some political economists who study mass media might be challenged to follow an approach suggested by Giddens in relating the process of structuration to the development of racial group identity. This process might be explored in the same ways in which it has been applied to the development of class-consciousness (Giddens 1982). Surely black people can be expected to develop a form of class consciousness that shares many of the fundamental aspects seen in its traditional form.

While critical political economists who study the mass media have tended to avoid conflating racial group with the fundamental class divisions derived from Marxian analysis, not all Marxists have been so restrictive in their analysis of class. Wright (1982) has been especially interested in exploring the problems that emerge when class analysis is pushed toward the limits that social development presents. He suggests that the "most obvious way in which racism intersects class relations is in the social processes which distribute people into class positions in the first place" (537). We need to extend this analysis to include the consumption of media goods and services.

Group Identity and Consumption

A variety of perspectives on the nature of identity share a common set of assumptions about the role that consumption, or the use of commodities, plays in the development of individual and collective identity (McRobbie 1994; Pietrykowski 1995). Researchers who pursue an understanding of identity formation "assume that we express some key aspects of our social identity through consumption patterns and preferences for food or art forms, through choice of media and music, and that these can be directly interpreted as signs of individual and collective identities" (Negus and Román-Velázquez 2000, 338). Unfortunately, too much of this work ignores the complex infrastructure that is involved in supplying those commodities through markets.

The primary focus of Stewart Ewen's (1976) analysis of the early history of advertising was the creation of a national culture of consumers at the same time that it shifted attention away from the conditions of productive labor. But he also pointed out the ways in which the cultivation of distinctive consumer identities was encouraged.

As Ewen notes, the so-called Progressives struggled with developing ways to extend their social control of labor beyond the factory into the community and into the household. With the assistance of these critical social theorists, businessmen "looked to move beyond their nineteenth-century characterization as captains of industry toward a position in which they could control the entire social realm. They aspired to become captains of consciousness" (19).

Over the historical period that Ewen describes, the advertising industry continued to push and pull its audiences toward a common identity as consumers. Advertisements lent support to the "Americanization" of immigrants and the smoothing out of differences that were associated with an ethnic past. However, it was not until the 1960s that the industry gave much notice to a black consumer who could not be integrated so easily into the American mainstream with the aid of hair dye and cosmetic surgery (Brooks 1995). Ewen, however, suggests that during the 1960s advertisers were responding to multiple sources of cultural resistance to their attempts at incorporation (1976, 218).

Segmentation and the cultivation of difference did not emerge as a corporate strategy until the multiplication of media channels and the development of reliable technologies of measurement made such distinctions profitable (Meehan 1993).

Some critical observers note that advertisers may not only "echo" or reflect the categories they find within the culture but may also be actively involved in creating them. Some marketers who actively seek to "exploit perceived opportunities in so-called ethnic markets may help to 'design,' 'invent,' or 'create' the groups involved by treating them, talking about them, and presenting them as a distinct and homogeneous population" (Cornell and Hartmann 1998, 188).

Yet we also recognize that individuals vary in the strength of their identification with the groups to which they have been assigned by traditional means (Bowker and Star 1999; Skerry 2000). Although most research exploring racial or ethnic identity treats it as a relatively stable construct (Cornell and Hartmann 1998), there is also good reason to consider its salience to be situational. Individual identity is composed of different functional components that become more or less important, depending on the nature of the interaction, tasks, or cues that are present at any given moment. This suggests that a generalized measure of racial identity, or "ethnic self-awareness," may not be a reliable predictor of an individual's response to the challenges or opportunities she encounters in different contexts—including mainstream and targeted media (Forehand and Deshpande 2001).

RACIAL IDENTITY AND MEDIA CONSUMPTION

I have granted that the development of segmentation as a marketing strategy may not be an intentionally racist act (Gandy 2000), but there is little doubt that it generates a racial effect.

Group membership can support cultural differentiation, but it is likely to be accompanied by social and economic stratification. This relationship is explored in an emerging discourse on the "membership theory of inequality" (Durlauf 1999, 161). This theory invites examination of the ways in which the characteristics of the members of a community or group are related to the quality and character of the opportunities that become available to the group's members. It is likely that for subordinate groups, differentiation may lead to greater misfortune.

For example, Lundberg and Startz (1998) argue that residential segregation reinforces the substantial economic inequality that exists between whites and African Americans. This outcome is explained in part by the character of the interactions that make up the day-to-day experiences of group members within the community.

This interaction effect is both the source and the result of polarization by race. It is not merely the polarization of attitudes and opinions that Sunstein (2001) notes with regard to the Internet, but the increasing disparity in varieties of social capital that have critical implications for the democratic project in general (Putnam 2001). I invite consideration of the degree to which this tendency toward polarization is shaped by the logic of advertiser-supported, racially targeted media.

Very few studies have explored the relations between black racial identity and media consumption (Davis and Gandy 1999). It is not surprising, therefore, that only a small number of projects have examined the relationship between racial identity and reliance on black-targeted media.

In attempting to understand how a racial group identity may interact with or substitute for a class identity, political scientists have examined the extent to which either of these forms of identity reliably predicts public policy preferences—especially policies that would have a significant impact on the lives of African Americans.

A relatively successful measure of racial group identity was developed by Dawson (1994). This measure assumed that the well-being of one's racial group could stand in for an individual's own well-being if her racial identification was strong. A measure of linked fate used by Dawson asked respondents to describe the extent to which what happens to black people in the country has something to do with what happens in their own life (Dawson 1994, 78).

RACIAL IDENTITY AND AFRICAN AMERICAN AUDIENCES

I have used Dawson's concept of linked fate to examine the relations between racial identity and media use among African Americans.

A rather large sample of African American adults (nearly 3,200) in four cities were interviewed by telephone between December 1998 and July 1999. Though it was quite large, this sample is clearly not representative of the African American population of the United States for a number of important reasons.

Because the primary study was designed to use black-formatted radio, the resulting sample systematically excluded African Americans living in predominantly white communities and those who don't ordinarily listen to black-formatted radio. Thus the sample is likely to misestimate the distribution of racial identity among black people in the United States.

We assumed that a critical orientation toward media was reflective of an oppositional black identity (Davis and Gandy 1999). Respondents were asked to indicate the extent to which they agreed with the statement: "The mass media tend to present black men as violent and threatening." Although residents of the four cities differed on a number of relevant dimensions, there were no significant differences between cities in this regard, and most respondents agreed with the statement to some degree.

If black political activists would use the commercial mass media to reach out to African Americans who are racially identified in ways that matter for the goal of collective mobilization, then it would be important for them to select the appropriate media vehicle. The same logic that applies to advertisers seeking the "right audience" applies to the activist seeking the audience most likely to respond to a mobilizing appeal.

In terms of linked fate, the best vehicle would appear to be the black press because of the positive association between reading these papers and racial identification ($r = .108$, $p = .000$). This relationship reflects the historical importance of the black press as a vehicle for black political mobilization in response to a history of racial oppression (Owen 1996). It is important to note, however, that in this sample, which is biased toward persons with some degree of black racial identity, nearly 60 percent of those who read newspapers at all, report that they *don't* usually read a black-targeted newspaper (58.9 percent), and racial group identity only explained about 1 percent of the variance in readership for the black press.

On the other hand, fewer than 10 percent of those who watch television appeared to avoid black television programs, while more than 60 percent reported viewing three or more programs with predominantely black casts each week.

Unfortunately, there was no statistically significant relationship between racial identity and the viewing of such programs, although there was a slight tendency for those who believe their fate is linked to that of other black people to watch more of these programs ($r = -.032$, $p = .077$).

This means that the media channels which attract African Americans with the greatest potential to be shaped into a racial class that might pursue a political agenda are not likely to attract a substantial share of that audience.

On the other hand, the costs of reaching this audience through television would be exceedingly high. Because these media outlets tend not to be owned by African Americans, we would expect them to be less willing to accept explicitly political content targeted to a racial class.

CONCLUSION

A great deal of work needs to be done. Scholars must work even harder at discovering ways in which the production and consumption of audiences defined by race and class govern the reproduction of economic and social disparity along similar lines.

We might begin examining the ways in which the valuation of "cultural capital" is shaped by the logic of segmented markets. Such an analysis would invite examination of both old and new media, especially in the face of continuing trends toward convergence and consolidation.

Although I share the concerns expressed by Guinier and others (Guinier and Torres 2002), who warn of the dangers of a color-blind political strategy, I also doubt that a racial identity based primarily on the consumption of commercial products can serve as the mobilizing force behind the revitalized movement for social justice that we so desperately need. We need to explore the possibility of an alternative.

REFERENCES

Ang, Ien. 1991. *Desperately Seeking the Audience*. London: Routledge.

Baker, C. Edwin. 1994. *Advertising and a Democratic Press*. Princeton: Princeton University Press.

———. 2002. *Media, Markets, and Democracy*. New York: Cambridge University Press.

Black Enterprise. 2002. *Black Enterprise* magazine subscriber profile. www.blackenterprise.com/SubscriberProfile.html.

Blackvoices.com. 2002. Advertisement. new.blackvoices.com/services/advertising.html.

Blais, Lynn. 1996. "Environmental Racism Reconsidered." *North Carolina Law Review* 75: 75–151.

Bowker, Geoffrey, and Susan Starr. 1999. *Sorting Things Out: Classification and Its Consequences*. Cambridge, Mass.: MIT Press.

Bowles, Samuel, and Herbert Gintis. 1992. "The Political Economy of Contested Exchange. In T. Wattenberg, ed., *Rethinking Power*, 196–224. Albany: State University of New York Press.

Brooks, Dwight E. 1995. "In Their Own Words: Advertisers' Construction of an African American Consumer Market, the World War II Era." *Howard Journal of Communications* 6, no. 1–2: 32–52.

Children's Partnership. 2000. "Online Content for Low-Income and Underserved Americans," May. www.childrenspartnership.org/pub/low_income.

Cohen, Julie. 1996. "A Right to Read Anonymously: A Closer Look at 'Copyright Management' in Cyberspace." *Connecticut Law Review* 28: 981.

Cornell, Stephen, and Douglas Hartmann. 1998. *Ethnicity and Race-Making Identities in a Changing World*. Thousand Oaks, Calif.: Pine Forge.

Croteau, David, and William Hoynes. 2001. *The Business of Media: Corporate Media and the Public Interest*. Thousand Oaks, Calif.: Pine Forge Press.

Davis, Jessica L., and Oscar H. Gandy. 1999. "Racial Identity and Media Orientation: Exploring the Nature of Constraint." *Journal of Black Studies* 29, no. 3: 367–97.

Dawson, Michael C. 1994. *Behind the Mule: Race and Class in African-American Politics*. Princeton: Princeton University Press.

Durlauf, Steven. 1999. "The Memberships Theory of Inequality: Ideas and Implications." In E. Brezis and P. Temin, eds., *Elites, Minorities, and Economic Growth*, 161–77. New York: Elsevier.

Ettema, James S., and Charles D. Whitney. 1994. *Audiencemaking: How the Media Create the Audience*. Thousand Oaks, Calif.: Sage.

Ewen, Stuart. 1976. *Captains of Consciousness: Advertising and the Social Roots of Consumer Culture*. New York: McGraw-Hill.

Forehand, Mark, and Rohit Deshpande. 2001. "What We See Makes Us Who We Are: Priming Ethnic Self-Awareness and Advertising Response." *Journal of Marketing Research* 38, no. 3: 336–48.

Flint, Joe. 2002. "NBC Reaps Profits by Shooting for Viewers with More Money." Wall Street Journal Online. online.wsj.com/article/O,,SB102184059241695760.djm,00.html.

Gandy, Oscar H. 1995. "It's Discrimination Stupid!" In J. Brook and I. Boal, eds., *Resisting the Virtual Life: The Culture and Politics of Information*, 35–37. San Francisco: City Lights.

———. 1998. *Communication and Race: A Structural Perspective*. New York: Oxford University Press.

———. 2000. "Audience Segmentation: Is It Racism or Just Good Business?" *Media Development* 2: 3–6.

Gandy, Oscar, and Nancy Signorielli. 1981. "Audience Production Functions: A Technical Approach to Programming." *Journalism Quarterly* 58: 232–40.

Garnham, Nicholas. 1990. *Capitalism and Communication: Global Culture and the Economics of Information*. Newbury Park, Calif.: Sage.

———. 1995. "Political Economy and Cultural Studies: Reconciliation or Divorce?" *Critical Studies in Mass Communication* 12: 62–71.

Giddens, Anthony. 1982. "Class Structuration and Class Consciousness." In A. Giddens and D. Held, eds., *Classes, Power, and Conflict: Classical and Contemporary Debates*, 157–74. Berkeley: University of California Press.

Grossberg, Lawrence. 1995. "Cultural Studies vs. Political Economy: Is Anybody Else Bored with This Debate? *Critical Studies in Mass Communication* 12: 72–81.

Guinier, Lani, and Gerald Torres. 2002. *The Miner's Canary: Enlisting Race, Resisting Power, Transforming Democracy*. Cambridge: Harvard University Press.

Hagen, Ingunn, and Janet Wasko. 2000. *Consuming Audiences? Production and Reception in Media Research*. Cresskill, N.J.: Hampton.

Hart, Joy, Stuart Esrock, Margaret D'Silva, and Kathy Werking. 2001. *American Communication Journal* 43. acjournal.org/holdings/vol4/iss3/articles/hart.htm.

Heider, Don. 2000. *White News: Why Local News Programs Don't Cover People of Color*. Mahwah, N.J.: Lawrence Erlbaum.

Hirsch, Paul M. 1968. "An Analysis of *Ebony:* The Magazine and Its Readers." *Journalism Quarterly* 45, no. 2: 261–70, 292.

Jhally, Sut, and Bill Livant. 1986. "Watching as Working: The Valorization of Audience Consciousness." *Journal of Communication* 363: 124–43.

Koschat, Martin, and William Putsis. 2000. "Who Wants You When You're Old and Poor? Exploring the Economics of Media Pricing." *Journal of Media Economics* 13, no. 4: 215–32.

Lessig, Lawrence. 1999. *Code and Other Laws of Cyberspace*. New York: Basic.

Livingstone, Sonia. 1998. "Audience Research at the Crossroads: The 'Implied Audience' in Media and Cultural Theory." *European Journal of Cultural Studies* 1, no. 2: 193–217.

Lundberg, Shelly, and Richard Startz. 1998. "On the Persistence of Racial Inequality." *Journal of Labor Economics* 16, no. 2: 292–323.

McRobbie, Angela. 1994. *Postmodernism and Popular Culture*. New York: Routledge.

Meehan, Eileen. 1993. "Commodity Audience, Actual Audience: The Blindspot Debate." In J. Wasko, V. Mosco, and M. Pendakur, eds., *Illuminating the Blindspots: Essays Honoring Dallas W. Smythe*, 378–97. Norwood, N.J.: Ablex.

"Money Income of Households: Distribution by Income Level and Selected Characteristics: 1999, Table 663." 2002. *Statistical Abstract of the United States 2001*, 434. Washington, D.C.: USGPO.

Mosco, Vincent. 1996. *The Political Economy of Communication: Rethinking and Renewal*. Thousand Oaks, Calif.: Sage.

Negus, Keith, and Patricia Román-Velázquez. 2000. "Globalization and Cultural Identities. In J. Curran and M. Gurevitch, eds., *Mass Media and Society*, 329–45. 3d ed. New York: Oxford University Press.

Ofori, Kofi A. 1999. *When Being No. 1 Is Not Enough: The Impact of Advertising Practices on Minority Owned and Minority Formatted Broadcast Stations*. Report to the Federal Communications Commission. Washington, D.C.: Civil Rights Forum on Communications Policy.

———. 2001. *Minority Targeted Programming: An Examination of Its Effect on Radio Station Advertising Performance.* Report to the National Black Media Coalition. Washington, D.C.: Ofori & Associates.

Owen, Reginald. 1996. "Entering the Twenty-First Century: Oppression and the African American Press." In V. Berry and C. Manning-Miller, eds., *Mediated Messages and African-American Culture: Contemporary Issues*, 96–116. Thousand Oaks, Calif.: Sage.

Pietrykowski, Bruce. 1995. "Beyond Contested Exchange: The Importance of Consumption and Communication in Market Exchange." *Review of Social Economy* 53, no. 2: 215.

Preston, Paschal. 2001. *Reshaping Communications: Technology, Information, and Social Change.* Thousand Oaks, Calif.: Sage.

Putnam, Robert. 2001. *Bowling Alone: The Collapse and Revival of American Community.* New York: Touchstone.

Reese, Shelly. 1997. "A World of Differences: When Marketing to Minorities, Selecting the Right Media Is as Important as Developing the Right Creative." *Marketing Tools*, August, 36.

Skerry, Peter. 2000. *Counting on the Census? Race, Group Identity and the Evasion Of Politics.* Washington, D.C.: Brookings Institution.

Smythe, Dallas. 1977. "Communications: Blindspot of Western Marxism." *Canadian Journal of Political and Social Theory* 1: 1–27.

Sunstein, Cass. 2001. *Republic.com.* Princeton: Princeton University Press.

Turow, Joseph. 1997. *Breaking Up America: Advertisers and the New Media World.* Chicago: University of Chicago Press.

Veblen, Thorstein. 1953. *The Theory of the Leisure Class.* New York: Mentor.

Webster, James, and Patricia Phalen. 1997. *The Mass Audience: Rediscovering the Dominant Model.* Mahwah, N.J.: Erlbaum.

Westin, Av. 2001. "You've Got to Be Carefully Taught." *Nieman Reports* 55, no. 1: 63.

Wildman, Steven S., and Theomary Karamanis. 1998. "The Economics of Minority Programming." In A. Garmer, ed., *Investing in Diversity: Advancing Opportunities for Minorities and Media*, 47–55. Washington, D.C.: Aspen Institute.

Wright, Eric Olin. 1982. "Race, Class, and Income Inequality." In E. Giddens and D. Held, eds., *Classes, Power, and Conflict: Classical and Contemporary Debates*, 520–44. Berkeley: University of California Press.

19

Feminist Theory and the Political Economy of Communication

Ellen Riordan

Over the past five years, there has been a positive response to incorporating feminist theories and methodologies into critical political economy in the field of media and communication studies. Conferences such as the International Association of Media and Communication Research (IAMCR) (Scotland 1998), International Communication Association (ICA) (San Francisco 1999), Union for Democratic Communications (UDC) (San Francisco 1998), and Capitalism and the Twenty-First Century (London 2002) have been exceptionally welcoming environments for alliance building between the approaches. What seemed to be a divisive topic in the previous decade—reaffirming links between critical political economy and cultural studies—appears to have lost some of its fiery rhetoric and deep-seated antagonism.[1]

In the interest of furthering our current understanding of the field, several media and communication scholars advocate a conciliatory attitude to scholarship and debate. As suggested by Graham Murdock (1995), "to make the best possible use of the gains delivered by these major strands of cultural analysis we must once again disregard the demarcation lines that separate cultural studies from critical political economy, and both from the sociology of culture" (94).

As Murdock implies, obstinacy keeps us from gaining new perspectives into left politics. Rather than abandon our entrenched theoretical paradigms,

Murdock suggests, we operate from within our theoretical paradigms but remove the stumbling blocks. More recently David Hesmondhalgh echoed Murdock's position. In *The Cultural Industries* (2002), Hesmondhalgh argues it would best serve leftist scholars to focus on the complexities of cultural contradictions and synthesize the best aspects of critical approaches in order to more fully understand tensions between capitalism and cultural production (42). In a climate seemingly receptive to collaboration, feminist political economy has been recognized, supported, and defended by those who may not necessarily claim a feminist subjectivity.

As Leslie Steeves and Janet Wasko (2002) point out in "Feminist Theory and Political Economy: Toward a Friendly Alliance,"

> though each field of study has become more complex in the past two decades in response to criticisms, it appears that the increased complexity has not produced a clear basis for merger. Rather, the two fields have taken different evolutionary paths, resulting in a more substantial paradigm shift in feminist scholarship compared to political economy. (16)

The authors' comment about a paradigm shift in feminist studies sheds some light on why feminist studies and political economy are not "natural" allies. The "substantial paradigm shift" in feminist scholarship referred to by Steeves and Wasko is the apparent move toward postmodern theory. Although the authors place no value judgment on this trend, it should be noted that postmodernism is highly contested territory in contemporary feminist scholarship, research, and politics. Not only do most postmodern assumptions within feminist theory preclude political-economic concerns, but also they complicate the field of feminist studies by introducing contradictions in core concepts such as women and gender. For this reason, feminist studies should be thought of as a field rather than a particular paradigm. Because heterogeneous theories and methodologies frequently grounded in opposing presuppositions make up feminist scholarship, the work of some feminist scholars at times seems to directly contradict the political projects of others.

While claiming to be a political economist can mean a variety of things, Steeves is correct to assert that the range between positions seems less antithetic. Most of us working out of a Marxist tradition refer to our work as "critical" political economy, a euphemism for assumptions grounded in Marxist theory. Yet it would be unfair and unrepresentative to suggest that critical signifies uniformity. Just as there are different types of feminists, so too are there distinct types of Marxists: classical, radical, neo—a few positions having different assumptions that come to mind. To further complicate matters, the term "neo-Marxist" frequently implies giving consideration to issues of identity such as race, gender, and sexuality, but not necessarily to all or equally to any one. The degree to which one attends to issues of identity, and how one builds on or compromises classical Marxist assumptions regarding social class, labor, and production varies a great deal.

In this chapter, I discuss basic issues regarding feminism and political economy in media and communication studies, and point to specific work in which scholars rely on the two. In the spirit of alliance building rather than paradigm critique, this chapter focuses on the effectiveness of this position. There has been much debate about the inadequacies and faults of both political economy and feminist cultural studies, but for many of us, working toward building a leftist political project, collaboration instead of tearing one another apart seems to be of utmost importance.

A JOINT CONCERN: GLOBALIZATION

Over the past five years dissatisfaction with global corporate domination has become increasingly visible. Public protests against corporate globalization and world trade have taken place in Seattle in 1999 against the World Trade Organization; in Davos, Switzerland, in January 2000 against the World Economic Forum; in Prague, Czechoslovakia, in September 2000 against the International Monetary Fund and World Bank; and most recently in Genoa, Italy, in July 2001 against the G-8. In these various protests taking place around the world, grassroots political activists with differing convictions disrupt meetings held by the world's economic elites in order to draw attention to some of the problems of globalization, such as corporations profiting at the expense of fair wage jobs for workers.

Because government regulations have relaxed since the 1980s, companies have merged into megacorporations, controlling large portions of global cultural production through synergistic practices (Wasko 1995, 249). For example, when Disney merged with ABC in 1995, the corporation used many of its newly acquired television networks to distribute Disney commodities. Although corporations are now claiming they overestimated (or overvalued) the economic rewards of synergy (i.e., AOL–Time Warner merger), synergy indeed allows for one concept or idea to be spun off into many commodities, in effect quelling the circulation and distribution of new and diverse ideas. This ability to distribute recycled culture en masse raises concerns. Even though many people in the United States view media commodities such as film, books, and magazines primarily as economic entities, citizens in other nations view such material products as central to the production and reproduction of their history and culture. For this reason, many outside the United States defend their right to exclude cultural industries and products from WTO negotiations (McPhail 2002, 215), while corporate elites find little problem with this. Even though not all feminist communication scholars focus on issues of globalization, most would agree that global production of culture has both positive and negative consequences, particularly for women. Given that only a handful of industrialized nations have the ability to produce and circulate culture globally, those who create cultural com-

modities and how culture shapes national identities are important considerations. A general concern for many feminists is that women, and particularly
women of color, have less access to resources and have little control of the
means of production.

Political economists and many feminists find numerous problems with
trends in globalization. Communication scholars such as Herbert I. Schiller
(1971) and Ariel Dorfman and Armand Mattelart (1975) were among the first
in the communication field to draw attention to the concern that Western media products contribute to a decline in local values and culture while simultaneously promoting the ideas associated with capitalism. Early articulations
of cultural imperialism have been critiqued extensively for not attributing autonomy and agency to people, and contemporary work of political economists and feminists alike tends to conceptualize media processes as complex
interactions between people and products.

Cultural feminists such as Barrett (2001), Radway (1984), Modleski (1984),
and Ang (1991) have made significant contributions to the literature of cultural domination, underscoring the point that audiences are not passive recipients; they actively engage texts, and therefore the relationship between
media corporations and audiences is complex and interactive. Other feminist
cultural scholars have noted a continuing unequal relationship between
women and men in cultural production (Gallagher 1980; Steeves 1993), suggesting that women's influence in the realm of cultural production along
with the circulation of symbolic ideas is underrepresented, even if their ideas
are not totally controlled. Despite critiques of cultural imperialism, one cannot discount that a disproportionate amount of cultural commodities are produced by predominantly male-controlled corporations in industrialized capitalist countries and then exported to other parts of the world. This position
does not necessarily discount the increasing number of media products coming out of smaller countries. Rather, it acknowledges the asymmetrical relationship between the relatively small number of imported films (and more
notably television shows into the United States), and the significantly larger
number of Hollywood exports to many other countries. As the work of feminists has suggested, the relationship between production and consumption
is skewed not only in terms of national origin but also of gender.

PUBLIC VERSUS PRIVATE SPHERES

Clearly, the power and control wielded by media corporations should be
taken seriously. Political economists have suggested this for years (Golding
and Murdock 1991; Garnham 1990), as have industry scholars (Bagdikian
1997; Compaine 1982). Yet many feminist media scholars have been hesitant
to venture into the field of media economics, industry analysis, and political
economy. Perhaps this is a result of what Lisa McLaughlin (1999) suggests is

a gendering of separate spheres, women scholars being drawn to the cultural (i.e., feminine realm), while male scholars are drawn to the political (i.e., masculine realm). This gendered division could result from what both Carey (1995) and Murdock (1995) alluded to as the separation of the fields of cultural studies and political economy along the lines of humanities and social science frequently played out in the field of communication research. While feminist sociologists continue to make contributions to political economy by theorizing economic structures affecting women's lives (Acker 1999; Edin and Lein 1997), feminist communication scholars tend to gravitate more toward issues of representation and identity, concerns usually theorized in cultural studies analyses based in the humanities and literary studies.

Not only is the duality of spheres that separates women into the private realm and men into the public realm observable in academia, it is also seen in daily life. Along with this duality comes the assumption that the public sphere is valued more than the domestic private sphere. Nancy Fraser's (1989) work illustrates this, showing how women have traditionally worked within the depoliticized private sphere while men have access to both private and public regions.

Even though it has been harshly critiqued, second wave feminism has contributed at least one essential insight: day-to-day moments and the private sphere of women's lives are indeed political and economic. According to this standpoint, as made apparent through second wave feminism, women's actions, however localized and "invisible," are political and economic, and therefore valuable, whether or not women hold public office, engage in legislation, or act as household wage earners.[2] Making connections from the everyday moments of women's lives back to the structural level of capitalism has been a difficult task for feminist communication scholars. This is one reason why many feminist communications scholars pay less attention to issues central to political economy. Yet avoiding the political economic context of daily life can be detrimental to women in oversimplifying the complex interlocking forms of oppression to which women are subjected.[3] Although Garnham (1995) would argue that we should privilege economic structure in the last instance, many feminists would counter with an assertion that privileging the economic oversimplifies the complexity of interlocking forms of oppression. An examination of gender, race, and sexuality as subjectivity does not have to be at the expense of the economic, particularly socioeconomic class. Feminist political economy seeks to understand how similar economic conditions can produce different experiences for women of color, gay men and lesbians, disabled women, and survivors of domestic violence.

POLITICAL ECONOMY IN COMMUNICATION

Political economists concern themselves less with consumption practices of individuals and more with production issues of cultural artifacts. For example,

Nicholas Garnham (1990) stressed the importance of cultural production and how artifacts are structured within the constraints of capitalism. Garnham's notion of "cultural materialism," derived from Raymond Williams, is a decidedly Marxist approach to the study of cultural production. Garnham (1979) argues that cultural commodities must be situated in their historical and material context to reveal not only the controlling interests of producers but also how "monopoly capitalism has been the exercise of political and ideological domination through the economic" (133). Economic structure according to Garnham is a core determinant of a given society. Feminist scholars, such as Marilyn Waring (1988, 1999), point out how capitalism naturalizes male bias because it values traditionally masculine ways of organization and knowing. This androcentric structure shapes our way of knowing and how we conceptualize questions. In essence, political economic research is much the same, as it often ignores the gendered nature of capitalism, privileging some aspects of the economic (i.e., production) rather than others (i.e., consumption).

To further understand capitalism and its relationship to the daily lives of people, political economists must focus on the meaning of consumption, not only as it results from a crisis of overproduction but also as it stems from the "pleasure" that many politically, economically, and socially disenfranchised groups derive from consuming. Understanding wants and desires as experienced by individuals and groups of people, as well as how this pathos combines with the crisis of overproduction, opens the way to changing social consciousness. Consumption is an integral part of the reproduction of capitalism, class inequalities, and women's oppression. The meaning and status conferred on consumption practices, although wildly varied across different groups and communities classified by race, class, sexuality, religious background, ethnicity, dis/ability, age, and so on, should be used as an entry point to understand how subjectivities are both economic and gendered.

FEMINISM IN COMMUNICATION

Defining feminism is nearly impossible; positions include liberal, radical, Marxist/social, psychoanalytic, poststructuralist, postmodern, ecofeminist, and postfeminist. This list does not account for all feminists, nor does it do justice to the blurring and complexity of feminist thought, which will not fit neatly into a single box. As with political economy, there are branches of feminism that are not critical in orientation, meaning they do not start with the assumption that social structures are inherently problematic. For example, liberal feminists fail to critique the inherent structure of capitalism as it relates to women's exploitation, even though they critique practices within this structure that oppress women.

Most feminists explicitly working in the area of political economy have been Marxist or socialist feminists. Marxist feminists reject the liberal claim that human nature is defined by rationality. Instead, they emphasize that human nature is defined by our labor or a need to produce our means of subsistence (Tong 1997, 39). While historical materialism offers an analysis of labor relations, class position, and exploitation, socialist feminists (as well as others) argue that Marxism does not adequately theorize gender relations (Hartman 1981). For Marxists, the exploitation of workers under the system of capitalism is privileged over the oppression of women under patriarchy. Feminist critiques of Marxism point to a major theoretical problem which assumes that the concept of class is gender neutral, when in fact it has a masculine bias (Acker 1999).[4]

The work of Marxist, neo-Marxist, and socialist feminists in media and communication research can be linked to both critical cultural studies and political economy. These types of feminist approaches look at the interplay between the structures of patriarchy and capitalism. Steeves (1987) argues that different assumptions about class, race, and gender shape different perspectives in a socialist feminist framework. Moreover, she insists that socialist feminists "assume the relative autonomy of ideological expressions in mass culture" (1987, 106). From the perspective of a cultural feminist, the economic base does not solely determine social practice. Instead, ideology expressed in political, economic, and social practices acts to produce and reproduce women's social status. Gender is a complex construction of deep-rooted social factors including race, class, sexuality, religious background, ethnicity, dis/ability, age, and so on. Thus an analysis isolating gender as a discrete variable may work to identify manifest differences in gender roles, but it fails to explicate the nature of these roles particularly since gender is linked to other social factors.

FEMINIST POLITICAL ECONOMY IN COMMUNICATION

Most feminist work is interdisciplinary with respect to theories and methods, and underlying assumptions frequently are not fixed. While feminists may not agree on what constitutes "woman," they repeatedly agree that the everyday moments in women's lives are valuable, important, and political. Yet the meaning ascribed to these terms is fiercely contested. Likewise, there is no single approach to political economy. Theoretical positions in the field range from classical (mostly descriptive) to critical (often more prescriptive). In addition to a continuum of theoretical approaches, political economy analyzes varied subject matter. Whether presenting an analysis of policy, regulation, corporate structure, labor, or production, political economic studies tend to examine the macrolevel rather than individual or microlevel.

While economists look at economic factors in determining the well-being of a society, critical political economists examine modes of production to understand social relations that indicate the relative health of a nation. Feminist political economist Marilyn Waring's research a year indicates how economics cannot adequately reveal the welfare of a nation because things such as women's reproductive labor (e.g., cooking, cleaning, subsistence farming, child care, etc.) is not counted as part of the gross domestic product (GDP) in the U.N. system of national accounts. Waring also shows that drug trafficking and child prostitution do count toward the GDP because these "transactions" go through the market. Waring's research clearly indicates how economics masks and naturalizes moral issues.

Feminist political economy in communication integrates an examination of capitalism and patriarchy. In addition to offering a critique of macrolevel social structures, feminist political economy stresses the importance of understanding issues of identity, subjectivity, pleasure, consumption, as well as visible and invisible labor in the context of women's daily lives. Even though both production and consumption are inextricably linked, feminist scholars and political economists tend to focus primarily on only one of these processes. Political economists tend to cut off their analysis when they reach consumption practices, and many feminists ignore production contexts of cultural artifacts. Drawing from both feminist and political economic theories offers ways to think about how knowledge is simultaneously gendered and economic. For example, while a political economic approach to the study of corporate-controlled production might examine social relations as shaped by capitalist exploitation such as labor conditions, a feminist political economic approach would look at how capitalist exploitation is also gendered and patriarchal, such as how women's work is often deskilled and underpaid. This is precisely what happens at megacorporations, where women from developing nations using highly technical machinery to assemble electronic parts are often concentrated in low-wage pink-collar jobs while male owners and managers earn substantially more for decision making (see Enloe 1995; Tracy 1999).

Whereas a political economic analysis might look at how the commodity audience is bought and sold, a feminist political economic analysis might look at how the process is also gendered. More specifically, a study may examine how corporations use women either as a commodity audience to sell to advertisers as a niche or as a sex object used to attract a demographic niche that becomes the commodity audience. As Meehan's (2002) research on the ratings industry points out, the assumptions behind advertisers' "desired" audience reveal institutional sexism where men are valued more than women (i.e., advertisers pay more for eighteen- to thirty-four-year-old males as a demographic group) and women become marginalized into niche markets despite their economic gains.

In addition to looking at gendered subjectivities within the framework of feminist political economy, several scholars have examined issues of race as they relate to both the media industry and basic civil rights. For example, Roopali Mukherjee's (2002) work examined the public policy process in

California, revealing how it became a site for producing and legitimating both racial and gendered identities. Mukherjee's analysis centers on the passage of the California Civil Rights Initiative (CCRI) in 1996 and how representations in the campaign perpetuated dominant racist and classist narratives and stereotypes. The campaign frequently employed the rhetoric of a gender-blind and color-blind meritocracy, while it simultaneously held up white women as models. Mukherjee argues that campaign tactics such as this furthered anti–affirmative action while silencing and delegitimating working-class women of color.

In her article "Periodical Pleasures," Amy Beer (2002) uses feminist political economic methods to investigate issues of racial identity. Beer argues that the construction of Latinas as desirable consumers attempts to correct historically negative stereotypes with positive representations, yet the process ultimately fails because it is founded on consumption rather than on social and political rights. Beer reasons that the profit-driven need to construct a model "Latina" identity forces magazine advertisers to group women from various ethnic groups into one homogenized Latina identity. While on the surface the images may appear positive (i.e., successful and upwardly mobile), Beer insists that they reinforce the invisibility of a large percentage of actual Latina women. Moreover, she suggests, these particular magazines geared toward a niche market, eighteen- to thirty-four-year-old Hispanic women, reinforce a promising correlation between economic and political power instead of offering real political power, and this subsequently contributes to the disenfranchisement of all Latinas.

Articulating a similar concern regarding the equation of increased consumption with improved human rights, Fred Fejes (2002) examines advertising trends in popular gay magazines. Fejes argues that upwardly mobile, well-educated gay men and lesbians are targeted by advertisers as niche markets and valued consumers, yet as a political group they are continually and systematically denied basic civil rights. While popular gay magazines may appear to be increasing the visibility of gay men and lesbians, Fejes insists they in fact do the opposite by reinforcing the invisibility of a large segment of the gay and lesbian population (i.e., working class) that is not deemed economically desirable by advertisers. Fejes suggests that social and sexual identities that do not match the desired audience profile are minimized or made totally invisible, and the political position of gays and lesbians is tenuous even though they count as consumers. Fejes points out how real lives of gay men and lesbians stand in stark contrast to images in ads, and this reinforces the invisibility of the real. As each of these studies illustrates, examining both production and consumption as integral parts of capitalist accumulation provides a way to theorize subjectivity from a cultural materialist perspective.

As evidenced by the studies mentioned above, scholars working in the area of feminist political economy integrate multiple methodologies to unlock complex relationships between highly abstract concepts of gender, race, class, and sexuality that have very real consequences for the lives of women and men. Feminist political economists often focus their investigations in specific areas while examining issues of identity. In *The Political Economy of Communication*, Vincent Mosco (1996) suggests three entry points for investigation: commodification, spatialization, and structuration. According to Mosco, commodification is predicated on the ideas derived from Marxist theory that a use value (the usefulness of the commodity to the consumer) is changed into an exchange value (what the commodity can command on the market). Spatialization, based on the ideas of Henri Lefebvre (1979), is concerned with issues surrounding the transformation of space and time by changes in technology and information; and structuration, originating in the work of Anthony Giddens (1984), deals with how to think about the impact of human agency on macrolevel structures. For cultural feminists, beginning with the commodity is often the most logical place because it is the site of both production and consumption. But areas of spatialization and structuration are equally important, spatialization because the media's potential to spread ideological messages is staggering and structuration because feminist analyses of microlevel events, such as media texts, can indeed change the nature of macrolevel structures, such as how the industry represents women.

A feminist political economy presents ways to move away from conceptualizing political economy as only looking at labor or class relations in order to broaden our understanding of accumulation and the reproduction of capitalism. As Acker (1999) suggests for Marxist sociologists, reconceptualizing political economy may mean rethinking class and its significance to a contemporary critique of capitalism. Perhaps such a reconceptualization means theoretical self-reflexivity that allows political economists to address issues of epistemology. Murdock (1995) and Hesmondhalgh (2002) seem to suggest that engaging different theoretical positions has the potential to strengthen rather than undermine the foundations of political economy. In order for feminist political economic analyses to offer more theoretical insight, scholars must reconceptualize the economic and broaden the objects of study to include individual experiences rather than focus primarily on macrolevel, institutional, and structural analyses. Women, as well as other marginalized groups, need to understand their lives as economic and shaped by both capitalism and patriarchy. In order to make this link, scholars must explicate how economics and gender are sutured into our smallest day-to-day actions. But this does not mean that the economic is solely determinant of those actions. It acknowledges the interplay between economics and class, race, gender, sexuality, and so on, as evident in the work of Mukherjee (2002), Beer (2002), and Fejes (2002).

Feminist political economy is committed to praxis, which includes dialogue across disciplinary boundaries. As this chapter suggested at the outset, the climate seems right for these types of exchanges. Feminist political economy has much to offer by way of examining interlocking forms of oppression such as gender, race, sexuality, and class. It attempts to address a concern in feminist studies about how to understand women's actions as resistance without dismissing them as subsumed under totalizing systems of patriarchy and capitalism, or without celebrating acts of resistance while ignoring the historical material conditions that make them possible. Understanding how pleasure and resistance can appear to be simultaneously yet contradictorily empowering and oppressive is at the crux of feminist political economic inquiries. By focusing on the complexities of cultural contradictions, feminism brings to political economy a way to look more broadly at the tensions between capitalism and culture as they become apparent in racialized, gendered, and sexed subjectivities.

CONCLUSION

The friction between feminism and political economy, especially noted in the *Critical Studies in Mass Communication* colloquy (1995), has subsided. Yet feminism remains at the margins of political economy, and political economic considerations are not central to most feminist media and communication scholarship. At the most recent IAMCR conference in Barcelona (July 2002) not one paper in the political economy section dealt explicitly with gender.[5] Similarly, in the gender section only one paper session was devoted to political economy, but with attention specifically to news media. The political economy section suggested that issues of globalization, information technology, and policy impact men and women in the same ways, although research indicates otherwise. The gender section suggested that feminist political economic studies are concerned only with the division of labor in news organizations, rather than women's access to information or the construction of gendered subjectivities. These session papers are hardly representative of the diverse scholarship currently under way that is informed by both political economy and feminist theory.

Some of the most promising feminist political economic scholarship continues to be in the area of cultural policy and women's access to technology. For example, Lisa McLaughlin (2002b) and Katharine Sarikakis (2002) are two scholars whose work deals with globalization and policy decisions as they affect women's status in the world information society. Additionally, Jo Ann Dumas's (2002) research focuses on the interplay of information technology and the role of women in facilitating social, political, and economic development in poor and rural communities. As the work of these scholars suggests, globalization, policy making, and technology introduce specific concerns for women and, given the predominance of transnational corporations that own the technologies and the state that controls them, it is essential that women's concerns be voiced.

In a somewhat different direction is the work of newer media and communication scholars who seem less concerned with adherence to particular paradigms and more focused on the ability to "poach," or draw from multiple theoretical paradigms for the purpose of critique. For example, Sasha Costanza-Chock's (2002) research, presented in the political economy section of IAMCR Barcelona, examined social movements and the use of online activism. Although Costanza-Chock does not necessarily focus on gender, his work relies on feminist theory, as well as queer theory, and thereby informs his understanding of connections between grassroots activism and marginalization. Constanza-Chock's work, as well as that of other newer scholars, introduces an interesting challenge: does a feminist political economy have to explicitly focus on gender or can it simply invoke a feminist sensibility informed by theory?

Five years ago the best direction for bringing feminism and political economy together was to explicitly introduce gender as a concern in political economic analyses. Yet this might not be the case today. The work of nascent political economic scholars does not necessarily revolve around gender as much as an epistemology informed by feminist theory and cultural concerns. Political economy in communication and media research has almost always been inclusive of analyses of culture to varying degrees. But emerging scholars in the field are finding new ways to incorporate multiple cultural theories, including feminist theory, into their analyses. The best direction for feminism and political economy is the one referred to at the beginning of this chapter and expressed in the thoughts of Murdock (1995) and Hesmondhalgh (2002): moving beyond political and personal barriers dividing critical scholars will produce fuller analyses. Perhaps the most fruitful direction for feminist political economy is for feminist theory to inform political economic analysis in the interest of revitalizing core assumptions, instead of necessarily placing women at the focal point of all analyses.

NOTES

1. While not all of feminist theory rests in the domain of cultural studies, a substantial body of work is committed to approaches that privilege culture.

2. Even though many women are household wage earners, women do not always see the political nature of their work because it is something that must be done for survival. This is another way in which the logic of capitalism that devalues women becomes naturalized and accepted.

3. See bell hooks, *Cultural Criticisms or Outlaw Culture: Resisting Representations* for a discussion of the interlocking forms of oppression of race, gender, and economics (1994). She refers to this as "White Supremacist Capitalist Patriarchy."

4. See Joan Acker (1999), "Rewriting Class, Race, and Gender: Problems in Feminist Rethinking," for a further elaboration of how feminists in sociology proceeded after they critiqued Marxism as male biased.

5. Norma Pecora's paper "Nickelodeon and the Export of Childhood," while not explicitly drawing on feminist theory, assumed a gendered concern about children.

REFERENCES

Acker, Joan. 1999. "Rewriting Class, Race, and Gender: Problems in Feminist Rethinking." In *Revisioning Gender*, ed. M. M. Ferree, J. Lorber, and B. Hess, 44–69. Thousand Oaks, Calif.: Sage.

Ang, Ien. 1991. *Desperately Seeking the Audience*. London: Routledge.

Bagdikian, Ben. 1997. *The Media Monopoly*. Boston: Beacon.

Barrett, Michele. 2001. "Feminism and the Definition of Cultural Politics." In *Feminism-Art-Theory: An Anthology 1968–2000*, ed. Hilary Robinson, 308–12. Oxford: Black Wells, 2001. Article first published in 1982.

Beer, Amy. 2002. "Periodical Pleasures." In *Sex and Money: Feminism and Political Economy in the Media*, ed. Eileen R. Meehan and Ellen Riordan, 164–80. Minneapolis: University of Minnesota Press.

Carey, James. 1995. "Abolishing the Old Spirit World." *Critical Studies in Mass Communication* 12, no. 1: 82–89.

Compaine, Benjamin. 1982. *Who Owns the Media?* White Plains, N.Y.: Knowledge Industry Publications.

Costanza-Chock, Sasha. 2002. "Mapping the Repertoire of Electronic Contention." Paper presented at the International Association of Media and Communication Research, Political Economy Section, Barcelona, July.

Dorfman, Ariel, and Armand Mattelart. 1975. *How to Read Donald Duck: Imperialist Ideology in the Disney Comic*. New York: International General.

Dumas, Jo Ann. 2002. "Information and Communications Technology (ICT) Policy and Gender Equity Policy for Access and Cultural Communication in Mali." Paper presented at the IAMCR conference, Barcelona, July.

Edin, Kathryn, and Laura Lein. 1997. *Making Ends Meet: How Single Mothers Survive Welfare and Low-Wage Work*. New York: Russell Sage Foundation.

Enloe, Cynthia. 1995. "The Globetrotting Sneaker." *Ms.*, March-April, 10–15.

Fejes, Fred. 2002. "Advertising and the Political Economy of Lesbian/Gay Identity." In *Sex and Money: Feminism and Political Economy in the Media*, ed. Eileen R. Meehan and Ellen Riordan, 196–208. Minneapolis: University of Minnesota Press.

Gallagher, Margaret. 1980. *Unequal Opportunities: The Case of Women and the Media*. Paris: UNESCO.

Garnham, Nicholas. 1979. "Contribution to a Political Economy of Mass Communication." *Media, Culture, and Society* 1: 123–46.

———. 1990. *Capitalism and Communication*. London: Sage.

———. 1995. "Political Economy and Cultural Studies: Reconciliation or Divorce?" *Critical Studies in Mass Communication* 12, no. 1: 62–71.

Giddens, Anthony. 1984. *The Constitution of Society: Outline of a Theory of Structuration*. Berkeley: University of California Press.

Golding, Peter, and Graham Murdock. 1991. "Culture, Communications, and Political Economy." In *Mass Media and Society*, ed. J. Curran and M. Gurevitch, 15–32. London: Edward Arnold.

Hartman, Heidi. 1981. "The Unhappy Marriage of Marxism and Feminism: Toward a More Progressive Union." In *Women and Revolution*, ed. Lydia Sargent, 1–41. Boston: South End.

Hesmondhalgh, David. 2002. *The Cultural Industries*. London: Sage.

hooks, bell. 1994. *Outlaw Culture: Resisting Representations*. New York: Routledge.

Lefebvre, Henri. 1979. "Space: Social Product and Use Value." In *Critical Sociology: European Perspectives*, 285–95. Irvington, N.Y.: Halsted.

McLaughlin, Lisa. 1993. "Feminism and the Public Sphere." *Media, Culture, and Society* 15, no. 4: 599–620.

———. 2002. "Global Subsistence Citizenship: Questions of Access and Institutionalization Before the World Summit on the Information Society." Paper presented at the Union for Democratic Communications Conference, Penn State University, October.

McPhail, Thomas. 2002. *Global Communication: Theories, Stakeholders, and Trends*. Boston: Allyn & Bacon.

Meehan, Eileen R. 2002. "Gendering the Commodity Audience: Critical media Research, Feminism, and Political Economy." In *Sex and Money: Feminism and Political Economy in the Media*, ed. Eileen R. Meehan and Ellen Riordan, 209–22. Minneapolis: University of Minnesota Press.

Modleski, Tania. 1984. *Loving with a Vengeance: Mass-Produced Fantasies for Women*. London: Methuen.

Mosco, Vincent. 1996. *The Political Economy of Communication*. London: Sage.

Mukherjee, Roopali. 2002. "Single Moms, Quota Queens, and the Model Majority: Putting 'Women' to Work in the California Civil Rights Initiative." In *Sex and Money: Feminism and Political Economy in the Media*, ed. Eileen R. Meehan and Ellen Riordan, 100–111. Minneapolis: University of Minnesota Press.

Murdock, Graham. 1995. "Across the Great Divide: Cultural Analysis and the Condition of Democracy." *Critical Studies in Mass Communication* 12, no. 1: 89–95.

Radway, Janice. 1984. *Reading the Romance: Women, Patriarchy, and Popular Literature*. Chapel Hill: University of North Carolina Press.

Sarikakis, Katharine. 2002. "Gender and the Global Information Society: A Broken Link?" Paper presented at the IAMCR conference, Barcelona, July.

Schiller, Herbert. 1971. *Mass Communications and American Empire*. Boston: Beacon.

Steeves, H. Leslie. 1987. "Feminist Theories and Media Studies." *Critical Studies in Mass Communication* 4, no. 2: 95–135.

———. 1993. "Gender and Mass Communication in a Global Context." In *Women in Mass Communication*, ed. Pamela Creedon. Newbury Park: Sage.

Steeves, H. Leslie, and Janet Wasko. 2002. "Feminist Theory and Political Economy: Toward a Friendly Alliance." In *Sex and Money: Feminism and Political Economy in the Media*, ed. Eileen R. Meehan and Ellen Riordan, 16–29. Minneapolis: University of Minnesota Press.

Tong, Rosemarie. 1997. *Feminist Thought: A Comprehensive Introduction*. London: Routledge.

Tracy, James F. 1999. "Whistle While You Work: The Disney Company and the Global Division of Labor." *Journal of Communication Inquiry* 23, no. 4: 374–89.

Waring, Marilyn. 1988. *If Women Counted*. San Francisco: Harper & Row.

———. 1999. *Counting for Nothing: What Men Value and What Women Are Worth*. Toronto: University of Toronto Press.

Wasko, Janet. 1995. *Hollywood in the Information Age: Beyond the Silver Screen*. Austin: University of Texas Press.

Index

Page references in italics indicate a figure or table.

ABC, 218, 344
Abrams v US, 71, 72, 73
Acker, Joan, 351
Adams, Henry, 56
Adler, Julius Ochs, 74
advertisers, 329–30
Aeropagitica (Milton), 67, 68, 77
Afghanistan, 3, 4, 125
African American audience, 331–33,
    336–38
African National Congress (ANC), 113,
    114, 118, 119
Aksoy, A., 133
Al-Jazeera, 25
Allen, Robert, 299
Allied Artists, 144
al Qaeda, 3, 4
Altschull, Herbert, 67
American Airlines, 224
*American Booksellers Association v
    Hudnut,* 77
American Civil Liberties Union (ACLU),
    76, 79
American Communist Party, 73
American Jewish Committee, 76
American Socialist Party, 73

America Online (AOL), 218, 232
Amino, Yoshihiko, 98–99, 101, 104, 105,
    106
Amnesty Committee, 118
Amnesty International, 123
Amsterdam Protocol, 187, 191
Andreessen, Marc, 296, 300, 302, 303,
    304
Ang, Ien, 345
Annan, Noel, 155
Anti-Defamation League, 76
"antiglobalization" movement, 223–24
AOL/CompuServe, 232
AOL–Time Warner, 146, 218, 310, 344
Apple, 290, 295
Arendt, Hannah, 76, 86
Artsworld, 159, 166, 167
Asahi Shimbun, 313
Association for Education in Journalism
    and Mass Communication (AEJMC),
    60
Athenian agora, 6, 31, 75, 79
AT&T, 5, 6, 218, 222, 293, 299
Atta, Mohammed, 224
audience: advertisers and, 329–30;
    African American viewers in, 331–33,

336–38; as a commodity, 327–41; as
consumers, 328–29; Hispanic viewers
in, 332; interest in, 9–10; race,
ethnicity, and class of viewers in,
330–38
Auerbach, Ken, 220
Austin, J. L., 66

Baistow, K., 14
bakumatsu, 108
Baltic International Telemedicine
   Network, 270
Barbrook, R., 31, 32
Barlow, John Perry, 288–89, 290, 294,
   295, 299, 300, 301
Barnett, S., 20, 22, 27, 28–29
Barrett, Michele, 345
Bart, Peter, 146
Barthes, R., 215
Bass, Gary Jonathan, 116
Batman, 140–41
BCE, 218
Beck, Ulrich, 224–25
Beena, Eric, 296
Beer, Amy, 350, 351
Bell, Daniel, 91, 211
Bellamy, Edward, 56
Benn, Tony, 26
Bentham, Jeremy, 1, 70, 79
Berlusconi, S., 24
Bertelsmann, 218
Birmingham Centre for Contemporary
   Cultural Studies, 15–16
Birmingham School, 13
BITNET, 288
Black Enterprise, 333
"The Black Silence of Fear" (Douglas),
   74
blackvoices.com, 333
Blair, Tony, 245
Blair Witch Project, 318
Blockbuster, 140
B'nai B'rith, 76
Bok, Derek, 50
Borah, William, 73
Bosnia, 122, 123, 124
Boston Globe, 302

Bourdieu, Pierre, 23–24, 35, 84, 86–87,
   250, 251, 253, 254
"bourgeois scholar," 45–46
Bradner, Scott, 300–301
Brand, Stuart, 295
Brandeis, Louis, 69, 72
*The Brass Check: A Study of American
   Journalism* (Sinclair), 56
Brennan, Irene, 16
Brennan, William, 69
Britain/United Kingdom: Annan
   Committee/Report of, 27, 153, 161;
   Arts Council of, 24; Broadcasting
   Standards Commission of, 152;
   BSkyB in, 153, 157, 167, 172, 188,
   203, 257; Cabinet Office of, 28;
   Channel 3 in, 159; Channel 4 in, 152,
   156, 159, 161, 163, 169, 191, 203,
   207; Channel 5 in, 152, 156, 159, 203;
   Communications Bill of 2002, 238;
   Competition Act 1998 of, 163, 167,
   169, 170; Conservative Party in, 172;
   Davies Panel of, 158, 159, 161, 165,
   169; Department of Culture, Media,
   and Sport of, 28, 152; Department of
   National Heritage of, 28; Department
   of Trade and Industry of, 28; Draft
   Communications Bill of, 159, 169–70;
   General Strike in, 203; Greater
   London Council of, 24; households
   with PCs/access to the Internet,
   249–50, 252, 254–58; Independent
   Review Panel on the Future Funding
   of the BBC, 158; Independent
   Television Commission (ITC) of, 152,
   154, 159; ISP market in, 229, 231–40;
   I Take My Place initiative, 256; Joint
   Parliamentary Scrutiny Committee of,
   151, 159; Labour Party in, 16, 26, 27,
   30; Leicester/Loughborough tradition
   of, 15; New Labour in, 27, 245; new
   media markets in, 228–41; New Right
   of, 27; Office of Communications
   (Ofcom) of, 28, 151, 152, 164, 169,
   170, 172, 238; Office of Fair Trading
   of, 152, 170; Office of
   Telecommunications in, 234, 235,

236; Peacock Committee/Report in, 153, 154, 155, 156, 157, 162, 169; People and Media Labor group in, 35; Pilkington Committee of, 153, 155; policy for public broadcasting, 151–77; Puttnam Committee of, 151, 154, 163; Radio Authority of, 152; Radiocommunications Agency of, 152; Royal Commission on the Press of, 15, 27; SurfTime in, 234, 235; U.K. Communications Act of, 170; "UK Online Computer Training" in, 254–55; Viewers and Listeners Association, 27

British Broadcasting Corporation (BBC), 17, 25, 27; BBC1 of, 160; BBC2 of, 14, 26, 160; BBC Technology and Resources of, 164; BBC Worldwide of, 164; broadcasting policy cycles of, 152–73; evolution of television systems of, 188–89; history of, 32–33; license fee of, 203; *Newsnight* of, 20; online access through, 257–58

British Journalism Review, 27

British Telecom, 30, 170, 234, 235, 236, 240

Brittan, Samuel, 155, 157, 171

broadband, 236–37, 248

broadcasting: dictatorial control of, 199; regulation of, 194–210. *See also* public service broadcasting; *specific country*

Brooks Fiber Property, 232

Brown, Gordon, 256

BSkyB, 153, 157, 167, 172, 188, 203, 257

Buchwald, Art, 138

Bulgaria, as EU candidate, 263, *264,* 265, 266, *275,* 277, 280, 281

Burke, Kenneth, 58

Bush, George H. W., 292, 293

Bush, George W., 4, 124, 125, 214

Business at the Speed of Thought (Gates), 215

cable television (CATV), 140–41, 262, 266

Cahier du Cinéma, 36

Cairncross, Frances, 213

California Civil Rights Initiative (CCRI), 350

Cambodia, 122

Cameron, A., 32

Campbell, Colin, 298

Canada: communication sectors of, 218; film industry of, 133; programming in, 207

Canal Plus, 183, 207

CanWest, 218

capitalism: communication and, 83–94; in media studies, 49; new media and, 228–41; socialism and, 97

Capitalism and Communication (Garnham), 133

Capitalism and the Twenty-First Century (conference), 342

"capitalism's Chernobyl," 224

Cardiff, David, 32

Carey, James, 58, 212, 214, 286, 346

Carlton, 157, 160

Carolco, 144

Carr Center for Human Rights Policy, 122

Carroll, Lewis, 249

Castells, Manuel, 30, 88, 91–93, 229, 247, 249

CEEC10, 263, 274, 276, 280

Central Europe, as EU candidate, 261, 263, 274, 276, 279, 280. *See also* CEEC10

Cerf, Vinton, 300

Chaffee, Zechariah, 72

Chechen war, 34

Cheney, Dick, 125

"*chi,*" 98

China, 47

Cisco, 221

"Civilization" (Mill), 70

Clark, J. M., 239

Clark, Jim, 301, 302, 304

Clinton, William J., 4, 6, 122, 123, 124, 125, 245, 300, 303

Cold War, 3, 58–59, 74, 112, 122, 295

Collins, Richard, 24, 25, 27, 28

Colt Telecom, 232

Columbia, 144

Columbia/Tri-Star, 143

The Coming Anarchy (Kaplan), 225

Coming to America, 138

communication: capitalist mode of production of, 87–90; corporate power integrating with, 217–19; critical scholarship of, 45–52; cultural materialism in, 346–47; economic transformation of, 83–94; feminism/feminist political economy in, 347–52; heuristic perspective of, 87; history of technology of, 33; impact of cyberspace on, 212–15; internationalized activity of, 89–90; "marketplace of ideas" and, 65–82; research of, 41–64

Communications Act of 1934, 204

Communist Party, 16, 21, 45, 73, 201

Compaine, Benjamin, 249, 252

Compaq, 290

competition, in public service broadcasting, 170–71

CompuServe, 287, 292

Computer Lib, 295

Computer Professionals for Social Responsibility, 295

computers/PCs: "haves" and "have-nots," 245, 289–90. *See also* Internet

Constantinople, war crimes process in, 116–17

Consumers Union, 57

Corner, John, 19

Corsi, M., 239

Costanza-Chock, Sasha, 353

Country of My Skull (Krog), 116

Coward, Noel, 14

Cox, Barry, 191

"critical political economy," 1–2

Critical Studies in Mass Communication, 352

Crown Castle, 190

cultural feminism, 345

The Cultural Industries (Hesmondhalgh), 343

Curran, James, 11, 16, 19, 20, 22, 25, 27, 28, 29, 31, 32

Curry, A., 20, 288

"cyberspace," 212–15, 288, 290, 294, 303

Cyprus, as EU candidate, 261, 262, *264, 271,* 278, 280

Czech Republic, as EU candidate, 263, *264,* 265, 266, *271, 275,* 280

Dahlgren, Peter, 19

Daily Mail, 29

Daniels, B., 143

Davies, Gavyn, 158

Davis, Aeron, 29

Dawson, Michael, 337

Declaration of Human Rights, 200

Defense Policy Board, 125

DEG, 144

"deregulation," 5, 47, 89

Dewey, John, 56, 57, 72, 80

Digital Classics, 166–67

digitalization: commodification and, 215–17; digital divide of, 245–60; participation and exclusion in, 244–60

digital television, 189–91

Diller, Barry, 299

Direct-TV, 218

Discovery, 159

Discrimination and Popular Culture (Thompson), 14

Disney/Disney Corporation, 134, 144, 145, 146, 218, 344

"Domesticating Cyberspace" (Stix), 299, 300

Dorfman, Ariel, 345

dot-coms, 4, 308, 309

Douglas, William O., 74, 77

Dreamworks, 144

DSL, 262, 317

Dumas, Jo Ann, 352

"dumbing down," 161

DVD market, 139–40

Dworkin, Ronald, 50

Eastern Europe: as EU candidate, 261, 263, 274, 276, 279, 280; media in, 21, 25. *See also* CEEC10

EBRD, 279

economics, "marketplace of ideas" and, 65–82
Economist, 80
eEurope Plus Action Plan, 261
Eizenstat, Stuart, 124
"electrical sublime," 212
Eliasson, G., 231
El Salvador, truth commission in, 114
e-mail, 287
Emancipation, the Media, and Modernity (Garnham), 31
Embassy, 144
Energis, 232
Engels, Friedrich, 195
Enlightenment project, 7, 9
Enron, 222
Erskine, Thomas, 67
ESPN, 218
Estonia, as EU candidate, 262, 263, *264,* 265, 266, *271,* 273, *275,* 277, 280, 281
"ethnic enmity," 29
ethnicity of audience, 330–38
European Bank for Reconstruction and Development (EBRD), 279
European Commission, 255
European Convention on Human Rights, 122
European Training Education, 279
European Union (EU), 3; defining boundaries of public television by, 185, *185,* 186–88; e-business/e-readiness trends in, 270, *272,* 273–75, *275,* 276–83; e-Europe in, 249, 255, 261; exports of, 265, *267;* exports to, *268;* ICT-based education in, 276–78; information society (IS) in candidate countries, 261–85; programming in, 207; public gateways to e-business in, 274
European Union Framework Directive, 168
Ewen, Stuart, 59, 335
ex ante regulation, 167–69
Express Newspapers Group, 309

"failed states," 124, 125, 126

Fairness Doctrine, 77, 78, 202
Falling Through The Net, 245
"false consciousness," 8
fax, introduction of, 34
FCC v Pacifica, 77
Federal Bureau of Investigation (FBI), 222
Federal Radio Commission, 202
Fejes, Fred, 350, 351
feminist theory and political economy, 342–55
"Feminist Theory and Political Economy: Toward a Friendly Alliance" (Steeves and Wasko), 343
film industry in the United States, 131–47, 147n1, 148–50
Financial Times, 151, 154, 158
Finland, *264,* 265
First Amendment, 77, 78, 79, 199
Fisher, George, 299
FMR Corporation, 232, 233
Forbes ASAP, 302–3
Fordist system, 216, 221
foreign direct investigation (FDI), 263
foreign television markets, 141–42
Forte Group, 29
Fortune, 211, 291
Fowler, Mark, 78
Fox, 143
France, state broadcasting in, 204
Fraser, Nancy, 346
Freedman, Des, 27
Freedom Forum, 247
Freedom House, 123
"freefone 0800," 234
Freeman, C., 229
Free Software project, 303
Free Trade Agreement (FTA), 219
Freeview, 190
FRIACO Hybrid, 235
Fukuyama, Frances, 212–13
fusetsuryu, 108

G-8, 230, 344
Gaber, I., 29
Gandy, Oscar, 9, 59

Garnham, Nicholas, theory and research of, 2, 7–8, 9, 11, 14, 16, 17–18, 19, 23, 24, 25, 26, 27, 30–31, 32, 35–36, 41, 52, 59, 86, 88, 93, 95–96, 133, 155, 157, 160, 162, 167, 168, 170, 171, 172–73, 207–8, 240, 331, 346, 347

Gates, Bill, 215, 244, 289, 299, 301, 303, 304

gay/lesbian audience, 350

"geek chic," 302

Geist, 96

gender in political economy, 342–56

General Agreement on Tariffs and Trade (GATT), 5, 219

General Electric, 218

Gerbner, George, 58

Gerbrandt, Larry, 144

Germany, 265; Basic Law of, 205; Federal Constitutional Court, 21, 205; State-controlled broadcasting in, 204–5; West Germany Basic Law, 21

Giddens, Anthony, 334, 351

Gilder, George, 213, 215, 222

Gitlin, Todd, 79

Glander, Timothy, 58

glasnost, 74

"global contagion," 3, 4

Global Crossing, 222

"globalitarian" ideology, 90

globalization, 90, 344–45

"global north," 318

"global social space," 86–87

"global south," 318

"God Is the Machine" (Kelly), 215

Goebbels, Josef, 58

Golding, Peter, 2, 59

Goodman, Paul, 58

Goodwin, Peter, 20

Gopher services, 287

Gorbachev, Mikhail, 74, 214, 290

Gordon, Thomas, 67

Gore, Al, 6, 245, 293, 294, 299, 300, 304, 305

Gore, Albert, Sr., 292–93

Graham, Andrew, 158

Gramsci, Antonio, 18–19, 197

Granada, 157, 160

Greece, *264, 275*

Greenspan, Alan, 75

"grounded truth," 8

Ground Zero, 225

Group of Eight's Digital Opportunities Task Force, 230

Grundrisse (Marx), 9–10

Guardian Media Group (GMG), 166

Guatemala, truth commission in, 112

Guback, Thomas, 133, 134, 142, 147

Guinier, Lani, 338

Guttmann, Amy, 50

Habermas, Jürgen, theory and research of, 7–8, 18–19, 35, 78, 80, 87, 98, 101–2, 103

Haiti, 122, 123, 124

Hall, Stuart, 18, 46–47, 305

Hambley, John, 166, 167, 172

Hambrecht and Quist, 302

Hand, Learned, 72

Hardt, Hanno, 58

Harper, Sue, 33

Harper's, 75

Harvard, communication and media studies at, 54

Hasselbach, Suzanne, 21

Hegel, Georg Wilhelm Friedrich, 80

Hertzberg, Hendrik, 126

Hesmondhalgh, David, 343, 351, 353

Hideyoshi, Toyotomi, 100

Higashijima, Makoto, 106, 107, 108, 109

Hills, Jill, 2, 20, 34

Hispanic audience, 332

History Channel, 159, 166

History of Britain, 160

Hitler, Adolf, 58

Hoffman-Riem, W., 205

Hollywood, political economic perspective of, 131–50

Hollywood Entertainment, 140

Hollywood in the Information Age (Wasko), 133

Holmes, Oliver Wendell, Jr., 66, 69, 71, 73, 80

Homebrew Computer Club, 295

home video, 139–40
Hoover, Herbert, 73, 202
Horton, Mildred, 75
Horwitz, Robert, 66
Households Below Average Income
   (HBAI), 249
HSBC Holdings, 233
Huettig, Mae, 133
Hull Telephones/Kingston
   Communications, 170
humanitarian interventionism, 126–27
human rights, abuses of, 111–30
Human Rights Violations Committee,
   118
Human Rights Watch, 123
Humphrey, Hubert H., 75
Hundt, Reed, 198
Hungary, as EU candidate, 263, *264,*
   265, *271, 275,* 277, 278, 280
Hunt, Chris, 167
Huntington, Samuel, 124
Hustler v Falwell, 77
Huston, G., 230–31
Hutchins Commission, 57

IBM, 281, 291, 293, 299, 301
ICI, 25
identity politics, 97–98
ie, 105
Ignatieff, Michael, 125, 126
Independent on Sunday, 29
Independent Television (ITV), 22, 26,
   156, 160, 183, 203
"informationalization," 89
information and communication
   technologies (ICTs), 261–85
"information society" (IS), 30, 31, 91–94,
   261–85
"information superhighway," 6, 290,
   292, 299, 303
Inkatha Freedom Party, 118
Innis, Harold, 51
intellectual property rights (IPR), 5
Interim Constitution of 1993, 113–14
International Association of Media and
   Communication Research (IAMCR),
   342, 352, 353

International Communication
   Association (ICA), 42, 60, 342
International Criminal Court, 125
The International Film Industry, 133
international human rights, 120–26
International Monetary Fund (IMF), 219,
   344
International Telecommunications
   Union (ITU), 219–20, 221
International Telegraph Union, 34
Internet, 6, 47, 244–45, 246, 286–306;
   access for minority users, 333;
   browsers for, 296–98; business
   models and revenue sources for,
   318–20; communication sectors in,
   218; diffusion patterns of users of,
   290; digital television access to, 190;
   dot-coms in, 209, 308; early online
   years of, 287–90; global journalism
   in, 19; Gopher services on, 287;
   impact on existing mass media,
   31–32, 307–20, *321,* 322–26; LANs
   access to, 298, 301; Mosaic browser
   for, 296–98, 299, 300, 301, 302, 303;
   "net native" companies of, 308, 309;
   Netscape on the, 296, 298, 301,
   302–3; revolution of, 5; role in the
   business culture, 286–306;
   technology systems for, 316–18; U.S.
   household access to, 244–60; "Viola"
   on the, 296, *297;* WWW protocol
   and, 297
Internet Corporation for Assigned
   Names and Numbers (ICANN),
   220–21
Internet Explorer, 296
Internet service providers (ISPs), 229,
   231, 232, 233, 234, 235
Internet Society, 300
Inu Houjouki, 108
Iraq, 3, 4, 122, 125
Italy, *275*
ITN, 163

Jackson, Andrew, 121, 122
Jacobs, Jane, 211
James, William, 69

Japan: advances in chip manufacturing by, 291, 293; *bakumatsu* of, 108; bourgeoisie society in, 96–110; *"chi"* land of, 98; *fusetsuryu* of, 108; *ie* in, 105; *joubun* in, 101; Kamakura in, 98, 99; *kanjin-hijiri* in, 108; *kanjin* in, 101, 106, 108; *kugai-mono* of, 101, 106; Kyoto in, 98, 99; Meiji Restoration in, 106; *muen* land in, 98, 99, 100, 101, 104, 105, 106, 107, 108, 109; "public sphere" in medieval history of, 96–110; *raku,* principles of, 98, 99, 100, 105; *sajiki* in, 107, 108; Tokyo war crime trials in, 116; *yuen* of, 100–101, 105
Jefferson, Thomas, 66, 67
Jenkins, S., 42
Jesus Christ, Superstar, 76
Jevons, W. Stanley, 80
Jobs, Steven, 295, 304
Johnson, Nicholas, 78
joubun, 101
Journal of Communication, 41, 60
Jowell, Tessa, 154

Kagan World Media, 144
kanjin, 101, 106, 108
kanjin-hijiri, 108
Kant, Immanuel, 86
Kaplan, Robert, 225
Keane, John, 19, 28
Keck, Margaret E., 123
Kelly, Kevin, 215
Kennedy School of Government, 54, 122
Keynes, John Maynard, 1, 61n7
Keyworth, George, 213
"killer app," 297, 303, 304
Kirch group, 183
Kissinger, Henry, 120, 121, 122, 123, 124
Klingender, F. D., 132–33
Kluge, Alexander, 194
Knight, D., 23
Kosovo, 122, 123, 124
Krog, Antjie, 116, 118, 119
Krol, Ed, 296
Kuehler, Jack, 299
kugai, 95–110

kugai-mono, 101, 106
Kurds, 122
Kurzweil, Ray, 212, 213
Kyoto protocol, 124

La Follette, Robert, 56
Lamont v Postmaster General, 77
Länder, 205
Land ohne Musik, 161
Laqueur, Thomas, 123
Lasch, Christopher, 52, 79
Latina, identity of, 350
Latin America, truth commissions in, 122
Latvia, as EU candidate, 263, *264,* 265, 266, 270, *271, 275,* 280
Lauren, Paul Gordon, 122
Lazarsfeld, Paul, 45, 46, 57
Leavisite, 14, 24
Leedy, D., 143
Lefebvre, Henri, 98, 99, 351
Legg, S., 132–33
Le Monde, 313
Lenin, Vladimir, 197
lesbian/gay audience, 350
Liberty Media Corporation, 218
Liddiment, David, 169
Lippmann, Walter, 57, 72
Lithuania, as EU candidate, *264,* 270, *271, 275*
Lorimar, 144
Lucent, 221
Lundberg, Shelly, 336
Lyon, Danny, 212

Macintosh, 296, 300
MacKenzie, D., 228
Magee, James, 72
Malone, John, 299
Malta, as EU candidate, 261, 262, *264,* 265, 266, *271,* 278
Malthus, Thomas, 1, 61n7
Mamdani, Mahmood, 117
Mansell, Robin, 2
"A Marketplace Approach to Broadcast Regulation" (Fowler and Brenner), 78
"marketplace of ideas," 65–82
Marshall, Alfred, 1, 80

"Marshall Plan" for the information society, 283
Marvin, Carolyn, 33
Marx, Karl, 1, 9–10, 46, 61n7, 69, 80, 97, 195
Marx, Leo, 212
Marxism, 15–18, 196, 197, 347–48
Marxism Today, 16
Mattelart, Armand, 2, 90, 345
McCarthy, Joe, 246
McCarthyism, 73, 74
McCaw, Craig, 299
McChesney, Robert, 2, 66
McConnell International, 274
McCullagh, Declan, 293
McKerrow, Raymie, 42
McLaughlin, Lisa, 345–46, 352
McLuhan, Marshall, 85, 92
McNally, Lord, 154
meaning of citizenship, 9
Mearsheimer, John, 125
media: cultural studies of, 48; digitalization, impact of, 215–23; economic transformation of, 43, 84–87; history and studies of, 32–35, 52–59; Internet, impact of, 307–20, *321,* 322–26; mass media organizations in, 309–11; new media and capitalism in, 228–41; political economy of film industry in, 131–50; social functions of, 85–87
"The Media and the Public Sphere" (Garnham), 7
Media, Culture, and Society, 13, 36
"media literacy," 14
Meehan, Eileen, 59, 328, 349
Meiklejohn, Alexander, 72
Menand, Louis, 72, 76
Mercosul, 3
Mercury Assets Management, 233
Merrill Lynch, 160, 161, 233
Merton, Robert, 57
Metzger, Geoff, 166
MGM/UA, 144
Miami Herald v Tornillo, 77
Michael, John, 51
Microsoft, 218, 244, 281, 287, 290, 291, 301, 302, 303

Middle East, satellite broadcasting in, 25
Miège, Bernard, 2, 216
Milken, Michael, 222
Mill, James, 70
Mill, John Stuart, 1, 65, 66, 69–71, 72, 73, 74, 77, 79, 80, 81
Miller, T., 133
Mills, C. Wright, 48, 58–59
Milton, John, 65, 66, 67, 68–69, 72, 73, 80–81
Minitel, 31
Mintz, B., 233
Miramax, 145
Mitchell, William, 213
Modleski, Tania, 345
Money behind the Screen (Klingender and Legg), 132–33
Morgan, Janet, 199
Mosaic, 296–98, 299, 300, 301, 302, 303
Mosco, Vincent, 1–2, 59, 83, 132, 351
Motion Picture Association of America (MPAA), 131, 137, 143
Motorola, 299
The Movies, 14
Movies and Money (Wasko), 133
MTV, 253, 288
muen, principles of, 98, 99, 100, 101, 104, 105, 106, 107, 108, 109
Mukherjee, Roopali, 349–50, 351
Murdock, George, 342–43
Murdock, Graham, 2, 10, 59, 346, 351, 353
Murroni, C., 25, 28

Nader, Ralph, 293
The Nation, 79
National Center for Supercomputing Applications (NCSA), 296, 301
National Commission on the Causes and Prevention of Violence, 77–78
National Communication Association (NCA), 42, 60
"National Information Infrastructure," 300
National Security Strategy, 125
National Telecommunications and Information Administration, 245

National Unity and Reconciliation Bill, 115
nation building, 124–27
"negative liberty," 111
Negroponte, Nicholas, 212, 213, 215
Nelson, Theodor, 295
neoliberalism, 49, 219
Nerone, J., 68
Netscape, 296, 298, 301, 302–3
Network World, 300
Neuromancer, 289, 294
Newbold, David, 73
New Data on the Digital Divide (National Telecommunications and Information Administration), 245
New Deal, 201
New Economy, 90
New Line Cinemas, 144
New Republican, 79
New School, 76
News Corp., 143, 146, 218
News International, 203
Newsnight, 20
New Socialist, 16
Newsweek, 294
New World Information and Communication Order (NWICO), 60
New York Times, 72–73, *73,* 74–75, 78, 125, 218, 294, 313
Nixon, Richard M., 75
Nobunaga, Oda, 100
nomenklatura, 21
nongovernmental organizations (NGOs), 126, 281
Nordic-style social market policies, 27
Norris, Pippa, 254
Nortel, 221, 223
North American Free Trade Agreement (NAFTA), 3, 219
North Atlantic Treaty Organization (NATO), 74
Norway, 48
NSFnet, 293
NTL Group Ltd., 232
Nuremberg trials, 111, 116, 119, 120

öffentliche Gewalt, 100

Öffentlichkeit, 66, 100
Office of Communications (Ofcom), 28, 151, 152, 164, 169, 170, 172, 238
Oftel, 169, 170
Ohmae, Kenichi, 213
O'Malley, T., 28
On Liberty (Mill), 69, 71, 77
Organization for Economic Cooperation and Development (OECD), 229–30, 280
Orion, 144
ORTF, 204
Osiel, Mark, 117
Over the Counter Bulletin Board Exchange, 310
Oxman, J., 229

PACT, 163, 169, 174
PACTS, 136
Paine, Thomas, 67
Pakistan, 125
Paradise Lost (Milton), 69
Paramount, 137, 138, 144
Park, M.-Y., 25
Park, Robert, 56
pay-per-view (PPV), 140
PBS, 145
PC, 296, 297, 300
Peacock, Alan, 153
Pendakur, Manjunath, 2, 59, 132, 133
Pentagon, 4
People, 303
The People and the Media (Labour Party), 26
"Periodical Pleasures" (Beer), 350
Pew Research Center, 246
Pietrykowski, Bruce, 335
Piore, M., 212
Poland, as EU candidate, 263, *264, 271, 275, 277, 279,* 280
political economy of communication, 2; components in study of, 43–64; defined, 1, 43; feminist theory and, 342–55; "mainstream" approach of, 46, 49
The Political Economy of Communication (Mosco), 1, 351

Political Quarterly, 152, 155
The Politics of Truth and Reconciliation in South Africa: Legitimizing the Post-Apartheid State (Wilson), 118
Pol Pot, 122
Polytechnic of Central London (PCL), 13, 14, 15, 16, 17, 32, 33
Porter, Vincent, 14, 16, 20, 21, 23, 27
Portugal, as EU candidate, *275*
Posen, Barry, 125
Powell, Adam Clayton, III, 247
Power, Samantha, 122
The Power Elite (Mills), 59
PPP protocol, 297
Prindle, D., 133
Printers' Ink, 58
"private sphere," 345–46
Prodigy, 287, 292
Progress and Freedom Foundation, 213
Progressive Era, 56
propaganda, 58–59
Prudential Corporation, 233
Public Broadcasting Service (PBS), 203
"public interest," 5
public service broadcasting: "crowding out" of, 165–67; role of competition in, 170–71; U.K. policy cycle of, 151–77
"public sphere," 3, 18, 24, 85; feminist theory and, 345–46; in Japan, 95–110; "marketplace of ideas" and, 65–82; private spheres and, 85, 345–46; theory of, 18–19. *See also* Athenian agora
public television: crises of, 181–82; freedom of expression and pluralism of, 170, 180; as a national education agency, 179; resources of, 184, *184,* 185, *185,* 186; revenue shares of, 182, *182;* role in democracy, 179, 186–87; trends and future of, 178–93
Putnam, Robert, 50, 251, 257
Puttnam, Lord, 151

Quarterly Report, 310
Quebecor, 218
Quirk, John, 286

R. A. V. v City of St. Paul, 77
race of audience, 330–38
Radway, Janice, 345
raku, principles of, 98, 99, 100, 105
Rattigan, Terence, 14
Rawls, John, 50
Reagan, Ronald, 202, 214, 290, 292
Red Lion, 77, 202
"Red Queen effect," 249
regulation: of broadcasting, 194–210; censorship argument of, 200; historical context of, 200–205; liberal critique of, 198–200; market distortion argument of, 198; Marxist critique of, 196–98; political control argument of, 199; role in democracy and citizenship, 206–8
religion, "marketplace of ideas" and, 76
Renan, Ernest, 119
Reparations and Rehabilitation Committee, 118
Report on Editorializing by Broadcast Licensees, 202
Republican Party, 73
RIAS, 74
Ricardo, David, 1, 61n7, 80
Rice-Davies, Mandy, 167
Risky Business: The Political Economy of Hollywood (Prindle), 133
Risse, Thomas, 124
The Road Ahead (Gates), 215, 244
"road kill on the information superhighway," 292
Robin, Kevin, 133
Rockefeller, David, 211
Rockefeller, Nelson, 211
Rockefeller Foundation, 57
Rogers Communication, 218
Rohatyn, Felix, 223
Rolling Stone, 294
Romania, as EU candidate, 262, 263, *264,* 265, *271, 275,* 277, 279
Roosevelt, Franklin, 201
Roosevelt, Theodore, 122
Rosetto, Louis, 294, 295
Ruggiero, Renato, 5, 11n2
Rumsfeld, Donald, 125

Russia, *275*
Rwanda, 29, 122

Sabel, C., 212
sajiki, 107, 108
Sakr, Naomi, 25
salon, 102
Salon.com, 309
Salon Media Group, 310
Sarikakis, Katharine, 352
SBC Communications, 218
Scannell, Paddy, 19–20, 32
Schiller, Dan, 2, 45, 57, 59
Schiller, Herbert, 2, 58, 59, 60, 345
Schlafly, Phyllis, 61n6
Schlesinger, Philip, 17
School-Net, 277
Schumpeter, Joseph, 47, 240
Schwartz, M., 233
Schwarzlose, Richard, 68
Scientific American, 300
Scott, J., 233
Screen, 15, 16
Sears Financial Network, 75
Seaton, Jean, 27, 28, 29, 31, 32, 34
Securities and Exchange Commission, 222
Seek for Education, Elevation, and Knowledge (SEEK), 76
"self-righting principle," 67
September 11, 2001, 3, 4, 113, 124, 125, 126, 127, 211–12, 224–25
Seymour, E., 22
Shaftesbury, Earl of, 67
Shaw Communication, 218
Shell Films, 14
Shichirobei, Yamamoto, 108
shopping channel, 299
Siino, Rosanne, 302
Sikkink, Kathryn, 123, 124
Silicon Graphics (SGI), 301
Silicon Valley, 291, 302, 304
Sillitoe, A., 14
Sills, S., 143
Simpson, Christopher, 58
Sinclair, Upton, 56
SLIP protocol, 297

Slovakia, as EU candidate, 262, *264,* 265, 270, *271, 275,* 280
Slovenia, as EU candidate, 262, 263, *264, 271,* 273, *275,* 277, 278, 279
small and medium-sized enterprises (SMEs), 263, 266, 269, 279
SmallCap market, 310
Smith, Adam, 1, 61n7, 80, 81, 123
Smith, Jeffery, 67, 68
SMTP, 297
Smythe, Dallas, 2, 21, 58, 59, 328
social class of audience, 330–38
socialism, capitalism and, 97
Socialist Review, 16
Socialist Workers Party, 16
The Sociological Imagination (Mills), 59
Soley, C., 28
Somalia, 122, 123, 124
Sony, 143, 146, 218
South Africa: African National Congress (ANC) of, 113, 114, 118, 119; Amnesty Committee of, 118; Human Rights Violations Committee of, 118; Inkatha Freedom Party in, 118; Interim Constitution of 1993 of, 113–14; National Party of, 113, 120; National Unity and Reconciliation Bill of, 115; Reparations and Rehabilitation Committee of, 118; Truth and Reconciliation Commission (TRC) in, 112, 113–20; *ubuntu* of, 113–14, 118
South African Broadcast Corporation (SABC), 115
Soviet Union, 45, 47, 58, 74, 200, 201, 291
Spain, *275*
Sparks, Colin, 16, 21, 25, 31–32
Sprint, 222
Stallman, Richard, 303
Startz, Richard, 336
Stay the Hand of Vengeance (Bass), 116
Steeves, Leslie, 343, 348
Sterne, Jonathan, 48
Strategic Computing Initiatives, 214
Strategic Defense system, 214
Structural Transformation of the Public Sphere (Habermas), 18

Sunstein, Cass, 50, 78–79, 336
SurfTime, 234, 235
A Survey of the "Have-Nots" in Rural and Urban America (National Telecommunications and Information Administration), 245
Sussman, Gerald, 59
Sweden, 48

Taliban, 3, 4
Tallinn Technical University, 281
Tedford, Thomas, 67
Teilhard de Chardin, Pierre, 212
telecommunications: deregulation of, 5, 47, 89; "harmonization" on policy of, 5; technology of, 30–32
Telecommunications Act of 1996, 6, 221
telemedicine, 270
television, 140, 141, 188–89; digital and cable television in, 140–41, 262, 266; evolution of systems of, 188–89. *See also* public television; *specific country, corporation, or station*
Texas v Johnson, 77
Thatcher, Margaret, 18, 24, 204
Theory of Political Economy (Jevons), 80
"they don't get it," 294–96
Thomas, Norman, 73, 74
Thompson, Mark, 161, 172
Through the Looking Glass (Carroll), 249
Time, 303
The Times, 16
Toffler, A., 213, 215
Toffler, H., 213, 215
Tombs, Matt, 166
Touchstone Pictures, 145
Touraine, Alain, 91
Travelocity.com, 224
Treaty of Westphalia, 112, 120, 126
Trebing, H., 229
Trenchard, John, 67
"trickle-down" digital access, 247–48
Truth and Reconciliation Commission, 112, 113–20
"truth commissions," 111–30

Tulloch, John, 28
Turkey, as EU candidate, 261, 262–63, *264,* 265, 266, 269, *271, 275,* 280
Tutu, Desmond, 114, 118, 119
Twentieth Century Fox, 144

ubuntu, 113–14, 118
U.K. Communications Act, 170
UK History, 166
"UK Online Computer Training," 254–55
Unilever, 25
Union for Democratic Communications (UDC), 342
United Kingdom. *See* Britain/United Kingdom
United Nations, 125; Charter of, 122; Commission on Human Rights of, 123
United States, media studies of political economy in, 41–64
Universal, 143, 144
Universal Declaration of Human Rights, 111, 122
University of Westminster, 13
University of Wisconsin–Madison, 51, 53
"urban form," 98
"urban sites," 98
Uruguay Round of the General Agreement on Tariffs and Trade (GATT), 5
U.S. Federal Communications Commission (FCC), 7, 198, 202, 204
U.S. News & World Report, 299, 300
U.S. Supreme Court, 77, *77,* 78
US v Rumely, 77
UUNET, 232

Variety, 146
"velvet revolutions," 3
Verio, 232
Verizon Communications, 218
Verkehr, 97
Viacom, 146, 218
Vickers, John, 162, 163
Vienna Institute for International Economic Studies (WIIW), 265
Vietnam War, 76, 203, 294, 295

Viewership Power Ratio, 160
Village Voice, 295
Viola, 296, *297*
Vivendi/Vivendi Universal, 143, 146, 218
Vogel, Harold, 135

Wall Street Journal, 291
Walt, Stephen, 125
Walt Disney Pictures, 145
Waltz, Kenneth, 121, 125
Wander, P., 42
WAP, 262
war crimes, 116–17
Waring, Marilyn, 347, 349
Warner, 144
Wasko, Janet, 2, 59, 343
Webster, Franck, 93
Wertheim, Margaret, 213
Westminster School, 11, 13–36; on
    communications technology, 30–32;
    on media history, 32–35; on media
    policy and performance, 26–30;
    reformist view of, 16–21; studies of
    market influence on media, 21–26
Westphalia, Treaty of, 112, 120, 126
Whalen, Grover A., 73
"What Is a Nation?" (Renan), 119
Who Owns the Media? (Guback), 133
Wilhelm, Anthony, 249
Will, George, 61n6
Williams, Raymond, 214, 347

Wilson, Richard, 118
Wilson, Woodrow, 121, 122
Winston, Brian, 34
Wired, 212, 214, 290, 293, 294, 295, 301,
    303–4
WNEW-TV, 75
Wohlstetter, Albert, 125
World Bank, 219, 344
WorldCom, 221–22, 232
World Economic Forum, 280, 344
World of Medieval Towns in Japan
    (Amino), 99
World's Fair, 73
World Trade Center (WTC), 4, 34,
    211–12, 225
World Trade Organization (WTO), 5,
    125, 219, 344
World War II, 121, 122, 123–24, 205
World Wide Web, 6, 245, 246, 296, 309
Wozniak, Steven, 295, 304
Wright, Eric, 334

Xerox PARC, 295
Xhosa, 114

Yeo, Tim, 157
yuen, 100–101, 105
Yugoslavia, as EU candidate, 29, 74

ZDF, 204
Zulu, 114

About the Contributors

Marc Bogdanowicz has a social sciences background. Before joining IPTS in April 2000, he worked as a senior researcher in two successive university departments with continuous participation in European activities, networks and observatories. Since 2001, Bogdanowicz has coordinated an "ICT and Enlargement" cluster of research activities as part of the IPTS prospective research actions on ICT.

Jean-Claude Burgelman is project leader at the ICT unit of the JRC-IPTS, on leave from his position as professor of communication technology policy at the Free University of Brussels. He directed for ten years the research center Studies on Media, Information and Telecommunications (www.vub.ac.be/SCOM/smit/smit.html). His latest books (as editor) are *Beyond Competition: Broadening the Scope of Telecommunication Policy; Communication, Citizenship, and Social Policy: Rethinking the Limits of the Welfare State;* and *e-Merging Media* (forthcoming).

Andrew Calabrese is associate professor at the University of Colorado in Boulder. In addition to many articles and book chapters about media and citizenship, and the public policies that govern the media industries, he edited *Information Society and Civil Society: Contemporary Perspectives on the Changing World Order* (1994, with Slavko Splichal and Colin Sparks) and *Communication, Citizenship and Social Policy* (1999, with Jean-Claude Burgelman). He serves on several editorial boards and is a founding board member of the European Institute for Communication and Culture (EURICOM).

Richard Collins is professor of media studies and head of sociology at the Open University. He is the author of several books and articles including *From Satellite to Single Market: New Communication Technology and European Public Service Television* (1998); *Culture, Communication, and National Identity: The Case of Canadian Television* (1990 and 1994); and (with Cristina Murroni) *New Media: New Policies* (1996). He worked with Nicholas Garnham at the Polytechnic of Central London from 1972 to 1989 with whom he (and Gareth Locksley) wrote *The Economics of Television: The UK Case* (1988).

James Curran is professor of communications at Goldsmiths College, London.

Oscar H. Gandy Jr. is the Herbert I. Schiller Term Professor at the Annenberg School for Communication at The University of Pennsylvania. His research and teaching are in the areas of privacy, public opinion, and policy formation. In addition, he pursues social and theoretical issues in the area of communication and race, which includes the strategic use of statistical representation.

Peter Golding is professor of sociology, codirector of the Communications Research Centre, and head of social sciences at the University of Loughborough. He writes and researches on media and social policy and on the social implications of new technologies. He is an editor of the *European Journal of Communication,* chair of the European Sociological Association media research network, and co-chair of the European Science Foundation program "Changing Media—Changing Europe."

Elissaveta Gourova has degrees in electronics and automatics engineering (MSc) and electrical engineering (Ph.D.) from the Technical University of Sofia. She formed part of the IPTS-JRC team working on the Enlargement (Futures) Project from 2000 to 2003. During this time, she made a considerable contribution to research on information society development in the candidate countries. She coauthored panel reports on information and communication technologies and on technology, knowledge, and learning. She also wrote a report providing insight into the skills of professionals and the job availability in the ICT sector in the candidate countries.

Tatsuro Hanada is a professor at the Institute of Socio-Information and Communication Studies, University of Tokyo.

Sylvia Harvey is professor of broadcasting policy at the University of Lincoln, United Kingdom, and the principal associate director of the AHRB Centre for

British Film and Television Studies. She coedited *Television Times* (1996); *The Regions, the Nations, and the BBC* (1993); and *Enterprise and Heritage: Cross Currents of National Culture* (1991) and is the author of *May '68 and Film Culture* (1978). She has published widely on aspects of film and television history and policy and is currently working on the topic of broadcasting regulation. She is a founder member of the International Documentary Festival (Sheffield, U.K.).

Robert Horwitz is professor of communication in the Department of Communication, University of California, San Diego. He is the author of two books: *Communication and Democratic Reform in South Africa* (2001) and *The Irony of Regulatory Reform: The Deregulation of American Telecommunications* (1989), as well as numerous articles and book chapters on communication law and policy.

Michèle Javary is research fellow at the Centre for Research in Innovation Management (CENTRIM), University of Brighton, and a member of the ESRC CoPs Centre, where she conducts research on innovation in the large capital goods sector. She is the author of the book *The Economics of Power, Knowledge and Time* (2002).

Robin Mansell is Dixons Chair in New Media and the Internet at the London School of Economics and Political Science, where she teaches and conducts research on the social, economic, and policy issues arising from innovations in information and communication technologies. Her books include *Networking Knowledge for Information Societies: Institutions and Intervention* (2002); *Inside the Communication Revolution: Evolving Patterns of Social and Technical Interaction* (2002); and *Mobilizing the Information Society: Strategies for Growth and Opportunity* (2000, with W. E. Steinmueller).

Robert McChesney is the author of eight books on media and politics, professor of communication at the University of Illinois at Urbana-Champaign, and host of the weekly talk show, Media Matters, on WILL-AM radio. McChesney also writes widely for both academic and nonacademic publications. He gives talks frequently on issues related to media and politics in the United States and world today.

Bernard Miège is professor of communication studies at the University Stendhal of Grenoble (France), where he teaches in communication theory, the industrialization of culture and information, and the development of the ICTs and news medias. He has written fourteen books, including (in English) *The Capitalization of Cultural Production* (1989).

Vincent Mosco is Canada Research Chair in Communication and Society at Queen's University, Kingston, Canada, and a research affiliate with the Harvard University Program on Information Resources Policy. He is the author of five books and editor or coeditor of eight on the mass media, telecommunications, computers, and information technology. His most recent books are *The Digital Sublime: Myth, Power, and Cyberspace* (forthcoming), *Continental Order? Integrating North America for Cybercapitalism* (2001, edited with Dan Schiller), and *The Political Economy of Communication: Rethinking and Renewal* (1996).

Graham Murdock is reader in the sociology of culture at Loughborough University. He has held visiting professorships in the United States, Belgium, Norway, Mexico, and, most recently, Sweden as the Bonnier Chair at the University of Stockholm. He has long-standing interests in the political economy of communications industries and the social organization and impact of new communications technologies. He is currently codirecting a panel study of digital access and participation. His recent books include, as coauthor, *Researching Communications* (1999) and, as coeditor, *Television across Europe* (2000).

John Durham Peters is F. Wendell Miller Distinguished Professor in the Department of Communication Studies at the University of Iowa. He is author of *Speaking into the Air: A History of the Idea of Communication* (2000).

Giuseppe Richeri is professor of communication studies at Università della Svizzera Italiana di Lugano (Switzerland), where he teaches media economics and the social history of communications. Formerly he taught at École National d'Administration in Paris and at Universidad Autonoma de Barcelona, where he held the UNESCO Communication Chair. He is author/editor of twelve books published in Italy and abroad, including *La television entre servicio publico y negocio* (1984); *La tv che conta: Televisione come impresa* (Baskerville, Bologna 1993); *Telecommunication: New Dynamics and Driving Forces* (1996); and *Il mercato televisivo italiano nel contesto europeo* (2003).

Ellen Riordan is visiting assistant professor at Gustavus Adolphus College in St. Peter, Minnesota. Her research focuses on feminist theory, political economy, and popular culture. She is coeditor of *Sex and Money: Feminism and Political Economy in the Media* (2002).

Colin Sparks is professor of media studies and director of the Communication and Media Research Institute of the University of Westminster.

Thomas Streeter studies media institutions, laws, and policies at the University of Vermont. His *Selling the Air: A Critique of the Policy of Commercial Broadcasting in the United States* (1996) won the McGannon Award for Social and Ethical Relevance in Communication Policy Research. He has taught at the University of Wisconsin and the University of Southern California, and has been a member of the School of Social Science at the Institute for Advanced Study, Princeton, New Jersey.

Janet Wasko is a professor and Knight Chair for Communication Research at the University of Oregon. She is the author of *Understanding Disney: The Manufacture of Culture* and *Hollywood in the Information Age*, and she has edited numerous books on the political economy of media and communications.